ERNEST HEMINGWAY: Critiques of Four Major Novels

604781 B

 SCRIBNER
RESEARCH
ANTHOLOGIES

Martin Steinmann, Jr., GENERAL EDITOR

CARLOS BAKER
Princeton University

ERNEST HEMINGWAY:
Critiques of Four Major Novels

004489

 SCRIBNER
RESEARCH
ANTHOLOGIES

CHARLES SCRIBNER'S SONS   New York

SBN 684-41157-1 (paper)

PRINTED IN THE UNITED STATES OF AMERICA

Library of Congress Catalog Card Number 62-17589

Preface

Each Scribner Research Anthology is a collection of written sources upon a single historical, literary, or scientific topic—the Hungarian Revolt, Shakespeare's *Julius Cæsar*, or extrasensory perception, for example. In addition to these sources, it contains (1) "Guide to Research," an account of the rationale and the methods of research and of research-paper writing (2) an introduction to the topic of the anthology, (3) suggested topics for controlled research, and (4) suggested sources and topics for library research.

Each anthology is designed to serve two purposes. First, each gives the student access to important sources—texts, documents, letters, diaries, essays, for instance—on a given topic. Some of these sources are otherwise available in only a few libraries, some (manuscripts and historical documents) in only one. In any case, the collection as a whole is not otherwise available in one volume. Second, each anthology gives the student either all his sources for a controlled-research paper or some of them for a library-research paper. Each anthology can be valuable either for readings in courses in history, literature, science, or humanities or as the basis for a research paper in these or in other courses.

A controlled-research paper—a paper in which the student's search for sources is limited to, and in certain ways controlled by, those sources contained in one anthology—is not so noble an undertaking as a library-research paper. But it is often more successful—more rewarding for the student and easier for his instructor to teach effectively and judge fairly. Its advantages for both student and instructor are often considerable.

For the student, it sometimes provides sources unavailable in his school library. And it enables him to learn a good deal about research (selection, interpretation, and evaluation of sources; quotation and paraphrase; and documentation) without prior instruction in use of the library (and, incidentally, without overtaxing the facilities and the resources of his library and without loss of, or damage to, sources either irreplaceable or difficult and expensive to replace).

For the instructor, it permits focus of class discussion upon a limited set of topics. It enables him to track down the student's sources conveniently. And—perhaps the greatest advantage of all—it enables him to judge both conveniently and exactly how well the student has selected, interpreted, and evaluated his sources and how well he has quoted and paraphrased them.

In many schools, a controlled-research paper is either a preliminary to or a part of a library-research paper. A library-research paper is probably the most difficult paper that the student can be assigned to write. The problems that confront him are not simply those common to any paper—organization, paragraphing, and transitions, for instance—and those (already mentioned) common to all research papers. He has, in addition, the problem of using the library well—of, for example, using the card catalogue, periodical indexes, and other reference works. But, if the instructor assigns a controlled-research paper as a preliminary to or, as it were, an early part of a library-research paper, the student need not come to grips with all these problems at once.

Each Scribner Research Anthology is compiled according to the following editorial principles. Each source that is not anonymous is prefaced by a biographical note on its author. At the foot of the same page is a bibliographical note. Each source is reprinted exactly as it appears in the original except for (1) some typographical peculiarities, (2) explanatory notes, given in brackets, and (3) omissions, indicated by ellipses (". . ."). And, finally, for each source that has pagination in the original, page numbers are given in brackets within the source itself—thus: "[**320/321**]," where everything before the slash (and after the preceding slash, if any) is from page 320, and everything after the slash (and before the next slash, if any) is from page 321. For a source hitherto unpublished, no page numbers are given; and the student who uses it should cite the page numbers of the Scribner Research Anthology. Footnotes to a source are given as in the original. Where the original pagination of a footnote is not evident, its page number precedes it in brackets.

MARTIN STEINMANN, JR.

Bingham Bay
Lake Gogebic
August, 1960

Guide to Research

THE IDEA OF RESEARCH

Research is the organized, disciplined search for truth; the aim of all research is to discover the truth about something. That thing may be a historical object like the Stonehenge monuments or a historical event like the Hungarian Revolt or the Battle of Waterloo. It may be a work of literature like Shakespeare's *Julius Cæsar* or Miller's *Death of a Salesman*. It may be a recurring event like the motions of the planets or the circulation of the blood. Or it may be an experimentally repeatable phenomenon like behavior of rats in a maze or perception apparently unaccounted for by the five senses. Archeology, history, literary criticism and scholarship, astronomy, physiology, and psychology—these are some of the many divisions of research. Indeed, all the sciences—physical, biological, and social—and all other scholarly disciplines share this organized, disciplined search for truth.

The search for truth has often been confused with such aims as confirming prejudice, instilling patriotism, and praising friends and blaming enemies. The attempt to prove the preconceived conclusion *that* one college is superior to another, for example, is not research (though the attempt to discover *whether* one college is so superior is). Research is hostile to prejudice.

General Methods of Research. The best general method of research is first-hand observation. But this method is not always possible and, when it is possible, not always practical.

The best method to begin discovering the truth about something is to observe that thing and the circumstances surrounding it. To discover the truth about *Julius Cæsar* or *Death of a Salesman*, get the play and read it, or go to the theatre and watch a performance. To discover the truth about the planets, observe them through your telescope. To discover the truth about the intelligence of rats, build a maze and run some rats through it.

This first-hand observation is not always possible, however. To discover the truth about the Battle of Waterloo, you can't observe the battle. The best that you or anyone else can do is to observe other persons' observations, the recorded observations of eye-witnesses: diaries, letters, and memoirs, for instance, of soldiers and generals who were in the battle. With more recent historical events—for example, the Hungarian Revolt—you are better off. You can watch films and listen to tape recordings. You may be able to interview people who were there. But these observations are still second-hand; and, on the whole, history can be observed only at second-hand. The sole exception is history that you have been part of. You may have fought in the Hungarian Revolt—though, if you did, you may be prejudiced.

Even when first-hand observation is possible, it is not always practical. You may have a copy of or tickets to *Julius Cæsar* or *Death of a Salesman* but not know enough about the principles of dramatic criticism to interpret the play unaided. You may have a telescope but not know how to use it or, if you do, not know what to make of what you observe through it. You may have some rats but not know how to build a maze or, if you do, not know enough about animal psychology to run your rats through it properly. The best that *you* can do under these circumstances is to supplement whatever first-hand observations you can make with observations of the first-hand observations of other people better-trained or better-equipped than you. Read *Julius Cæsar* or *Death of a Salesman* and also critics' interpretations of the play. Observe the planets, if you can, and read treatises on astronomy. Do what you can with your rats, and read reports of experiments with rats. After all, no one can master the special methods and come by the special equipment of all scholarly disciplines. Indeed, few people can do this with more than one discipline, and then not before they're thirty. But all people who want a liberal education should try to discover as much of the truth about as many scholarly disciplines as their abilities and their circumstances permit. Indeed, the achievement of this is what is meant by "a liberal education."

Primary and Secondary Sources. As the foregoing account of the general methods of research suggests, there is, ultimately, only one source of the truth about something—the thing, the event, or the phenomenon itself: the Stonehenge monuments, the Hungarian Revolt, or the Battle of Waterloo; the text of *Julius Cæsar* or *Death of a Salesman;* the motions of the planets or the circulation of blood; extrasensory perceptions or rats running in a maze. Such a source is a *primary* source. And, in historical research, where the thing itself (the Hungarian Revolt or the Battle of Waterloo) cannot be observed at first hand, a report of an eyewitness or a film or a tape recording is also counted as a *primary* source. But any other second-hand source (an interpretation of *Julius Cæsar* or *Death of a Salesman,* a treatise on astronomy, a report of an experiment with rats) is a *secondary* source.

A primary source is, of course, better. But, if a primary source is unavailable to you (if it is a book, perhaps your school library does not have it) or if you are not trained or equipped to use it (you don't know how to run rats through a maze or you have no telescope), then a secondary source must do. In any case, except for the most mature scientists and scholars, a good secondary source is useful and often indispensable.

It is worth noticing that being primary or being secondary is not an intrinsic characteristic of the source itself. It is, rather, a relationship that either exists or does not exist between a given source and a given topic of research. Consequently, a given source may be primary in relation to one given topic but secondary in relation to another. Two examples may serve to make this important point clear. Edward Gibbon's *The Decline and Fall of the Roman Empire* (1776-1788) is a secondary source in relation to the topic of the Roman Empire but a primary source in relation to that of eighteenth-century English prose style or that of eighteenth-century historiography. Samuel Taylor Coleridge's *Lectures on Shakespeare* (1811-1812) is a secondary source in relation to the topic of Shakespeare's plays but a primary source in relation to that of nineteenth-century principles of dramatic criticism or that of Shakespeare's reputation.

It is worth noticing also that a given source may be primary or secondary in relationship to more than one topic. James Joyce's novel *A Portrait of the Artist as a Young Man* is a primary source in relation not only to the topic of the structure of *A Portrait of the Artist as a Young Man* (and dozens of other topics on the novel itself) but also to the topic of use of the stream-of-consciousness technique in twentieth-century fiction.

THE RESEARCH PAPER

A research paper is a paper giving the results of research, the methods by which they were reached, and the sources, primary or secondary, which were used. A research paper attempts to tell the truth about a topic, and also tells how and where this truth was discovered. As we have seen, the sources of a research paper may be either written sources (literary texts and historical documents, for example) or sources of other kinds (experiments, for example). Since a research paper written in school is almost always based upon written (printed) sources, we shall here discuss only that kind. A research paper based upon written sources may be either a library-research paper or a controlled-research paper. A library-research paper is a research paper for which your search for sources is limited to those sources contained in the libraries available to you; a controlled-research paper, to those sources contained in one anthology —to those contained in this volume, for example. Here we shall emphasize the latter kind.

Finding Your Topic. The first step in writing a research paper based upon written sources, whether a library-research or a controlled-research paper, is finding a topic. We say "finding a topic" rather than "choosing a topic" because the process is more like finding a job than choosing a sandwich from a menu. Unless your instructor assigns you a topic, which he may do, you must look for one; and the one you find may not be just what you want but the best one that you can find. But, if you look long and carefully, you may find a topic that so well suits your interests, your capacities, and the time and the space at your disposal that your paper will almost surely be a success.

Finding a topic is the most important single step in writing a research paper, and the things that you should have in mind when looking for a topic are (1) your interests, (2) your capacities, and (3) the time and the space at your disposal. If you are interested in a topic, if you know something about the special methods of research that the topic requires, and if your topic is narrow enough to require no more time than you have for research and no greater development than you can give it in a paper of the length assigned you, then the paper that results will probably be satisfactory. For example, the topic of figures of speech in *Julius Cæsar* may interest you greatly. But, if it does, you must ask yourself whether you know enough about figures of speech to do research on them and, if you do, whether this topic is narrow enough. Even the topic of metaphors in the play would be too broad for most

papers; metaphors in Brutus' soliloquies might be about right. In any case, before you take a topic for a paper, you should do some reading on that topic; otherwise, you won't know whether it is interesting, within your ability to handle, and within the scope of your assigned paper.

Once you think that you've found a topic, take great care in phrasing it. The best phrasing is a question or a series of closely related questions. Better than "The character of Brutus" is "To what extent is Brutus motivated by self-interest and to what extent by the public interest?" The latter is not only more narrow and more precise; it provides you with a criterion of relevance in selecting your sources. At the end of this volume, you will find a list of suggested topics, intended to call your attention to topics that might not occur to you. But these topics are suggestive rather than definitive or precise.

Finding Your Sources. Finding sources for a library-research paper and finding ones for a controlled-research paper, though different in several respects, are alike in certain others. Finding sources in the library requires knowledge of how to use the card catalogue, periodical indexes, special bibliographies, reserve shelves, and encyclopedias. Finding sources in this volume or a similar one does not. But, in either case, you must have a clear idea of what you are looking for; and you must be prepared to put up with a high ratio of looking to finding. In other words, you must have not only criteria of relevance but also a willingness to do a good deal of skimming and a good deal more of careful reading, some of it fruitless.

The basic criterion of relevance you provide by careful phrasing of your topic, a problem discussed in the preceding section. The other criteria you provide by making a preliminary or tentative outline —perhaps in the form of subtopics, perhaps in the form of questions. Such an outline is not to be used for your paper. The outline for your paper will probably be quite different and, in any event, cannot be made until after you find your sources and take your notes. This preliminary outline guides your research and, as we shall see, provides you with the subtopic headings necessary for your note-cards (see "Taking Your Notes," page xi).

Making Your Working Bibliography. Once you have found a promising source ("promising" because, though it seems to be relevant, it may turn out not to be) you want to make some record of it so that, once you have completed your search for sources, you can turn back to it, read it, and, if it turns out to be relevant, take notes on it. This record of promising sources is your *working* bibliography. It is so called for two reasons: first, because you work with it as you proceed with your research and the writing of your paper, adding promising sources to it and discarding irrelevant ones; and, second, because this designation distinguishes it from your final bibliography, which appears at the very end of your research paper and contains only sources actually used in the paper. For a controlled-research paper, your working bibliography may be nothing more elaborate than a series of check marks in the table of contents of your research anthology or a list of page numbers. For a library-research paper, however, you need something quite different.

A working bibliography for a library-research paper is a collection of three-by-five cards each representing a promising source and each containing full information about that source. Once you have completed your research, written your paper, and discarded all promising but (as they turned out) irrelevant sources, this bibliography is identical with your final bibliography. Having a separate card for each source enables you to add and to discard sources easily and to sort and arrange them easily in any order you please. Eventually, when this bibliography becomes identical with your final bibliography, you will arrange sources alphabetically by authors' last names. Having full information about each source on its card enables you

to turn back to it easily—to locate it in the library without first looking it up again. You find this information in the card catalogue, periodical indexes, or other bibliographical aids; or, when browsing through the shelves or the stacks of the library and coming upon a promising source, you find it in or on the source itself—for example, on the spine and the title page of a book.

If the source is a *book,* you should put the following information on the three-by-five working-bibliography card:

(1) the library call number,
(2) the author's (or authors') full name (or names), last name first for the first author,
(3) the title of the book,
(4) the name of the city of publication,
(5) the name of the publisher (*not* the printer), and
(6) the year of publication (often found on the other side of the title page).

See the example of such a card on the opposite page (note the punctuation carefully).

If the source is a *periodical article,* you should put the following information on the three-by-five working-bibliography card:

(1) the author's (or authors') full name (or names),
(2) the title of the article,
(3) the name of the periodical,
(4) the volume number,
(5) the week, the month, or the season of publication, together with the year, and
(6) the page numbers covered by the article.

See the example of such a card on the opposite page (note the punctuation carefully).

These two forms take care of the two standard cases. For special cases—such things as books with editors or translators as well as authors, books published in several editions or in several volumes, and daily newspapers—see any good handbook of composition.

860.3
J23

Jones, John A., and William C.
Brown. A History of
Serbia. New York: The
Rowland Press, Inc., 1934.

WORKING-BIBLIOGRAPHY CARD FOR A BOOK

Smith, Harold B. "Fishing
in Serbian Waters." Journal
of Balkan Sports, VII
(May, 1936), 26-32.

WORKING-BIBLIOGRAPHY CARD FOR A PERIODICAL ARTICLE

Taking Your Notes. Once you have found sources, entered them in your working bibliography, read them, and found them relevant, taking notes requires your exactly following a standard procedure if your notes are going to be useful to you when you come to write your paper. An extra five minutes given to taking a note correctly can save you a half hour in writing your paper. Here is the standard procedure:

(1) Take all notes on four-by-six cards. Never use notebooks, loose sheets of paper, or backs of old envelopes.

(2) Limit each note to information on a single subtopic of your preliminary outline *and* from a single source. It follows from this that you may have many cards on the same subtopic and many cards from the same source but that you may never have one card on more than one subtopic or from more than one source.

(3) On each card, in addition to the note itself, put

    (a) the appropriate subtopic heading in the upper left-hand corner.

    (b) the name of the source (usually the author's last name will do) in the upper right-hand corner, and

    (c) the page number (or numbers) of that part (or those parts) of the source that you have used in taking your note. If you have used more than one page, indicate your page numbers in such a way that, when you come to write your paper, you can tell what page each part of the note comes from, for you may not use the whole note.

(If you follow these first three rules, you will be able, when you come to outline and to organize your paper, to sort your notes in any way you please—by subtopic, for example—and to arrange them in any order you please. Such flexibility is impossible if you take your notes in a notebook. If you follow the third rule, you will also be able to document your paper—write footnotes, for example—without again referring to the sources themselves.)

(4) In taking the note itself, paraphrase or quote your source or do both; but do only one at a time, and use quotation very sparingly.

Paraphrase and quotation require special care. Anything between paraphrase and quotation is not acceptable to good writers: you either paraphrase or quote, but do nothing in between. To paraphrase a source (or part of a source) is to reproduce it in words and word orders substantially different from the original. When you paraphrase well, you keep the sense of the original but change the language,

retaining some key words, of course, but otherwise using your own words and your own sentence patterns. To quote a source (or part of a source) is to reproduce it exactly. When you quote well, you keep both the sense and the language of the original, retaining its punctuation, its capitalization, its type face (roman or italic), and its spelling (indeed, even its misspelling).

Omissions and additions require special care. If, when quoting, you wish to omit some of the original, you may do so only if the omission does not change the sense of the original (never leave out a "not," for example!) *and* if it is indicated by ellipses (three spaced periods: ". . ."). If you wish to add something to the original, you may do so only if the addition does not change the sense of the original (never add a "not"!) *and* it is indicated by square brackets. The most usual additions are explanations ("They [i.e., the people of Paris] were alarmed") and disclaimers of errors in the original, indicated by the Latin *"sic,"* meaning "thus" ("Colombis [*sic*] discovered America in 1592 [*sic*]"). You must, of course, carry these ellipses and square brackets from your note-cards to your paper. And, if you type your paper, brackets may be a problem, for most typewriter keyboards do not include them. If your keyboard does not, you may do one of two things—either use the slash ("/") and underlining ("__" and "——") in such a way as to produce a bracket ("⌐" and "⌐") or draw brackets in with a pen. In any event, don't substitute parentheses for brackets.

In your paper, quotations no longer than three or four lines are to be enclosed within a set of quotation marks and run into your text; longer ones are to be set off from the text, without quotation marks, by indention from the left-hand margin and, especially in typewritten copy, by single-spacing. But never use either of these devices unless the language is exactly that of the original.

Your usual treatment of a source should be paraphrase; use quotation only if the

Fly-fishing   Smith

Smith says that fly-fishing is a method of fishing used chiefly by wealthy Serbians and foreign tourists, that the flies used are generally imported from Scotland, and that "Serbian trout are so snobbish that they won't glance [27/28] at a domestic fly."

[Query: How reliable is the information in this rather facetious article?]

NOTE-CARD

language of the original is striking (strikingly good or strikingly bad), if it is the very topic of your research (as in a paper on Shakespeare's style), or if it is so complex (as it might be in a legal document) that you don't want to risk paraphrasing it.

Let us look at the sample note-card above. The topic of research is methods of fishing in Serbia; the subtopic that the note deals with is fly-fishing in Serbia; the source is Harold B. Smith's article "Fishing in Serbian Waters," from the *Journal of Balkan Sports* (see the second of the two working-bibliography cards on page xi).

Note the subtopic heading ("Fly-fishing") in the upper left-hand corner; the name of the source, abbreviated to the author's last name ("Smith"), in the upper right-hand corner; the page numbers ("[27/28]"), indicating that everything, both paraphrase and quotation, up through the word "glance" is from page 27 and that everything after that word is from page 28; the sparing and appropriate use of quotation; and the bracketed query, to remind the note-taker that he must use this source with caution.

Writing Your Paper. Many of the problems of writing a research paper based upon written sources—organization, the outline, the thesis paragraph, topic sentences, transitions, and the like—are problems of expository writing generally. Here we shall discuss only those problems peculiar to such a paper. Two of these problems—paraphrase and quotation—we discussed in the preceding section. Two others remain: reaching conclusions and avoiding the scissors-and-paste organization.

When you come to make the outline for your paper and to write your paper, you will have before you three things: (1) your *preliminary* outline, containing ordered subtopics of your topic; (2) your working bibliography; and (3) your note-cards. These are the *immediate* results of your research; they are not the *final* results. They are only the raw material out of which you must fashion your paper. At best, they are an intermediate stage between finding your topic and making your final outline. The preliminary outline will not do for the final outline. The working bibliography will almost certainly require further pruning. And the note-cards will require sorting, evaluation, organization, pruning, and exercise of logic and common sense. All this needs to be done, preferably before you make your final outline and begin to write your paper, though almost inevitably some of it will remain to bedevil you while you are writing it. To put the matter in another way, you are, with these things before you, a Sherlock Holmes who has gathered all his clues but who has reached no conclusions from them, who has not come to the end of his search for truth. You must discard irrelevant clues, ones that have no bearing on the questions that you want answered. You must arbitrate the claims of conflicting or contradictory clues. You must decide which one of several probable conclusions is the most probable.

Once you have reached your conclusions, you must organize your paper and set forth this organization in your final outline. Organization and the outline are, of course, problems common to all expository writing. But a problem peculiar to the research paper is avoiding the scissors-and-paste organization—avoiding a paper that looks as though you had cut paraphrases and quotations out of your note-cards, pasted them in columns on paper, and connected them only with such phrases as "Jones says" and "On the other hand, Brown says." Such an organization is the result of a failure to reach conclusions (with the consequence that there is nothing but "Jones says" to put in between paraphrases and quotations); or it is a failure to see the necessity of giving the conclusions reached *and* the reasoning by

which they were reached (with the consequence that, though there is something to put between paraphrases and quotations, nothing is put there, and the reader is left to write the paper for himself).

Documenting Your Paper. To document your paper is to give the source of each paraphrase and quotation that it contains, so that your reader can, if he wishes to, check each of your sources and judge for himself what use you have made of it. To give the source is usually to give (1) either the information that you have about that source in your working bibliography (except that the name of the publisher of a book is usually not given) or the information that accompanies each source in a research anthology *and* (2) the information about page numbers that you have in your notes. This information you may give either formally or informally, as your instructor decides.

Formal documentation is given in footnotes. For a full discussion of footnotes, see any good handbook (one cheap and widely accepted one is *The MLA Style Sheet*). The form of footnotes is similar to, but not identical with, the form of bibliographical entries. With these three sample footnotes, compare the two sample working-bibliography cards on page xi:

[1] John A. Jones and William C. Brown, *A History of Serbia* (New York, 1934), p. 211.
[2] Harold B. Smith, "Fishing in Serbian Waters," *Journal of Balkan Sports,* VII (May, 1936), 27.
[3] Smith, pp. 27-28.

Informal documentation is given in the text of the paper, usually parenthetically, as in this example:

Fly-fishing in Serbia is chiefly a sport of wealthy Serbians and foreign tourists (Harold B. Smith, "Fishing in Serbian Waters," *Journal of Balkan Sports,* VII [May, 1936], 27), though in some mountain districts it is popular among the peasants (John A. Jones and William C. Brown. *A History of Serbia* [New York, 1934], p. 211). The flies used are generally imported from Scotland; indeed, Smith facetiously adds, "Serbian trout are so snobbish that they won't glance at a domestic fly" (pp. 27-28).

As this example suggests, however, informal documentation can be an annoying distraction. It probably works out best in papers that use only a few sources. In such papers, there are few occasions for long first-references to sources: for example, "(Harold B. Smith, "Fishing in Serbian Waters," *Journal of Balkan Sports,* VII [May, 1936], 27)." But there are many occasions for short succeeding-references: for example, "(Smith, pp 27-28)" or "(pp. 27-28)." Occasionally, informal documentation may be profitably combined with formal, as in a paper about Shakespeare's *Julius Cæsar.* In such a paper, references to the play might well be given informally —for example, "(III.ii.2-7)"—but references to critics formally.

How many footnotes (or parenthetical documentations) do you need in your paper? The answer is, of course, that you need as many footnotes as you have paraphrases or quotations of sources, unless you group several paraphrases or quotations *from the same page or consecutive pages of a given source* in such a way that one footnote will do for all. One way to do this grouping—almost the only way— is to introduce the group with such a sentence as "Smith's views on fly-fishing are quite different from Brown's" and to conclude it with the raised numeral referring to the footnote. Your reader will understand that everything between the introductory sentence and the numeral comes from the page or the successive pages of the source indicated in the footnote.

Making Your Final Bibliography. Your paper concludes with your final bibliography, which is simply a list of all the sources—and only those sources—that you actually paraphrase or quote in your paper. In other words, every source that you give in a footnote (or a parenthetical documentation) you include in your final bibliography; and you include no other sources (inclusion of others results in what is unfavorably known as "a padded bibliography"). The form for entries in your final bibliography is identical with that for ones in your working bibliography, given above. You should list these sources alphabetically by authors' last names or, if a source is anonymous, by the first word of its title, but not by "a," "an," or "the." For example:

BIBLIOGRAPHY

Jones, John A., and William C. Brown, *A History of Serbia.* New York: The Rowland Press, Inc., 1934.
"Serbian Pastimes." *Sports Gazette,* XCI (October 26, 1952), 18-19, 38, 40-42.
Smith, Harold B. "Fishing in Serbian Waters." *Journal of Balkan Sports,* VII (May, 1936), 26-32.

MARTIN STEINMANN, JR.

Contents

Introduction

The purpose of this book is to enable students to examine with care and understanding a part of the distinguished legacy of Ernest Hemingway. On the morning of July 2, 1961, readers the world over were suddenly compelled to reckon with the fact that his writing career was at an end. Luckily for those who survived him, he had managed to complete four major novels in the forty years of his writing life. These are *The Sun Also Rises* (1926); *A Farewell to Arms* (1929); *For Whom the Bell Tolls* (1940); and *The Old Man and the Sea* (1952). Besides these he had brought to publication two other novels, upwards of fifty short stories, several volumes of non-fiction, some poems, and a play. A few other works may be expected to appear posthumously. For present purposes, however, it has seemed best to concentrate on his work in the novel, reaching out to embrace the short stories wherever their themes or methods can illuminate his longer fiction.

This work is complete, substantial, and psychologically complex. In style, theme, subject, and narrative method, as well as in their multiple relations to the short stories, Hemingway's four chief novels offer many opportunities and problems to the research student. Moreover, for better or for worse, Hemingway's work has been much written about, so that the student of literature, whether he confines his efforts to "controlled research"—using only the writings of Hemingway and the critical materials in this volume—or whether he goes farther afield into "library research" and enlarges the scope of his investigation, is not likely to feel the lack of something important to write about. No matter what secondary materials he uses, however, it is a good maxim for any student of literature that he should keep the novel or the story central in his consciousness at all times.

The guidebook which follows offers a wide variety of critical commentary on the four major novels as well as a few synoptic essays which draw their materials from the whole range of Hemingway's work. Some of the critiques, like that of James T. Farrell, are broadly sociological in their orientation; others consider moral, political, and religious questions; still others concern themselves with matters of characterization, structure, style, and narrative techniques. The only item from the pen of Hemingway himself is the original conclusion of *A Farewell to Arms,* here published for the first time. Students of the novel should find it instructive to compare this rejected conclusion with the one that was actually published.

The suggested topics for controlled research look back to the critical interpretations and beyond these, always, to Hemingway's work itself. Other topics are suggested for those who have access to a library. Although these by no means exhaust the possible lines of investigation, they are meant to assist the serious researcher to a better comprehension of Hemingway's aims, methods, and achievements as a writer of fiction.

Princeton, New Jersey   Carlos Baker
February, 1962

Postscript: The editor wishes to extend special thanks to the scholars whose work is here reprinted; and very special thanks to Dr. G. B. Tennyson and Mr. J. C. D. Marshall, to whom he is much indebted for technical and other assistance, and to Dorothy S. Baker, whose help and good counsel have been constant and invaluable.

PART ONE

THE SUN ALSO RISES

The Sun Also Rises*

JAMES T. FARRELL, best known as the author of the Studs Lonigan trilogy, has written many other novels, short stories, essays, and books of criticism.

Ernest Hemingway's first novel, *The Sun Also Rises,* has been generally heralded as the definitive account of a war-wearied lost generation. In the light of this interpretation it is interesting to note that this novel was published in 1926, and that the time of its action is 1925. For these years fall within the most hopeful period of the post-Versailles world.

At that time there were many signs (at least in the eyes of superficial observers) to suggest that the world was returning to normalcy. After 1923, European capitalism seemed to have been restabilized, following the shocks of war, revolution, and dangers of revolution. At least to some, Germany looked like a going concern: the Weimar Republic was considered firmly secure. Hope was being revived in cartels as the means of achieving peaceable allocation of markets and equitable access to sources of raw materials. The epoch of disarmament talks, peace pacts, peace conferences had begun. America was in the full sweep of a tremendous economic boom, leading many to believe that this country was paving the way toward a new era of unprecedented world prosperity.

It may seem paradoxical that in such a period a novel of war disillusionment, nihilistic in outlook, should have become an international success.

However, this paradox is only superficial. With signs of a return to world prosperity there were growing evidences of [20/21] pacifism. In particular, the youth which had been too young to have been in the trenches was deeply pacifistic. Disillusionment with the war was more or less accepted. In addition, a re-examination of the character of disillusionment portrayed in *The Sun Also Rises* suggests that this mood had become a way of feeling and acting; in fact, a social habit. By 1925 those who had been morally unhinged or physically maimed during the war had had a number of years in which to make some kind of adjustment to the postwar world. The period of the first difficult readjustment had passed. Such, for instance, is the case of the chief protagonist in *The Sun Also Rises.* Jake Barnes, impotent as a result of wounds suffered on the Italian front, has more or less reconciled himself to his condition.

Whenever there is a widespread mood of disillusionment caused by an event as catastrophic as a world war, that mood is bound to be nihilistic and rather adolescent in character unless it serves as the basis for a radical and progressive political orientation that aims to change and better the world. This is illustrated in *The Sun Also Rises.*

The characters express their bitterness, their feelings of disenchantment, with calculated bravado. Their conversation is reduced to enthusiastic small talk about their escapades. And this talk, as well as their actions, is largely a matter of pose and gesture. They act like people who have not fully grown up and who lack the self-

---

*James T. Farrell, "The Sun Also Rises," *The League of Frightened Philistines* (New York: Vanguard Press, Ltd., 1945), pp. 20-24. Copyright 1945 by Vanguard Press, Ltd. Reprinted by permission of the publishers.

awareness to realize this; in fact, they possess no desire to grow up.

The Sun Also Rises influenced younger persons more widely than it did members of Hemingway's own generation. He may have reflected the feelings of many who fought in the war; but most of these men were finding some way of settling down and adjusting themselves in the nineteen-twenties. Some were doing creative writing, some finding editorial jobs, some launching themselves in careers that later won them Pulitzer prizes in poetry and so on. This novel struck deeper chords in the youth of the Twenties.

Hemingway's first books had hardly been published when he had imitators all over America; furthermore, boys and girls on [21/22] campus after campus began to talk like Hemingway characters. One need not go into detail to describe certain features of the Twenties; these are too fresh in our minds. Suffice it to say that by and large younger people were revolting against the standards and conventions of their elders, against the accepted notions of middle-class society. At the same time they were nonpolitical in their revolt. Add to this the deep pacifism of the decade, and one can easily understand why this novel struck such chords of response among young people, why Hemingway suddenly became the influence he did become at the time.

His influence was not merely superficial. It played a liberating and salutary role on those who would become the next generation of writers, and, more so, numerically, on readers. The hopes of those days have now been proved a snare by history. The nihilistic character of Hemingway's writing helped to free younger people from these false hopes. And although this novel (and many of his early stories as well) is set against a European background, Hemingway helped focus the eyes of younger people sharply on American life.

His writing was exciting and possessed of an extraordinary power of suggestiveness; it won over the reader to the feeling that he was actually participating in the lives of very real men and women. His use of dialogue helped enormously to create this impression. Others, notably Ring Lardner, preceded Hemingway in exploring and revealing the literary possibilities of the use of American vernacular, but he used it with amazing skill and originality. Both his suggestiveness in conveying a sense of life and his use of dialogue tended to turn the attention of youth toward common American experiences and to the speech expressing them on city streets and farms.

But Hemingway's influence, though so widespread, at the same time has been one that seems quickly to have exhausted itself. For Hemingway is a writer of limited vision, one who has no broad and fertile perspective on life. Younger writers were influenced—even seduced—by his moods; and they could grasp from him a sense of the great possibilities to be discovered in the true and simple treatment of common subject matter and [22/23] in the use of ordinary speech. But once they had learned these lessons, they could gain little more from Hemingway.

The Europe described in *The Sun Also Rises* is a tourist's Europe of the Twenties. Cafés, restaurants, hotels, particularly of the Left Bank, are the setting. When the action shifts to Spain, it is to permit a magnificent description of bull fights and a fiesta. The mood and attitude of the main characters is that of people on a vacation. They set out to do what people want to do on a vacation: they have love affairs, they drink, go fishing, and see new spectacles. Written in the first person, the book unfolds from the standpoint of a spectator's attitude. Jake, the narrator, is a newspaper man; his is an occupation that naturally tends to develop the point of view of the spectator. Jake is constantly looking at the other characters, at himself, at the scenery of Spain, at the bull fight, at everything that occurs or comes within his view.

The main characters have only a meager past. They are escaping from their past and usually do not wish even to talk or to think of it. They live for the present, constantly searching for new and fresh sensations. They do not really think; even Jake scarcely thinks about himself or about his own impotence. These people feel quite alike. They form a small clique, stoically accepting the ills of their life.

Robert Cohn, however, is an outsider. He is with them because of his doglike love for Lady Brett Ashley. Unlike the others, he is unable to drown his feelings in banalities, small talk, and new spectacles. Cohn's difference from the others is one of the central points of the novel. This contrast is stated overtly when Lady Brett says that Cohn is "not one of us," and when Jake thinks that Cohn has behaved badly by pursuing Lady Brett. Focused against Cohn, Jake's simple, stoical attitude is enforced more strongly. The attitude of Jake is one of the basic attitudes in Hemingway's writings.

Hemingway's realism is, by and large, one which deals with sensations—with shocks to the senses. He has tended to reduce life to the effect that sights, scenes, and experiences make upon the nervous system; and he has avoided complicated types of [23/24] response. Herein we find one of the major factors revealing his limitations as a writer.

In his most representative work he has saved himself from the crudities of simple behaviorism because of his gift of suggestiveness and his developed skill of understatement. The moral outlook in his work is on a plane of equal simplicity with his characters and subject matter. It amounts to the attitude that an action is good if it makes one feel good. Such an outlook on characters and events suggests that a development of greater understanding—broader range of feeling and sympathy, greater depth of imagination—is practically precluded.

This has been the case in Hemingway's career. He arrived on the literary scene absolute master of the style he has made his own; his attitudes were firmly fixed at that time. And he said pretty much what he had to say with his first stories and his first two novels.

As a novelist, it is my opinion that the best of Ernest Hemingway is still to be found in *The Sun Also Rises.* Its freshness has not faded with time. It remains one of the very best American novels of the Twenties.

The Sun Also Rises: A Commentary*

PHILIP YOUNG, Professor of American Literature at Pennsylvania State University, is the author of a critical study of Hemingway, as well as an introductory pamphlet on Hemingway's life and work and a number of critical essays on American literature.

The Sun Also Rises, which appeared in 1926, reintroduces us to the hero. In Hemingway's novels this man is a slightly less personal hero than Nick was, and his adventures are to be less closely identified with Hemingway's, for more events are changed, or even "made up." But he still projects qualities of the man who created him, many of his experiences are still either literal or transformed autobiography, and his wound is still the crucial fact about him. Even when, as Robert Jordan of *For Whom the Bell Tolls,* he is somewhat disguised, we have little or no trouble in recognizing him.

Recognition is immediate and unmistakable in *The Sun Also Rises.* Here the wound, again with its literal and symbolic meanings, is transferred from the spine to the genitals: Jake Barnes was emasculated in the war. But he is the same man, a grown Nick Adams, and again the actual injury func- [54/55] tions as concrete evidence that the hero is a casualty. He is a writer living in Paris in the twenties as, for example, Harry was; he was, like Nick, transplanted from midwestern America to the Austro-Italian front; when things are at their worst for him, like Fraser he cries in the night. When he refuses the services of a prostitute, and she asks, "What's the matter? You sick?" he is not thinking of his impotence alone when he answers, "Yes." He is the insomniac as before, and for the same reasons: "I blew out the lamp. Perhaps I would be able to sleep. My head

started to work. The old grievance." And later he remembers that time, which we witnessed, when "for six months I never slept with the light off." He is the man who is troubled in the night, who leaves Brett alone in his sitting room and lies face down on the bed, having "a bad time."

In addition, Jake like Nick is the protagonist who has broken with society and with the usual middle-class ways; and, again, he has made the break in connection with his wounding. He has very little use for most people. At times he has little use even for his friends; at times he has little use for himself. He exists on a fringe of the society he has renounced; as a newspaper reporter he works just enough to make enough money to eat and drink well on, and spends the rest of his time in cafés, or fishing, or watching bullfights. Though it is not highly developed yet, he and those few he respects have a code, too. Jake complains very little, although he suffers a good deal; there are certain things that are "done" and many that are "not done." Lady Brett Ashley also knows the code, and distinguishes people according to it; a person is "one of us," as she puts it, or is not—and most are not. The whole trouble with Robert Cohn, the boxing, maladroit Jew of the novel, is that he is not. He points up the code most clearly by so lacking it: he will not [55/56] go away when Brett is done with him; he is "messy" in every way. After he has se-

*Philip Young, "The Sun Also Rises: A Commentary," *Ernest Hemingway* (New York: Holt, Rinehart and Winston, Inc., copyright © 1952), pp. 54-60. Reprinted by permission of Holt, Rinehart and Winston, Inc.

verely beaten up Romero, the small young bullfighter, and Romero will not give in, Cohn cries, wretchedly proclaims his love for Brett in public, and tries to shake Romero's hand. He gets that hand in the face, an act which is approved as appropriate comment on his behavior.

Cohn does not like Romero because Brett does. She finally goes off with the bullfighter, and it is when she leaves him too that she makes a particularly clear statement of what she and the other "right" people have salvaged from the wreck of their compromised lives. She has decided that she is ruining Romero's career, and besides she is too old for him. She walks out, and says to Jake:

"It makes one feel rather good deciding not to be a bitch. . . . It's sort of what we have instead of God."

In early editions, *The Sun Also Rises* had on its title page, in addition to the passage on futility in *Ecclesiastes* from which the title is taken, Gertrude Stein's famous "You are all a lost generation." The novel provides an explanation for this observation, in addition to illustrating it in action. As in the story called "In Another Country," the picture of the hero wounded and embittered by his experience of violence is broadened to include other people. Brett Ashley, for example, and her fiancé Mike Campbell are both casualties from ordeals similar to those which damaged Jake. Brett has behind her the very unpleasant death of her first fiancé; Mike's whole character was shattered by the war. *A Farewell to Arms* can be read as background to the earlier novel: some of Brett's past is filled in by Catherine Barkley, whose fiancé had been blown to bits in the war, and most of Jake's by Frederic Henry. [56/57]

The fact that characters in *The Sun Also Rises* are recognizable people, taken from "real life," does not contradict the fact that they are in this pattern. Various personages known to Paris of the twenties have thought that they recognized with-

out difficulty the originals—Donald Ogden Stewart, Harold Stearns, Harold Loeb, Lady Duff-Twisden, Ford Madox Ford, and Pat Guthrie—and even Jake had his counterpart in actuality. But Hemingway, like most authors, has changed the characters to suit his purposes, and it is clear that whatever his origins, Jake, for instance, owes most to the man who created him, and is the hero.

He is the hero emasculated, however, and this must primarily account for the fact that he does not always seem entirely real. As he feels befits his status, he is largely a passive arranger of things for others, who only wants to "play it along and just not make trouble for people." But as narrator, at least, he is convincing, and if there is something blurred about him it helps to bring the participants into a focus that is all the sharper. Hemingway has always been good with secondary characters, finding them in a bright flash that reveals all we need know. Here, as he somehow manages to make similar people easily distinguishable, the revelations are brilliant. One remembers Brett and Cohn longest, for they get the fullest development, but Count Mippipopolous is wonderful, and wonderful too—save for their anti-Semitism, largely missing from the twenty-five cent edition, which advertises that "Not one word has been changed or omitted"—are Mike and Bill.

Chiefly it is Hemingway's ear, a trap that catches every mannerism of speech, that is responsible for the fact that these wastrels come so alive and distinct. That famous ear also caught a great many "swells" and "grands" that have [57/58] dated—for slang is one thing almost certain to go bad with the passage of time—and some of the dialogue of camaraderie ("Old Bill!" "You bum!") is also embarrassing. But taken as a whole the talk is superb and, as a whole, so is the rest of the writing in the book. Hemingway's wide-awake senses fully evoke an American's Paris, a vacationer's Spain. Jake moves through these places with the awareness of a professional soldier reconnoitering new terrain. The action is always foremost, but it is supported by real country and real city. The conversational style, which gives us the illusion that Jake is just telling us the story of what he has been doing lately, gracefully hides the fact that the pace is carefully calculated and swift, the sentences and scenes hard and clean. This is true of the over-all structure, too: the book is informal and relaxed only on the surface, and beneath it lies a scrupulous and satisfying orchestration. It is not until nearly the end, for example, when Cohn becomes the center of what there is of action, that opening with him seems anything but a simply random way of getting started. This discussion of Cohn has eased us into Jake's life in Paris, and especially his situation with Brett. Suddenly the lines are all drawn. An interlude of trout fishing moves us smoothly into Spain and the bullfights. At Pamplona the tension which all try to ignore builds up, slowly, and breaks finally as the events come to their climax simultaneously with the fiesta's. Then, in an intensely muted coda, a solitary Jake, rehabilitating himself, washes away his hangovers in the ocean. Soon it is all gone, he is returned to Brett as before, and we discover that we have come full circle, like all the rivers, the winds, and the sun, to the place where we began.

This is motion which goes no place. Constant activity has brought us along with such pleasant, gentle insistence **[58/59]** that not until the end do we realize that we have not been taken in, exactly, but taken nowhere; and that, finally, is the point. This is structure as meaning, organization as content. And, as the enormous effect the book had on its generation proved, such a meaning or content was important to 1926. The book touched with delicate accuracy on something big, on things other people were feeling, but too dimly for articulation. Hemingway had deeply felt and understood what was in the wind. Like Brett, who was the kind of woman who sets styles, the book itself was profoundly creative, and had the kind of power that is prototypal.

But for another generation, looking backward, this quality of the novel is largely gone out of it. The pessimism is based chiefly on the story of a hopeless love, and for Jake this is basis enough. But his situation with Brett sometimes seems forced—brought up periodically for air that it may be kept alive—as if Hemingway, who must have been through most of Jake's important experiences, but not exactly this one, had to keep reminding himself that it existed. And worse: though the rest of the pessimism rises eloquently out of the novel's structure, it does not seem to rise out of the day-to-day action at all. There is a gaping cleavage here between manner and message, between joy in life and a pronouncement of life's futility. Jake's disability excepted, always, the book now seems really the long *Fiesta* it was called in the English edition, and one's net impression today is of all the fun there is to be had in getting good and lost.

And yet *The Sun Also Rises* is still Hemingway's *Waste Land*, and Jake is Hemingway's Fisher King. This may be just coincidence, though the novelist had read the poem, but once again here is the protagonist gone impotent, and his land gone sterile. Eliot's London is Hemingway's Paris, **[59/60]** where spiritual life in general, and Jake's sexual life in particular, are alike impoverished. Prayer breaks down and fails, a knowledge of traditional distinctions between good and evil is largely lost, copulation is morally neutral and, cut off from the past chiefly by the spiritual disaster of the war, life has become mostly meaningless. "What shall we do?" is the same constant question, to which the answer must be, again, "Nothing." To hide it, instead of playing chess one drinks, mechanically and always. Love is a possibility only for the two who cannot love; once again homosexuality intensifies this atmosphere of sterility; once more the Fisher King is also a man who fishes. And again the author plays with quotations from the great of the past, as when in reply to Jake's remark that he is a taxidermist Bill objects, "That was in another country. And besides all the animals were dead."

To be sure, the liquor is good, and so are the food and the conversation. But in one way Hemingway's book is even more desperate than Eliot's. The lesson of an "asceticism" to control the aimless expression of lust would be to Jake Barnes only one more bad joke, and the fragments he has shored against his ruins are few, and quite inadequate. In the poem a message of salvation comes out of the life-giving rain which falls on western civilization. In Hemingway's waste land there is fun, but there is no hope. No rain falls on Europe this time, and when it does fall, in *A Farewell to Arms,* it brings not life but death.

Place, Fact, and Scene in *The Sun Also Rises**

CARLOS BAKER, Professor of English at Princeton University, has written critical studies of Shelley and Hemingway, a novel, and a number of essays and reviews.

"The job of the last twenty-five years was for the writer or artist to get what there was to be got (artistically) out of the world extant."

—*Ezra Pound*[1]

"A writer's job is to tell the truth," said Hemingway in 1942.[2] He had believed it for twenty years and he would continue to believe it as long as he lived. No other writer of our time has so fiercely asserted, so pugnaciously defended, or so consistently exemplified the writer's obligation to speak truly. His standard of truth-telling has been, moreover, so high and so rigorous that he has very rarely been willing to admit secondary evidence, whether literary evidence or evidence picked up from other sources than his own experience. "I only know what I have seen," is a statement which comes often to his lips and pen. What he has personally done, or what he knows unforgettably by having gone through one version of it, is what he is interested in telling about. This is not to say that he has refused to invent freely. But he has always made it a sacrosanct point to invent in terms of what he actually knows from having been there.

The primary intent of his writing, from first to last, has been to seize and project for the reader what he has often called "the way it was." This is a characteristically simple phrase for a concept of extraordinary complexity, and Hemingway's conception of its meaning has subtly changed several times in the course of his career—always in the direction of greater complexity. At the core of the concept, however, one can invariably discern the operation of three esthetic instruments: the sense of place, the sense of fact, and the sense of scene.

The first of these, which is clearly a passion with Hemingway, [48/49] is the sense of place. "Unless you have geography, background," he once told George Antheil, "you have nothing."[3] You have, that is to say, a dramatic vacuum. Few writers have been more place-conscious. Few have so carefully charted out the geographical groundwork of their novels while managing to keep background so conspicuously unobtrusive. Few, accordingly, have been able to record more economically and graphically the way it is when you walk through the streets of Paris in search of breakfast at a corner café. Or when your footfalls echo among surrounding walls on the ancient cobblestones of early morning Venice, heading for the market-place beside the Adriatic. Or when, at around six o'clock of a Spanish dawn, you watch the bulls running from the corrals at the Puerta Rochapea through the streets of Pamplona towards the bullring.

"When I woke it was the sound of the rocket exploding that announced the release of the bulls from the corrals at the

[1] Ezra Pound, quoted in Samuel Putnam, *Paris Was Our Mistress*, New York, 1947, p. 154.
[2] *Men at War*, New York, 1942, introduction, p. xv.
[3] George Antheil, *Bad Boy of Music*, p. 278.

*Carlos Baker, "Place, Fact, and Scene in *The Sun Also Rises*," *Hemingway: The Writer as Artist* (Princeton, N. J.: Princeton University Press, 1956), pp. 48-59. Copyright 1956 by the Princeton University Press.

edge of town. . . . Down below the narrow street was empty. All the balconies were crowded with people. Suddenly a crowd came down the street. They were all running, packed close together. They passed along and up the street toward the bullring and behind them came more men running faster, and then some stragglers who were really running. Behind them was a little bare space, and then the bulls, galloping, tossing their heads up and down. It all went out of sight around the corner. One man fell, rolled to the gutter, and lay quiet. But the bulls went right on and did not notice him. They were all running together."[4]

This scene is as morning-fresh as a design in India ink on clean white paper. First is the bare white street, seen from above, quiet and empty. Then one sees the first packed clot of runners. Behind these are the thinner ranks of those who move faster because closer to the bulls. Then the almost comic stragglers, who are "really running." Brilliantly behind these shines the "little bare space," a desperate margin for error. Then the clot of running bulls—closing the design, except of course for the man in the gutter making himself, like the designer's initials, as inconspicuous as possible. [**49/50**]

The continuing freshness of such occasions as this might be associated with Hemingway's lifelong habit of early waking. More likely, the freshness arises because Hemingway loves continental cities, makes it almost a fetish to know them with an artist's eye, and has trained himself rigorously to see and retain those aspects of a place that make it *that place,* even though, with an odd skill, he manages at the same time to render these aspects generically.

As with the cities—and Hemingway's preference is for the Latin cities—so with the marshes, rivers, lakes, troutstreams, gulfstreams, groves, forests, hills, and gullies, from Wyoming to Tanganyika, from the Tagliamento to the Irati, and from Key West to the Golden Horn. "None can care for literature itself," said Stevenson,

somewhere, "who do not take a special pleasure in the sound of names." Hemingway's love of names is obvious. It belongs to his sense of place. But like the rest of his language, it is under strict control. One never finds, as so often happens in the novels of Thomas Wolfe or the poetry of Carl Sandburg, the mere riot and revel of place-names, played upon like guitar-strings for the music they contain. Hemingway likes the words *country* and *land.* It is astonishing how often they recur in his work without being obtrusive. He likes to move from place to place, and to be firmly grounded, for the time being, in whatever place he has chosen. It may be the banks of the Big Two-Hearted River of Northern Michigan or its Spanish equivalent above Burguete. It may be the Guadarrama hilltop where El Sordo died, or the Veneto marshes where Colonel Cantwell shot his last mallards from a duckblind. Wherever it is, it is solid and permanent, both in itself and in the books.

The earliest of his published work, descriptively speaking, shows an almost neoclassical restraint. Take a sample passage from *The Sun Also Rises,* not his earliest but fairly representative. This one concerns the Irati Valley fishing-trip of Jake Barnes and Bill Gorton.

"It was a beech wood and the trees were very old. Their roots bulked above the ground and the branches were twisted. We walked on the road between the thick trunks of the old beeches and the sunlight came through the leaves in light patches on the [**50/51**] grass. The trees were big, and the foliage was thick but it was not gloomy. There was no undergrowth, only the smooth grass, very green and fresh, and the big gray trees were well spaced as though it were a park. 'This is country,' Bill said."[5]

It is such country as an impressionist might paint almost exactly in the terms, and the subdued colors, which Hemingway employs. More than this, however, is the fact that in such a paragraph Dr.

[4] *SAR,* pp. 165-166.
[5] *SAR,* p. 120.

Samuel Johnson's Imlac could find little to criticize. Even the arrangement of the beech trees themselves, like the choice of the words, is clean and classical. The foliage is thick, but there is no gloom. Here is neither teeming undergrowth nor its verbal equivalent. The sage of Johnson's *Rasselas* advises all aspirant poets against numbering the streaks of the tulip or describing in detail the different shades of the verdure of the forest. Young Hemingway, still an aspirant poet, follows the advice. When he has finished, it is possible to say (and we supply our own inflection for Bill Gorton's words) : "This is country."

For all the restraint, the avoidance of color-flaunting adjectives, and the plainsong sentences (five compound to one complex), the paragraph is loaded with precisely observed fact: beech wood, old trees, exposed roots, twisted branches, thick trunks, sun-patches, smooth green grass, foliage which casts a shade without excluding light. One cannot say that he has been given a generalized landscape—there are too many exact factual observations. On the other hand, the uniquenesses of the place receive no special emphasis. One recognizes easily the generic type of the clean and orderly grove, where weeds and brush do not flourish because of the shade, and the grass gets only enough light to rise to carpet-level. Undoubtedly, as in the neoclassical esthetic, the intent is to provide a generic frame within which the reader is at liberty to insert his own uniquenesses—as many or as few as his imagination may supply.

Along with the sense of place, and as a part of it, is the sense of fact. Facts march through all his pages in a stream as continuous as the refugee wagons in Thrace or the military camions on the road from the Isonzo. Speculation, whether by the author or by the characters, is ordinarily kept to a minimum. But facts, [51/52] visible or audible or tangible facts, facts baldly stated, facts without verbal paraphernalia to inhibit their striking power, are the stuff of Hemingway's prose.

Sometimes, especially in the early work, the facts seem too many for the effect apparently intended, though even here the reader should be on guard against misconstruing the intention of a given passage. It is hard to discover, nevertheless, what purpose beyond the establishment of the sense of place is served by Barnes's complete itinerary of his walk with Bill Gorton through the streets of Paris.[6] The direction is from Madame Lecomte's restaurant on the Île St. Louis across to the left bank of the Seine, and eventually up the Boulevard du Port Royal to the Café Select. The walk fills only two pages. Yet it seems much longer and does not further the action appreciably except to provide Jake and Bill with healthy after-dinner exercise. At Madame Lecomte's (the facts again), they have eaten "a roast chicken, new green beans, mashed potatoes, a salad, and some apple pie and cheese." To the native Parisian, or a foreigner who knows the city, the pleasure in the after-dinner itinerary would consist in the happy shock of recognition. For others, the inclusion of so many of the facts of municipal or gastronomic geography—so many more than are justified by their dramatic purpose—may seem excessive.

Still, this is the way it was that time in Paris. Here lay the bridges and the streets, the squares and the cafés. If you followed them in the prescribed order, you came to the café where Lady Brett Ashley sat on a high stool at the bar, her crossed legs stockingless, her eyes crinkling at the corners.

If an imaginative fusion of the sense of place and the sense of fact is to occur, and if, out of the fusing process, dramatic life is to arise, a third element is required. This may be called the sense of scene. Places are less than geography, facts lie inert and uncoordinated, unless the imagination runs through them like a vitalizing current and the total picture moves and quickens. How was it, for example, that second day of the San Fermin fiesta in

---

[6] *SAR*, pp. 79-80.

the Pamplona bullring after Romero had killed the first bull?

"They had hitched the mules to the dead bull and then the whips cracked, the men ran, and the mules, straining forward, [52/53] their legs pushing, broke into a gallop, and the bull, one horn up, his head on its side, swept a swath smoothly across the sand and out the red gate." [7]

Here are a dead bull, men, mules, whips, sand, and a red gate like a closing curtain —the place and the facts. But here also, in this remarkably graphic sentence, are the seven verbs, the two adverbs, and the five adverbial phrases which fuse and co-ordinate the diverse facts of place and thing and set them in rapid motion. If one feels that the sentence is very satisfying as a scene, and wishes to know why, the answer might well lie where it so often lies in a successful lyric poem—that is, in our sense of difficulty overcome. Between the inertness of the dead bull when he is merely *hitched* (a placid verb) and the smooth speed with which the body finally *sweeps* across the sand and out of sight, come the verbs of sweating effort: *crack, run, strain,* and *break.* It is precisely at the verb *broke* that the sentence stops straining and moves into the smooth glide of its close. The massing, in that section of the sentence, of a half-dozen *s*'s, compounded with the *th* sounds of *swath* and *smoothly,* can hardly have been inadvertent. They ease (or grease) the path of the bull's departure.

The pattern in the quoted passage is that of a task undertaken, striven through, and smoothly completed: order and success. For another graphic sentence, so arranged as to show the precise opposites— total disorder and total failure—one might take the following example from *Death in the Afternoon.* The protagonist is a "phenomenon," a bullfighter who has lost his nerve.

"In your mind you see the phenomenon, sweating, white-faced, and sick with fear, unable to look at the horn or go near it, a couple of swords on the ground, capes all around him, running in at an angle on the bull hoping the sword will strike a vital spot, cushions sailing down into the ring and the steers ready to come in." [8]

In this passage, place has become predicament. The facts, thrown in almost helter-skelter, imply the desperate inward fear which is responsible for the creation of the outward disorder. Verbs are held to a minimum, and their natural naked power is [53/54] limited with qualifications. The phenomenon is *unable to look,* and *hoping to strike,* not *looking* and *striking.* He runs, but it is at a bad angle. The disorder of the swords on the ground and the capes all around is increased by the scaling-in of seat-cushions from the benches, the audience's insult to gross cowardice. The author-spectator's crowning insult is the allusion to the steers, who by comparison with the enraged bull are bovine, old-womanly creatures. On being admitted to the ring, they will quiet and lead away the bull the phenomenon could not kill.

The sense of place and the sense of fact are indispensable to Hemingway's art. But the true craft, by which diversities are unified and compelled into graphic collaboration, comes about through the operation of the sense of scene. Often, moving through the Latin language countries, watching the crowd from a café table or a barrera bench, Hemingway seems like a lineal descendant of Browning's observer in *How It Strikes a Contemporary.*

> You saw go up and down Valladolid
> A man of mark, to know next time you saw . . .
> Scenting the world, looking it full in face.

Although they are clearly fundamental to any consideration of Hemingway's esthetic aims, place, fact, and scene are together no more than one phase of a more complex observational interest. The skillful writer can make them work in harmony, with place and fact like teamed horses under the dominance of the sense

[7] *SAR*, p. 175.
[8] *DIA*, p. 226.

of scene. The result is often as striking and satisfactory to watch as a good chariot race. But the event is, after all, mainly an extrinsic matter. These are not Plato's horses of the soul.

The complementary phase is inward: a state of mind causally related to the extrinsic events and accurately presented in direct relation to those events. When Samuel Putnam asked Hemingway in the late twenties for a definition of his aims, the answer was: "Put down what I see and what I feel in the best and simplest way I can tell it." [9] Taken as absolute standards, of course, best- [54/55] ness and simplicity will often be at variance, a fact of which Hemingway at that date was apparently becoming more and more conscious. But his aim from the beginning had been to show, if he could, the precise relationship between what he saw and what he felt.

It is characteristic of Hemingway, with his genuine scorn for overintellectualized criticism, that he has himself refused to employ critical jargon in the presentation of his esthetic ideas. It is also evident, however, that early in his career, probably about 1922, he had evolved an esthetic principle which might be called "the discipline of double perception." The term is not quite exact, since the aim of double perception is ultimately a singleness of vision. This is the kind of vision everyone experiences when his two eyes, though each sees the same set of objects from slightly disparate angles, work together to produce a unified picture with a sense of depth to it. According to Hemingway, he was trying very hard for this double perception about the time of his return from the Near East in the fall of 1922. Aside from knowing "truly" what he "really" felt in the presence of any given piece of action, he found that his greatest difficulty lay in putting down on paper "what really happened in action; what the actual things were which produced the emotion" felt by the observer. No wonder that he was finding it hard to get "the real thing, the sequence of motion and fact which made

the emotion." Whatever that real thing was, if you stated it "purely" enough and were likewise lucky, there was a chance that your statement of it would be valid, esthetically and emotionally valid, forever. [10]

Fundamental to the task is the deletion of one's own preconceptions. Such and such was the way it *ought* to be, the way you *assumed* it was. But "oughts" and "assumptions" are dangerous ground for a man to stand on who wishes to take the word of no one else, and to achieve in esthetics what René Descartes thought he had achieved in philosophy, namely, a start at the start. The hope was that the genuinely serious and determined writer-observer might be able in time to penetrate behind the illusions which all our preconceptions play upon the act of clear [55/56] seeing.

It would then become his task to perfect himself in the discipline of double perception. To make something so humanly true that it will outlast the vagaries of time and change, yet will still speak directly to one's own changing time, he must somehow reach a state of objective awareness between two poles, one inward-outward and the other outward-inward. The first need (though not always first in order of time) is the ability to look within and to describe that complex of mixed emotions which a given set of circumstances has produced in the observer's mind. The other necessity is to locate and to state factually and exactly that outer complex of motion and fact which produced the emotional reaction.

This second class of things and circumstances, considered in their relations to the emotional complexes of the first class, would be precisely what T. S. Eliot called "objective correlatives." [11] His statement calls them variously "a set of objects, a situation, a chain of events which shall be the formula of that particular emotion; such that when the external facts, which

[9] Samuel Putnam, *op. cit.*, pp. 128-129.
[10] *DIA*, p. 2.
[11] T. S. Eliot, *The Sacred Wood*, London, 1920, pp. 92-93.

must terminate in sensory experience, are given, the emotion is immediately evoked." He states further that the idea of artistic "inevitability" consists in the "complete adequacy of the external to the emotion." Mr. Eliot's generic description fits Hemingway's customary performance. Yet it may be noticed that Eliot's most frequent practice, as distinguished from his theoretical formulation, is to fashion his objective correlatives into a series of complex *literary* symbols. These are designed to elicit a more or less controlled emotional response from the reader (like the Wagnerian passage in *The Waste Land*), depending to some degree on the extent of his cultural holdings. With Hemingway, on the other hand, the objective correlatives are not so much inserted and adapted as observed and encompassed. They are to be traced back, not to anterior literature and art objects, but to things actually seen and known by direct experience of the world.

Hemingway's method has this special advantage over Eliot's—that one's ability to grasp the emotional suggestions embodied in an objective correlative depends almost solely on two factors: the reader's sensitivity to emotional suggestion, and the degree [**56/57**] of his imaginative and sympathetic involvement in the story which is being told. With Eliot these two factors are likewise emphatically present, but a third is added. This third, which in a measure controls and delimits the first two, is the factor of "literary" experience. One's emotional response to the Wagnerian passage cannot be really full unless he knows its origin, can see it in both its original and its new and secondary context, and can make certain quick comparisons between the two. Some, though not all, of Eliot's correlatives accordingly show a "twice-removed" quality which in a measure pales and rarefies them. They cannot always achieve the full-bloodedness and immediacy of correlatives taken directly from the actual set of empirical circumstances which produced in the author the emotion which he is seeking to convey

to the reader.

The objective correlatives in Hemingway appear to be of two main types, arbitrarily separable though always working together in a variety of ways. The first may be called *things-in-context:* that particular arrangement of facts in their relations to one another which constitutes a static field of perception. The second type may be called *things-in-motion,* since the arrangement of facts in their relations one to another is almost never wholly static. One might call any combination of the two types by the generic term of *what happened,* where the idea of happening implies a sequence of events in a certain order in time, though any event in the sequence can be arrested to form a static field of observation. If you have *what happened* in this special sense, you will have a chance of reproducing, in a perspective with depth, "the way it was."

To write for permanence, therefore, is to find and set down those things-in-context and things-in-motion which evoked a reaction in the writer as observer. Yet even the presence of both of these correlatives will not suffice to produce the total effect unless one also knows and says what he "really felt" in their presence. The important corollary idea of selection, meaning the elimination of the irrelevant and the unimportant at both poles, is clearly implied in Hemingway's phrase, "stated purely enough." During the five years of his early apprenticeship and the next five in which he developed his skills with such remarkable rapidity, the disci- [**57/58**] pline of double perception was for Hemingway the leading esthetic principle. It is hard to imagine a better—or more difficult—task for the young writer to attempt. Although other principles and other skills have since arisen to complement and supplement this first one, it still occupies one whole side of his attention as an artist.

The basis of Hemingway's continuing power, and the real backbone of his eminence, is in practical esthetics. "Pure" cr theoretical esthetics, of that special bloodless order which can argue to all hours without a glance at concretions, holds little interest for an artist of so pragmatic and empirical a cast of mind. One might even doubt that theoretical esthetics is of real interest to any genuine artist, unless in his alter ego he happens also to be a philosophical critic. If that is true, his artistic life is always in some danger, as Hemingway's is not. In esthetics as in his personal philosophy, he has labored hard to stay free of the wrong kind of illusion, and out from under the control of any cut-and-dried system, always trying instead to keep his eye trained on the thing in itself and the effect of the thing in himself. The actual, he wrote in 1949, is "made of knowledge, experience, wine, bread, oil, salt, vinegar, bed, early mornings, nights, days, the sea, men, women, dogs, beloved motor cars, bicycles, hills and valleys, the appearance and disappearance of trains on straight and curved tracks . . . cock grouse drumming on a basswood log, the smell of sweetgrass and fresh-smoked leather and Sicily." [12] Given the knowledge and experience of these and their unnamed equivalents, the artist can be at home in the world. If he is a practical esthetician whose aim is to "invent truly," he is on firm ground. By experience he knows what will do. By observation he knows what will go—like the eminently practical Aristotle of the *Poetics*.

It was once remarked, though not by Aristotle, that the province of esthetics is the true and the beautiful, the province of morality the good. Of Hemingway as a moral writer there will be much to say. It is clear that the strongest conviction in Heming- [**58/59**] way the esthetician—the principle underlying his sense of place and fact and scene, the principle supporting his "discipline of double perception"—is the importance of telling truth.

[12] Introd. to Elio Vittorini's novel, *In Sicily*, New York, 1949.

The Death of Love in *The Sun Also Rises**

MARK SPILKA teaches English and American literature at the University of Michigan and has written extensively in the field of his interest.

One of the most persistent themes of the twenties was the death of love in World War I. All the major writers recorded it, often in piecemeal fashion, as part of the larger postwar scene; but only Hemingway seems to have caught it whole and delivered it in lasting fictional form. His [238/239] intellectual grasp of the theme might account for this. Where D. H. Lawrence settles for the shock of war on the Phallic Consciousness, or where Eliot presents assorted glimpses of sterility, Hemingway seems to design an extensive parable. Thus, in *The Sun Also Rises,* his protagonists are deliberately shaped as allegorical figures: Jake Barnes and Brett Ashley are two lovers desexed by the war; Robert Cohn is the false knight who challenges their despair; while Romero, the stalwart bullfighter, personifies the good life which will survive their failure. Of course, these characters are not abstractions in the text; they are realized through the most concrete style in American fiction, and their larger meaning is implied only by their response to immediate situations. But the implications are there, the parable is at work in every scene, and its presence lends unity and depth to the whole novel.

Barnes himself is a fine example of this technique. Cut off from love by a shell wound, he seems to suffer from an undeserved misfortune. But as most readers agree, his condition represents a peculiar form of emotional impotence. It does not involve distaste for the flesh, as with Law- rence's crippled veteran, Clifford Chatterley; instead Barnes lacks the power to control love's strength and durability. His sexual wound, the result of an unpreventable "accident" in the war, points to another realm where accidents can always happen and where Barnes is equally powerless to prevent them. In Book II of the novel he makes this same comparison while describing one of the dinners at Pamplona: "It was like certain dinners I remember from the war. There was much wine, an ignored tension, and a feeling of things coming that you could not prevent happening." This fear of emotional consequences is the key to [239/240] Barnes's condition. Like so many Hemingway heroes, he has no way to handle subjective complications, and his wound is a token for this kind of impotence.

It serves the same purpose for the expatriate crowd in Paris. In some figurative manner these artists, writers, and derelicts have all been rendered impotent by the war. Thus, as Barnes presents them, they pass before us like a parade of sexual cripples, and we are able to measure them against his own forbearance in the face of a common problem. Whoever bears his sickness well is akin to Barnes; whoever adopts false postures, or willfully hurts others, falls short of his example. This is the organizing principle in Book I, this alignment of characters by their stoic qualities. But, stoic or not, they are all incapable of love, and in their sober moments they seem to know it.

*Mark Spilka, "The Death of Love in *The Sun Also Rises,"* *Twelve Original Essays on Great American Novels,* ed., Charles Shapiro (Detroit, Mich.: Wayne State University Press, 1958), pp. 238-256. Copyright 1958 by the Wayne State University Press. Reprinted by permission of the publishers.

For this reason they feel especially upset whenever Robert Cohn appears. Cohn still upholds a romantic view of life, and since he affirms it with stubborn persistence, he acts like a goad upon his wiser contemporaries. As the narrator, Barnes must account for the challenge he presents them and the decisive turn it takes in later chapters. Accordingly, he begins the book with a review of Cohn's boxing career at Princeton. Though he has no taste for it, college boxing means a lot to Cohn. For one thing, it helps to compensate for anti-Semitic treatment from his classmates. More subtly, it turns him into an armed romantic, a man who can damage others in defense of his own beliefs. He also loves the pose of manhood which it affords him and seems strangely pleased when his nose is flattened in the ring. Soon other tokens of virility delight him, and he often confuses them with actual manliness. He likes the idea of a mistress more than he likes his actual mistress; or [**240/241**] he likes the authority of editing and the prestige of writing, though he is a bad editor and a poor novelist. In other words, he always looks for internal strength in outward signs and sources. On leaving Princeton, he marries "on the rebound from the rotten time . . . in college." But in five years the marriage falls through, and he rebounds again to his present mistress, the forceful Frances Clyne. Then, to escape her dominance and his own disquiet, he begins to look for romance in far-off countries. As with most of his views, the source of this idea is an exotic book:

He had been reading W. H. Hudson. That sounds like an innocent occupation, but Cohn had read and reread "The Purple Land." "The Purple Land" is a very sinister book if read too late in life. It recounts splendid imaginary amorous adventures of a perfect English gentleman in an intensely romantic land, the scenery of which is very well described. For a man to take it at thirty-four as a guidebook to what life holds is about as safe as it would be for a man of the same age to enter Wall Street direct from a French convent, equipped with a complete set of the more practical Alger books. Cohn, I believe, took every word

of "The Purple Land" as literally as though it had been an R. G. Dun report.

Cohn's romanticism explains his key position in the parable. He is the last chivalric hero, the last defender of an outworn faith, and his function is to illustrate its present folly—to show us, through the absurdity of his behavior, that romantic love is dead, that one of the great guiding codes of the past no longer operates. "You're getting damned romantic," says Brett to Jake at one point in the novel. "No, bored," he replies, because for this generation [**241/242**] boredom has become more plausible than love. As a foil to his contemporaries, Cohn helps to reveal why this is so.

Of course, there is much that is traditional in the satire on Cohn. Like the many victims of romantic literature, from Don Quixote to Tom Sawyer, he lives by what he reads and neglects reality at his own and others' peril. But Barnes and his friends have no alternative to Cohn's beliefs. There is nothing here, for example, like the neat balance between sense and sensibility in Jane Austen's world. Granted that Barnes is sensible enough, that he sees life clearly and that we are meant to contrast his private grief with Cohn's public suffering, his self-restraint with Cohn's deliberate self-exposure. Yet, emasculation aside, Barnes has no way to measure or control the state of love; and though he recognizes this with his mind and tries to act accordingly, he seems no different from Cohn in his deepest feelings. When he is alone with Brett, he wants to live with her in the country, to go with her to San Sebastian, to go up to her room, to keep her in his own room, or to keep on kissing her—though he can never really act upon such sentiments. Nor are they merely the yearnings of a tragically impotent man, for eventually they will lead Barnes to betray his own principles and to abandon self-respect, all for the sake of Lady Ashley. No, at best he is a restrained romantic, a man who carries himself well in the face of love's impossibilities, but who seems to share with Cohn a common (if hidden) weakness.

The sexual parade continues through the early chapters. Besides Cohn and his possessive mistress, there is the prostitute Georgette, whom Barnes picks up one day "because of a vague sentimental idea that it would be nice to eat with someone." Barnes introduces her to his friends as his [242/243] fiancée, and as his private joke affirms, the two have much in common. Georgette is sick and sterile, having reduced love to a simple monetary exchange; but, like Barnes, she manages to be frank and forthright and to keep an even keel among the drifters of Paris. Together they form a pair of honest cripples, in contrast with the various pretenders whom they meet along the Left Bank. Among the latter are Cohn and Frances Clyne, the writer Braddocks and his wife, and Robert Prentiss, a rising young novelist who seems to verbalize their phoniness: "Oh, how charmingly you get angry," he tells Barnes. "I wish I had that faculty." Barnes's honest anger has been aroused by the appearance of a band of homosexuals, accompanied by Brett Ashley. When one of the band spies Georgette, he decides to dance with her; then one by one the rest follow suit, in deliberate parody of normal love. Brett herself provides a key to the dizzy sexual medley. With a man's felt hat on her boyish bob, and with her familiar reference to men as fellow "chaps," she completes the distortion of sexual roles which seems to characterize the period. For the war, which has unmanned Barnes and his contemporaries, has turned Brett into the freewheeling equal of any man. It has taken her first sweetheart's life through dysentery and has sent her present husband home in a dangerous state of shock. For Brett these blows are the equivalent of Jake's emasculation; they seem to release her from her womanly nature and expose her to the male prerogatives of drink and promiscuity. Once she claims these rights as her own, she becomes an early but more honest version of Catherine Barkley, the English nurse in Hem-

ingway's next important novel, *A Farewell to Arms*. Like Catherine, Brett has been a nurse on the Italian front and has lost a sweetheart in the war; but for her [243/244] there is no saving interlude of love with a wounded patient, no rigged and timely escape through death in childbirth. Instead she survives the colossal violence, the disruption of her personal life, and the exposure to mass promiscuity, to confront a moral and emotional vacuum among her postwar lovers. With this evidence of male default all around her, she steps off the romantic pedestal, moves freely through the bars of Paris, and stands confidently there beside her newfound equals. Ironically, her most recent conquest, Robert Cohn, fails to see the bearing of such changes on romantic love. He still believes that Brett is womanly and therefore deeply serious about intimate matters. After their first meeting, he describes her as "absolutely fine and straight" and nearly strikes Barnes for thinking otherwise; and a bit later, after their brief affair in the country, he remains unconvinced "that it didn't mean anything." But when men no longer command respect, and women replace their natural warmth with masculine freedom and mobility, there can be no serious love.

Brett does have some respect for Barnes, even a little tenderness, though her actions scarcely show abiding love. At best she can affirm his worth and share his standards and perceptions. When in public, she knows how to keep her essential misery to herself; when alone with Barnes, she will express her feelings, admit her faults, and even display good judgment. Thus her friend Count Mippipopolous is introduced to Barnes as "one of us." The count qualifies by virtue of his war wounds, his invariable calmness, and his curious system of values. He appreciates good food, good wine, and a quiet place in which to enjoy them. Love also has a place in his system, but since he is "always in love," the place seems rather shaky. Like Jake and Brett [244/245] and perhaps Georgette, he simply bears himself well among the postwar ruins.

The count completes the list of cripples who appear in Book I. In a broader sense, they are all disaffiliates, all men and women who have cut themselves off from conventional society and who have made Paris their permanent playground. Jake Barnes has introduced them, and we have been able to test them against his stoic attitudes toward life in a moral wasteland. Yet such life is finally unbearable, as we have also seen whenever Jake and Brett are alone together, or whenever Jake is alone with his thoughts. He needs a healthier code to live by, and for this reason the movement in Book II is away from Paris to the trout stream at Burguete and the bull ring at Pamplona. Here a more vital testing process occurs, and with the appearance of Bill Gorton we get our first inkling of its nature.

Gorton is a successful writer who shares with Barnes a love for boxing and other sports. In Vienna he has helped to rescue a splendid Negro boxer from an angry and intolerant crowd. The incident has spoiled Vienna for him, and, as his reaction suggests, the sports world will provide the terms of moral judgment from this point onward in the novel. Or, more accurately, Jake Barnes's feelings about sports will shape the rest of the novel. For, with Hemingway, the great outdoors is chiefly a state of mind, a projection of moral and emotional attitudes onto physical arenas, so that a clear account of surface action will reproduce these attitudes in the reader. In "Big Two-Hearted River," for example, he describes Nick Adams' fishing and camping activities along a trout stream in Michigan. His descriptions run to considerable length, and they are all [245/246] carefully detailed, almost as if they were meant for a fishing manual. Yet the details themselves have strong emotional connotations for Nick Adams. He thinks of his camp as "the good place," the place where none of his previous troubles can touch him. He has left society behind him, and, as the story begins, there is even a burnt town at his back, to signify his disaffiliation. He has also walked miles to reach an arbitrary campsite, and this is one of the ways in which he sets his own conditions for happiness and then lives up to them. He finds extraordinary pleasure, moreover, in the techniques of making coffee and pitching camp, or in his responses to fishing and eating. In fact, his sensations have become so valuable that he doesn't want to rush them: they bring health, pleasure, beauty, and a sense of order which is sorely missing in his civilized experience; they are part of a healing process, a private and imaginative means of wiping out the damages of civilized life. When this process is described with elaborate attention to surface detail, the effect on the reader is decidedly subjective.

The same holds true, of course, for the fishing trip in *The Sun Also Rises*. As Barnes and Gorton approach "the good place," each item in the landscape is singled out and given its own importance. Later the techniques of fishing are treated with the same reverence for detail. For, like Nick Adams, these men have left the wasteland for the green plains of health; they have traveled miles, by train and on foot, to reach a particular trout stream. The fishing there is good, the talk free and easy, and even Barnes is able to sleep well after lunch, though he is usually an insomniac. The meal itself is handled like a mock religious ceremony: "Let us rejoice in our blessings," says Gorton. "Let us utilize the fowls of the air. Let us utilize the produce of [246/247] the vine. Will you utilize a little, brother?" A few days later, when they visit the old monastery at Roncesvalles, this combination of fishing, drinking, and male camaraderie is given an edge over religion itself. With their English friend, Harris, they honor the monastery as a remarkable place, but decide that "it isn't the same as fishing"; then all agree to "utilize" a little pub across the way. At the trout stream, moreover, romantic love is given the same comparative treatment and seems sadly foolish before the immediate joys of fishing:

It was a little past noon and there was not much shade, but I sat against the trunk of two of the trees that grew together, and read. The book was something by A. E. W. Mason, and I was reading a wonderful story about a man who had been frozen in the Alps and then fallen into a glacier and disappeared, and his bride was going to wait twenty-four years exactly for his body to come out on the moraine, while her true love waited too, and they were still waiting when Bill came up [with four trout in his bag].... His face was sweaty and happy.

As these comparisons show, the fishing trip has been invested with unique importance. By sticking closely to the surface action, Barnes has evoked the deeper attitudes which underlie it and which make it a therapeutic process for him. He describes himself now as a "rotten Catholic" and speaks briefly of his thwarted love for Brett; but with religion defunct and love no longer possible, he can at least find happiness through private and imaginative means. Thus he now constructs a more positive code to follow: as with Nick Adams, it brings him health, pleasure, beauty and order, and helps to wipe out the damage of his troubled life in Paris. [247/248]

Yet somehow the code lacks depth and substance. To gain these advantages, Barnes must move to Pamplona, which stands roughly to Burguete as the swamp in "Big Two-Hearted River" stands to the trout stream. In the latter story, Nick Adams prefers the clear portion of the river to its second and more congested heart:

In the swamp the banks were bare, the big cedars came together overhead, the sun did not come through, except in patches; in the fast deep water, in the half light, the fishing would be tragic. In the swamp fishing was a tragic adventure. Nick did not want it.... There were plenty of days coming when he could fish the swamp.

The fishing is tragic here because it involves the risk of death. Nick is not yet ready for that challenge, but plainly it will test his manhood when he comes to face it. In *The Sun Also Rises* Barnes makes no such demands upon himself; but he is strongly attracted to the young bullfighter, Pedro Romero, whose courage be-

fore death lends moral weight to the sportsman's code.[1]

So Pamplona is an extension of Burguete for Barnes: gayer and more festive on the surface, but essentially more [248/249] serious. The spoilers from Paris have arrived, but (Cohn excepted) they are soon swept up by the fiesta: their mood is jubilant, they are surrounded by dancers, and they sing, drink, and shout with the peasant crowd. Barnes himself is among fellow *aficionados;* he gains "real emotion" from the bullfights and feels truly elated afterwards. Even his friends seem like "such nice people," though he begins to feel uneasy when an argument breaks out between them. The tension is created by Brett's fiancé, Mike Campbell, who is aware of her numerous infidelities and who seems to accept them with amoral tolerance. Actually he resents them, so that Cohn (the perennial Jewish scapegoat) provides him with a convenient outlet for his feelings. He begins to bait him for following Brett around like a sick steer.

Mike's description is accurate enough. Cohn is always willing to suffer in public and to absorb insults for the sake of true love. On the other hand, he is also "ready to do battle for his lady," and when the chance finally comes, he knocks his rivals down like a genuine knight-errant. With Jake and Mike he has no trouble, but when he charges into Pedro's room to rescue Brett, the results are disastrous: Brett tells him off, the bullfighter refuses to stay knocked down, and no one will shake hands with him at the end, in accord with

[1] Hemingway's preoccupation with death has been explained in various ways: by his desire to write about simple, fundamental things; by his "sadomasochism"; or, more fairly and accurately, by his need to efface an actual war wound, or to supplant the ugly, senseless violence of war with ordered, graceful violence. Yet chiefly the risk of death lends moral seriousness to a private code which lacks it. The risk is arbitrary; when a man elects to meet it, his beliefs take on subjective weight and he is able to give meaning to his private life. In this sense, he moves forever on a kind of imaginative frontier, where the opposition is always Nature, in some token form, where the stakes are always manliness and self-respect, and where death invests the scene with tragic implications. In *The Sun Also Rises*, Romero lives on such a frontier, and for Barnes and his friends he provides an example of just these values.

prep-school custom. When Brett remains with Pedro, Cohn retires to his room, alone and friendless.

This last encounter is the high point of the parable, for in the Code Hero, the Romantic Hero has finally met his match. As the clash between them shows, there is a difference between physical and moral victory, between chivalric stubbornness and real self-respect. Thus Pedro fights to repair an affront to his dignity; though he is badly beaten, [**249/250**] his spirit is untouched by his opponent, whereas Cohn's spirit is completely smashed. From the beginning Cohn has based his manhood on skill at boxing, or upon a woman's love, never upon internal strength; but now, when neither skill nor love supports him, he has bludgeoned his way to his own emptiness. Compare his conduct with Romero's, on the following day, as the younger man performs for Brett in the bull ring:

Everything of which he could control the locality he did in front of her all that afternoon. Never once did he look up. . . . Because he did not look up to ask if it pleased he did it all for himself inside, and it strengthened him, and yet he did it for her, too. But he did not do it for her at any loss to himself. He gained by it all through the afternoon.

Thus, where Cohn expends and degrades himself for his beloved, Romero pays tribute without self-loss. His manhood is a thing independent of women, and for this reason he holds special attractions for Jake Barnes.

By now it seems apparent that Cohn and Pedro are extremes for which Barnes is the unhappy medium. His resemblance to Pedro is clear enough: they share the same code, they both believe that a man's dignity depends on his own resources. His resemblance to Cohn is more subtle, but at this stage of the book it becomes grossly evident. Appropriately enough, the exposure comes through the knockout blow from Cohn, which dredges up a strange prewar experience:

Walking across the square ₁o the hotel everything looked new and changed. . . . I felt as I felt once coming home from an out-of-town football game. I was carrying a suitcase with my football [**250/251**] things in it, and I walked up the street from the station in the town I had lived in all my life and it was all new. They were raking the lawns and burning leaves in the road, and I stopped for a long time and watched. It was all strange. Then I went on, and my feet seemed to be a long way off, and everything seemed to come from a long way off, and I could hear my feet walking a great distance away. I had been kicked in the head early in the game. It was like that crossing the square. It was like that going up the stairs in the hotel. Going up the stairs took a long time, and I had the feeling that I was carrying my suitcase.

Barnes seems to have regressed here to his youthful football days. As he moves on up the stairs to see Cohn, who has been asking for him, he still carries his "phantom suitcase" with him; and when he enters Cohn's room, he even sets it down. Cohn himself has just returned from the fight with Romero: "There he was, face down on the bed, crying. He had on a white polo shirt, the kind he'd worn at Princeton." In other words, Cohn has also regressed to his abject college days: they are both emotional adolescents, about the same age as the nineteen-year-old Romero, who is the only real man among them. Of course, these facts are not spelled out for us, except through the polo shirt and the phantom suitcase, which remind us (inadvertently) of one of those dreamlike fantasies by the Czech genius Franz Kafka, in which trunks and youthful clothes are symbols of arrested development. Yet there has already been some helpful spelling out in Book I, during a curious (and otherwise pointless) exchange between Cohn and another expatriate, the drunkard Harvey Stone. After first calling Cohn a moron, Harvey asks him to say, without thinking about it, what he would rather do if he could do anything he [**251/252**] wanted. Cohn is again urged to say what comes into his head first, and soon replies, "I think I'd rather play football again with what I know about handling myself, now." To which Harvey responds: "I misjudged you. . . . You're not a moron. You're only a case of arrested development."

The first thought to enter Cohn's mind here has been suppressed by Barnes for a long time, but in Book II the knockout blow releases it: more than anything else, he too would like to "play football again," to prevent that kick to his head from happening, or that smash to the jaw from Cohn, or that sexual wound which explains either blow. For the truth about Barnes seems obvious now: he has always been an emotional adolescent. Like Nick Adams, he has grown up in a society which has little use for manliness; as an expression of that society, the war has robbed him of his dignity as a man and has thus exposed him to indignities with women. We must understand here that the war, the early football game, and the fight with Cohn have this in common: they all involve ugly, senseless, or impersonal forms of violence, in which a man has little chance to set the terms of his own integrity. Hence for Hemingway they represent the kinds of degradation which can occur at any point in modern society— and the violence at Pamplona is our current sample of such degradation. Indeed, the whole confluence of events now points to the social meaning of Jake's wound, for just as Cohn has reduced him to a dazed adolescent, so has Brett reduced him to a slavish pimp. When she asks for his help in her affair with Pedro, Barnes has no integrity to rely on; he can only serve her as Cohn has served her, like a sick romantic steer. Thus, for love's sake, he will allow her to use him as a go-between, to disgrace him with his friend Montoya, to [252/253] corrupt Romero, and so strip the whole fiesta of significance. In the next book he will even run to her rescue in Madrid, though by then he can at least recognize his folly and supply his own indictment: "That was it. Send a girl off with one man. Introduce her to another to go off with him. Now go and bring her back. And sign the wire with love. That was it all right." It seems plain, then, that

Cohn and Brett have given us a peacetime demonstration, postwar style, of the meaning of Jake's shell wound.

At Pamplona the demonstration continues. Brett strolls through the fiesta with her head high, "as though [it] were being staged in her honor, and she found it pleasant and amusing." When Romero presents her with a bull's ear "cut by popular acclamation," she carries it off to her hotel, stuffs it far back in the drawer of the bed table, and forgets about it. The ear was taken, however, from the same bull which had killed one of the crowd a few days before, during the dangerous bull-run through the streets; later the entire town attended the man's funeral, along with drinking and dancing societies from nearby communities. For the crowd, the death of this bull was a communal triumph and his ear a token of communal strength; for Brett the ear is a private trophy. In effect, she has robbed the community of its triumph, as she will now rob it of its hero. As an *aficionado,* Barnes understands this threat too well. These are decadent times in the bull ring, marred by false esthetics; Romero alone has "the old thing," the old "purity of line through the maximum of exposure": his corruption by Brett will complete the decadence. But mainly the young fighter means something more personal to Barnes. In the bull ring he combines grace, control, and sincerity with manliness; in the fight with Cohn he proves [253/254] his integrity where skill is lacking. His values are exactly those of the hunter in "Francis Macomber," or of the fisherman in *The Old Man and the Sea.* As one of these few remaining images of independent manhood, he offers Barnes the comfort of vicarious redemption. Brett seems to smash this as she leaves with Pedro for Madrid. To ward off depression, Barnes can only get drunk and retire to bed; the fiesta goes on outside, but it means nothing now: the "good place" has been ruined.

As Book III begins, Barnes tries to reclaim his dignity and to cleanse himself of the damage at Pamplona. He goes to San Sebastian and sits quietly there in a café, listening to band concerts; or he goes swimming there alone, diving deep in the green waters. Then a telegram from Brett arrives, calling him to Madrid to help her out of trouble. At once he is like Cohn again, ready to serve his lady at the expense of self-respect. Yet in Madrid he learns to accept, emotionally, what he has always faintly understood. As he listens to Brett, he begins to drink heavily, as if her story has driven home a painful lesson. Brett herself feels "rather good" about sending Pedro away: she has at least been able to avoid being "one of these bitches that ruins children." This is a moral triumph for her, as Barnes agrees; but he can scarcely ignore its implications for himself. For when Brett refuses to let her hair grow long for Pedro, it means that her role in life is fixed: she can no longer reclaim her lost womanhood; she can no longer live with a fine man without destroying him. This seems to kill the illusion which is behind Jake's suffering throughout the novel: namely, that if he hadn't been wounded, if he had somehow survived the war with his manhood intact, then [**254/255**] he and Brett would have become true lovers. The closing lines confirm his total disillusionment:

"Oh, Jake," Brett said, "we could have had such a damned good time together."
Ahead was a mounted policeman in khaki directing traffic. He raised his baton. The car slowed suddenly pressing Brett against me.
"Yes," I said. "Isn't it pretty to think so?"

"Pretty" is a romantic word which means here "foolish to consider what could *never* have happened," and not "what can't happen now." The signal for this interpretation comes from the policeman who directs traffic between Brett's speech and Barnes's reply. With his khaki clothes and his preventive baton, he stands for the war and the society which made it, for the force which stops the lovers' car, and which robs them of their normal sexual roles. As Barnes now sees, love itself is dead for their generation. Even without

his wound, he would still be unmanly, and Brett unable to let her hair grow long.

Yet, according to the opening epigraphs, if one generation is lost and another comes, the earth abides forever; and according to Hemingway himself, the abiding earth is the novel's hero. Perhaps he is wrong on this point, or at least misleading. There are no joyous hymns to the seasons in this novel, no celebrations of fertility and change. The scenic descriptions are accurate enough, but rather flat; there is no deep feeling in them, only fondness, for the author takes less delight in nature than in outdoor sports. He is more concerned, that is, with baiting hooks and catching trout than with the Irati River and more pleased with the grace and skill of the bullfighter than with the bull's magnificence. In fact, it is the bullfighter who seems to [**255/256**] abide in the novel, for surely the bulls are dead like the trout before them, having fulfilled their roles as beloved opponents. But Romero is very much alive as the novel ends. When he leaves the hotel in Madrid, he "pays the bill" for his affair with Brett, which means that he has earned all its benefits. He also dominates the final conversation between the lovers, and so dominates the closing section. We learn here that his sexual initiation has been completed and his independence assured. From now on, he can work out his life alone, moving again and again through his passes in the ring, gaining strength, order, and purpose as he meets his own conditions. He provides no literal prescription to follow here, no call to bullfighting as the answer to Barnes's problems; but he does provide an image of integrity, against which Barnes and his generation are weighed and found wanting. In this sense, Pedro is the real hero of the parable, the final moral touchstone, the man whose code gives meaning to a world where love and religion are defunct, where the proofs of manhood are difficult and scarce, and where every man must learn to define his own moral conditions and then live up to them.

PART TWO

A FAREWELL TO ARMS

A Farewell to Arms*

RAY B. WEST, JR., Professor of English at San Francisco State College, is author and editor of many studies in American and English literature, with special emphasis on long and short fiction.

I

Ernest Hemingway's first three important works were *In Our Time,* a collection of curiously related short stories; *The Sun Also Rises,* his first serious and successful novel; and *A Farewell to Arms*. All three deal with the same subject: the condition of man in a society upset by the violence of war. The short stories, while complete (almost idyllic) within themselves, take on an added dimension when viewed against the animal-cruelty of the connecting war scenes. *The Sun Also Rises,* although set in the postwar period, is conditioned by the wartime disability of its principal figure, Jake Barnes. But the setting for *A Farewell to Arms* is the war itself, and the romance of Frederic Henry and Catherine Barkley, their attempt to escape the war and its resulting chaos, is a parable of twentieth-century man's disgust and disillusionment at the failure of civilization to achieve the ideals it had been promising throughout the nineteenth century. While the relation of one story to another in *In Our Time* is more or less arbitrary, while the meandering action of the ex-patriots' excursion into Spain in *The Sun Also Rises* is at most emblematic, the sequence of events in *A Farewell to Arms* is ordered and logical to an extreme which (outside of Henry James) is the exception in the American novel.

As a matter of fact, the physical form of *A Farewell to Arms* more nearly resembles the drama than it does the majority of American works of fiction. It is composed of five separate books, each composed of a series of scenes, and each scene broken into sections which might be likened to stage direction and dialogue. Thus, in section one we have the introduction of all major characters, the general war setting, and a statement of the problems involved; in section two, the development of the romance between Frederic and Catherine; in section three, the retreat at Caporetto and the decision of Frederic to escape the chaos of war; in section four, the supposed escape, the rowing of Frederic and Catherine across the lake into Switzerland; and in section five, the hope of sanctuary which, through a reversal reminiscent again of the drama, comes to a climax in the ironic scene of Catherine's death while giving birth to their child.

As Robert Penn Warren has pointed out (*Kenyon Review:* Winter, 1947), *A Farewell to Arms,* while not a religious book in the usual sense, depends upon a consciousness of the religious problems of our time. Its subject is [622/623] the search for truth—for ethical standards to replace those which seemed impossible under the wartime conditions which it depicts. The use of the Christian religion is not, however, confined to the conventional uses of the ordinary religious novel, in which the characters are evaluated according to their acceptance or rejection of orthodox views. Rather, it is ironically

*Ray B. West, Jr., "A Farewell to Arms," The Art of Modern Fiction, eds., Ray B. West, Jr. and Robert W. Stallman (New York: Holt, Rinehart and Winston, Inc., 1949), pp. 622-633. Reprinted by permission of Holt, Rinehart and Winston, Inc.

implied, for instance, that Catherine, who is repeatedly portrayed as one with no orthodox religious sense, is really on the side of the priest, whose orthodoxy is beyond question. It is implied, too, that the priest's religious sensibility, like the sensibility of all of the participants in the novel's action, is heightened by the events of the war. After the difficult summer, during which Frederic was confined in the hospital, all of the men in his group have been softened. "Where are all the good old priest-baiters?" Rinaldi asks. "Do I have to bait this priest alone without support?"[1] Frederic could see that the baiting which had gone on earlier did not touch the priest now. In talking with the priest he makes a distinction which is important to our interpretation of all the characters: even the priest is now not only technically a Christian, he is more like Our Lord. "It is," Frederic says, "in defeat that we become Christians."

On the other hand, it is not merely the humility of defeat, but the result of active participation (a firsthand acquaintance with the objective facts instead of the abstract theories of warfare) which makes all the difference. Outward forms divorced from action do not suffice, as when the soldier under Frederic refuses to believe that the Austrians were going to attack, because, as he said, "What has been done this summer cannot have been done in vain." Frederic thinks: "I was always embarrassed by the words sacred, glorious, and sacrifice and the expression in vain. We had heard them, sometimes standing in the rain almost out of earshot, so that only the shouted words came through, and had read them, on proclamations that were slapped up by billposters over other proclamations, now for a long time, and I had seen nothing sacred, and the things that were glorious had no glory and the sacrifices were like the stockyards at Chicago if nothing was done with the meat except to bury it. There were many words that you could not stand to hear and finally only the names of places had dignity." When the words became separated from the acts they were meant to describe, then they meant nothing; the slaughter of war was less than the slaughter of animals in the stockyard. The names of places had dignity because the places still had some objective reality. Likewise, the acts of Rinaldi when he is practicing his craft, of Dr. Valentini (but not of the incompetent physicians), have dignity because they are done surely and skillfully—to some purpose. The early stages of Frederic and Catherine's courtship were like moves in a [623/624] chess game or a game of bridge; later it became something different, so different that even the outward form of marriage could make no difference. Catherine asks: "What good would it do to marry now? We're really married. I couldn't be any more married." Even the war, when Frederic was no longer participating, "seemed as far away as the football games of some one else's college." No activity has meaning unless the participant is emotionally involved; this is the real test, like the names of places. There is Christianity and there are true Christians. There is incompetence and competence. There is marriage and there is true love. In a story in *In Our Time,* we have the picture of a bullfighter who is defeated and derided by the crowd, but he is really "The Undefeated" (the title of the story), because he is only outwardly not inwardly defeated. As we have seen, in "The Short Happy Life" even death does not defeat Francis Macomber, for it is in death that he triumphs.

But what is the real distinction between the failures—the defeated—and the *genuine* men and women in the novel—what critics have come to call "the initiated"? Rinaldi (who is one of them) says to Frederic at the time when Frederic returns to the front: "You puncture me when I become a great Italian thinker. But I know many things I can't say." Frederic, when he is talking to the priest after his return

[1] This passage and all the following passages in this analysis are reprinted from *A Farewell to Arms* by Ernest Hemingway and are used by permission of the publishers, Charles Scribner's Sons. Copyright 1929, Charles Scribner's Sons; renewal copyright © 1957, Ernest Hemingway.

from the hospital, says: "I never think and yet when I begin to talk I say the things I have found out in my mind without thinking." There are times when Catherine "feels" immoral, but most of the time she "feels" that her love is sanctified. The peasants and the defeated soldiers have wisdom because they are not misled by the empty forms. Hemingway seems to be saying, like William Wordsworth, that such men are by circumstance closer to reality —and thus to wisdom. In the book which followed *A Farewell to Arms—Death in the Afternoon*—Hemingway says, "Morals are what you feel good after." Brett Ashley in *The Sun Also Rises* decides to give up a love affair because it makes her *feel* good "deciding not to be a bitch." The test of morals is the unadulterated sensibility—the sensibility not misled by the empty forms of patriotism, religion, and love: the sensibility of Rinaldi when he does not attempt to be a great Italian thinker; the sensibility of Dr. Valentini, who knows at once what is to be done and does it without quibble and consultation; the sensibility of the peasants; the sensibility of Catherine, who learns from her love for Frederic that it is all right, who says: "Everything we do seems so innocent and simple. I can't believe we do anything wrong." Even the sensibility of Frederic, which is the developing moral sense of the novel, is superior to Rinaldi's because it has greater scope—the surgeon is happy only when he is working. "I know more than you," Rinaldi says, and Frederic agrees with him. "But you will have a better time. Even with remorse you will have a better time."

It is this limiting quality in Frederic's character which points to the prin- [624/ 625] cipal problem of the novel. Rinaldi calls it remorse. Frederic cannot completely escape the forms of his early training, though he makes a systematic progress throughout the book. Before he was wounded he had attempted to accept Catherine's philosophy that death is the end, but his experience seemed to prove otherwise, for in her antireligious position

Catherine is as orthodox as the priest. Frederic says: "I felt myself rush bodily out of myself and out and out and out and all the time bodily in the wind. I went out swiftly, all of myself, and I knew I was dead and that it had all been a mistake to think you just died." This is Hemingway's mysticism which triumphed in *For Whom the Bell Tolls* and which was at its lowest ebb in his curious little essay "A Natural History of the Dead." Frederic does not love God, but he is afraid of him in the night sometimes. Because he does not "belong," he and Catherine cannot find sanctuary in the church the evening they are waiting for the train, though an Italian couple does. Yet Frederic is much more anxious about the absence of the marriage ceremony than Catherine, and when the child is born dead he is disturbed because it had not been baptized. The limitations of Frederic's religious sensibility (a symbol for the religious sensibility of our time) are depicted in two scenes, the first in his failure to visit the home of the priest at Abruzzi, where "You would like the people and though it is cold it is clear and dry"; the second is the incident at the church:

There were streetcar tracks and beyond them was the cathedral. It was white and wet in the mist. We crossed the tram tracks. On our left were the shops, their windows lighted, and the entrance to the galleria. There was a fog in the square and when we came close to the front of the cathedral it was very big and the stone was wet.

"Would you like to go in?"

"No," Catherine said. We walked along. There was a soldier standing with his girl in the shadow of one of the stone buttresses ahead of us and we passed them. They were standing tight up against the stone and he had put his cape around her.

"They're like us," I said.

"Nobody is like us," Catherine said. She did not mean it happily.

"I wish they had some place to go."

"It mightn't do them any good."

"I don't know. Everybody ought to have some place to go."

"They have the cathedral," Catherine said.

(XXIII, 157)

Catherine and Frederic have a hotel room (the "lost generation"), while the

Italian soldier and his girl have the cathe-dral; the priest has his cold, clear, dry country; the atheists have their houses of prostitution. The priest's country appeals to Frederic, and he is sorry he did not visit it while he was on leave: [**625/626**]

> I had wanted to go to Abruzzi. I had gone to no place where the roads were frozen and hard as iron, where it was clear cold and dry and the snow was dry and powdery and hare-tracks in the snow and the peasants took off their hats and called you Lord and there was good hunting. I had gone to no such place but to the smoke of cafés and nights when the room whirled and you needed to look at the wall to make it stop, nights in bed, drunk, when you know* that that was all there was, and the strange excitement of waking and not knowing who it was with you, and the world all unreal in the dark and so exciting that you must resume again unknowing and not caring in the night, sure that this was all and all and all and not caring.
>
> (III, 13)

Here is the symbol of Frederic's predica-ment, a key passage, since it represents the religious contrast. The priest's religion is his clear, cold country; Catherine's re-ligion is her love, which, as Count Greffi says, "is a religious feeling," or, as Cath-erine tells Frederic: "You're my religion. You're all I've got." Frederic is the mod-ern hero, lost between two worlds, the world of tradition and certainty which he cannot wholly relinquish, and the exciting but uncertain world of the twentieth cen-tury, where you only occasionally find something substantial to look at to make everything stop whirling, where you live for the moment, giving yourself up to sen-sations, for it is through the senses that you discover truth: the strong man giving equal odds to his weaker opponent, the boxer, the hunter, the bullfighter, the sol-dier, and the lover; the strong man aware that the only order in the universe is that which he himself can supply, but aware, too, that such order is transitory, that per-haps the highest possible values consist in pure sensation which seeks out new order and a stoicism which transcends physical defeat.

II

At the beginning Frederic wavers between reason and sensibility, between formal re-ligion and "true" Christianity, between the empty forms of love and true love. He has been thrust into a world of violent ac-tion in which choice is eventually to be-come necessary. An English critic has called Frederic "a curiously passive hero," but this is true only in the sense that Thomas Mann's Herr Friedemann was passive. The Hemingway hero is, theoret-ically, passive, because he is allied to nature through his unreason, but his par-ticular dilemma usually has all the ap-pearances of active seeking.

Frederic's relationship to Catherine in Book I is like a game of bridge where you pretend to be playing for stakes, but do not know what the stakes are. At the end of the section Frederic is wounded, but not seriously. It is the first hint that what he had called "the picturesque front" was capable of becoming something else. It is a foreshadowing of the retreat at Caporetto. [**626/627**]

In Book II the action takes place in the American hospital at Milan, and almost at once we know that the formal relationship (love like a bridge game or a game of chess) has ended. Frederic thinks:

> God knows I had not wanted to fall in love with her. I had not wanted to fall in love with any one. But God knows I had and I lay on the bed in the room of the hospital in Milan and all sorts of things went through my head but I felt wonderful . . .
>
> (XIV, 100)

We are introduced to the incompetent doctors and to the professional patriots like Ettore. Frederic, although he cannot reject Ettore as completely as Catherine, does reject his own decoration, because he knows that he is not a hero. The silver medal repeats the pattern of the empty form. A new action is suggested in this book by Catherine's fear of death. She is afraid of the rain, she says, and when

* *sic;* "knew" in Hemingway.

pressed by Frederic for an explanation, admits that it is because she sometimes sees herself dead in it. Frederic is unbelieving. "And sometimes I see you dead in it," she adds. "That's more likely," Frederic says. "No it's not, darling. Because I can keep you safe. I know I can. But nobody can help themselves." Here is one of the secrets of the passivity of Hemingway's characters. Later in the section, when Catherine admits that she is going to have a baby:

> "You aren't angry are you, darling?"
> "No."
> "And you don't feel trapped?"
> "Maybe a little. But not by you."
> "I didn't mean by me. You must be stupid. I meant trapped at all."
> "You always feel trapped biologically."
>
> (XXI, 148)

"Biologically," in the Hemingway world, covers just about everything; there is nothing you can do about life but accept it with stoicism. This is an anticipation of the final scenes in the novel, but Frederic, fortunately, did not realize how final the trap was:

> Poor, poor dear Cat. And this was the price you paid for sleeping together. This was the end of the trap. This was what people got for loving each other.
>
> (XLI, 341-342)

In this book, however, the threat is taken only seriously enough to provoke discussion of death and the conditions of man's dying. Frederic has quoted the line, "The coward dies a thousand deaths, the brave but one"; Catherine replies: "The brave dies perhaps two thousand deaths if he's intelligent. He simply doesn't mention them."

There is an indication that Frederic is very little different from Catherine in his fear of death. They are in a café and it is raining. He quotes Andrew **[627/628]** Marvell: "But at my back I always hear/ Time's wingéd chariot hurrying near." He wants to talk facts. Where will the baby be born? Catherine refuses (stoically) to discuss it. "Then don't worry, darling," she tells him. "You were fine until now and now you're worrying."

The tone of this section suggests death, but the reader does not know, any more than do Catherine and Frederic, whose death it is to be. Frederic returns to the front, where there are rumors of a new attack by the Austrians. Catherine awaits the time when she will have her baby. Both are, in a sense, trapped—trapped by the war, by their love, and (though they are unaware of it) by death.

At the very beginning of Book III we are introduced to the town of Caporetto. Frederic "remembered it as a little white town with a campanile in a valley. It was a clean little town and there was a fine fountain in the square." This is where the summer fighting has ended. One of Hemingway's most constant symbols of the goal which his heroes seek is—to utilize the title of one of his stories—a "Clean, Well-Lighted Place." War has undoubtedly destroyed the "clean little town," but this is just an additional indication of war's ugliness. Caporetto is the point where the Austrians succeed in breaking through and turning Frederic's "picturesque front" into a machine of destruction. There are only isolated examples of decency and order in the retreat; the whole atmosphere is one of anarchy and confusion.

Malcolm Cowley has likened Frederic's plunge into the river to escape execution as a baptism—a symbol of Frederic's entering the world of the initiated, but this is true only in so far as it refers to his decision (his rebirth) concerning the war. The chapters preceding, where Frederic returns to the front and meets his old comrades, indicates both how much he had learned through his stay at the hospital (the baptism of love) and how much the members of his company have learned through the difficult fighting of the summer (their baptism of fire), but the final consecration does not come until later when Frederic is confronted by love and death at the same time. The retreat does, however, represent a major phase in his initiation. Frederic is in the position of the fat gray-haired little lieutenant-colonel whom the carabinieri were questioning at the bridge:

The questioners had all the efficiency, coldness and command of themselves of Italians who are firing and are not being fired on.
"Your brigade?"
He told them.
"Regiment?"
He told them.
"Why are you not with your regiment?"
He told them.
"Do you not know that an officer should be with his troops?"
He did. [628/629]
That was all. Another officer spoke.
"It is you and such as you that have let the barbarians onto the sacred soil of the fatherland."
"I beg your pardon," said the lieutenant-colonel.
"It is because of treachery such as yours that we have lost the fruits of victory."
"Have you ever been in a retreat?" the lieutenant-colonel asked.

(XXX, 239)

The military police are firing but are not being fired on. They are like religious persons who have never been tempted, condemning the sinner who has succumbed; the police have the hollow shell of patriotism, using such phrases as "the sacred soil of the fatherland" and "the fruits of victory," but it is punctured by the lieutenant-colonel's simple question: "Have you ever been in a retreat?" The carabiniere's brave words have no relation to the reality of the situation, while the condemned man's question goes right to the heart of it. Frederic rationalizes his own situation as follows:

You had lost your cars and your men as a floorwalker loses the stock of his department in a fire. There was, however, no insurance. You were out of it now. You had no more obligation. If they shot the floorwalkers after a fire in the partment in a fire. There was, however, no insurance. You were out of it now*, certainly the floorwalkers would not be expected to return when the store opened again for business. They might seek other employment; if there was any other employment and the police did not get them.
    Anger was washed away in the river along with any obligation. Although that ceased when the carabiniere put his hands on my collar. I would like to have had the uniform off *although I did*

not care much about the outward forms [our** italics] [.] I had taken off the stars, but that was for convenience. It was no point of honor. I was not against them. I was through. I wished them all the luck. There were the good ones, and the brave ones, and the calm ones, and the sensible ones, and they deserved it. But it was not my show any more and I wished this bloody train would get to Mestre and I would eat and stop thinking. I would have to stop.

(XXXII, 248)

The fighter obeys the rules until they are suspended or no longer enforced; then he gets out of the ring (cf. Margot Macomber in "The Short Happy Life"). With the retreat at Caporetto, the Austrian front ceased to be "the picturesque front"; it is no longer subject to the traditional rules of "honorable" warfare. Frederic, too, for the time being ceases to be the "curiously passive hero." He cannot escape the war until he escapes from Italy with Catherine, and to escape is to struggle.

Yet according to the standards of Frederic Henry's world, such a decision is in itself dangerous. His reasoning is too pat, his assurance too great. The determination to struggle becomes a kind of "tragic flaw"—a brash modern pride which tempts fate as the occupants of Stephen Crane's little boat [629/630] tempt the seven mad gods of the sea. Hemingway hints at this in the beginning of Book IV. In the hotel at Stresa, where Frederic went to find Catherine, the barman asks him questions about the war.

"Don't talk about the war," I said. The war was a long way off. Maybe there wasn't any war. There was no war here. Then I realized it was over for me. But I did not have the feeling that it was really over. I had the feeling of a boy who thinks of what is happening at a certain hour at the schoolhouse from which he has played truant.

(XXXIV, 262)

The war is not over. Even after the successful effort to leave Italy and enter Switzerland, the war (which is really a symbol for the chaos of nature—the bio-

* "partment . . . now." *sic;* "department store because they spoke with an accent they had always had, then" in Hemingway.
** I.e., West's.

logical trap) catches up with Frederic and Catherine. It is significant that Frederic's reason tells him he can escape—that he *has* escaped; his sensibility suggests that he is only playing truant. Frederic felt like a masquerader in his civilian clothes. That is to say, in the modern sense, all happiness is a form of truancy. The months in Switzerland were idyllic. Even the snow came late, almost as though Frederic had ordered nature's cooperation.

The trap is sprung in Book V. Catherine's confinement is difficult, and the birth when it does come is finally performed through a Caesarean operation. The child is born dead. Catherine herself dies soon afterward. Yet, though it is Catherine who dies, *A Farewell to Arms* is not her tragedy. Unlike Francis Macomber and unlike Manuelo in "The Undefeated," she does not *become* admirable in her dying; she *remains* admirable according to the rules of decorum which Hemingway has set up:

The nurse opened the door and motioned with her finger for me to come. I followed her into the room. Catherine did not look up when I came in. I went over to the side of the bed. The doctor was standing by the bed on the opposite side. Catherine looked at me and smiled. I bent down over the bed and started to cry.
"Poor darling," Catherine said very softly. She looked gray.
"You're all right, Cat," I said. "You're going to be all right."
"I'm going to die," she said; then waited and said, "I hate it."
I took her hand.
"Don't touch me," she said. I let go of her hand. She smiled. "Poor darling. You touch me all you want."
"You'll be all right, Cat. I know you'll be all right."
"I meant to write you a letter to have if anything happened, but I didn't do it."
"Do you want me to get a priest or any one to come and see you?"
"Just you," she said. Then a little later, "I'm not afraid. I just hate it."
(XLI, 353-354)

Catherine had had the perception of death early, but it had come to [**630/631**] Frederic only since learning of the doctor's fears. During the operation he thought she was dead: "Her face was

gray." Catherine knows intuitively that she is going to die. Frederic senses it, but his reason will not allow him to accept it, as she does, as ". . . just a dirty trick."

I knew she was going to die and I prayed that she would not. Don't let her die. Oh, God, please don't let her die. I'll do anything for you if you won't let her die. Please, please, please, dear God, don't let her die. Dear God, don't let her die. Please, please, please don't let her die. God please make her not die. I'll do anything you say if you don't let her die. You took the baby but don't let her die. That was all right, but don't let her die. Please, please, dear God, don't let her die.
(XLI, 353)

Frederic's hope that he could prevent her from dying is as illusory as his belief that he could escape the war by signing a separate peace. In a sense, Frederic is a depiction of the narrator's figure in "The Open Boat," who, when he realizes that there is no tangible thing to hoot, feels the desire to confront a personification and indulge in pleas. It isn't until he has accepted the terrible reality of Catherine's death that he is truly initiated: "It was like saying good-by to a statue." This is the biological trap—sprung. Catherine has been right from the beginning. Early in the novel, in speaking of her English lover who was killed in France, she says: "I thought perhaps he couldn't stand it and then of course he was killed and that was the end of it." "I don't know," Frederic said. "Oh, yes," Catherine emphasizes. "That's the end of it."

These are the limits, then, as circumscribed by nature: death is the end of life. After death there is only the lifeless statue. It was this conclusion (or something like it) which caused Gertrude Stein to say of Ernest Hemingway that he belonged to the "lost generation," lost because the comfortable morality of the nineteenth century had been denied them after 1914. Frederic Henry attempts to believe in the validity of warfare, but even the peasant soldiers under him know better. When he puts his trust in religion or in his love for Catherine he is also defeated. He reasons it out as follows:

That was what you did. You died. You did not know what it was about. You never had time to learn. They threw you in and told you the rules and the first time they caught you off base they killed you.

(XLI, 350)

In "The Short Happy Life of Francis Macomber" the emphasis was upon man's final victory over death. That view is represented here in the stoical death of Catherine, but the emphasis is upon futility. In a striking image which represents the key scene in the novel, we have Frederic thinking about an experience he has had: [**631/632**]

Once in camp I put a log on top of the fire and it was full of ants. As it commenced to burn, the ants swarmed out and went first toward the centre where the fire was; then turned back and ran toward the end. When there were enough on the end they fell off into the fire. Some got out, their bodies burnt and flattened, and went off not knowing where they were going. But most of them went toward the fire and then back toward the end and swarmed on the cool end and finally fell off into the fire. I remember thinking at the time that it was the end of the world and a splendid chance to be a messiah and lift the log off the fire and throw it out where the ants could get off onto the ground. But I did not do anything but throw a tin cup of water on the log, so that I would have the cup empty to put whiskey in before I added water to it. I think the cup of water on the burning log only steamed the ants.

(XLI, 350)

The relationship of this parable to Catherine's predicament is unmistakable. For her there is likewise no messiah to come to the rescue. Death is the end of it, and the only value in death is man's knowledge of it. In Ernest Hemingway's novels, those who live well die like heroes. They are the initiated. But the initiation of Frederic Henry comes gradually. He learns about war, love, and finally death. Catherine's death is the final stage in his initiation.

III

If this conclusion is true, we might ask: "Why the title: *A Farewell to Arms*"? The title suggests in its obvious implications that the author saw his subject as concerned primarily with the war. In that case, we might say either that we are wrong in our conclusions or that the author was wrong in his selection of title. This raises the question of Ernest Hemingway's method—his style. Hemingway's sensibility, when it is functioning at its highest point, has always worked upon an immediate objective level which translates ideas into terms of concrete things: life as a baseball game where each error is punished by death or compared to the struggle of ants on a burning log, the comparison of a hero's death with the slaughter of animals at a stockyard. In each case we are aware of the double implication, the idea and the image; and the emotional force of the idea is intensified by the shock supplied by the image. This is the more complicated form of Hemingway's noted "understatement." At the time of Catherine's operation, while the doctor has gone to make his preparations, Frederic is left to administer the anesthesia. He has been told that the correct amount would register upon the dial at number 2, but when Catherine is in extreme pain, he says, "I turned the dial to three and then four. I wished the doctor would come back. I was afraid of the numbers above two." The statement "I wished the doctor would come back" is understatement. The use of the machine- [**632/633**] image suggests Catherine's immediate danger. Another author might have examined in great detail both Catherine's illness and the emotion which Frederic was experiencing at that time; but from the simple, quiet statement, reinforced by the dial registering the numbers above two, we get the full force of Frederic's terror in a few strokes.

That Hemingway was aware of this quality is evidenced by the statement which he once made that what he was attempting to get was a "fifth dimension" in his prose; not the ordinary dimensions of exposition and description, but the full quality of the emotional experience. This is not an unusual characteristic of a work of art; it is merely Ernest Hemingway's means of explaining his own intention; but it suggests the caution a reader should exercise in taking the author's words or sentences at their most obvious level of meaning. Perhaps this is true also of the title, *A Farewell to Arms*. Someone has suggested somewhere that the "Arms" referred not to the war, but to the arms of Catherine; thus suggesting that what the novel was about, really, was Frederic's loss of his love. This is as limited an interpretation as that which sees the novel as only a "war novel." A more valid interpretation would see the title as completely ironic. Frederic has attempted to escape from the obligations which life imposes. He did not wish to fall in love, but he did. He attempted to escape the war, but he felt like a schoolboy who was playing truant. His life with Catherine in Switzerland and the life which they anticipated after the war were relatively devoid of conflict. Catherine and Frederic had said farewell to the life of action and struggle, but ironically their greatest test—the attempt to save the life of Catherine—came at the very moment when they seemed to have achieved a successful escape.

What the novel says, finally, is that you cannot escape the obligations of action—you cannot say "farewell to arms"; you cannot sign a separate peace. You can only learn to live with life, to tolerate it as "the initiated" learn to tolerate it.

The Religion of Death in *A Farewell to Arms**

JAMES F. LIGHT teaches literary studies at Indiana State Teachers College in Terre Haute.

One way of looking at Ernest Hemingway's *A Farewell to Arms* is to see its close involvement in four ideals of service.[1] Each of these ideals is dramatized by a character of some importance, and it is between these four that Lt. Henry wavers in the course of the novel. The orthodoxly religious ideal of service is that of the Priest, who wishes to serve God but who asserts as well the broader concept of service: "When you love you wish to do things for. You wish to sacrifice for. You wish to serve."[2] Another selfless ideal of service is that of the patriot Gino, who wishes to serve his country so fully that he is willing to die for it A third is the code of Catherine Berkeley [*sic*], who wishes to serve her lover and who sees in such service her personal substitute for conventional religion. The last is the ideal of Rinaldi, who, as a doctor, wishes to serve mankind by alleviating the wounds of war. Each is an initiate to the subordination of self, and in this they differ from the selfishness of the king and the officers who ride in cars and throw mud on the men, or from the hero Ettore, who sees war as an accident suitable for promotion and self-glorification. In no other way, despite the contention of such a perceptive and influential critic as Robert Penn Warren, are they really initiates. They are not so in their greater discipline —Catherine is hysterical early in the novel and Rinaldi is a nervous wreck in the middle. They are not so in their talk, for though Rinaldi and Valenti [*sic*], another doctor and another so-called initiate, may possess a similar "bantering, ironical tone," the Priest and Catherine are far removed from any such tone; nor do they have any greater awareness than others "of the issue of meaning in life."[3] They act instinctively rather than intellectually, and the one instinct they have in common— the attraction toward the ideal of service —is, from the context and the conclusion of the novel, a foolish selflessness without intellectual worth.

The Priest, Gino, Catherine, and Rinaldi do, however, live by the ideal of service, and the dramatic tension of the novel is largely based on Lt. Henry's wavering toward each ideal and eventual rejection of all four. Toward the Priest's ideal, Henry's attitude is at first one of sympathy but of rejection. He does not bait the Priest with the other priest-baiters early [169/170] in the novel, but neither does he stay with the Priest when the other officers leave for the whore houses near by. Nor does he visit the high, cold, dry country, the Priest's home, where he is invited to go on his leave. Instead he goes to the large cities, the ironic "centres of culture and civilization" (p. 8), where he lives the life of sensation and feels

[1] Robert Penn Warren discusses two of these ideals, those of Catherine and the Priest, in his introduction to Scribner's Modern Standard Authors edition of *Farewell*. Anyone familiar with Mr. Warren's essay will see that though I disagree with much of its interpretation of *Farewell*, I at the same time am indebted to it deeply.
[2] Ernest Hemingway, *A Farewell to Arms*, Intro. Robert Penn Warren (Scribner's Modern Standard Authors, 1949), p. 75. Subsequent page references to *Farewell* are from this edition and are incorporated in the text.
[3] Warren, Introduction to Hemingway's *A Farewell to Arms*, p. xxxi.

* James F. Light, "The Religion of Death in *A Farewell to Arms*," *Modern Fiction Studies*, VII (Summer, 1961), 169-173. Reprinted by permission of the author and the Purdue Research Foundation.

"that this was all and all and all and not caring" (p. 13). After he is wounded and has found real love with Catherine, however, Lt. Henry comes closer to the Priest, so that when he returns to duty he can reject the priest-baiting of Rinaldi and instead of going to town—and the whore houses—he can visit with the Priest. The implication apparently is that the love Henry has found in Catherine has somehow made him more sympathetic to the kind of selfless love that the Priest avows. By the end of the novel, however, Henry has thoroughly rejected the Priest and his ideal of service to God. He does, however, give that ideal a test. Where the Priest had earlier prayed for the end of the war—"I believe and I pray that something will happen. I have felt it very close" (pp. 184-5).—Henry now prays that Catherine not die. Basic and repetitive in the prayer is the implication of some necessary reciprocal relation between man and God: you do this for me and I'll do this for you. Thus Henry prays: "Oh, God, please don't let her die. I'll do anything for you if you won't let her die. . . . Please, please, please don't let her die. . . . I'll do anything you say if you don't make her die" (p. 341). Catherine, however, does die, just as, despite the Priest's prayers, the war continues. The implication is that the Priest's ideal of service lacks reciprocity, and the knowledge of its lack is not unique to Henry. Huck Finn had earlier, in the novel that Hemingway has said is the origin of all modern American literature, felt the same flaw; for he had seen, by pragmatic test, the inefficacy of prayer, and he had discerned that the Priest's—or Miss Watson's—ideal of service was a one-way street with no advantage for the human individual. For Lt. Henry this lack of reciprocity makes for the image of a God who in his eternal selfishness is the origin of human selfishness, so that man in his selfishness most accurately reflects God. This concept of the divine selfishness is portrayed in Henry's remembrance, as Catherine is dying, of watching some ants burning on a log. Henry envisions the

opportunity for him to be "a messiah and lift the log off the fire" (p. 339). Divinity, however, does not ease the pain of man's existence, and Henry does not save the ants. Instead, selfishly—and in so doing he is reflecting the divine selfishness which is so antithetical to the Priest's ideal of service—Henry throws "a tin cup of water on the log, so that I would have the cup empty to put whiskey in before I added water to it" (p. 339).

A second ideal of service is that dramatized by the patriot Gino. He believes the "soil is sacred" (p. 190) and that the deaths in the war were not "in vain" (p. 191). He will not talk of losing the war and Lt. Henry feels he understands Gino's "being a patriot. He was born one" (p. 191). Though Lt. Henry never has Gino's simple love of country, he does for a good part of the novel act and talk as a "patriot." The priest applies the term to Lt. Henry (p. 74), and its justification, despite the fact that Lt. Henry is not [170/171] defending his own country, is shown in an early conversation of Lt. Henry with the mechanic Passini. Passini believes there is nothing worse than war, but Lt. Henry contradicts this by saying, "Defeat is worse" (p. 52). When Passini disagrees, Lt. Henry continues by arguing in patriotic cliches: the enemy "come after you. They take your home. They take your sister" (p. 52). Passini says people should defend their own homes, and sisters should be kept in the house. The disagreement concludes with Lt. Henry saying that the war is bad but it must be finished. Passini answers, "It doesn't finish. There is no finish to a war" (p. 52). The innocence of Lt. Henry is revealed when he says, "Yes, there is" (p. 52). In terms of the ultimate despair of the book, with its cry that life itself, from birth to death, is perpetual war, Lt. Henry's statement shows a naivete that Lt. Henry must—and does—lose. His loss begins when the real danger and killing of the war become apparent. (Earlier he had felt the war "seemed no more dangerous to me myself than war in the movies" [p. 38].) His loss of innocence is most obvious when he feels himself completely separated from the patriot Gino and responds to Gino's cliches by the famous passage that begins, "I was always embarrassed by the words sacred, glorious, and sacrifice, and the expression in vain . . ." (p. 191). Because he has lost his patriotism, Lt. Henry, later, has no intellectual qualms about deserting and making a "separate peace" (p. 252).

A third ideal of service is the ideal by which Catherine lives. She dramatizes the service of secular lovers to one another, and she lives and dies by this code. Completely selfless in her attitude toward her lover, she needs no marriage ceremony and dreams of uniting herself so completely to Lt. Henry—her religion she calls him at one time—that the two become truly one. The depth of the desire to serve is shown in the last chapter. There, Lt. Henry takes Catherine's hand. She knows that she is going to die and also feels that her recent agony in childbirth and her impending death are the final results for her of the sexual desires of Henry. Therefore, she lashes out: "Don't touch me" (p. 341). Then, despite her bitterness, she adds, "Poor darling. You touch me all you want" (p. 342). This is perfect selflessness, still concerned with others, still trying to serve even while dying, and it is this kind of service that Henry learns about from Catherine. Thus while rowing Catherine to Switzerland, Henry can blister his hands to the point of real pain, and then can jestingly refer to his own hands as similar to those of Christ. Later, when Catherine is dying, Henry desperately wishes to serve, and this he does in some small way by giving her gas to ease her pain. Of this act, he feels, "It was very good of the doctor to let me do something" (p. 328). Later Henry asks such questions as, "Do you want anything, Cat?" and "Can I get you anything?" (p. 342). Henry, however, can do nothing, and the ineffectuality of the service of secular lovers is made apparent in the last para-

graph of the novel when Henry finds he can't even effectively say goodbye.

The fourth ideal of service is that of Rinaldi. Rinaldi is a good doctor, one for whom work is the sole justification for life. It is Rinaldi to whom Henry is closest at the beginning of the novel—Rinaldi says they are blood brothers—for both are not only living a life of non-thinking sensation, but [171/172] more important both are involved in the service of healing man's body. After Henry has been wounded and has returned to duty, however, there is a change. Henry finds that the Priest now is more sure of himself, while Rinaldi, convinced that he has syphilis, is tense and irritable. The cause for the change is the way in which the war has been going. Many men have been killed and many wounded, and these facts have made the Priest—concerned with man's soul—feel more necessary, while at the same time, they have made Rinaldi—concerned with man's body—feel his own futility. The difference is made clear when Rinaldi attempts to bait the priest, as in earlier days, and is unsuccessful in weakening the Priest's placidity. His lack of success, though his insults go even beyond those of the earlier time, and his feeling that Henry is betraying him and is now on the Priest's side enrage Rinaldi, and he yells at Henry that he can't side with the Priest: "You can't do it. You can't do it. I say you can't do it. You're dry and you're empty and there's nothing else. There's nothing else I tell you. Not a damned thing. I know, when I stop working" (p. 180). The complete materialist —he calls himself "the snake of reason" (p. 176)—Rinaldi, after this scene, disappears physically from the novel, but his role as the worker for the cure of man's body is assumed later by another doctor, the one who cares for Catherine in her childbirth. Like Rinaldi, this doctor is also ineffectual in his attempt at service, and his feeling of his failure leads to apologetics [*sic*] which Henry rejects. Henry is left with the failure of all the ideals of service. In addition he is left with the knowledge of the one thing man can believe in: death. Catherine becomes a "statue"—which suggests some pagan deity—and the novel ends on the word *rain,* a word which symbolically stands for two things, paradoxically intertwined, in the novel. One is spring and new birth. The other is the thaws of spring that begin the war anew and anew bring death. In the beginning of life, then, is the fact of death, and the sexual urge is the biological trap which leads to death. Death is the basic fact of life, and there is nothing more deserving of worship.

It is no wonder that in Hemingway's next book, *Death in the Afternoon,* he states—and it is a thorough rejection of any ideal of service—that "what is moral is what you feel good after and what is immoral is what you feel bad after."[4] Hemingway feels good after seeing a bullfight, and for him it is "very moral."[5] The reason is that in the bullfight one confronts in a pure way the ultimate fact of death. Man's problem is to dominate death as the bullfighter's is to dominate the bull, and the way toward domination is to see life, like the bullfight, as an art form, with certain rules which the "manly" man will obey. The basic offense against the "rules" of the bullfight is for the bullfighter to pretend to be in the area of danger while in reality he avoids that area and is perfectly safe. The basic offense against the "rules" of life as an art form is to show self-pity, an offense so great that Hemingway could, when he saw it in his friend Scott Fitzgerald, write a reprimanding letter in which he pointed out that all men "are bitched from the start" and [**172/173**] no man has any right to whine.[6] To avoid the area of danger in the bullfight is to avoid real domination of the bull; to whine in life is to avoid domination of death. The lack of domination makes for messiness—impure art—in either the bullfight or life. Such messiness is a form of cheating, and in life "when you get the damned hurt use it—don't cheat with it."[7]

Watching the bullfights, Hemingway gains a feeling of "life and death, mortality and immortality."[8] Though he himself is vague about the reason he gains these feelings, it seems clear that the feeling of immortality does not come from any orthodox Christian reason. Instead it arises because the bullfighter, when he enters the area of danger, shows his contempt for death, becomes victorious over it, and gains in his victory a small immortality. The same kind of contempt for death is evident in the way in which Catherine meets her end, for she recognizes her death as a "dirty trick" (p. 342) but winks at the joke. She has not been broken by death, despite her feeling to the contrary, and she has therefore gained victory and immortality. This is the only kind of immortality man can know; it is gained by bravery and stoicism, not selfless service to God (the Priest), country (Gino), beloved (Catherine), or mankind (Rinaldi). Such a limited immortality is a poor substitute for victory over death through everlasting life; but it is the only kind of immortality, the only kind of religion, the Hemingway of *Farewell* can believe in.

4 Ernest Hemingway, *Death in the Afternoon* (Scribner's, 1932), p. 4.
5 Hemingway, *Death in the Afternoon,* p. 4.
6 Letter from Ernest Hemingway to F. Scott Fitzgerald. Quoted in Arthur Mizener, *The Far Side of Paradise* (Houghton-Mifflin, 1951), p. 238.
7 Letter from Hemingway to Fitzgerald. Quoted in Mizener, *The Far Side of Paradise,* p. 238.
8 Hemingway, *Death in the Afternoon,* p. 4.

Hemingway's Other Style*

CHARLES R. ANDERSON, Professor of English at The Johns Hopkins University, has written extensively about American literature. Among his books are *Melville in the South Seas, Emily Dickinson's Poetry: Stairway of Surprise,* and the Centennial Edition of the poems of Sidney Lanier.

On the surface Hemingway's prose is hard and bare, secular and insistently non-literary. This observation is such a commonplace it would be inexcusable to repeat it at this late date except as a sounding board for observations of a very different order. Its purpose here is to serve as a starting point for examining passages written in an opposing style—warmly human, richly allusive, and at least suggestive of spiritual values. They are indeed rare, but they are usually crucial. And much of their effectiveness comes from contextual contrast with the prevailing mode in which Hemingway's fictions are written—the "purified," stripped, athletic prose for which he has long been famous. Undue admiration for this, as if simplicity were somehow superior to complexity in literature, has tended to make critics neglect his other style. Further, these lyric passages are so submerged beneath the tough exterior that many readers have overlooked them altogether.

A close look at one example, the brief dream sequence during the retreat from Caporetto in *A Farewell to Arms*,[1] will illustrate both [434/435] the technique and the function of such passages. It comes in Chapter 28 at the main turning point in the narrative. For what began as an orderly retreat quickly degenerates into a rout, and by the end of Chapter 30, in the chaos at the Tagliamento River crossing, Lieutenant Henry has deserted from the Italian army. War, the first theme of the book, drops out from this point on and the second theme, love, emerges as the dominant one. This has been amply prepared for in the chapters just prior to the dream sequence, and they must now be combed for the threads that are woven by sleep into such a richly symbolic fabric.

In Chapter 23 during the hero's convalescence from battle wounds, at the base hospital in Milan, his love for Catherine Barkley had first matured and ripened. It reached a climax on his last evening before returning to the front, when the lovers found their only available rendezvous in a cheap hotel opposite the railroad station. For the first few minutes, depressed by the tawdry surroundings, her spirits sank: "I never felt like a whore before," she said (158). But refreshed by a dinner of woodcock and wine, and renewed by love's feast, she decided that the red plush and mirrors were just right. He summed it up: "We felt very happy and in a little time the room felt like our own home. My room at the hospital had been our own home . . . in the same way" (159). With a tenderness just concealed under the clipped surface, their talk turned to her pregnancy and the serious problem of bearing their child in a world dislocated by war. Her only lament was that they were never settled in their "home" very long, but she concluded characteristically

[1] For convenience the edition in Scribner's Modern Standard Authors series is used. Page references are given in parentheses in the text, following each quotation or citation.

* Charles R. Anderson, "Hemingway's Other Style," *Modern Language Notes,* LXXVI (May, 1961), 434-442. Reprinted by permission of the author and The Johns Hopkins Press.

with chin up: "I'll have a fine home for you when you come back" (162). War not only disrupts peace and the chances of domestic happiness, but makes more urgent the note of transiency as a threat to love. What really lifts the whole scene up is the very brief literary allusion, made by Lieutenant Henry in the midst of their talk:

> But at my back I always hear
> Time's wingèd chariot hurrying near.   (161)

This quotation from Marvel [sic], enriching enough in itself, is made more complex by being strained through the ironic discords of its echo in Eliot's *Wasteland* [sic], as has been recently pointed out.[2] At this high [**435/436**] point the tryst is broken abruptly by the arrival of the midnight train and the lovers are separated, in the rain.

Time is running out with the Italian defenses at the Austrian frontier too. On rejoining his corps, Henry finds the morale in a state of collapse, profanity and obscenity increasing with the general spread of war weariness. Though it is still autumn the winter rains have already set in, torrential and unending. Rain, a pervasive symbol throughout the novel for the depression and destruction of war, now becomes a deluge that washes away the resistance of the Italian army as it had previously eroded all the values of civilization. Less than a week after his return the combined German and Austrian forces launch a major offensive, the front gives way, and the long retreat begins. Since this is not a historical novel, the focus narrows to the three hospital cars under command of Lieutenant Henry. Their withdrawal is orderly at first, and the only two events that break the routine are seemingly trivial ones but pertinent to the present analysis: the comic evacuation of the soldiers' whorehouse at Gorizia on the first day (195), and the episode of the two young girls that occurs late that night (202), when the retreating column is stalled in the mud on the road to Udine.

The driver of one of the hospital cars has given the adolescent sisters a ride and is playfully making passes at them. As they sob in terror he asks if they are virgins, and both nod their heads vigorously, " 'Don't worry,' he said. 'No danger of ———,' using the vulgar word. 'No place for ———.' . . . Both the girls seemed cheered" (203). After witnessing this and deciding that all is well, Henry returns to his car and falls asleep.

This full rehearsal of the context in which the dream sequence takes place—bringing back to the reader's mind all he would be aware of when he had reached this point—has been necessary in order to show the dream's intricate relation to the main themes of the novel. Now for the passage itself:

> It was still raining hard. . . . Those were a couple of fine girls with Barto. A retreat was no place for two virgins. Real virgins. Probably very religious. If there were no war we would probably all be in bed. In bed I lay me down my head. Bed and board. Stiff as a board in bed. Catherine was in bed now between two sheets, over her and under her. Which side did she sleep on? Maybe she wasn't asleep. Maybe she was lying thinking about me. Blow, blow, ye western wind. Well, it blew and it wasn't the small rain but big rain down that rained. It rained all night. You knew it rained down that rained. Look at it. Christ, that my love were in my arms and I in my bed again. That my love Catherine. That my sweet love Catherine down might rain. Blow her again to me. Well, we were in it. Every one was [**436/437**] caught in it and the small rain would not quiet it. "Goodnight, Catherine," I said out loud. "I hope you sleep well. If it's too uncomfortable, darling, lie on the other side," I said "I'll get you some cold water. In a little while it will be morning and then it won't be so bad. I'm sorry he makes you so uncomfortable. Try and go to sleep, sweet."
> (204)

The dream device here adopted offers several advantages. Substantively, it affords the hero an escape from the horrors of war

[2] Donna Gerstenberger, "The *Waste Land* in *A Farewell to Arms*," *MLN*, LXXVI (1961), 24-25. It should be added, to complete the record, that Hemingway also echoes these lines at the end of the novel, just before Catherine's sudden death: "We knew the baby was very close now and it gave us both such a feeling as though something were hurrying us and we could not lose any time together" (321).

and reunion with his beloved, at least in spirit. Stylistically, it frees him from the requisite soldier talk, whether of bravura or nihilism, and permits a change of pace into tender, allusive, and lyrical language. Structurally, with the sprung syntax and free association of ideas characteristic of dreams, it justifies the author in abandoning the logic of prose for the indirection and symbolism of poetry. Hemingway takes full advantage of all these possibilities.

The key sentence in this passage, though written as prose, he undoubtedly expected the attentive reader to recognize as a direct quotation from an anonymous sixteenth-century lyric, "The Lover in Winter Plaineth for the Spring":

O Western wind, when wilt thou blow
That the small rain down can rain?
*Christ, that my love were in my arms
And I in my bed again!*[3]

With this clue, which has passed unnoticed by previous critics, the complex significance of the paragraph begins to unfold. It opens with the pouring rain that has turned late October into the winter of discontent, for the despairing Italians in retreat and for the hero separated from his love by a war that has become meaningless. (Only a dozen pages before, p. 191, had come the well-known rejection of his earlier idealism: "I had seen nothing sacred, and the things that were glorious had no glory and the sacrifices were like the stockyards at Chicago if nothing was done with the meat except to bury it.") In contrast to this, the last image before his eyes as he drops off to sleep suggests two different kinds of love: the sexual desire of men stranded in the loneliness of war (Barto's comic threat of seducing the two little girls), and the love of God ("Real virgins. Probably very religious"). Even the former is difficult of fulfillment during a disastrous military retreat, so that the soldier's twofold obsession—to sleep, and to sleep with a woman—is reduced for the moment to the [437/

438] former ("If there were no war we would all probably be in bed"). And in such a time and place the latter, sacred love, is simply unthinkable, unless one's thoughts revert to childhood's prayer in the sanctity of the home, which is exactly what they do in the next sentence: "In bed I lay me down my head." By the inverted word order of what would otherwise seem like a gratuitously incongruous element in this dream, unobtrusively but surely he invokes the familiar

Now I lay me down to sleep,
I pray the Lord my soul to keep;
If I should die before I wake,
I pray the Lord my soul to take.

"If I should die" is certainly applicable to a soldier surrounded on all sides by death; in terms of the whole novel it applies to Catherine too, looking forward to his reiterated cry "What if she should die?" as she lay actually dying in childbirth at the end (331). But in the context of the dream itself it recalls the little girls praying God to keep them pure.

This surprise reappearance of the young virgins Barto had made a proposal to, "using the vulgar word," leads to more elaborate word-play: "Bed and board. Stiff as a board in bed." The first of these, in spite of its triteness, has a double significance: it is the minimum that a husband is required by custom to provide for his family, and negatively it is the legal term defining the first stage of divorce (*a mensa et thoro,* "from bed and board")—which exactly describes Henry's present involuntary separation from Catherine. The second phrase is a prurient pun; the board, by an ingenious scrambling of the first phrase, becomes stiffened into a phallic symbol of his longing for her. Readers conditioned by Freud have probably never failed to catch this, but too much taken with Hemingway's sexual frankness they may have been thrown off the trail of what follows. For it is when the hero's thoughts turn to his true love ("Catherine was in

[3] *The Oxford Book of English Verse* (Oxford, 1925), p. 53, marked "16th C.?" (Italics mine.)

bed now") that his dream opens out into its full significance, which goes far beyond mere eroticism.

The crescendo begins with "Blow, blow, ye western wind," ushering in the complaint of the lover in winter, though the phrases from the old lyric are fragmentary and garbled at first. "Well, it blew and it wasn't the small rain but the big rain down that rained. It rained all night." When he was last with Catherine it had been raining too, but only a gentle rain that lent an air of privacy to their rendezvous, and though at night also a very different kind of night from the [438/439] present disastrous one. In view of the whole novel's weather symbolism these were ominous symptoms, it is true, for a similar light rain will be falling on the spring night at Lausanne when Catherine dies (335-343). Indeed, there are only two memorable scenes in the book when it is *not* raining, and these are the two most vividly associated with a life of peace and love: first, near the beginning, the chaplain-priest's account of his home in the bright cool air of the Abruzzi mountains, where "a man may love God" without feeling foolish and where "the spring . . . was the most beautiful in Italy" (74-76) ; second, near the conclusion, at the chalet in the Swiss Alps where Catherine and Henry have their only real life together, their love soaring into an idyll in the clear winter sunshine for a few months before it goes down to its tragic end (299-327). But midway in the novel there is still a great distinction in his mind between the "big rain" symbolizing the general destruction of war and the "small rain" that merely plagued their love without dampening it. For the soldier in Italy as well as the poet in England, both winter-bound, it is the western wind that will bring the light spring rains and the end of separation. Caught in the deluge brought by the north wind (*tramonto*), Lieutenant Henry quite naturally invokes through the old lyric the western wind that will bring the renewal of life and love, unaware of the tragic irony that for the doomed lovers it

will be only a "false Spring" (321).

In his present war-dream he can only look back to the Milan episode, when in spite of the small rain it was not "winter" for them in either inner or outer climate, as a dream of love to be repeated. So his yearning (perhaps his foreboding too) wrings a cry of anguish from him: "Christ, that my love were in my arms and I in my bed again." This certainly strikes the note of physical passion, as it rightly should, since *A Farewell to Arms* is one of the great love stories of the century. But there are other meanings not too far submerged beneath the surface of the dream language. Even the exclamation "Christ," when uttered by sensitive souls under high emotional tension, hovers halfway between prayer and profanity. "Time's wingèd chariot," quoted earlier and echoed later, is what gives urgency to this soldier's plea for one more night with his beloved. And when the love of man for woman reaches the point of demanding expression in poetry, this in itself is a token of aspiration above the flesh. For all his worldly pose he has been concerned for some time with this dual aspect of his affair. [439/440]

Early in the book, in that same conversation with the priest mentioned above, they were discussing sacred and profane love. Lieutenant Henry's mind was preoccupied with his changing attitude toward Catherine, which had begun on the level of sexual desire, differing only in behavioral pattern from that which the other soldiers satisfied through prostitutes. That kind of thing is only passion and lust, the priest said, remembering the ribald talk at mess. It is utterly different from the love of God: "When you love you wish to do things for. You wish to sacrifice for. You wish to serve." When Henry asked, "If I really loved some woman would it be like that?" (75), the celibate would not venture an answer. But the development of his love for Catherine in the ensuing months has been clearly in this direction and its progress is actually recorded in the dream, from the symbol of carnal desire at the beginning to his solicitude for her and the child at the end. Even in the lyric he quoted there are overtones of a spiritual sort. The old poet surely knew of the traditional medieval symbol of Christ as the gentle rain, falling on the earth in spring to make it green and fertile again. So there is in these lines at least a suggestion of heavenly love cast in earthly terms, though the poem is secular in mode. And if Hemingway were not aware of this, how else explain the cryptic line, "That my sweet love Catherine down might rain"? As a man who confesses he does not know how to love God, she is the one he worships, her grace what he implores. Only her love raining down on him can make the earth green again with spring, and the downward flow of her delivery in childbirth will bring the renewal of life in the fruitfulness of love.

With the free association of ideas expected in dreams, this sequence is followed out by the next sentence, "Blow her again to me," since it suggests the whole context of a cradlesong in *The Princess,* from which it is lifted:

Sweet and low, sweet and low,
 Wind of the western sea,
Low, low, breathe and blow,
 Wind of the western sea!
Over the rolling waters go,
Come from the dying moon, and blow,
 Blow him again to me;
While my little one, while my pretty one, sleeps. . . .

For those who think of Hemingway as exclusively a spokesman for the hardboiled this must come as a shock, a lullaby from Tennyson! But there it is inescapably in the text, and it actually measures the [440/441] final motion of the dream, from the most basic sexual desire to the highest sentiments of home and married love. By changing one pronoun he makes the quotation his own, shifting the scene from a mother waiting for the return of a sailor-father to his "babe in the nest," and fitting it to the exigencies of a novel where the soldier yearning for his beloved simply prays that the same western wind will turn winter into spring and "Blow *her* again to

me." In terms of Tennyson's lullaby the reunion will take place "Under the silver moon"; in terms of the novel it will come after the torrential rains of the dark night of war are over ("In a little while it will be morning"). Meanwhile they can merely wait and dream. Catherine and Henry's child, still in the womb and not yet part of their life, is referred to only indirectly ("I'm sorry he makes you so uncomfortable"), but his coming accounts at least in part for the new tenderness of the lover, now directed solely to the pregnant mother. "Try and go to sleep, sweet," he ends his lullaby. The reader, from memory, can fill in all the rest—from "Sweet and low" to "sleep, my pretty one, sleep."

The protective device of the dream, which insulates him from the need to be hard, is enhanced by the fact that though he was talking out loud in his sleep it was in English, incomprehensible to his Italian companions. On waking, Lieutenant Henry is plunged back into the deluge of war, engulfed in death and disaster, profanity and obscenity and all the rest. So the lyrical interlude, cut off as abruptly as it began, stands in sharp contrast to the tough style which immediately takes over again, beginning with a four letter expletive from his driver: "——," Piani said. "They've started again" (205). This continues, with increasing disintegration of all values, to the end of the retreat two chapters later. But the dream is not lost, merely locked in the hero's heart, and its major affirmations reappear twice in muted form. Once, while escaping from the enemy, as his men fall away from him one by one crying "Peace" and "Home," Henry asks the remaining loyal one why he did not run with the others. " 'I should think a married man would want to get back to his wife," I said. "I would be glad to talk about wives" [*sic*] (229). Again, while escaping from his own battle police, who would have shot him if he had not broken from them and dived into the river. Now lying on the floor of a freight car, temporarily safe but half-dazed, he falls into a kind of daydream: "I could remember Catherine but I knew I would get crazy if I thought about her . . . so I would not think about [**441/442**] her, only about her a little, . . . lying with Catherine on the floor of the car. Hard as the floor of the car . . . and lonesome inside and alone with wet clothing and hard floor for a wife" (240). Home and married love! Throughout, such words have come to represent all that men dream of as not-war, just as war is the desolate world of not-home, where love can only take its chances. And these same words, strangely enough, have been more often on his lips than on hers—the sentiment of the hardened soldier even more than of the expectant mother. After the loss of his idealism for a cause, they become the measure of all his conduct to the end of the book. But the alert reader of the dream passage already knows the high place these terms hold on Lieutenant Henry's index of values. Flesh or spirit? Flesh *and* spirit.

It would be imprudent to draw sweeping conclusions from the interpretation of a single passage in one novel, but it might be provocative of further close readings to suggest them. When Hemingway dispensed with the lyrical mode altogether, it may be ventured, he could be guilty of abject parody of his own athletic style, as in *Across the River and Into the Trees.* When he allowed it to become too dominant the result could be spongy, as in the Hispanic rhetoric and soft ideology of *For Whom the Bell Tolls.* Most recently, it could be suggested of *The Old Man and the Sea,* he achieved a real measure of success by going all the way into romantic fable, and this may indeed be the beginning of a new direction yet to be coped with. But the Hemingway still mostly admired and argued over is the author of the early fictions—*The Sun Also Rises, A Farewell to Arms,* and half-a-dozen of the best short stories. If their impudent manner and their surface nihilism had been all they had to offer, they would have dropped from the lists long ago. Perhaps their staying power derives not from their tough exterior alone but also from their tender spots of sensibility carefully nurtured in a dehumanized world—those passages of muted lyricism that provide both a measure and a meaning for the protective toughness. Rare and brief as they are, they achieve a special resonance by being sounded against the hard polished surface of his typical prose. It was by laying one style against the other that Hemingway became a modern writer for our century, rather than merely the spokesman for a lost generation.

The Mountain and the Plain*

CARLOS BAKER. For information about the author, see "Place, Fact, and Scene in *The Sun Also Rises*," by Carlos Baker, reprinted on page 11.

"Learn about the human heart and the human mind in war from this book."
—*Hemingway, in another connection.*[1]

I. LANDSCAPE IN GORIZIA

The opening chapter of Hemingway's second novel, *A Farewell to Arms,* is a generically rendered landscape with thousands of moving figures. It does much more than start the book. It helps to establish the dominant mood (which is one of doom), plants a series of important images for future symbolic cultivation, and subtly compels the reader into the position of detached observer.

"In the late summer of that year we lived in a house in a village that looked across the river and the plain to the mountains. In the bed of the river there were pebbles and boulders, dry and white in the sun, and the water was clear and swiftly moving and blue in the channels. Troops went by the house and down the road and the dust they raised powdered the leaves of the trees. The trunks of the trees too were dusty and the leaves fell early that year and we saw the troops marching along the road and the dust rising and leaves, stirred by the breeze, falling and the soldiers marching and afterward the road bare and white, except for the leaves."

The first sentence here fixes the reader in a house in the village where he can take a long view across the river and the plain to the distant mountains. Although he does not realize it yet, the plain and the mountains (not to mention the river and the trees, the dust and the leaves) have a fundamental value as symbols. The autumnal tone of the language is important in establishing the autumnal mood of the chapter. The landscape itself has the further importance of serving as a general setting for the whole first part of the novel. Under these values, and of basic structural importance, are the elemental images which compose this remarkable introductory chapter.

The second sentence, which draws attention from the moun- **[94/95]** tainous background to the bed of the river in the middle distance, produces a sense of clearness, dryness, whiteness, and sunniness which is to grow very subtly under the artist's hands until it merges with one of the novel's two dominant symbols, the mountain-image. The other major symbol is the plain. Throughout the substructure of the book it is opposed to the mountain-image. Down this plain the river flows. Across it, on the dusty road among the trees, pass the men-at-war, faceless and voiceless and unidentified against the background of the spreading plain.

In the third and fourth sentences of this beautifully managed paragraph the march-past of troops and vehicles begins. From the reader's elevated vantage-point, looking down on the plain, the river, and the road, the continuously parading men

[1] Hemingway, *Men at War*, introd., p. xx.

*Carlos Baker, "The Mountain and the Plain," Hemingway: The Writer as Artist (Princeton, N. J.: Princeton University Press, 1956), pp. 94-116. Copyright 1956 by the Princeton University Press.

are reduced in size and scale—made to seem smaller, more pitiful, more pathetic, more like wraiths blown down the wind, than would be true if the reader were brought close enough to overhear their conversation or see them as individualized personalities.

Between the first and fourth sentences, moreover, Hemingway accomplishes the transition from late summer to autumn—an inexorability of seasonal change which prepares the way for the study in doom on which he is embarked. Here again the natural elements take on a symbolic function. In the late summer we have the dust; in the early autumn the dust and the leaves falling; and through them both the marching troops impersonally seen. The reminder, through the dust, of the words of the funeral service in the prayer-book is fortified by the second natural symbol, the falling leaves. They dry out, fall, decay, and become part of the dust. Into the dust is where the troops are going—some of them soon, all of them eventually.

The short first chapter closes with winter, and the establishment of rain as a symbol of disaster. "At the start of the winter came the permanent rain and with the rain came the cholera. But it was checked and in the end only seven thousand died of it in the army." Already, now in the winter, seven thousand of the wraiths have vanished underground. The permanent rain lays the dust and rots the leaves as if they had never existed. There is no excellent beauty, even in the country around Gorizia, that has not some sadness to it. And there is hardly a natural beauty in [95/96] the whole first chapter of *A Farewell to Arms* which has not some symbolic function in Hemingway's first study in doom.

II. NOT IN OUR STARS

To call *A Farewell to Arms* a "first" study in doom might seem unfair to *The Sun Also Rises*. But the total effect of the first novel, whatever its author's intention, is closer to that of tragicomedy than of tragedy. The tragic sense of life exists in the undertones of *The Sun Also Rises*. Its surface tone is, however, somewhere within the broad range of the comic. Reading it, one is oftener reminded of the tragi-comic irony of a work like Chaucer's *Troilus and Criseyde* than, say, the tragic irony of the Greeks and the Elizabethans. The operation of pity—again as in Chaucer—is carefully equivocal, somehow in itself a phase of irony, and under a restraint so nearly complete that it can scarcely move. Possibly because of the nature of the material, possibly because of the cultivated habit of understatement, one does not find in *The Sun Also Rises* the degree of emotional commitment which becomes visible in *A Farewell to Arms*.

After the experience of writing and revising his first novel, Hemingway worked more wisely and more slowly on his second. The preparation of the first draft took six months instead of six weeks. It was begun in Paris about the first of March, 1928. Through the spring and summer the work went on in Key West, where Hemingway made himself relax by deep-sea fishing while writing some 40,000 words. He continued the draft in Piggott, Arkansas, and Kansas City, Missouri, where he ran the total number of words to something like 87,000. The book was completed in preliminary form near Big Horn, in Sheridan County, Wyoming, about the end of August, 1928.

Following a brief interlude, he began revision, an extremely painstaking job of cutting and rewriting which filled another five months. On January 22, 1929, he wrote Perkins that the final draft stood complete in typescript, and by mid-February it had been decided to serialize the book in *Scribner's Magazine,* beginning with the number of May, 1929. Still Hemingway was dissatisfied. In Paris during the spring he continued to labor over [96/97] the galley-proofs of the magazine version, rewriting some portions and keeping them by him until the last possible moment. Book-proof reached him in Paris on June 5, 1929.[2] By the twenty-fourth, when he had finally satisfied himself that everything possible had been done, he was able to report to Perkins that he had at last achieved a "new and much better ending" for his novel. There is a persistent tradition that the present ending was rewritten seventeen times before Hemingway got the corrected galley-proof aboard the boat-train.

In the midst of life, runs the Book of Common Prayer, we are in death. "During the time I was writing the first draft," said Hemingway in 1948, "my second son Patrick was delivered in Kansas City by Caesarean section, and while I was rewriting my father killed himself in Oak Park, Illinois. . . . I remember all these things happening and all the places we lived in and the fine times and the bad times we had in that year. But much more vividly I remember living in the book and making up what happened in it every day. Making the country and the people and the things that happened I was happier than I had ever been. Each day I read the book through from the beginning to the point where I went on writing and each day I stopped when I was still going good and when I knew what would happen next. The fact that the book was a tragic one did not make me unhappy since I believed that life was a tragedy and knew it could only have one end. But finding you were able to make something up; to create truly enough so that it made you happy to read it; and to do this every day you worked was something that gave a greater pleasure [97/98] than any I had ever known. Beside it nothing else mattered." [3]

The appearance of *A Farewell to Arms* in book form on September 27, 1929, marked the inception of Hemingway's still lengthening career as one of the very few great tragic writers in twentieth-century fiction. His next book, *Death in the Afternoon*, furthered his exploration into the esthetics of tragedy. Through the 1930's he continued at intervals to wrestle with the problem. *To Have and Have Not*

(though with limited success) examined the tragic implications of social and political decay. *For Whom the Bell Tolls* attacked a similar problem on an epic and international scale. Ten years after that, at the age of fifty, Hemingway rounded out a full twenty years of work in tragedy with his character-study of Colonel Richard Cantwell.

The position occupied by *A Farewell to Arms* among Hemingway's tragic writings may be suggested by the fact that he once referred to the story of Lieutenant Frederick Henry and Catherine Barkley as his *Romeo and Juliet.*[4] The most obvious

[2] Details on the composition are drawn from the following letters: *EH to MP*, 3/17/28, 3/21/28, 6/7/28, ca. 9/5/28, 9/28/28, 1/8/29, 1/10/29, 1/22/29, 6/7/29, 6/24/29. Also EH to Bridges, 5/18/29; and *MP to EH*, 5/24/29, and 7/12/29. At the time he began *FTA*, Hemingway had been for some time at work on another novel—"a sort of modern *Tom Jones*," which was up to nearly 60,000 words when he dropped it in favor of the story of Frederick Henry and Catherine Barkley. On Thanksgiving Day, 1927, he told Perkins that he had completed 17 chapters of the *Tom Jones* work and was only a third through. He had decided to change the narrative method to the third person, having "got tired of the limitations" imposed by first-person narrative. But *FTA*, like *SAR*, used the first-person method. Hemingway did not begin to employ the third person consistently until the middle 1930's.

[3] See Hemingway's introduction, dated June 30, 1948, to the illustrated edition of *FTA*, New York, Scribner's, 1948, pp. vii-viii. Hemingway seems to be in error when he gives the impression that the original publication date was "the day the stock market crashed"—that is, October 30, 1929. The book had been published September 27th. For an excellent review of *FTA* following publication, see Malcolm Cowley, *New York Herald Tribune Books*, October 6, 1929, pp. 1 and 6.

[4] The *Romeo and Juliet* comment is quoted by Edmund Wilson in "Ernest Hemingway: Bourdon Gauge of Morale," which first appeared in the *Atlantic Monthly* 164 (July 1939), pp. 36-46. The essay was collected in *The Wound and the Bow*, New York, 1941, and reprinted by J. K. M. McCaffery, ed., *Ernest Hemingway, The Man and His Work*, New York, 1950, pp. 236-257. Further page-references to this essay will be to the McCaffery reprint only.

It is of some interest to notice that Bertrand Russell on an American lecture tour denounced the novel as a piece of Victorianism. See Irene and Allen Cleaton, *Books and Battles*, New York, 1937. Compare further the opinion of Oliver Allston (Van Wyck Brooks) that *FTA* is another version of the Evangeline story. See *The Opinions of Oliver Allston*, New York, 1941, p. 173.

Boston and Italy had other opinions. The serialization of the novel began in *Scribner's Magazine* in May 1929 (Vol. 85, pp. 493 ff.) and ran to October (Vol. 86, pp. 20 ff.). One startling event of the summer was the banning of the June and July issues from public sale on the orders of Chief of Police Michael H. Crowley of Boston. The result, however unhappy [98/99] for censorship, was in-parallel is [**98/99**] that Henry and Catherine, like their Elizabethan prototypes, might be seen as star-crossed lovers. Hemingway might also have been thinking of how rapidly Romeo and Juliet, whose affair has begun as a mere flirtation, pass over into the status of relatively mature lovers. In the third place, he may have meant to imply that his own lovers, caught in the tragic pattern of the war on the Austrian-Italian front, are not far different from the young victims of the Montague-Capulet family feud.

Neither in *Romeo and Juliet* nor in *A Farewell to Arms* is the catastrophe a direct and logical result of the immoral social situation. Catherine's bodily structure, which precludes a normal delivery for her baby, is an unfortunate biological accident. The death of Shakespeare's lovers is also precipitated by an accident—the detention of the message-bearing friar. The student of esthetics, recognizing another kind of logic in art than that of mathematical cause-and-effect, may however conclude that Catherine's death, like that of Juliet, shows a kind of artistic inevitability. Except by a large indirection, the war does not kill Catherine any more than the Veronese feud kills Juliet. But in the emotional experience of the novel, Catherine's dying is directly associated and interwoven with the whole tragic pattern of fatigue and suffering, loneliness, defeat and doom, of which the war is itself the broad social manifestation. And one might make a similar argument about *Romeo and Juliet*.

In application to Frederick and Catherine, the phrase "star- [**99/100**] crossed lovers" needs some qualification. It does not mean that they are the victims of an actual malevolent metaphysical power. All their crises are caused by forces which human beings have set in motion. During Frederick's understandably bitter ruminations while Catherine lies dying in the Lausanne hospital, fatalistic thoughts do, quite naturally, cross his mind. But he does not, in the end, blame anything called "Fate" for Catherine's death. The

pain of her labor reminds him that her pregnancy has been comfortable and apparently normal; the present biological struggle is perhaps a way of evening things up. "So now they got her in the end. You never got away with anything." But he immediately rejects his own inference: that is, that her sufferings in labor are a punishment for sinful pleasures. Scientifically considered, the child is simply a by-product of good nights in Milan—and there is never a pretence that they were not good. The parents do not happen to be formally married; still, the pain of the child-bearing would have been just as it is even if they had been married fifty times. In short, the pain is natural, inevitable, and without either moral or metaphysical significance. The anonymous "they" is nothing but a name for the way things are.

A little later Frederick Henry bitterly compares the human predicament first to a game and then to a swarm of ants on a log in a campfire. Both are homely and unbookish metaphors such as would naturally occur to any young American male at a comparable time. Living now seems to be a war-like game, played "for keeps," where to be tagged out is to die. Here again, there is a moral implication in the idea of being caught off base—trying to steal third, say, when the infield situation and the number of outs make it wiser to stay on second. "They threw you in and told you the rules and the first time they caught you off base they killed you." One trouble, of course, is that the player rarely has time enough to learn by long experi-

creased sales for the book. A poet in *The Daily Oklahoman* felt that.

　　Scribner's may have larger circulation
　　Since Boston with its codfish and its beans
　　Deems Hemingway a menace to the nation.

Both the novel and the film were banned in Italy by Mussolini's government. It was felt that they showed Italian military valor in an ugly light. The film, which Hemingway resented as a falsification of his intention, was released in December 1932. Samuel Putnam notes that up to 1947 Hemingway was still popular with Italian anti-fascists. (*Paris Was Our Mistress*, p. 132.)

　　FTA is the only one of Hemingway's works to appear in three media. The novel was successfully dramatized by Lawrence Stallings, and presented at the National Theatre, September 22, 1930. See *New Republic* 64 (October 8, 1930), pp. 208-209.

ence; his fatal error may come in the second half of the first inning, which is about as far as Catherine seems likely to go. Even those who survive long enough to learn the rules may be killed through the operation of chance or the accidents of the game. Death may, in short, come "gratuitously" without the slightest reference to "the rules."

It is plainly a gratuitous death which comes to the ants on the [**100/101**] burning log in Frederick's remembered campfire. Some immediately die in flame, as Catherine is now dying. Others, like Lieutenant Henry, who has survived a trench-mortar explosion, will manage to get away, their bodies permanently scarred, their future course uncertain—except that they will die in the end. Still others, unharmed, will swarm on the still cool end of the log until the fire at last reaches them. If a Hardyan President of the Immortals takes any notice of them, He does little enough for their relief. He is like Frederick Henry pouring water on the burning campfire log—not to save the ants but only to empty a cup.

Catherine's suffering and death prove nothing except that she should not have become pregnant. But she had to become pregnant in order to find out that becoming pregnant was unwise. Death is a penalty for ignorance of "the rules": it is also a fact which has nothing to do with rule or reason. Death is the fire which, in conclusion, burns us all, and it may singe us along the way. Frederick Henry's ruminations simply go to show that if he and Catherine seem star-crossed, it is only because Catherine is biologically double-crossed, Europe is war-crossed, and life is death-crossed.[5]

III. HOME AND NOT-HOME

As its first chapter suggests, the natural-mythological structure which informs *A Farewell to Arms* is in some ways comparable to the Burguete-Montparnasse, Catholic-Pagan, and Romero-Cohn contrasts of *The Sun Also Rises*. One has the impression, however, of greater assurance, subtlety, and complexity in the second novel, as if the writing of the first had strengthened and consolidated Hemingway's powers and given him new insights into this method for controlling materials from below.

Despite the insistent, denotative matter-of-factness at the surface of the presentation, the subsurface activity of *A Farewell to Arms* is organized connotatively around two poles. By a process of accrual and coagulation, the images tend to build round the opposed concepts of Home and Not-Home. Neither, of course, is truly conceptualistic; each is a kind of poetic intuition, charged [**101/102**] with emotional values and woven, like a cable, of many strands. The Home-concept, for example, is associated with the mountains; with dry-cold weather; with peace and quiet; with love, dignity, health, happiness, and the good life; and with worship or at least the consciousness of God. The Not-Home concept is associated with low-lying plains; with rain and fog; with obscenity, indignity, disease, suffering, nervousness, war and death; and with irreligion.

The motto of William Bird's Three Mountains Press in Paris, which printed Hemingway's *in our time*, was "Levavi oculos meos in montes." The line might also have served as an epigraph for *A Farewell to Arms*. Merely introduced in the first sentence of the first chapter, the mountain-image begins to develop important associations as early as Chapter Two. Learning that Frederick Henry is to go on leave, the young priest urges him to visit Capracotta in the Abruzzi. "There," he says, "is good hunting. You would like the people and though it is cold, it is clear and dry. You could stay with my family. My father is a famous hunter." But the lowlander infantry captain interrupts: "Come on," he says in pidgin Italian to Frederick Henry. "We go whorehouse before it shuts."[6]

---

[5] On Catherine's bad luck, see *FTA*, pp. 342, 350.
[6] *FTA*, pp. 9, 13.

After Henry's return from the leave, during which he has been almost everywhere else on the Italian peninsula *except* Abruzzi, the mountain-image gets further backing from another low-land contrast. "I had wanted," says he, "to go to Abruzzi. I had gone to no place where the roads were frozen and hard as iron, where it was clear cold and dry and the snow was dry and powdery and haretracks in the snow and the peasants took off their hats and called you Lord and there was good hunting. I had gone to no such place but to the smoke of cafés and nights when the room whirled and you needed to look at the wall to make it stop, nights in bed, drunk, when you knew that that was all there was."

Throughout Book I, Hemingway quietly consolidates the mountain-image. On the way up towards the Isonzo from Gorizia, Frederick looks across the river and the plain to the Julian and Carnic Alps. "I looked to the north at the two ranges of moun- [102/103] tains, green and dark to the snow-line and then white and lovely in the sun. Then, as the road mounted along the ridge, I saw a third range of mountains, higher snow mountains, that looked chalky white and furrowed, with strange planes, and then there were mountains far beyond all these that you could hardly tell if you really saw." [7] Like Pope in the celebrated "Alps on Alps arise" passage, Hemingway is using the mountains symbolically. Years later, in "The Snows of Kilimanjaro," he would use the mighty peak of East Africa as a natural image of immortality, just as in *The Green Hills of Africa* he would build his narrative in part upon a contrast between the hill-country and the Serengetti Plain. When Frederick Henry lowers his eyes from the far-off ranges, he sees the plain and the river, the war-making equipment, and "the broken houses of the little town" which is to be occupied, if anything is left of it to occupy, during the coming attack. Already now, a few dozen pages into the book, the mountain-image has developed associations; with the man of God and his

homeland, with clear dry cold and snow, with polite and kindly people, with hospitality, and with natural beauty. Already it has its oppositions: the lowland obscenities of the priest-baiting captain, cheap cafés, one-night prostitutes, drunkenness, destruction, and the war.

When the trench-mortar explosion nearly kills Henry, the priest comes to visit him in the field-hospital, and the Abruzzi homeland acquires a religious association. "There in my country," says the priest, "it is understood that a man may love God. It is not a dirty joke." Repeating, for emphasis, the effect of the priest's first account of the highland country, Hemingway allows Frederick to develop in his mind's eye an idyllic picture of the priest's home-ground.

"At Capracotta, he had told me, there were trout in the stream below the town. It was forbidden to play the flute at night . . . because it was bad for the girls to hear. . . . Aquila was a fine town. It was cool in the summer at night and the spring in Abruzzi was the most beautiful in Italy. But what was lovely was the fall to go hunting through the chestnut woods. The birds were all good [103/104] because they fed on grapes, and you never took a lunch because the peasants were always honored if you would eat with them in their houses. . . ." [8]

By the close of Book I, largely through the agency of the priest, a complex connection has come clear between the idea of Home and the combination of high ground, cold weather, love, and the love of God. Throughout, Hemingway has worked solely by suggestion, implication, and quiet repetition, putting the reader into potential awareness, readying him for what is to come.

The next step is to bring Catherine Barkley by degrees into the center of the image. Her love affair with Henry begins as a "rotten game" of war-time seduction. Still emotionally unstable and at loose nervous ends from her fiancé's death, Cath-

[7] *FTA*, p. 48.
[8] *FTA*, p. 78.

erine is a comparatively easy conquest. But in the American hospital at Milan, following Henry's ordeal by fire at the front not far from the Isonzo, the casual affair becomes an honorable though unpriested marriage. Because she can make a "home" of any room she occupies—and Henry several times alludes to this power of hers—Catherine naturally moves into association with ideas of home, love, and happiness. She does not really reach the center of the mountain-image until, on the heels of Frederick's harrowing lowland experiences during the retreat from Caporetto, the lovers move to Switzerland. Catherine is the first to go, and Henry follows her there as if she were the genius of the mountains, beckoning him on. Soon they are settled into a supremely happy life in the winterland on the mountainside above Montreux. Catherine's death occurs at Lausanne, after the March rains and the approaching need for a good lying-in hospital have driven the young couple down from their magic mountain—the closest approximation to the priest's fair homeland in the Abruzzi that they are ever to know.

The total structure of the novel is developed, in fact, around the series of contrasting situations already outlined. To Gorizia, the Not-Home of war, succeeds the Home which Catherine and Frederick make together in the Milan Hospital. The Not-Home of the grim retreat from the Isonzo is followed by the quiet and happy retreat which the lovers share above Montreux. Home ends [**104/105**] for Frederick Henry when he leaves Catherine dead in the Lausanne Hospital.

Developed for an esthetic purpose, Hemingway's contrasting images have also a moral value. Although he has nothing to say about the images themselves, Mr. Ludwig Lewisohn is undoubtedly correct in saying that *A Farewell to Arms* "proves once again the ultimate identity of the moral and the esthetic." In this critic's view, Hemingway "transcended the moral nihilism of the school he had himself helped to form" by the very intensity of his feelings for the contrast of love and war. "The simply wrought fable," Lewisohn continues, ignoring all the symbolic complexities yet still making a just appraisal, "has two culminations—the laconic and terrible one in which the activity of the battle police brings to an end the epically delineated retreat of the Italian army with its classically curbed rage and pity . . . and that other and final culmination in Switzerland with its blending in so simple and moving a fashion of the eternal notes of love and death." The operation of the underlying imagery, once its purposes are understood, doubly underscores Mr. Lewisohn's point that there is no moral nihilism in the central story of *A Farewell to Arms.*[9]

The use of rain as a kind of symbolic obligato in the novel has been widely and properly admired. Less apparent to the cursory reader is the way in which the whole idea of climate is related to the natural-mythological structure. (Hemingway's clusters of associated images produce emotional "climates" also, but they are better experienced than reduced by critical descriptions.) The rains begin in Italy during October, just before Henry's return to Gorizia after his recovery from his wounds. The rains continue, at first steadily, then intermittently, throughout the disastrous retreat, Henry's flight to Stresa, and the time of his reunion with Catherine. When they awaken the morning after their reunion night, the rain has stopped, light floods the window, and Henry, looking out in the fresh early morning, can see Lake Maggiore in the sun "with the mountains beyond." Towards these mountains the lovers now depart.

Not until they are settled in idyllic hibernation in their rented chalet above Montreux are they really out of the rain. As if to [**105/106**] emphasize by climatic accompaniment their "confused alarums of struggle and flight," the rain has swept over them during their escape up the lake in an open boat. Once in the mountains,

[9] *Expression in America*, New York, 1932, p. 519.

however, they are out of the lowlands, out of danger, out of the huge, tired debacle of the war. Above Montreux, as in the priest's homeland of Abruzzi, the ridges are "iron-hard with the frost." The deep snow isolates them, and gives them a feeling of domestic safety, tranquillity, and invulnerability.

For several months the rainless idyll continues. "We lived through the months of January and February and the winter was very fine and we were very happy. There had been short thaws when the wind blew warm and the snow softened and the air felt like spring, but always the clear, hard cold had come again and the winter had returned. In March came the first break in the winter. In the night it started raining."

The reader has been prepared to recognize some kind of disaster-symbol in the return of the rains. Much as in *Romeo and Juliet,* several earlier premonitions of doom have been inserted at intervals. "I'm afraid of the rain," says Catherine in the Milan Hospital one summer night, "because sometimes I see me dead in it." In the fall, just before Henry returns to the front, they are in a Milan hotel. During a break in the conversation the sound of falling rain comes in. A motor car klaxons, and Henry quotes Marvell: "At my back I always hear Time's wingèd chariot hurrying near." He must soon take a cab to catch the train that will project him, though he does not know it yet, into the disaster of the great retreat. Months later, in Lausanne, the Marvell lines echo hollowly: "We knew the baby was very close now and it gave us both a feeling *as though something were hurrying us and we could not lose any time together.*" (Italics added.) The sound of the rain continues like an undersong until, with Catherine dead in the hospital room (not unlike that other happy one where their child was conceived), Henry walks back to the hotel in the rain.[10] [106/107]

One further reinforcement of the central symbolic structure is provided by the contrast between the priest and the doctor, the man of God and the man without God. In line with the reminiscence of *Romeo and Juliet,* it may not be fantastic to see them respectively as the Friar Lawrence and the Mercutio of Hemingway's novel. The marked contrast between the two men becomes especially apparent when Henry returns to the Gorizia area following his discharge from the hospital.

The return to Gorizia is a sharp comedown. After the "home-feeling" of the hospital and the hotel in Milan, the old army post seems less like home than ever. The tenor of life there has noticeably changed. A kind of damp-rot afflicts morale. The major, bringing Henry up to date on the state of affairs, plays dismally on the word *bad.* It has been a "bad summer." It was "very bad" on the Bainsizza plateau: "We lost three cars. . . . You wouldn't believe how bad it's been. . . . You were lucky to be hit when you were. . . . Next year will be worse. . . ." As if he were not fully convinced by the Major's despair, Henry picks up the word: "Is it so bad?" The answer is yes. "It is so bad and worse. Go get cleaned up and find your friend Rinaldi."

With Rinaldi the doctor, things also are bad, a fact which has been borne in upon the major so strongly that he thinks of Rinaldi when he mentions the word *bad.* Things are not bad for Rinaldi from a professional point of view, for he has operated on so many casualties that he has become "a lovely surgeon." Still, he is not the old Mercutio-like and mercurial Rinaldi. If mercury enters into his picture at all it is because he has syphilis, or thinks he has. He is treating himself for it and is beginning to entertain certain delusions of persecution. Except for his work, and the temporary opiates of drink and prostitutes, both of which interfere with his work, Rinaldi, the man of the plain, the man without God, is a man without resources.

[10] *FTA,* pp. 135, 165, 267, 326, and 332 show, in order, the various premonitions and the obligato use of rain. Malcolm Cowley was one of the first of Hemingway's critics to point to his symbolic use of weather. See *The Portable Hemingway,* New York, 1944, introd., p. xvi.

With the priest, the man from the Abruzzi highlands, tacitly reintroduced as a contrast for Rinaldi, things are not so bad. "He was the same as ever," says Henry at their meeting, "small and brown and compact-looking." He is much more sure of himself than formerly, though in a modest way. When Rinaldi, in the absence of the foul-mouthed captain, takes up the former indoor [107/108] game of priest-baiting, the priest is not perturbed. "I could see," says Henry, "that the baiting did not touch him now."

Out of the evils of the past summer the priest has even contrived to gather a nascent hope. Officers and men, he thinks, are gentling down because they "realize the war" as never before. When this happens, the fighting cannot continue for very much longer. Henry, playing half-heartedly the *advocatus diaboli,* argues that what the priest calls "gentling down" is really nothing but the feeling of defeat: "It is in defeat that we become Christian . . . like Our Lord." Henry is maintaining that after the fearless courage of His ministry, Our Lord's gentleness and His refusal to fight against the full brunt of the experience on Calvary became the ideal of Christian meekness. If Peter had rescued Christ Jesus from the Garden, suggests Henry, Christian ethics might be something different. But the priest, who is as compact as he looks, knows otherwise. Our Lord would not have changed in any way. From that knowledge and belief comes the priest's own strength. He has resources which Dr. Rinaldi, the man without God, does not possess.[11]

The priest-doctor contrast is carried out in the sacred-versus-profane-love antithesis which is quietly emphasized in the novel. Through the agency of Rinaldi the love affair begins at a fairly low level. The doctor introduces Frederick to Catherine, and takes a jocularly profane view of the early infatuation, seeming to doubt that it can ever be anything but an unvarnished war-time seduction. On the other hand, the background symbols of home and true love and high ground suggest that the lovers' idyllic life in Switzerland is carried on under the spiritual aegis of the priest. Neither Rinaldi nor the priest appears in the latter part of the book. But when, having been driven to the lowlands by the rains of spring, Catherine enters the hospital, it is naturally enough a doctor who takes over. And though this doctor does all he can to save her life, Catherine dies.

Projected in actualistic terms and a matter-of-fact tone, telling the truth about the effects of war in human life, *A Farewell to Arms* is entirely and even exclusively acceptable as a naturalistic [108/109] narrative of what happened. To read it only as such, however, is to miss the controlling symbolism: the deep central antithesis between the image of life and home (the mountain) and the image of war and death (the plain).

IV. THE FEMALE OF THE SPECIES

Coleridge once made the questionable remark that in Shakespeare "it is the perfection of woman to be characterless. Every one wishes a Desdemona or Ophelia for a wife—creatures who, though they may not always understand you, do always feel [for] you and feel with you."[12] To make so inordinate a generalization, Coleridge was obliged to ignore the better than half of Shakespeare's "perfect" women who are anything but characterless.

The modern reader, brought up on similar generalizations about the heroines of Hemingway, may wish to reconsider the problem. The most frequent adverse comment on Hemingway's fictional heroines is that they tend to embody two extremes, ignoring the middle ground. This fact is taken to be a kind of sin of omission, the belief being that most of their real-life sisters congregate and operate precisely in

[11] On the low morale among the Italian troops, see *FTA*, pp. 174-175. On Rinaldi's affliction, see p. 181. On the priest's firmness, see pp. 183-184.
[12] Coleridge, *Table Talk,* in *Works,* ed. Shedd, vol. 6, p. 349.

the area which Hemingway chooses not to invade at all.

The strictures of Mr. Edmund Wilson may be taken as typical of a recurrent critical position. He puts the argument in terms of a still-to-be-written chapter on the resemblances between Hemingway and Kipling. The two writers seem to him to share in "certain assumptions about society" with particular reference to the position of women. Kipling and Hemingway show, says Mr. Wilson, "much the same split attitude toward women. Kipling anticipates Hemingway in his beliefs that 'he travels fastest who travels alone' and that 'the female of the species is more deadly than the male'; and Hemingway seems to reflect Kipling in the submissive infra-Anglo-Saxon women that make his heroes such perfect mistresses. The most striking example of this is the amoeba-like little Spanish girl, Maria, in *For Whom the Bell Tolls*. Like the docile native 'wives' of English officials in the early stories of [**109/110**] Kipling, she lives only to serve her lord and to merge her identity with his; and this love affair with a woman in a sleeping-bag, lacking completely the kind of give and take that goes on between real men and women, has the all-too-perfect felicity of a youthful erotic dream."[13]

The relevance of this commentary is that it underscores the idea of the two extremes in Hemingway's fictional treatment of women. In one group are the "deadly" females. Their best-realized (because most sympathetically presented and most roundly characterized) representative is Brett Ashley. The horrible example would presumably be someone like Margot Macomber, who is really and literally deadly. In varying degrees—and the fact that it is a matter of degree ought to be noticed—these women are selfish, corrupt, and predatory. They are "bad" for the men with whom they are involved. At the other extreme would stand the allegedly docile and submissive mistress-types, of whom Catherine Barkley and Maria are the conspicuous examples. These, for Mr. Wilson, are incredible wish-projections,

youthfully erotic dream-girls, or impossibly romantic ideals of wife-hood. They bear, it seems, little resemblance to the women with whom one is acquainted. Where now, Mr. Wilson seems to be asking, are the day-by-day vagaries, the captious bickerings, the charming or enraging anfractuosities which combine to produce the "normal" or "real" married state? The greater number of the female kind obviously occupy some realm intermediate between the Becky Sharps and the Amelia Sedleys, between the pole of Goneril and Regan and the pole of Ophelia and Desdemona. By his failure, or his tacit refusal, to depict realistically the occupants of this realm and to use them as the heroines of his fiction, Hemingway has somehow failed in his obligation to present things as they are.

This point of view naturally affects Mr. Wilson's judgment of *A Farewell to Arms*. On the whole he finds the novel to be "a less serious affair" than Hemingway's previous work. Catherine Barkley and Frederick Henry, at least during the period of their Swiss idyll, strike him as "not in themselves convincing as human personalities." For him their relationship is merely an [**110/111**] idealization, "the abstraction of a lyric emotion."[14] Mr. Cowley evidently shares this view. "To me," writes Mr. Cowley, "[Catherine] is only a woman at the beginning of the book, in her near madness"—as if, perhaps, some degree of emotional instability were a criterion of credibility in the portrait of a fictional heroine.[15]

For those who find it hard to accept Mr. Wilson's view of Catherine as an abstraction and of Maria as an amoeba, four practical points might well be made. The first has to do with the relation of Brett Ashley and Catherine Barkley to what Mr. Wilson might call the Great Infra-Anglo-Saxon tradition of fictional heroines. It is of some interest to observe that Mr. Wilson's strictures on the heroines of Heming-

[13] McCaffery, *op. cit.*, p. 254, note.
[14] *ibid.*, p. 242.
[15] Malcolm Cowley to CB, 10/20/51.

way could be applied with equal justice, not only to the heroines of Kipling but also to a considerable number of other heroines throughout the history of English and American fiction. Hemingway shares with many predecessors an outlook indubitably masculine, a certain chivalric attitude not without ironic overtones, and a disinclination to interest himself in what may be called the prosaisms of the female world.

The second point is that through a method of comparative portraiture, Hemingway carefully establishes a moral norm of womanly behavior. Then, whether by ethical intent or by temperamental attitude, he uses the established norm as a means of computing various degrees of departure from it. Depending on their own views in this area, readers may find Hemingway's "norm-women" less interesting and less credible than their "abnormal" cousins. For the inveterate reader of fiction and narrative poetry it is perhaps a psychological truism that the *femme fatale,* the general type of the temptress, seems more "interesting" than the stable heroine.

In the early work of Hemingway the point is well illustrated by the contrast between Brett and Catherine. There are, to begin with, certain resemblances. Like Brett, Catherine is an Englishwoman; like Brett, she is beautiful, tall, and blonde. She talks as Brett does, stressing certain words which in print are italicized. [111/112] Like Brett, she has lost her own true love early in the war, and her emotions, like her way of life, have become confused as a result of the bereavement. But here the resemblances stop.

Brett's neurosis drives her from bar to bar, from man to man, and from city to city. None of it is any good: her polygamy, with or without benefit of justices of the peace, leads only to more of the same, as one drink leads to another in the endless round. Brett is not "good" for the men she knows. Romero wants her to let her hair grow out, to become more feminine, to marry and live with him. The basic abnor-

mality at work in Brett opposes such feminization. She is the short-haired companion of men, wearing a man's felt hat, calling herself a "chap." She does not really like other women, and neither has nor wishes to have any real friends among them. She is never happier than in the Pamplona wineshop, the center of raucous masculine singing, as if she were a half-woman half in love with damnation.

Catherine Barkley, on the other hand, is all woman. At once dependent and independent, she half-mothers, half-mistresses Frederick Henry. She wants no other life than with him, no other man than he. She drinks little and displays none of Brett's geographical restlessness. She is temperamentally monogamous. Where she is, home is. Even the red-plush hotel room in Milan (which for several minutes makes her feel like a whore) is changed by her presence until she herself can feel at home in it. "In a little while," says her lover, "the room felt like our own home. My room at the hospital had been our own home and this room was our home too in the same way." Trying at first to help her out of the harlot-feeling, Henry kisses her and assures her, "You're my good girl." "I'm certainly yours," says Catherine, wryly. But she is also, and preeminently, a "good girl"—even more so, for example, than Hardy's Tess, who was so designated on the title page.[16] As if Hemingway were looking back for contrast to the Circean figure of his first novel, Rinaldi refers to Catherine as "your lovely cool . . . English goddess." But she is a woman, not a goddess. She rescues, pities, comforts, companions, and sustains, just as she in turn is rescued from the "craziness" induced [112/113] by her lover's death when she has finally involved herself sufficiently in Henry's growing love. Her hair is long; she dresses like a woman and gets on well with other women like her friend Ferguson. Yet she is evidently happiest alone with her husband. She would be unhappy and possibly frightened on the wine-cask

[16] On Catherine's connection with the "home-feeling," see *FTA*, p. 163. Rinaldi's remark on her goddess-like qualities is on p. 71.

in Pamplona. She is at ease in Milan in the midst of a war because she is a young woman in the midst of love. Like Maria, she is a completing agent for the hero, and is in turn completed by her association with him. But Brett, on the other hand, is an agent of depletion, as she herself realizes, and as her unselfish renunciation of Romero is presumably meant to show.[17]

The third point to be made about Hemingway's heroines is that they are, on the whole, an aspect of the poetry of things. It is perhaps a sign of an attitude innately chivalric that they are never written off, as sometimes happened in Kipling, as mere bundles of rags, bones, and hanks of hair. Even Margot Macomber, in the bottomless slough of her bitch-hood, is seen to be "damned beautiful." The treatment of Catherine, like that of Brett, shows in Hemingway a fundamental indisposition to render his heroines "reductively." And if one argues that he nowhere seems to commit himself to the emancipation of women, or to become in the usual sense of the term an ardent feminist, the answer would be, perhaps, that his women are truly emancipated only through an idea or ideal of service. His heroines, to make the statement exactly, are meant to show a symbolic or ritualistic function in the service of the artist and the service of man.

The final point grows naturally out of the preceding ones. It is, in brief, that all of Hemingway's heroines, like all of his heroes, are placed in a special kind of accelerated world. We do not see them puttering in their kitchens, but only dreaming of that as a desirable possibility. They are never presented as harassed mothers; their entire orientation tends to be, in this connection, [113/114] premarital. Wars and revolutions, the inevitable enemies of peace and domesticity, set them adrift or destroy their lives. Yet they contrive to embody the image of home, the idea if not the actuality of the married state, and where they are, whatever the outward threats, home is.

Mr. Wilson's feeling that Catherine is not convincing as a human personality, his belief that her love affair with Frederick Henry is an "abstraction of lyric emotion," may be partly explained by the fact that a majority of the characters in the first two novels are oddly rootless. With a few notable exceptions like Robert Cohn, Brett Ashley, or the priest from Abruzzi, they seem on the whole to possess no genealogies or previous biographies. We know nothing about Henry's background, and next to nothing about Catherine Barkley's. Like Jake Barnes, Bill Gorton, and Dr. Rinaldi, they seem to come from nowhere, move into the now and here, and depart again for nowhere after the elapsed time of the novels. They have substance and cast shadows, but they lack the full perspective and chiaroscuro that one finds among most of the people in *For Whom the Bell Tolls*. We are seldom permitted to know them in depth. The inclination is to accept them for what they do more than for what they are. They are the men and women of action, the meaning of whose lives must be sought in the kind of actions in which they are involved, very much, again, as in *Romeo and Juliet*.

This feeling about the characters can be accounted for in two different ways. One has to do with Hemingway's esthetic assumptions as of 1928–1929; the other is a natural consequence of the kind of stories he chose to tell. His working assumption that character is revealed through action will, if rigorously adhered to, produce the kind of fiction in which characterization-in-depth is in a measure sacrificed to the exigencies of narrative movement. Even there, however, it is advisable to notice that a close reading of any of the early books reveals far more in the way of nuances of light and shade, or

---

[17] Mr. Theodore Bardacke has an interesting essay on "Hemingway's Women" in McCaffery, *op. cit.*, pp. 340-351. Among its contributions is a discussion of Hemingway's "symbolic" use of long and short hair as a mark of femininity or the relative lack of it. The point is of special interest in connection with Maria, who has been raped and shorn by the fascists. The growing-out of her hair is a reminder of her gradual return to mental and physical health under the double tutelage of Pilar and Roberto.

in subtle shifts of motivation, than one at first imagined was there. This half-concealed power is easily explained by what is now acknowledged in all quarters: Hemingway's carefully controlled habit of understatement. As for the second explanation, it might be pointed out that nearly all of the im- [114/115] portant characters in the first two novels are "displaced persons"—either men fighting a war far from their former home-environments, or aliens in foreign lands whose ties with nearly everything they have known before are now severed—for better or for worse, but severed.

These two explanations, the esthetic and the "geographical," may throw some further light into the reasons behind Mr. Wilson's strictures. If Hemingway had not yet met head-on the problem of characterization-in-depth, perhaps it was unfair to ask a writer who had done so much so brilliantly that he should do so much more. He had developed a memorably individualized style—whittled it, as MacLeish said, from the hard wood of a walnut stick. He showed an unerring ability to keep his narratives in motion. Finally, he had achieved mastery of that special combination of naturalistic and symbolic truth-telling which was the despair of those who could (and so frequently did) imitate his style and his narrative manner.

In the absence of other evidence, it is probably wisest to assume that Hemingway knew what he was doing. That he could draw a character fully, roundedly, and quickly is proved by a dozen minor portraits in the first two books—Cohn's acidulous mistress, for example, or Brett's friend Mippipopoulos [sic], or the wonderful old Count Greffi, with whom Henry plays at billiards and philosophy in the hotel at Stresa, or the Milanese surgeon who does the operation on Henry's leg after the affair of the trench mortar, a surgeon who seems, and is, four times as good as the three old-maiden doctors who have wisely wagged their heads an hour before and advised Henry to wait six months for the operation. These are only four examples, but they are enough to show that the ability to draw character was by no means lacking in the Hemingway of 1929. If he went no deeper into the backgrounds of his displaced persons, he went as deeply as he needed to do for the purposes of his narrative. And the paring-out of the superfluous had always been one of his special addictions.

There is, finally, a *tendenz* in *A Farewell to Arms* which helps to account for the opinion that Hemingway has somehow failed in his attempt to present Catherine as a credible characterization. In a large and general way, the whole movement of the novel [115/116] is from concretion towards abstraction. This became apparent in our consideration of the wonderfully complex opening chapter, and the importance of the observation is enhanced by what happens in the closing chapters of the book. The fact that the whole story is projected in actualistic terms ought not finally to obscure the symbolic mythos on which it is built and from which a great part of its emotional power derives. Catherine may be taken as an English girl who has a Juliet-like liaison with a young American officer. Similarly, one may read the novel as a naturalistic narrative of what happened to a small group of people on the Italian front during the years 1917–1918.

In the central antithesis between the image of life, love, and home (the mountain), and the image of war and death (the plain), Catherine however has a symbolic part to play. It is indeed required of her that she should become, as the novel moves on towards its dénouement, more of an abstraction of love than a down-to-earth portrait of an actual woman in love and in pain. The truly sympathetic reader may feel that she is a woman, too. But if she does move in the direction of abstraction, one might argue that the *tendenz* of the novel is in this respect symbolically and emotionally justified. For when Frederick Henry has closed the door of the hospital room in order to be alone with his dead wife Catherine, he learns at once, as if by that act, the finality and totality of his loss. It is the loss of a life, of a love, of a home. Saying good-bye is "like saying good bye to a statue." The loved woman has become in death an abstract unvital image of her living self, a marble memorial to all that has gone without hope of recovery. Her death exactly completes the symbolic structure, the edifice of tragedy so carefully erected. This structure is essentially poetic in conception and execution. It is achieved without obvious insistence or belaboring of the point, but it is indubitably achieved for any reader who has found his way into the true heart of the book. And it is this achievement which enables Hemingway's first study in doom to succeed as something far more than an exercise in romantic naturalism. Next to *For Whom the Bell Tolls,* it is his best novel.

Hemingway's Ambiguity: Symbolism and Irony*

E. M. HALLIDAY, formerly on the faculty of North Carolina State College, is now serving on the editorial staff of *American Heritage*.

I

One of the curious things about *The Old Man and the Sea* was the sense of awe that it created in its author, its publisher, and (to judge by many of the reviewers) its readers. "Don't you think it is a strange damn story that it should affect all of us (me especially) the way it does?"[1] wrote Hemingway to one of *Life's* editors. And Scribner's dust jacket responded like a good Greek chorus, "One cannot hope to explain why the reading of this book is so profound an experience."[2]

There has always been a certain mystery about Hemingway's effects in his best writing. From *In Our Time* (1925), with its puzzling "chapters" connecting (or separating) the stories, through *For Whom the Bell Tolls* (1940), with its oddly equivocal interpretation of the Spanish civil war, his best has evoked a somewhat doubtful sound from critics who nevertheless were at pains to recommend. Something, it was felt, was being missed; or if not missed, then sensed too vaguely for critical description. *A Farewell to Arms* (1929), declared Edward Hope in the New York *Herald Tribune*, was "one of those things—like the Grand Canyon—that one doesn't care to talk about."[3] Despite such reverent throwing up of hands by early critics many things were aptly observed; but the emphasis was heavily on Hemingway the realist, whose bright fidelity to perceptible surfaces of life was accomplished through living dialogue and a prose finely engineered to the accurate rendering of sensuous experience. And the brilliance of his reflected surface together with the roughness of the things he preferred to write about—fishing, hunting, skiing, bull-fighting, boxing, horse-racing, and war—perhaps made it difficult to see one of the cardinal facts about Hemingway: that essentially he is a philosophical writer. His main [1/2] interest, in representing human life through fictional forms, has consistently been to set man against the background of his world and universe, to examine the human situation from various points of view.

Not that he has a "system," for on the final questions Hemingway has always shown himself a skeptic. "It seemed like a fine philosophy," Jake Barnes says to himself at one bitter point in *The Sun Also Rises*. "In five years . . . it will seem just as silly as all the other fine philosophies I've had."[4] Like Jake, Hemingway has been "technically" a Roman Catholic, but the metaphysical doctrines of Christianity seem never to have taken a convincing hold. His most devout characters are only devoutly mystified by the universe: both Anselmo, the good old man of *For Whom the Bell Tolls,* and Santiago, of *The Old Man and the Sea,* disclaim their religiosity, and their Hail-Marys are uttered mechanically enough to evoke a chilly memory of the sleepless waiter in "A Clean,

[1] Quoted in *Time*, LX, No. 9, 48 (Sept. 1, 1952).
[2] *The Old Man and the Sea* (New York, 1952).
[3] Quoted on the flyleaf of *A Farewell to Arms*, Bantam Edition (New York, 1954).
[4] *The Sun Also Rises* (New York, 1926), p. 153.

* E. M. Halliday, "Hemingway's Ambiguity: Symbolism and Irony," *American Literature*, XXVIII (March, 1956), 1-22. Reprinted by permission of the author and Duke University Press.

Well-Lighted Place," who prayed, "Hail nothing, full of nothing, nothing is with thee."[5] The parable of the doomed ants on the burning log, in *A Farewell to Arms*,[6] has been thought to represent Hemingway's *Weltanschauung* at its most pessimistic; but there is no reason, actually, to think that there has since been a fundamental change in his view of life. "Everything kills everything else in some way,"[7] reflects the old Cuban fisherman of the latest book; and even the small bird that rests momentarily on his fishing line may fall to the hawks before reaching land, at best must take its chance "like any man or bird or fish."[8] The world, it seems, still breaks everyone, and only the earth and the Gulf Stream abide after the vortex of human vanities has subsided forever.

Given Hemingway's suspicion of ultimate doom and his passionate fondness for being alive, it is no surprise that his philosophical preoccupation is primarily ethical. Extinction may well be the end of all, as the writer of Ecclesiastes repeatedly remarked, but for Hemingway and his heroes this merely emphasizes the need to live each moment properly and skilfully, to sense judiciously the texture of every fleeting act and perception. The focus is conduct: "Maybe [2/3] if you found out how to live in it you learned from that what it was all about,"[9] says Jake Barnes. It is not accidental that the French existentialists have shown a strong feeling for Hemingway's work. Like them he has been poised in his hours of despair on the edge of nothingness, the abyss of nonmeaning which confronts most of the characters in the stories of *Winner Take Nothing* (1933) ; and like them he has looked in his hours of hope to a salvation built out of individual human courage around a code, at once rational and intuitive, of strict, often ritualistic behavior. *"Nous sommes foutus . . . comme toujours,"* says Golz, the Loyalist general commanding the attack with which Jordan's mission is coordinated in *For Whom the Bell Tolls.* *". . . Bon. Nous ferons notre petit possi-* *ble."*[10] As it was for Socrates and Jeremy Taylor, although for quite different reasons, dying well is for Hemingway the crucial corollary to living well. So Robert Jordan fights off an impulse to kill himself to end the anguish of a badly broken leg and avoid possible capture. "You can do nothing for yourself but perhaps you can do something for another,"[11] he tells himself; yet we are to understand that he has died well not just because of his sacrifice, but because he has not abandoned the principle of fortitude. In the image of the crucifixion which has haunted Hemingway from "Today Is Friday" (1926) to *The Old Man and the Sea,* it is the unique courage of the forsaken and crucified man-God that takes his attention. "I'll tell you," says a Roman soldier in the earlier work, "he looked pretty good to me in there today."[12] We are part of a universe offering no assurance beyond the grave, and we are to make what we can of life by a pragmatic ethic spun bravely out of man himself in full and steady cognizance that the end is darkness.

II

Undoubtedly Hemingway's preoccupation with the human predicament and a moral code that might satisfactorily control it, in itself partly accounts for the sense of hidden significance which many have experienced in reading him. Obscured as this preoccupation has been by his choice of particular fictional materials and by his manner, which has always eschewed explication, it could neverthe-[3/4] less almost always be felt: it was impossible to avoid the impression that this writer was dealing with something of final importance to us all. Like the Eliza-

---

[5] *The Short Stories of Ernest Hemingway* (New York, 1938), p. 481.
[6] *A Farewell to Arms* (New York, 1932), p. 350.
[7] *The Old Man and the Sea*, p. 117.
[8] *Ibid.*, p. 61.
[9] *The Sun Also Rises*, p. 153.
[10] *For Whom the Bell Tolls* (New York, 1940), pp. 428, 430.
[11] *Ibid.*, p. 466.
[12] *The Short Stories*, p. 457.

bethans whom he evidently loves, he never lets us quite forget that death awaits every man at some turn perhaps not far along the way. And like nobody but Hemingway —that is, in his peculiar and distinguished manner as an artist—he continually reminds us that (as he expressed it once to Maxwell Perkins) it is our "performance en route"[13] that counts for good or bad.

But what is the essence of his peculiar manner? It is a manner of implication, clearly, as he himself has said in various notes of self-criticism of which the figure in *Death in the Afternoon* is perhaps the most striking: "The dignity of movement of an ice-berg is due to only one-eighth of it being above water."[14] The question is what mode of narrative technique he exploits in order to make the ice-berg principle operative in his work. I do not remember seeing the word "symbolism" in critical writing about Hemingway before 1940, nor have I seen more than one review of *The Old Man and the Sea* that did not lean heavily on the word. The number of exegeses that explain Hemingway as a symbolist has increased geometrically since Malcolm Cowley suggested in 1944 that he should be grouped not among the realists, but "with Poe and Hawthorne and Melville: the haunted and nocturnal writers, the men who dealt in images that were symbols of an inner world."[15] It was a startling and pleasing suggestion. Mr. Cowley advanced it rather tentatively and did not press his discovery very far; but it was taken up with something like a hue and cry by other critics who, it seemed, had been testily waiting for the scent and were eager to get on with the hunt. Literary conversation soon began to reflect the new trend: I recall hearing it asserted on two proximate occasions that the sleeping bag in *For Whom the Bell Tolls* is an "obvious" symbol of the womb; and that a ketchup bottle in "The Killers" patently symbolizes blood. By 1949 it was no great surprise to open an issue of the *Sewanee Review* to an essay by Caroline Gordon called "Notes on Hemingway and Kafka."[16] It would have been surprising

only if the analysis had not hinged on a comparison between the two writers as symbolists. [4/5]

Is Hemingway genuinely a symbolist? I think he uses certain techniques of symbolism, but I think he does so in a very limited and closely controlled way, and that failure to recognize the controls leads —already has led—to distortions of his meaning and misappreciations of his narrative art. As a sample, Miss Gordon's essay is instructive on this point. Starting calmly, as her title suggests, with the assumption that Hemingway is a symbolist, she proceeds to compare him, not very favorably, with Kafka. And it turns out that Hemingway's trouble is simple—he is not *enough* of a symbolist: "this plane of action is for him a slippery sub-stratum glimpsed intermittently. It does not underlie the Naturalistic plane of action solidly, or over-arch it grandly, as Kafka's Symbolism does."[17]

But this is mistaking an artistic discipline for a fault. Hemingway has not attempted Kafka's kind of symbolism and fallen short: it is something foreign to Hemingway's art. The Kafka story used by Miss Gordon as the basis for her comparison is "The Hunter Gracchus," a carefully elaborated allegory revolving around the life of Christ—that is to say, there are two distinct and parallel narrative lines, the primary, which operates within the confines of a more or less realistic world, and the secondary, which operates within the realm of religious myth and in this case is assumed by the author to be a prior possession on the part of the reader. Incidentally, Miss Gordon forces her comparison from both sides, claiming for Kafka, as something he shares with Hemingway, "a surface which is strictly Naturalistic in detail."[18] But this claim must rest on a

[13] Quoted by Perkins in *Scribner's Magazine*, LXXXI, 4 (March, 1927).
[14] *Death in the Afternoon* (New York, 1932), p. 192.
[15] Introduction to *The Portable Hemingway* (New York, 1944), p. vii.
[16] *Sewanee Review*, LVII, 214-226 (Spring, 1949).
[17] *Ibid.*, p. 226.
[18] *Ibid.*, p. 222.

curious understanding of the phrase "in detail" since the story on the "Naturalistic" level offers, among other attractions, a corpse that is mysteriously still alive, and a German-speaking dove the size of a rooster.

Hemingway, as far as I know, has never written an allegory—notwithstanding the bright interpretations of *The Old Man and the Sea* that illuminated cocktail parties a few years ago when it was published in *Life*—and for a very good reason. In successful allegory, the story on the primary level is dominated by the story on the secondary level, and if the allegorical meaning is to be kept clear, its naturalistic counterpart must pay for it by surrendering realistic probability in one way or another. A strain is imposed on the whole [5/6] narrative mechanism, for mere connotative symbolism will not do to carry the allegory: there must be a denotative equation, part for part, between symbols and things symbolized in order to identify the actors and action on the allegorical level. The extreme difficulty of satisfactorily conducting the dual action throughout a prolonged narrative is classically illustrated by *The Faerie Queene* and by *The Pilgrim's Progress*. The allegorist who admires realism is constantly pulled in two directions at once, and is very lucky when he can prevent one or the other of his meanings from unbalancing him.

Still, Hemingway has used the symbolism of association to convey by implication his essential meaning from the time of his earliest American publication. It may well be that this was inevitable for a writer starting out with Hemingway's determination to communicate, as he put it (in *Death in the Afternoon*) "what really happened in action; what the actual things were which produced the emotion that you experienced."[19] Nothing could more clearly differentiate Hemingway's kind of realism from Zolaesque naturalistic description than this early statement of intent. Everything is to depend on judicious discrimination of objective details: *what really happened* is not by any means

everything that happened; it is only "the actual things . . . which produced the emotion that you experienced." As a matter of fact "produced" is a little too strict, as Hemingway demonstrates again and again in *The Sun Also Rises* and *A Farewell to Arms,* where he depends heavily on the technique of objective epitome—a symbolist technique, if you like—to convey the subjective conditions of his characters. The details selected are not so much those which *produce* the emotion as those which epitomize it; it is the action of the story which has produced the emotion. Thus at the crisis of *The Sun Also Rises,* when Jake Barnes presents Brett to Pedro Romero—a Pandarism for which he is obliged to hate himself—his agonized feelings are not discussed, but are nevertheless most poignantly suggested by the perceptions he reports:

> When I came back and looked in the café, twenty minutes later, Brett and Pedro Romero were gone. The coffee-glasses and our three empty cognac-glasses were on the table. A waiter came with a cloth and picked up the glasses and mopped off the table.[20] [6/7]

In *A Farewell to Arms,* Frederic Henry goes dully out for breakfast from the Swiss maternity hospital where Catherine Barkley is fighting for life in ominously abnormal labor:

> Outside along the street were the refuse cans from the houses waiting for the collector. A dog was nosing at one of the cans.
> "What do you want?" I asked and looked in the can to see if there was anything I could pull out for him; there was nothing on top but coffee-grounds, dust and some dead flowers.
> "There isn't anything, dog," I said.[21]

There is, of course, a larger sense, germane to all good fiction, in which Hemingway may be said to be symbolic in his narrative method: the sense which indicates his typical creation of key characters who are representative on several levels.

[19] *Death in the Afternoon*, p. 2.
[20] *The Sun Also Rises*, p. 194.
[21] *A Farewell to Arms*, p. 336.

We thus find Jake Barnes's war-wound impotence a kind of metaphor for the whole atmosphere of sterility and frustration which is the *ambiance* of *The Sun Also Rises;* we find Catherine Barkley's naïve simplicity and warmth the right epitome for the idea and ideal of normal civilian home life to which Frederic Henry deserts; we find the old Cuban fisherman in some way representative of the whole human race in its natural struggle for survival. But the recent criticism of Hemingway as symbolist goes far beyond such palpable observations as these, and in considering the fundamental character of his narrative technique I wish to turn attention to more ingenious if not esoteric explications.

Professor Carlos Baker, in *Hemingway: The Writer as Artist* (1952), has established himself as the leading oracle of Hemingway's symbolism. His book is, I think, the most valuable piece of extended Hemingway criticism that we yet have, and to a large extent its contribution is one of new insights into the symbolist aspect of his subject's narrative method. He is sweeping: "From the first Hemingway has been dedicated as a writer to the rendering of Wahrheit, the precise and at least partly naturalistic rendering of things as they are and were. Yet under all his brilliant surfaces lies the controlling Dichtung, the symbolic underpainting which gives so remarkable a sense of depth and vitality to what otherwise might be flat two-dimensional portraiture."[22] This may fairly be said to represent Mr. Baker's major thesis, and he develops and supports [7/8] it with remarkable energy and skill. I do not wish to disparage his over-all effort—he is often very enlightening—but I do wish to argue that he has been rather carried away by his thesis, and that therein he eminently typifies the new symbolist criticism of Hemingway which in its enthusiasm slights or ignores other basic aspects of Hemingway's technique.

Mr. Baker's chapter on *A Farewell to Arms* is an original piece of criticism, and it solidly illustrates his approach. He finds

that the essential meaning of this novel is conveyed by two master symbols, the Mountain and the Plain, which organize the "Dichtung" around "two poles": "By a process of accrual and coagulation, the images tend to build round the opposed concepts of Home and Not-Home. . . . The Home-concept, for example, is associated with the mountains; with dry-cold weather; with peace and quiet; with love, dignity, health, happiness, and the good life; and with worship or at least the consciousness of God. The Not-Home concept is associated with low-lying plains; with rain and fog; with obscenity, indignity, disease, suffering, nervousness, war and death; and with irreligion."[23] It is in terms of these antipodal concepts that Mr. Baker analyzes the semantic structure of *A Farewell to Arms,* a structure which he finds effective chiefly because of the adroit and subtle development of the correspondingly antipodal symbols, the Mountain and the Plain. He argues that from the first page of the story these are set up in their significant antithesis, that they are the key to the relationships among several of the leading characters, and that the central action—Frederic Henry's desertion from the Italian Army to join Catherine Barkley, the British nurse—can be fully appreciated only on this symbolic basis. "*A Farewell to Arms,*" he concludes, "is entirely and even exclusively acceptable as a naturalistic narrative of what happened. To read it only as such, however, is to miss the controlling symbolism: the deep central antithesis between the image of life and home (the mountain) and the image of war and death (the plain)."[24]

Clearly there is some truth in this. The "deep central antithesis" cannot be denied, I would think, by anyone with an acceptable understanding of the book. The question at issue is one of technique; to what extent, and how precisely, is the central antithesis in fact engineered around

[22] Carlos Baker, *Hemingway: The Writer as Artist* (Princeton, 1952), p. 289.
[23] *Ibid.,* pp. 101, 102.
[24] *Ibid.,* pp. 108, 109.

the Mountain and the Plain as symbols? [8/9]

One thing is noticeable immediately: as in virtually all of Hemingway, anything that can possibly be construed to operate symbolically does no violence whatsoever to the naturalism (or realism) of the story on the primary level. Nothing could be a more natural—or more traditional—symbol of purity, of escape from the commonplace, in short of elevation, than mountains. If thousands of people have read the passages in *A Farewell to Arms* which associate the mountains "with dry-cold weather; with peace and quiet; with love, dignity, health, happiness and the good life" without taking them to be "symbolic" it is presumably because these associations are almost second nature for all of us. Certainly this seems to be true of Frederic Henry: it is most doubtful that in the course of the novel he is ever to be imagined as consciously regarding the mountains as a symbol. This of course does not prove that Hemingway did not regard them as such, or that the full understanding of this novel as an art structure does not perhaps require the symbolic equation, *mountain* equals *life and home*. It does, however, point differentially to another type of symbolism, where the character in question is shown to be clearly aware of the trope, as when Catherine Barkley says she hates rain because "sometimes I see me dead in it,"[25] or when Frederic Henry says of his plunge into the Tagliamento, "Anger was washed away in the river along with any obligation."[26]

But Mr. Baker has claimed a most exact and detailed use by Hemingway of the Mountain-Plain symbolism, and his ingenious interpretation deserves closer attention. Like many other critics he is an intense admirer of the novel's opening paragraph, which, he says, "does much more than start the book. It helps to establish the dominant mood (which is one of doom), plants a series of important images for future symbolic cultivation, and subtly compels the reader into the position of detached observer."[27] He proceeds to a close analysis of this paragraph:

The second sentence, which draws attention from the mountainous background to the bed of the river in the middle distance, produces a sense of clearness, dryness, whiteness, and sunniness which is to grow very subtly under the artist's hands until it merges with one of the novel's two dominant symbols, the mountain-image. The other major symbol is the plain. [9/10] Throughout the sub-structure of the book it is opposed to the mountain-image. Down this plain the river flows. Across it, on the dusty road among the trees, pass the men-at-war, faceless and voiceless and unidentified against the background of the spreading plain.[28]

This is highly specific, and we are entitled to examine it minutely. Mr. Baker says the river is "in the middle distance" in the direction of the mountains with the image of which, as he sees it, the symbolic images of the river are to merge into one great symbol. But is the river really in the middle distance? The narrator tells us he can see not only its boulders but its *pebbles,* "dry and white in the sun." The river must, of course, flow from the mountains, but in the perspective seen from the house occupied by Frederic Henry, it would appear to be very close at hand— closer than the plain, and quite in contrast to the distant mountains. And this raises the question of whether the clearness, dryness, whiteness, and sunniness offered by the river are in fact artfully intended to be associated with the mountain-image and what it is held to symbolize; or, disregarding the question of intent, whether they do in fact so operate in the artistic structure. Why must the river images be disassociated from the images of the plain across which the river, naturally, flows? Because the river images are of a kind which, if they work as symbols, are incongruent with what Mr. Baker has decided the Plain stands for; they must instead be allocated to the Mountain. This is so important to his thesis that the river shifts

[25] *A Farewell to Arms*, p. 135.
[26] *Ibid.*, p. 248.
[27] Baker, *op. cit.*,
[28] *Ibid.*, pp. 94-9

gracefully, but without textual support, into "the middle distance," closer to the mountains.

And what of the soldiers on the road? Since they must be firmly associated with the Plain ("war and death"), it is against that background that Mr. Baker sees them in Hemingway's opening paragraph—it would not do to see them against the background of the river, with its Mountain images. But let us look again at the paragraph.

In the late summer of that year we lived in a house in a village that looked across the river and the plain to the mountains. In the bed of the river there were pebbles and boulders, dry and white in the sun, and the water was clear and swiftly moving and blue in the channels. Troops went by the house and down the road and the dust they raised powdered the leaves of the trees. [**10/11**]

Mr. Baker says the road is across the river, as of course it would have to be if we are to see the figures of the soldiers against the background of the plain. Hemingway does not say the road is across the river. Indeed, everything indicates the opposite arrangement: a house on a road running along the near side of the river, across which the plain stretches out to the mountains. "Sometimes in the dark," begins the third paragraph of the novel, "we heard the troops marching under the window. . . ." The truth is that a strong part of Mr. Baker's initially persuasive exegesis of the opening paragraph of *A Farewell to Arms* hangs on a reading that the written words will not support. This is not to deny that the paragraph establishes a mood of doom by its somber tone and the epitomic symbols of dust and falling leaves: what I am questioning is the over-all symbolic organization of the novel's structure in terms of the Mountain and the Plain, which Mr. Baker argues as a prime illustration of his unequivocal judgment of Hemingway as symbolist artist.

As a matter of fact, the plain presented in the opening pages of *A Farewell to Arms* is as troublesome as the river when it comes to supporting Mr. Baker's inter-

pretation. There are plains in many countries that could well serve as symbols of emptiness, desolation, disaster, and death —we have some in the American West. But this does not appear to be that sort of plain: quite the contrary. "The plain," Frederic Henry narrates in the opening words of the second paragraph, "was rich with crops; there were many orchards of fruit trees. . . ." Mr. Baker tells us neither how these images of fertility and fruition are to fit in with "rain and fog; with obscenity, indignity, disease, suffering, nervousness, war and death," nor how we should symbolically interpret the conclusion of the sentence, ". . . and beyond the plain the mountains were brown and bare." One can easily grant that as the novel unfolds the impression of war itself grows steadily more saturated with a sense of doomsday qualities: that was an essential part of Hemingway's theme. But to what degree is this impression heightened by the use of the Plain as symbol? The simple exigencies of history prevent exclusive association of the war with the plain as opposed to the mountains, as the narrator indicates on the first page: "There was fighting in the mountains and at night we could see flashes from the artillery." Yet if Mr. Baker is right we would expect to find, despite this difficulty, a salient artistic emphasis of the Plain in symbolic association with all those [**11/12**] images which his interpretation sets against those coalescing around the Mountain symbol.

Mr. Baker makes much of the fact that Frederic Henry, during his leave, fails to take advantage of the offer of his friend the chaplain and go to the high mountain country of the Abruzzi, "where the roads were frozen and hard as iron, where it was clear cold and dry and the snow was dry and powdery. . . . I had gone to no such place but to the smoke of cafés and nights when the room whirled and you needed to look at the wall to make it stop, nights in bed, drunk, when you knew that that was all there was."[29] Here, Mr. Baker

[29] *A Farewell to Arms*, p. 13.

claims, "the mountain-image gets further backing from another lowland contrast."[30] Granting the familiar association here of mountain-country with certain delectable and longed-for experiences, one would like to see, in support of the Mountain-Plain explication, a clearer identification of the contrasting, soldier-on-leave experiences, with the lowland or plain. And while wondering about this, one reads on in *A Farewell to Arms* and soon finds Frederic Henry and Catherine Barkley in Milan, where Henry is recuperating from his wound. They are having a wonderful time. They are in love, have frequent opportunities to be alone together in the hospital room, go often to the races, dine at the town's best restaurants, and in general lead an existence that makes the most pleasant contrast imaginable to the dismal life at the front. "We had a lovely time that summer,"[31] says the hero. What has happened here to the Mountain-Plain machinery? It does not seem to be operating; or perhaps it is operating in reverse, since Milan is definitely in the plain. Mr. Baker passes over these pages of the novel rather quickly, remarking that Catherine here "moves into association with ideas of home, love and happiness."[32] He seems to be aware of the difficulty, although he does not mention it as such: "She does not really [*sic*] reach the center of the mountain-image until, on the heels of Frederick's harrowing lowland experiences during the retreat from Caporetto, the lovers move to Switzerland. Catherine is the first to go, and Henry follows her there as if she were the genius of the mountains, beckoning him on."[33]

This is romantically pleasant, but inaccurate. Catherine does not [12/13] go to Switzerland, but to the Italian resort village of Stresa, on Lake Maggiore. Stresa, moreover, although surrounded by mountains, is itself distinctly lowland: you can pedal a bicycle from Milan or Turin without leaving nearly flat country. Still, it can be allowed that the lovers are not free of the contaminating shadow of war until they have escaped up the lake to Switzer-

land and established themselves in their little chalet above Montreux. Here, again, the associations all of us are likely to make with high-mountain living assert themselves—clear, cold air; magnificent views; white snow; peace and quiet—and the hero and heroine are shown to be happily aware of these. The rain, however, which they have both come to regard as an omen of disaster, grants no immunity to the mountain; it refuses to preserve a unilateral symbolic association with the plain. Mr. Baker knows this, but does not discuss the extent to which it obscures his neat Mountain-Plain antithesis, making the point instead that "the March rains and the approaching need for a good lying-in hospital have driven the young couple down from their magic mountain" to "the lowlands"[34] of Lausanne. Here again observation is fuzzy to the point of distortion: Lausanne happens to stand on a series of steep hills and is an extraordinarily poor specimen of a City of the Plain. This is clear, incidentally, without reference to an atlas, since there are several allusions to the hills and steep streets of Lausanne in the novel itself.[35] But Mr. Baker is caught up in his symbolic apparatus, and if one symbol of death (rain) has failed to stay where it belongs in his scheme (on the plain) he still is persuaded to see the topography of Switzerland in a light that will not darken his thesis.

What all this illustrates, it seems to me, is that Mr. Baker has allowed an excellent insight into Hemingway's imagery and acute sense of natural metonymy to turn into an interesting but greatly overelaborated critical gimmick. It is undeniable that in the midst of the darkling plain of struggle and flight which was the war in Italy, Frederic Henry thinks of the Swiss Alps as a neutral refuge of peace and happiness—surely millions must have lifted their eyes to those mountains with like

[30] Baker, *op. cit.*, p. 102.
[31] *A Farewell to Arms*, p. 119.
[32] Baker, *op. cit.*, p. 104.
[33] *Ibid.*
[34] *Ibid.*, pp. 104, 108.
[35] See, for instance, pp. 328, 331, 334.

thoughts during both World Wars. But in so far as this is symbolism it belongs to our race and culture; and if it is to be sophisticated into a precise scheme of artistic implication [**13/14**] revolving around two distinct polar symbols, the signals transmitted from artist to reader must be more clearly semaphored than anything Mr. Baker has been able to point to accurately. I do not believe this is derogatory to Hemingway. Sensitive as always to those parts of experience that are suggestive and connotative, he used the mountain metaphor which is part of our figurative heritage to deepen the thematic contrast in *A Farewell to Arms,* between war and not-war. But nowhere did he violate realism for the sake of this metaphor; nor did he, as I read the novel, set up the artificially rigid and unrealistic contrast between the Mountain and the Plain which Mr. Baker's analysis requires.

Mr. Baker himself has summed up the sequel to his investigation of *A Farewell to Arms.* "Once the reader has become aware of what Hemingway is doing in those parts of his work which lie below the surface, he is likely to find symbols operating everywhere. . . ."[36] Mr. Baker does find them everywhere, and they not infrequently trip him into strangely vulnerable judgments. Finding an unprecedented display of symbolism in *Across the River and into the Trees* (1950), for instance, he is willing to accord that disappointing novel a richly favorable verdict: "a prose poem, with a remarkably complex emotional structure, on the theme of the three ages of man. . . . If *A Farewell to Arms* was his *Romeo and Juliet* . . . this . . . could perhaps be called a lesser kind of *Winter's Tale* or *Tempest*."[37]

III

But we are not interested so much in the narrative technique of Hemingway's weakest work as we are in what happens in his best. To see symbolism as the master device of the earlier novels and short stories

tends to obscure another and more characteristic type of ambiguity which makes his best work great fiction in the tacit mode. I mean Hemingway's irony. The extent to which the ironic method has packed his fiction with substrata of meaning has not yet, I think, been adequately appreciated in published criticism. And it needs to be appreciated; for irony as a literary device is singularly suited to the view of life which Hemingway has consistently dramatized now for a quarter of our century in such manner as to distinguish him as a writer. [**14/15**]

If you look at Hemingway's earliest American publication in a medium of general circulation you are struck by this irony of view and method, just as it is strikingly there in *The Old Man and the Sea.* "Champs d'Honneur" was the title of one of six short poems printed in *Poetry* for January, 1923:

> Soldiers never do die well;
>   Crosses mark the places—
> Wooden crosses where they fell,
>   Stuck above their faces.
> Soldiers pitch and cough and twitch—
>   All the world roars red and black;
> Soldiers smother in a ditch,
>   Choking through the whole attack.[38]

One of the most interesting things about this is the strong ironic tension set up between the title and the verse itself; the harsh incongruity between the traditional notion of the soldier's heroic death and the grim reality. A tough irony of situation is also the keynote of *In Our Time* (1925), not only as clue to the individual meanings of most of the stories that make up the book, but as the very principle upon which it was composed. Many readers have tried to puzzle out a nice relationship between each story and the narrative fragment, numbered as a "chapter," which precedes it. But the principle in fact was irrelevance; what Hemingway did was to take the numbered sketches of *in our time*

---

[36] Baker, *op. cit.,* p. 117.
[37] *Ibid.,* pp. 264, 287.
[38] *Poetry,* XXI, 195 (Jan., 1923). Reprinted with the permission of Mrs. Ernest Hemingway.

(Paris, 1924) and intersperse them with the longer stories to give a powerfully ironic effect of spurious order supporting the book's subject: modern civil disruption and violence seen against the timeless background of everyday human cross-purposes.

The ironic gap between expectation and fulfillment, pretense and fact, intention and action, the message sent and the message received, the way things are thought or ought to be and the way things are—this has been Hemingway's great theme from the beginning; and it has called for an ironic method to do it artistic justice. All of his work thus far published deserves study with special attention to this method.

I do not think, for example, that a reader must understand the symbolic pattern Mr. Baker claims for *A Farewell to Arms* in order [15/16] to get the main point of the story; but unless he understands the irony of Catherine Barkley's death he surely has missed it completely. Long before this denouement, however, irony has drawn a chiaroscuro highlighting the meaning of the book. There is from the beginning the curious disproportion between Frederic Henry's lot in the army and his frame of mind. A noncombatant, he lives in comfortable houses, eats and drinks well, makes frequent visits to a brothel maintained exclusively for officers, and has extensive leaves urged on him by a sympathetic commanding officer. Despite such pleasures he is malcontent; and the more this fact emerges the more it becomes evident that his mood is a reflection not of his personal fortune, but of the whole dismal panorama of civilization disjointed by war. His manner of narration is already ironical: "At the start of the winter came the permanent rain and with the rain came the cholera. But it was checked and in the end only seven thousand died of it in the army."[39] Healthy in body, the hero is afflicted by a paralysis of the will, a torpor brought on by too many months of living close to the war; and this is the reason for his paradoxical failure to visit

the home of his friend the chaplain while he is on leave: "I myself felt as badly as he did and could not understand why I had not gone. It was what I had wanted to do. . . ."[40] Even the one constructive effort he has been regularly capable of, the performance of his duty as an ambulance officer, has begun to seem absurdly inconsequential to him: when he returns from leave he finds that his absence apparently has made no difference whatever.

As the war wears on, its grotesqueries receive more attention; it begins to be felt, indeed, that they are perhaps after all indigenous to life itself, and only emphasized by war. Henry is given a protective St. Anthony by the heroine: "After I was wounded I never found him. Some one probably got it at one of the dressing stations."[41] The ambulance unit which he commands makes elaborate preparations to receive wounded soldiers during a forthcoming attack: while they are waiting—and eating cheese and spaghetti—in a dugout, an enemy shell lands squarely on top of them, thus making Lt. Henry himself part of the first load of wounded going to [16/17] the rear. For this, he learns, he is to receive a bronze medal; his friend Rinaldi hopes it may be silver.

The episode in Milan, so recalcitrant to Mr. Baker's symbolist scheme, has an integral function in the ironic structure of the narrative. Recuperating far behind the lines, the hero becomes part of the incongruously pleasant civilian scene which always—to the incredulous and bitter astonishment of most combat soldiers—goes on while men die at the front. Yet to add a further ironic twist to this, there is Hemingway's satirical portrait of Ettore, the American-Italian who is a "legitimate hero" in the Italian Army. Not only does he see the social life of wartime Milan as perfectly normal, but it is clear that his view of the war as a whole is the reverse of Henry's: "Believe me, they're fine to have," he says, exhibiting his wound

[39] *A Farewell to Arms*, p. 4.
[40] *Ibid.*, p. 13.
[41] *Ibid.*, p. 47.

stripes. "I'd rather have them than medals. Believe me, boy, when you get three you've got something."[42]

Back at the front for only two days, Henry finds himself mixed up in the nightmarish retreat from Caporetto. Hemingway's famous description of this debacle is a stringent comment on the bewildering stupidity and chaos of war, but he takes the occasion to inject again a shot of special irony. With one ambulance mired to the hubs on a rainsoaked back road, Lt. Henry shoots a sergeant who, in his anxiety to keep up with the retreat, tries to get away on foot instead of staying to cut brush for the spinning wheels. The sergeant is only wounded, but he is quickly dispatched, with Henry's acquiescence, by Bonello, one of the ambulance drivers. "All my life I've wanted to kill a sergeant,"[43] Bonello says proudly; but a few hours later he too deserts, to let himself be captured by the enemy. The climax of this grim comedy is of course Frederic Henry's own desertion. Threatened with military justice akin to that he so summarily had dealt the sergeant, he dives into the Tagliamento River; and his sarcastic remarks on his would-be executioners ring with hyperironic overtones against the baffle of the earlier incident:

I saw how their minds worked; if they had minds and if they worked. They were all young men and they were saving their country. . . . The questioners had that beautiful detachment and devotion to stern justice of men dealing in death without being in any danger of it.[44][**17/18**]

There are many other ironic strokes in *A Farewell to Arms*, but it is this series, identifying the activities of war with all that is brutal and meaningless in human life, that gives the novel its predominantly ironic texture. The catastrophe, Catherine Barkley's shocking death, has the ambivalent effect of partly canceling this identification while at the same time violently reinforcing the total effect of irony. It is as if the author had said, "Do not imagine that the kind of cruelty and disruption I have shown you are confined to war:

they are the conditions of life itself." It is thus only at the end that the full ironic ambiguity of the title springs into view.

The title of Hemingway's other great war novel is likewise an index of its strongly ironic theme. It was strange how many reviewers and critics underweighed the epigraph from Donne and the meaningful paradox of the whole sentence furnishing the title: "And therefore never send to know for whom the bell tolls: it tolls for thee." Appraisals from both Right and Left accused Hemingway of having gone over to the other side, while certain critics less politically biased found that his theme was confused or that it had backfired. "At the center of *For Whom the Bell Tolls*," wrote Maxwell Geismar, "there is a basic confusion of Hemingway's intention. The novel attempts to be a constructive statement on human life. Yet Hemingway's underlying sense of destruction often contradicts this."[45]

But Hemingway was not confused. As always, he wanted to show something true about human life (not necessarily something "constructive") ; and he had come to take a more complex view of humanity at war than he projected in *A Farewell to Arms*. "A plague on both your houses"— the prevailing mood of Frederic Henry— has been replaced by Robert Jordan's unillusioned sense of the community of the human predicament. No man is an island, it turns out; but the storms that sweep the human continent are of such force, and the quakes that rack its surface so disruptive, that none of us can depend on better fortune than that of Jordan, who died making his own small and paradoxical effort to maintain its integrity. His affiliation with the Loyalists is no simple partisan allegiance; and to extend and support the hero's explicit awareness of the inevitable contradictions of his position, Hemingway poses a series of situations pregnant with irony. [**18/19**]

Outstanding is Pilar's account of the

[42] *Ibid.*, p. 130.
[43] *Ibid.*, p. 222.
[44] *Ibid.*, pp. 240, 241.
[45] *Writers in Crisis* (Boston, 1942), p. 81.

start of "the movement" in Pablo's home town, with its unflinching report of the steadily mounting sadism which infused the execution of the local Fascists. There is a remarkable tone to this report, as if Pilar were at confession, anxious to tell the whole truth and omitting not even the most shameful details, yet seeking at the same time to make it understood how these grisly acts could have occurred among normally decent Spanish peasants. She tells how, at first, many of the peasants were sickened by Pablo's plan to flail the Fascists down between a double line of men leading to the edge of a steep cliff. But within the ironic frame of the entire episode, in relation to the book, there are lesser ironies: for it is the cowardly behavior of the Fascists themselves that brings these peasants to a pitch of mob hatred and violence equal to Pablo's inveterate cruelty.

Throughout all this the reader is never allowed to forget that it is the Loyalists who are committing the atrocities described, and that the leaders of the massacre are the very people with whom Jordan is now allied. Robert Penn Warren cites the irony of this, but he suggests that *For Whom the Bell Tolls* is not Hemingway's best novel "primarily because . . . Hemingway does not accept the limitations of his premises . . . the irony . . . runs counter to the ostensible surface direction of the story."[46] So it does—but this is the nature of irony; and this is why it is so valuable to Hemingway in his intense effort to dramatize fully the implications of Donne's epigraph in relation to the ironical self-destruction which is civilized warfare. It is a mistake to think of *For Whom the Bell Tolls* as a document of social optimism in its intent, as opposed to the dark pessimism of Hemingway's earlier books. The darkness is relieved, deliberately, only by a faint existentialist glimmer: the general human enterprise seems very likely to end in failure, but each of us must do what he can—"*Nous ferons notre petit possible.*"

It is to this end that the irony of the

Loyalist massacre of the Fascists, which early in the book sets the theme of human sacrifice in a highly critical perspective, is complemented by the irony of the denouement. For the central action—the blowing of the bridge—which is responsible for the deaths of El Sordo, Anselmo, Fernando, [19/20] and, indeed, Robert Jordan, is rendered a strategic failure by the loose tongues of their comrades behind the lines.

To these two fundamental veins of irony many scenes provide tributary support: three may be cited as exemplary. There is the one in which Jordan reads the letters found in the pockets of a Fascist cavalryman he has just shot, and discovers he is from a Spanish town that Jordan knows well:

> How many is that you have killed? he asked himself. I don't know. Do you think you have a right to kill any one? No. But I have to. . . . But you like the people of Navarra better than those of any other part of Spain. Yes. And you kill them. Yes. . . . Don't you know it is wrong to kill? Yes. But you do it? Yes. And you still believe absolutely that your cause is right? Yes.[47]

This irony of Jordan's self-conscious ambivalence is heightened by juxtapositions of which he knows nothing. In the midst of El Sordo's great last fight, we are suddenly given a decidedly sympathetic portrait of Lt. Berrendo, second in command of the Fascist cavalry. Julian, his best friend, has just been killed by Sordo, and Captain Mora, the blustering officer in command, is shouting blasphemies at the hilltop in an effort (which carries its own small irony, in view of his imminent death) to prove that no one is left alive up there. Later, after Mora has become El Sordo's "Comrade Voyager," Berrendo reluctantly has his troopers decapitate the dead guerrillas for "proof and identification," and the Fascists start back towards their headquarters:

[46] Introduction to *A Farewell to Arms* (New York, 1949), p. xxv.
[47] *For Whom the Bell Tolls*, pp. 303-304.

Then he thought of Julian, dead on the hill, dead now, tied across a horse there in the first troop, and as he rode down into the dark pine forest, leaving the sunlight behind him on the hill, riding now in the quiet dark of the forest, he started to say a prayer for him again.[48]

At this point Anselmo, watching from a hillside, sees them ride past; and on his way back to the guerrilla cave he crosses El Sordo's hilltop where he finds the headless bodies of his comrades: ". . . as he walked he prayed for the souls of Sordo and of all his band. It was the first time he had prayed since the start of the movement."[49] The episode thus ends in ironic equilibrium, with both sides petitioning Heaven. But we have not yet seen our last of Lt. Berrendo. It is he who looms in the sights of Robert Jordan's machine gun in [**20/21**] the last paragraph of the story, lending the finale an ironic depth that protects it from false heroics. For these two young soldiers, preponderant as our sympathy may be for one rather than the other, the same bell tolls. The novel is Hemingway's fullest work so far in scope and artistic realization, and to its fulfillment the ambiguity of irony contributes an essential part.

IV

It would be foolish to argue that the work of any first-rate writer owes its success exclusively or even predominantly to any one narrative artifice. Hemingway has used techniques of symbolism and techniques of irony and used them well; what we want in criticism is an even view of his use of these and other artistic resources that does not exaggerate one at the expense of others. A point deserving great attention and emphasis about this writer is his devotion to the implicit rather than the explicit mode: and both symbolism and irony truly serve this artistic purpose. Hemingway, in fact, stirs thought as to the interrelationship of these two kinds of ambiguity. It is remarkable how often they operate together in his stories: an

ironic fact, perception, or event on the primary level may epitomize an irony in a broader context, and thus doubly deserve selection and accurate report by the narrator. As an illustration of his early effort to communicate "what really happened in action," Hemingway tells in *Death in the Afternoon* how he worked on the problem of accurately depicting a certain bullfight incident:

. . . waking in the night I tried to remember what it was that seemed just out of my remembering and that was the thing that I had really seen and, finally, remembering all around it, I got it. When he stood up, his face white and dirty and the silk of his breeches opened from waist to knee. it was the dirtiness of the rented breeches, the dirtiness of his slit underwear and the clean. clean, unbearably clean whiteness of the thighbone that I had seen, and it was that which was important.[50]

Clearly, it was the startling irony of the contrast that struck Hemingway here as "important"; but certainly (if not so clearly) there is also the symbolic suggestion of another contrast going far beyond the physical—the ironically pathetic gap, perhaps, between the matador's professional failure and his untouched inner pride which is the subject of "The Undefeated."

In a fictional narrative the double operation, ironic and symbolic, [**21/22**] can often be seen more sharply: take *The Old Man and the Sea*, where in effect the same subject is dramatized. The old fisherman's physical triumph in catching the great fish is ironically cut down—or transmuted—into spiritual triumph by the marauding sharks who leave him with only the skeleton of the largest marlin ever seen in Cuba. Without working out the metaphor in precise terms it can be said that the irony of the event itself would hardly be so effective without the broadening and deepening of its implication through symbolic suggestion.

It may be true that all perceptions are reducible finally to perceptions of likeness

48 *Ibid.*, p. 326.
49 *Ibid.*, p. 327.
50 *Death in the Afternoon*, p. 20.

or perceptions of difference. Perhaps this offers a clue to the effectiveness of both symbolism and irony for a writer who, like Hemingway, makes it his life's business to tell a truth, as he once put it, "truer . . . than anything factual can be."[51] With all his famous skill in writing with his eye upon the object, he understood from the beginning that it was only the object in relationship to other objects and to the observer that really counted: significance is, in short, a matter of likeness and difference. This is to speak broadly; and to apply the generalization to symbolism and irony requires a good deal of qualification. Yet symbolism does depend essentially on likeness, and irony on difference; and as artistic tools both are means of interpreting imaginatively, and with the flexibility of implication, a complex reality. Symbolism signifies through a harmony, irony through a discord; symbolism consolidates, irony complicates; symbolism synthesizes, irony analyzes.

For all of this, I would not like to see Hemingway go down in new literary histories as either "a symbolist" or (less likely, if somewhat more appropriately) "an ironist." Taken at face value the denomination "symbolist" has meanings in the common language of criticism that are quite inapplicable to him. But beyond this, Hemingway uses symbolism, as I have tried to show, with a severe restraint that in his good work always staunchly protects his realism. So likewise does he use irony. It is the ambiguity of life itself that Hemingway has sought to render, and if irony has served him peculiarly well it is because he sees life as inescapably ironic. But if we must classify him let us do him justice: with all his skilful use of artistic ambiguity, he remains the great *realist* of twentieth-century American fiction.

[51] Introduction to *Men at War* (New York, 1952), p. xi.

The Original Conclusion to *A Farewell to Arms**

ERNEST HEMINGWAY

It seems she had one hemorrhage after another. They couldn't stop it.

I went into the room and stayed with Catherine until she died. She was unconscious all the time, and it did not take her very long to die.

There are a great many more details, starting with my first meeting with an undertaker, and all the business of burial in a foreign country and going on with the rest of my life—which has gone on and seems likely to go on for a long time.

I could tell how Rinaldi was cured of the syphilis and lived to find that the technic learned in wartime surgery is not of much practical use in peace. I could tell how the priest in our mess lived to be a priest in Italy under Fascism. I could tell how Ettore became a Fascist and the part he took in that organization. I could tell how Piani got to be a taxi-driver in New York and what sort of a singer Simmons became. Many things have happened. Everything blunts and the world keeps on. It never stops. It only stops for you. Some of it stops while you are still alive. The rest goes on and you go on with it.

I could tell you what I have done since March, nineteen hundred and eighteen, when I walked that night in the rain back to the hotel where Catherine and I had lived and went upstairs to our room and undressed and slept finally, because I was so tired—to wake in the morning with the sun shining in the window; then suddenly to realize what had happened. I could tell what has happened since then, but that is the end of the story.

* Ernest Hemingway. Printed here for the first time and by permission of Mrs. Ernest Hemingway.

PART THREE

FOR WHOM THE BELL TOLLS

An American in Spain*

LIONEL TRILLING, Professor of English at Columbia University, has written critical studies of Matthew Arnold and E. M. Forster, a novel, and many essays in criticism. The latter have been partly collected in *The Liberal Imagination* and *The Opposing Self*.

To anyone at all interested in its author's career—and who is not?—*For Whom the Bell Tolls* will first give a literary emotion. For here, we feel at once, is a restored Hemingway writing to the top of his bent. He does not, as in the period of *To Have and Have Not* and *The Fifth Column*, warp or impede his notable talent with the belief that art is to be used like the automatic rifle. He does not substitute political will for literary insight nor arrogantly pass off his personal rage as social responsibility. Not that his present political attitude is coherent or illuminating; indeed, it is so little of either that it acts as the anarchic element in a work whose total effect is less impressive than many of its parts. Yet at least it is flexible enough, or ambiguous enough, to allow Hemingway a more varied notion of life than he has ever before achieved.

With the themes that bring out his craft most happily Hemingway has never been so good—no one else can make so memorable the events of physical experience, how things look and move and are related to each other. From the beginning of the novel to the end, one has the happy sense of the author's unremitting and successful poetic effort. So great is this effort, indeed, that one is inclined to feel that it is at times even too great, that it becomes conscious of itself almost to priggishness and quite to virtuosity. About some of the very good moments—they are by now famous —one has the uneasy sense that they are rather too obviously "performances": I

mean moments so admirable as the account of the massacre of the fascists by the republicans, as well as moments so much less good because so frankly gaudy as the description of the "smell of death" —the really superlative passages, such as the episode of El Sordo on his hill or Andres making his way through the republican lines, which are equal to Tolstoy in his best battle-manner, are more modestly handled. And the sense of the writer doing his duty up to and beyond the point of supererogation is forced on us in the frequent occurrence of the kind of [639/ 640] prose of which Hemingway has always allowed himself a small, perhaps forgivable, amount when he wishes to deal with emotions which he considers especially difficult, delicate, or noble. This kind of writing, obtrusively "literary," oddly "feminine," is most frequently used for the emotions of love and it is always in as false and fancy taste as this:

> Now as they lay all that before had been shielded was unshielded. Where there had been roughness of fabric all was smooth with a smoothness and firm rounded pressing and a long warm coolness, cool outside and warm within, long and light and closely holding, closely held, lonely, hollow-making with contours, happy-making, young and loving and now all warmly smooth with a hollowing, chest-aching, tight-held loneliness that was such that Robert Jordan felt he could stand it. . . .

Yet the virtuosity and the lapses of taste are but excesses of an effort which is, on the whole, remarkably successful. And if

*Lionel Trilling, "An American in Spain," *The Partisan Reader*, eds., William Philips and Philip Rahv (New York: Dial Press, Inc., 1946), pp. 639-644. Reprinted by permission of the author.

we cannot help thinking a little wryly about how much tragic defeat, how much limitation of political hope, was necessary before Hemingway could be weaned from the novel of arrogant political will, neither can we help being impressed by what he has accomplished in the change.

I speak first and at some length of the style of *For Whom the Bell Tolls* because it seems to me that the power and charm of the book arise almost entirely from the success of the style—from the success of many incidents handled to the full of their possible interest. The power and charm do not arise from the plan of the book as a whole; when the reading is behind us, what we remember is a series of brilliant scenes and a sense of having been almost constantly excited, but we do not remember a general significance. Yet Hemingway, we may be sure, intended that the star-crossed love and heroic death of Robert Jordan should be a real tragedy, a moral and political tragedy which would suggest and embody the tragedy of the Spanish war. In this intention he quite fails. The clue to the failure is the essential inner dullness of his hero. Robert Jordan does not have within himself what alone could have made tragedy out of this remarkable melodrama—he does not in himself embody the tensions which were in the historical events he lived through. His fate is determined by the moral and political contradictions of the historical situation, but he himself explicitly refuses to recognize these contradictions, he stands apart from them. And since it is Jordan's fate that must provide whatever intellectual architectonic the novel is to have, the novel itself [**640/641**] fails, not absolutely but relatively to its possibility and to its implied intention.

This failure illustrates as well as anything could the point of Philip Rahv's essay, "The Cult of Experience in American Writing" (*Partisan Review*, November-December 1940). For here again we have the imbalance which Mr. Rahv speaks of as characteristic of the American novel—on the one hand the remarkable perception of sensory and emotional fact, on the other hand an inadequacy of intellectual vitality. Consider as an illuminating detail the relation which Hemingway establishes between Robert Jordan and the leaders he admires, Goltz the general and Karkov the journalist. Both are cynical and exceptionally competent men, wholly capable of understanding all the meanings of the revolutionary scene. But they are Europeans and Robert Jordan is not; like the hero of Henry James's *The American*, he knows that there are machinations going on around him, very wrong but very wonderful, which he will never be able to understand. Nor does he really want to understand as his friends do. He wants, he says, to keep his mind in suspension until the war is won. He wants only to feel emotions and ideals, or, as a technician and a brave man, to *do* what he is told. The thinking is for others. Yet, like a Henry James character again, he must penetrate the complex secret; but he has no wish to use it, only to *experience* it, for he likes, as he says, the feeling of being an "insider," which is what one becomes by losing one's American "chastity of mind," telling political lies with the Russians in Gaylord's Hotel.

Hemingway himself, it would seem, has a full awareness of the complex actuality of the situation. Again and again, and always pungently, he brings to our notice the tensions and contradictions of a revolutionary civil war—describes the cynicism and intrigue and shabby vice of the Russian politicos, pointedly questions the political virtue of La Pasionaria, paints André Marty, in a brilliant and terrifying scene, as a homicidal psychopath under the protection of the Comintern, speaks out about the sins of Loyalist leaders and has only a small and uncertain inclination to extenuate the special sins of the Communists. Indeed, there is scarcely a charge that anti-Stalinists might have made during the war whose truth Hemingway does not in one way or another avow. Yet by some failure of mind or of seriousness, he cannot permit these political facts to become integral with the book by entering importantly into the mind of the hero. Robert Jordan, to be sure, thinks a good deal about all these things, but almost always as if they were not much more than—to use the [**641/ 642**] phrase of another antifascist—a matter of taste. He can, in Mr. Rahv's sense of the word, *experience* all the badness, but he cannot deal with it, he dare not judge it.

In the end it kills him. And Hemingway knows, of course, that it kills him and is at pains to make it clear that, of all the things that prevent Robert Jordan's dispatch from arriving in time to halt the ill-fated attack, it is the atmosphere of Gaylord's Hotel that is ultimately culpable; it is Marty's protected madness that seals Jordan's fate. Were this kept in focus we should have had a personal tragedy which would have truly represented the whole tragedy of the Spanish war—the tragedy, that is, which was not merely a defeat by a superior force but also a moral and political failure; for tragedy is not a matter of fact, it is a matter of value. To Robert Jordan his own death is bitter enough, but only as the ultimate incident of his experience. Of its inherent meaning, of its significance in relation to its cause, he has no awareness. Nor is his lack of awareness an intentional irony of which the reader is to be conscious. Hemingway lets the casual [*sic*] significance fade, and Jordan's death becomes very nearly a matter of accident. The book seems to wish to say that the loving and brave will be separated and killed unless men realize their unending community; but it is not only a lack of community that kills Robert Jordan, it is all that is implied by Gaylord's Hotel and André Marty.

It is almost terrifying to see where an author can be led in unintentional falsification by his devotion to naked "experience." Hemingway knows that his hero must die in *some* moral circumstance; he lamely and belatedly contrives for Robert Jordan a problem of—courage. And so we get what we all like, and rightly like, a good fighting death, but in the face of all that Jordan's death truly signifies, this is devastatingly meaningless. Courage, we are told in a last word, is all: and every nerve responds to the farewell, the flying hoofs, the pain and the pathos, but we have been shuffled quite away from tragedy, which is not of the nerves but of judgment and the mind.

The major movement of the novel is, then, a failure, and a failure the more to be regretted because it has so many of the elements of great success. There is another movement of the novel that cannot be judged by quite the same standards of political intelligence—I mean all that part which deals with the guerrilla bands of the mountains. To judge this, one has to understand its genre; one has to see this part of the story as a social romance. I should like to draw on Mr. Rahv again: he remarks in another of his essays ("Paleface and Redskin," *Kenyon Review,* Summer, 1939) that Hemingway may well be under- [**642/643**] stood as a descendant of Natty Bumppo. Certainly in each of Hemingway's heroes there is a great deal of the Leatherstocking blood, though "crossed" (as Leatherstocking himself would say) with the gentler, more sensitive blood of Uncas. And as Leatherstocking-Uncas, the perfect scout, Robert Jordan is all decision, action, and good perception, far more interesting and attractive than in his character of looker-on at the political feats of the Russians where he is a kind of Parsifal, the culpable innocent who will not ask the right questions. But more than the character of this hero takes its rise from Cooper—more, too, than Hemingway's "sense of terrain" which Edmund Wilson speaks of as being like Cooper's. For when we think of how clear a line there is between Uncas, Chingachgook and Tamenund, the noble Indians, and El Sordo and Anselmo and the rest of the guerrilla band, we see how very like Cooper's is Hemingway's romantic sense of the social and personal virtues.

With Cooper, however, the social idealization is more formal, more frankly "mythical"—he does not quite require that we really believe in his Indians, only learn from them. But Hemingway does want us to believe in his guerrillas with their strange, virtuous Indian-talk, and he wants us to love them. We cannot truly believe in them. And we cannot quite love them because we sense, as we usually do in a love affair between a writer and a virtuous nation or people or class—such as between Kipling and the sahibs or, to speak of a minor but socially interesting writer of today, between Angela Thirkell and the English upper middle class—that there is pretty sure to appear, sooner or later, a hatred of the outlander. If one cannot make an identification with Hemingway's guerrillas—and it is difficult—they suggest their own unique and superior moral charm rather than the human community the novel undertakes to celebrate.

There is something pretty suspect, too, in the love-story of this novel, which has so stirred and charmed the reviewers. By now the relation between men and women in Hemingway's novels has fixed itself into a rather dull convention according to which the men are all dominance and knowledge, the women all essential innocence and responsive passion. These relationships reach their full development almost at the moment of the first meeting and are somehow completed as soon as begun. Most significant, one feels of love in the Hemingway novels that it can exist at all only because circumstances so surely doom it. We do not have to venture very deep into unexpressed meanings to find a connection between Hemingway's social myth and the pattern of his love stories—in both there is a desperation [**643/644**] which makes a quick grab for simple per-fection. This desperation makes understandable the compulsive turning to courage as the saving and solving virtue. The whole complex of attitudes is, we might say, a way of responding to the imminent idea of death.

I am by no means in agreement with the many critics who, in writing about Hemingway, have expressed their annoyance that anyone should deal with death except as a simple physical fact. I am far from sure that our liberal, positive, progressive attitudes have taught us to be emotionally more competent before the idea of death, but only more silent; and I certainly do not assume that anyone is committing a political misdemeanor when he breaks our habit of silence. Yet in Hemingway's response to the idea of death there is something indirect and thwarted, as though he had not wholly escaped our reticences to meditate freely upon the theme, as could, say, a death-haunted man like John Donne, from whom Hemingway takes the epigraph and title of his novel. For Donne, death is the appalling negation and therefore the teacher of the ego. For Hemingway, death is the ego's final expression and the perfect protector of the personality. It is a sentimental error from which Donne was saved by his great power of mind. And it was from Donne's truer response to death that he learned the true nature of the ego, how little it can exist by itself, how "no man is an *Ilande* intire of itselfe." Hemingway, so much at the service of the cult of experience, debars himself from what Donne learned from his contemplation of death. As a consequence, it is the isolation of the individual ego in its search for experience that Hemingway celebrates in this novel that announces as its theme the community of men.

Style in *For Whom the Bell Tolls**

The late **J O S E P H   W A R R E N   B E A C H** (1880-1957) was a poet, critic, and Professor of English at the University of Minnesota. Besides writing several critical studies of English poetry and American fiction, he was the author of books on Hardy and Henry James.

. . . War is but one of many circumstances which has led vast numbers of thinking men, in our times, to distrust abstractions and ideologies. And esthetic taste has evolved along parallel lines. A disposition to behaviorism in fiction has carried with it an indisposition to the use of adjectives and metaphysical terminology. Our artists in fiction have tried to see how far they can go with a mere notation of objective facts. And they have re-discovered the important esthetic principle of economy. They have found that, other things being equal, the best effect is that achieved with the greatest economy of means. There is, for one thing, the great gain of avoiding the obvious. The sentiment is not wanting in Hemingway. But he finds that he can give more point to his sentiment if he does not dress it out in fine language. And all the more so because this method requires more skill than that which depends on fine language for making its point. It requires that the facts shall be so rightly ordered that they will speak for themselves. This is a challenge to the serious artist. The undiscriminating reader may miss the intention and confuse this work with pulp. But if the thing is done with skill and subtlety, the discriminating reader will not long miss it; and he will receive a pleasure proportioned to the difficulty of the undertaking. He will recognize that this writer has what we call "style." For style, in the larger sense, depends less on the words that are used to get an effect than on the right ordering of the words.

The matter goes beyond esthetics in the narrow sense. There is a significant remark in *The Sun Also Rises*. Brett is trying to tell Jake about the way she feels on having given up her Spanish lover. It is for her an edifying experience, something which in earlier times would have been called a "spiritual" experience, for it is a state of the spirit with Brett. But [111/112] Jake doesn't like to have these things dragged out into the vulgar light of words. He tries to shut her up. He says, "You'll lose it if you talk about it." That is a deep saying and one to which any man must respond who cares more for actual states of the spirit than for their verbal equivalents. States of the spirit are fragile and tenuous affairs; and in general we feel that the less said about them the better, lest they be cheapened and lost. Man is given to spiritual vanity; and words are liars. This saying of Jake's is as good a clue as we can find to Hemingway's distrust of verbalism, and his reticence on the subject of spiritual states.

Hemingway's system is an interesting one. He has got some very good results with it; and he has begotten a large school of writers, some of whom have got good results. It represents but a small segment of the great circle of what can and has been done in the field of prose fiction. I shouldn't want to see it erected into a

* Joseph Warren Beach, "Style in *For Whom the Bell Tolls*," *American Fiction, 1920-1940* (New York: The Macmillan Company, 1941), pp. 111-119. Republished, New York: Russell and Russell, Inc., 1960. Reprinted with the permission of Russell and Russell, Inc.

dogma and occupy the whole field. I shouldn't want to see all our storytellers bound by the self-denying ordinance to which Hemingway has bound himself. But it is, as it happens, a characteristic feature of our fiction today; and with several of our writers, like Caldwell and Steinbeck, it has proved consistent with high distinction. Like many present-day composers, they have achieved new dimensions in esthetics by taking advantage of limitations, part temperamental, part deliberately assumed, which need not be imposed on all the world.

Hemingway would, I think, be the first to agree to this reservation. He has shown, in *For Whom the Bell Tolls*, that he is capable of applying his own system without too rigid a dogmatism. His subject here— an episode from the fight for republican principles—calls for the frequent delineation of states of mind more exalted and more complex than had often been in question in his earlier work. He is obliged to distinguish types among the foreign communist leaders, [112/113] and still more types among the guerilla bands in the mountains—gypsies, peasants, village workmen, women. Robert Jordan has been assigned a task of great difficulty and danger, and the problem is, with each person he deals with: how far can he be trusted to follow orders, to understand the requirements of the situation, and to risk his life without flinching? A man's comprehension of the issues of the war, his devotion to the Republic, are but two factors in an equation that involves his personal pride and pride of race, his tribal attitudes, his appetites, his notions of right and wrong, and a dozen other imponderables.

There is the conviction of the old man Anselmo that killing is a sin; he is a brave and stanch Republican, and he knows that killing is necessary to win the war, but he can only do it under orders and with tears running down his cheeks. There is Pablo, the leader of this band, who has a natural bent for killing and cruelty and has performed great services for the Republic, but who has been softened by easy life in the mountain camp and thinks more of successful retreat than of holding the enemy. He is kept in line only by his inability to stand the thought of being alone; he will risk death rather than isolation. There is Fernando, stiff and conventional, who shrinks from the gross language of his comrades, but who is brave and firm in the face of danger, and can be relied on to perform whatever duty requires. There is Pablo's woman, a good cook, formidable master of invective, jealous and passionate, but absolutely devoted to a leader she can trust, and the most tough and resolute of all the comrades. I can only hint the psychological complexities with which the young American has to deal in his Spanish aids, beginning with the vanity and anarchical independence of the Spanish character in general, and including other more lovable racial traits.

And then there are the complexities of his own nature, which he must rule in the interest of his major objectives. He is a college professor and enough of an intellectual to have [113/114] doubts and misgivings in regard to every value to which his soul is wedded. He is able to master his doubts by virtue of some instinct or power of will; but first he must meet them, and this means a series of sharp debates within himself. In his personal reflections and in his talk with others, states of mind are the ultimate subject throughout—ideals, loyalties, cases of conscience, and the ins and outs of human motivation. And all this gives to the Spanish novel an appreciably more intellectual cast than the staple of his writing. It is more obviously concerned throughout with attitudes and reactions which have their relevance in a system, or at any rate a complex, of ethical evaluations.

It is true that Hemingway still takes pains to keep free from abstractions and sentimental elaborations. He tries to dispense with adjectives, and particularly the sort which serve to inflate the subject rather than render its substance. He tries to express his ethical values in terms of concrete objects, actions, and effects. He tries to keep his sentences simple, by reducing a train of thought to its component elements and ranging them in sequence rather than in the complicated patterns of logical subordination. But in all these matters he allows himself more latitude than formerly. He will not be hamstrung even by rules of his own making. Robert Jordan must admonish himself to keep straight in his thinking on the subject of killing men in war. "Because if you are not absolutely straight in your head you have no right to do the things you do for all of them are crimes and no man has a right to take another man's life unless it is to prevent something worse happening to other people." Here the author has allowed himself in a single sentence four separate conjunctions indicating reasons and conditions. Even in nature-description there is some syntactical build-up allowed, as in his account of Jordan's feeling about the hour of dawn. "He loved this hour of the day always and now he watched it; feeling it gray within him, as though he were a part of the slow lightening [114/115] that comes before the rising of the sun; when solid things darken and space lightens and the lights that have shone in the night go yellow and then fade as the day comes." There is in that a broader, more lingering cadence than is customary in his choppy writing, evidence of a ripeness that has come to him with his larger subject.

Not all the talk of the ragged band is in obscenities or in words of one syllable. There is much that is in a tone of dignified self-respect, and there is the formality and elevation of republican ideology. They are all agreed that they must first win the war; but there is some difference of opinion as to what should be done with the undesirables. Agustín would have them shoot the anarchists and communists "and all this *canalla* except the good Republicans." But Anselmo disagrees. "That we should win this war and shoot nobody. That we should govern justly and that all should participate in the benefits accord-

ing as they have striven for them. And that those who have fought against us should be educated to see their error."

Hemingway has undertaken in this book a linguistic feat of the first magnitude. Nearly all the dialogue is supposed to be talk in Spanish rendered in English, and his effort is to suggest throughout the flavor of the native idiom. I don't know how it will seem to a reader not trained in languages, but to me the effect is charming, picturesque and dramatic. Hemingway's ordinary English is so American, so modern, and so uncompromisingly vernacular that it would hardly do on the tongue of these Spaniards, whose language is in many ways so much more stately and at the same time has its own vernacular idioms that are often more racy than the American equivalents. The stateliness is largely a matter of the longer and fuller words that betray the Latin origin. Of a foreign name hard to remember: "It is a name I could never dominate." Of reinforcements from another camp: "Advising them in time, it should be possible to unite fifty rifles of a [115/116] certain dependability." "How dependable?" "Dependable within the gravity of the situation" (*dentro de la gravidad*).

Such expressions are well enough in their way, lending a quaint dignity to the characters and reminding us of their Roman heritage. But they need to be used with discretion, as I think they are. The genius of the foreign language is heard more often in homelier and more intimate turns of idiom chosen for some raciness of flavor. Pithy understatement: "less bad" for "excellent," or "why not?" for "yes indeed." Crispness and succinctness with gravity: "I go down now with Anselmo"; "Go now to thy bridge"; "Thus should men move" (that is, like the owl by night, the wings beating quickly, but with no noise of feathers as the bird hunts). Pride and elevation of feeling suggested by inverted word order: " 'For us will be the bridge and the battle, should there be one,' Robert Jordan said and saying it in the dark, he felt a little theatrical but it sounded well in Spanish." Sober precision of statement: " 'It should be of the highest interest,' Anselmo said and hearing him say it honestly and clearly and with no pose, neither the English pose of understatement nor any Latin bravado, Robert Jordan thought he was very lucky to have this old man. . . ." (But it *is* understatement, is it not? Referring to an enterprise in which they stand the greatest chance of giving their lives for the Republic—"it should be of the highest interest . . ."!)

But let me give, with publisher's permission, a longer passage of consecutive dialogue so that the reader may feel how much strength is lent to the situation by the native idioms lovingly cherished by Hemingway and faithfully transcribed in English. Fernando has been seriously wounded and has been borne by two of his comrades to a steep bank which they have to scale in making their escape. He asks them to leave him where he can still get in a shot or two at the enemy. Fernando is a stiff and pedantic person, but the soul of loyalty and courage. [**116/117**]

"Leave me here," Fernando said. "It hurts much and there is much hemorrhage inside. I feel it in the inside when I move."

"Let us get thee up the slope," Primitivo said. "Put thy arms around our shoulders and we will take thy legs."

"It is inutile," Fernando said. "Put me here behind a stone. I am as useful here as above."

"But when we go," Primitivo said.

"Leave me here," Fernando said. "There is no question of my travelling with this. Thus it gives one horse more. I am very well here. Certainly they will come soon."

"We can take thee up the hill," the gypsy said. "Easily."

He was, naturally, in a deadly hurry to be gone, as was Primitivo. But they had brought him this far.

"Nay," Fernando said. "I am very well here. What passes with Eladio?"

The gypsy put his finger on his head to show where the wound had been.

"Here," he said. "After thee. When we made the rush."

"Leave me," Fernando said. Anselmo could see he was suffering much. He held both hands against his groin now and put his head back against the bank, his legs straight out before him. His face was gray and sweating.

"Leave me now please, for a favor," he said. His eyes were shut with pain, the edges of his lips twitching. "I find myself very well here."

All this, of course, is incidental to Hemingway's main purpose, which is to picture the Spanish character as exhibited in certain obscure and humble adherents of the republican cause. The Spanish character, and especially that of the Spanish peasant, has exercised for years a strong fascination on Hemingway's imagination. And he has made the three days of this Homeric episode the framework for a magnificent delineation of his subject in all its variegated picturesqueness and strength of appeal— the pride and dignity and gravity, the grossness and cruelty, the homely earthiness and lofty gallantry, the loyalty and treachery, the passionate intensity of feeling, and the resolute devotion and idealism of the Spanish race. This is the subject for a chapter by itself. [**117/118**] I have only space to say that Hemingway has here shown an unsuspected genius for character-creation. Most impressive of his Spanish characters are Pablo and Pilar by virtue of their heroic stature and colorfulness taken in combination with all-too-human weaknesses and contradictions which make them so appallingly unpredictable in speech and action. But the canvas is crowded with minor figures *muy simpatico* and nicely individualized, from the stanch and tender-hearted Anselmo to the crazy commissar Marty, the heresy-hunter of the Communist party, brief apparition of the night before the attack.

There is no space for developing this theme. Instead, I will make one further remark on the Spanish flavoring of the dialogue in which the mountain band give outward expression to their character. The reader will note the constant use in their speech of the second-person singular "thee" and "thou," which alternate with the plural "you," as the feeling of the speaker fluctuates between affectionate intimacy with the person addressed and a more formal and distant attitude. It is the same fluctuation that is seen in the speech of young Hamlet and Gertrude, felt now as his mother and most intimate friend and now as Queen of Denmark and party to his father's murder. It is true that in Shakespeare's time the singular and plural forms were both current, and there was nothing foreign and poetic in the use of "thee" and "thou." They were the homely forms, and "you" was for stateliness and formality. In a contemporary writer in English "thee" and "thou" are archaic, suggestive of poetry and the Bible. Hemingway is of course aware of this, and has taken deliberate advantage of it to give to his dialogue an elevation of tone which is suited to his present subect. Any reader familiar with the English Bible or with the English prayerbook is certain to be affected in some degree by the solemnity of feeling associated with these now obsolete forms.

But that is not the whole story. Hemingway is surely rely- [118/119] ing on the literary culture of his readers to respond to the other range of associations established by these forms as they are still used in German and the Latin languages. Along with the Biblical solemnity go the intimacy and familiarity of the second-person singular in these languages, the homeliness and earthiness of forms that suggest not the ceremony of aristocratic life but the friendliness and warmth and familiarity of the plain people. This is a stroke of great subtlety and daring. Hemingway has managed by the use of this idiomatic device to link together in our feeling the secular homeliness of the republican cause with the poetry of religious sentiment. And, moreover, since "thee" and "thou" is the language of lovers, it is another means of establishing a connection between the two idealisms which run parallel through the story of Robert Jordan, the idealism of love and the idealism of political sentiment. "I love thee," Jordan declares to Maria, "as I love all that we have fought for. I love thee as I love liberty and dignity and the rights of all men to work and not be hungry. I love thee as I love Madrid that we have defended and as I love all my comrades that have died."

And so it is that, while still resisting the temptations of rhetoric, Hemingway has by no means neglected the resources of language. By skillful use of the idioms of a foreign tongue and the poetic associations of the Bible, he has added another "dimension" to his English prose.

The Background of a Style*

MARK SCHORER, Professor of English at the University of California in Berkeley, is the author of a critical study of William Blake, a biography of Sinclair Lewis, and many novels, short stories, and essays in criticism.

What was for long the sign of Ernest Hemingway's work—the curious tension between subject matter and style, between the themes of violence and the perfectly controlled prose—has gone. Hemingway was extraordinary among modern prose writers for exactly this reason, that he pressed his style into the service of his subject matter in a rather special way: the style was the immediate representation of the moral attitude of the author toward his material, it objectified the author's values and thus in itself was comment in writing otherwise unhampered by comment. When, however, the subject matter began to change—from violent experience itself to the expressed evaluation of violence—the manner began to change. The separation seems to take place in the story, "The Snows of Kilimanjaro," but it is in the novel *To Have and Have Not,* that the fumbling transition is clearest. The first third of this book is superb narrative in the old manner; but as Hemingway lets himself into the theme proper thereafter, the book begins to break down, and the end is a debacle, the noisy collapse of a style and technique simply unable to support their matter. Before, the style in itself was moral comment; with a change in moral attitude, that style was necessarily disrupted. In *For Whom the Bell Tolls* we may witness a new style, less brilliant but more flexible, as it integrates itself. That is a very exciting literary spectacle.

The Sun Also Rises was a representation of the life that Hemingway lived and enjoyed and out of which his values came. The characters in this novel—without belief, without relation to a cultural or national past, without ideological relation to the future—submerge themselves in extravagant sensation and view life as a losing game, a sport like bullfighting which, while it is more nearly tragedy than sport because death is inevitable, is interesting only if it observes strict rules. Hemingway epitomized this not very difficult matter when, in an author's note in *Scribner's Magazine,* he once said, "I've known some very wonderful [101/102] people who even though they were going directly to the grave . . . managed to put up a very fine performance enroute." This "fine performance" is the sporting attitude, and it is dramatized in the gesture of Lady Ashley when she gives up her lover: "You know I feel rather damned good, Jake . . . it makes one feel rather good deciding not to be a bitch. . . . It's sort of what we have instead of God." Jake has himself observed that morality is what makes you feel good afterwards. Brett feels "rather damned good" because she has behaved according to the tenets of that negative morality, that emphasis on the "performance en route," the *manner* of living, which the group has substituted for belief.

The preoccupation with bullfighting is not accidental; bullfighting is at once the most violent and the most stylized of sports. Its entire excitement depends on the degree to which the matador exposes himself to death *within the rules.* It dis-

*Mark Schorer, "The Background of a Style," *Kenyon Review*, III (Winter, 1941), 101-105. Reprinted by permission of the author.

regards consequences, regards performance. Both are important. Courage, or unconcern for disaster, is a moral virtue: the
best bullfighter works closest to the horns;
the best man disregards present and impending catastrophe. Syphilis, the occupa-
tional disease of bullfighters, "of all people who lead lives in which a disregard of
consequences dominate," is nearly com-
mended. A blundering display of courage,
however, is absurd: the matador should
"increase the amount of the danger of
death"

within the rules provided for his protection. . . . it
is to his credit if he does something that he knows
how to do in a highly dangerous but still geometrically possible manner. It is to his discredit if he
runs danger through ignorance, through disregard
of the fundamental rules. . . .

Courage stylized, *style,* then, matters finally, and the experienced spectator looks
for this; "what they seek is honesty and
true, not tricked, emotion and always
classicism and the purity of execution of
all the suertes, and . . . they want no sweet-
ening." Since the performance is a matter
of the fighter's honor, bullfighting is a
moral art, and style a *moral* matter.

So far, about morals, [writes Hemingway] I know
only that what is moral is what you feel good
after and what is immoral is what you feel bad
after and judged by these moral standards . . . the
bullfight is very moral to me. . . .

In *The Sun Also Rises,* Romero, who
"fakes" nothing in the fight, who has "the
old thing, the holding of his purity of line
through the maximum of exposure," is the
one character who makes the others feel
fine: he is the representation of artistic,
hence of moral excellence. [**102/103**]

All this carried directly over into Hemingway's concept of prose and into his own
prose. The definition of morality and
Brett's dramatization of it; the important
counterpoint between danger and performance; the concept of art as moral inso-
far as its style is "honest" or "true" or
"pure"—this complex is translated as follows:

It is much more difficult than poetry. . . . It can be
written, *without tricks* and *without cheating. With
nothing that will go bad afterwards.* . . . First,
there must be talent. . . . Then there must be discipline. . . . Then there must be . . . an *absolute conscience* as unchanging as the standard meter in
Paris, to prevent *faking.*

The style which made Hemingway famous
—with its ascetic suppression of ornament
and figure, its insistence on the objective
and the unreflective (for good fighters do
not talk), its habit of understatement (or
sportsmen boast), the directness and the
brevity of its syntactical constructions, its
muscularity, the sharpness of its staccato
and repetitive effects, "the purity of its
line under the maximum of exposure,"
that is, its continued poise under the
weight of event or feeling—this style is an
exact   transfiguration   of   Hemingway's
moral attitude toward a peculiarly violent
and chaotic experience. His style, in effect,
is what he had instead of God.

Until God came.

Now that the evidence is in, the position
taken by Edmund Wilson some time ago
in *The Atlantic Monthly* is indefensible.
Mr. Wilson argued that Hemingway's political persuasion was no persuasion at all,
but a simple transfer from object to object
of the desire to kill: kudu to fascist. No
one would seriously contend, I think, that
the very motive of *For Whom the Bell
Tolls* is not a tremendous sense of man's
dignity and worth, an urgent awareness of
the necessity of man's freedom, a nearly
poetic realization of man's *collective* virtues. Indeed, the individual vanishes in the
political whole, but vanishes precisely to
defend his dignity, his freedom, his virtue.
In spite of the ominous premium which
the title seems to place on individuality,
the real theme of this book is the relative
unimportance of individuality and the superb importance of the political whole.
(For fascists are men, too, and even when
the bell tolls for them, it tolls for me, I
believe; but the fascists in this book have
scarcely any meaning as personalities,
merely represent The Enemy.) Hemingway's title portends nothing more than

that which we have all known: that the doom of Republican Spain was our doom. This novel is no *War and Peace,* no *Dynasts;* it is realistic, political, and deeply [**103/104**] partisan. The defects of characterization are the conventional defects of partisan novels, in which personalities always threaten to vanish in abstractions, as, half the time, the woman Pilar becomes a Spanish Gaea, Robert Jordan any vaguely attractive American, and Maria that perfect sexual creature of the private Hemingway mythology. As in so many partisan novels it is the minor characters, who bear no burden but their own, who are excellent: Sordo, the good old man Anselmo, the insane Marty, the politically exhausted Pablo, this last a magnificent portrait, and a dozen more. About their cause, which is his, Hemingway writes with a zealot's passion. And the old mould is as useless to him—as meaningless—as the old insistence on the individual's isolation, on the private pursuit of his pleasures, and on the exercise of his wholly private virtues. If the early books pled for sporting conduct on violent occasions, this book pleads the moral necessity of political violence. A different thing; indeed, a different writer.

Here is none of the grace of *The Sun Also Rises,* none of the precise perfection of stories such as *A Clean, Well-Lighted Place.* This is by no means a perfect technical performance. The severe compression of the old work gives way to nearly complete relaxation. The first effect of this relaxation is evident in the pace of the narrative itself, which is leisurely. The second effect is in the fulness of detail, which Hemingway's sentences can suddenly accommodate. And the third effect is in the sentences themselves, which employ a wide variety of cadences, almost entirely new, and which are short and long, truncated and sinuous, bare or copious as they are needed. To my taste, this syntactical loosening up is almost excessive, for it quickly ramifies in many directions. Understatement is gone and overstatement too often replaces it; we are reminded of Hemingway's own remark that "the dignity of movement of an iceberg is due to only one-eighth of it being above water." The older objectivity of style held the narrative in check in a way that this narrative is not held in check; and to this fact we may attribute many long passages of reflection not particularly well-written and not particularly necessary to the story, long reveries with which the older Hemingway would have had nothing to do. This easy method of exposition is a technical device which the older style made a luxury; here it is everywhere, and largely wasted.

Thus we gain and we lose. Because it is another story, this story could not have been told at all in the older style, and so, in the future, the [**104/105**] flexibility of this new style, with its broader subject matter, gives us a bigger writer. How much do we care if, in relaxing, this style also sprawls sometimes, sometimes even snores a little in the sun? It is possible that moral greatness and the best manners are incompatible.

Review of *For Whom the Bell Tolls**

ALVAH C. BESSIE, veteran and historian of the Abraham Lincoln Brigade in the Spanish Civil War, is also a well-known poet and novelist.

"No man is an *Iland,* intire of it selfe; every man is a peece of the *Continent,* a part of the *maine;* if a *Clod* bee washed away by the *Sea, Europe* is the lesse, as well as if a *Promontorie* were, as well as if a *Mannor* of thy friends or of *thine owne* were; any mans *death* diminishes me, because I am involved in *Mankinde;* And therefore never send to know for whom the *bell* tolls; It tolls for *thee.*"

This is the quotation from John Donne which Ernest Hemingway sets as a rubric for his new novel, and this is the touchstone by which that novel must be evaluated. Since we must assume that Donne was speaking of the universal brotherhood of man, of the inter-relationship of human life and its indivisibility, we have a right to expect that Hemingway's long novel of the war in Spain will illuminate that text and not obscure it, will demonstrate the novelist's realization of the significance of that war, and find him at the peak of his achievement. For that war, which Hemingway witnessed at close hand, is being revealed with every day that passes to have been a touchstone and a turning point in human history which those who had foresight in 1936 stated it would be: "the cause of all advanced and progressive mankind."

Ernest Hemingway's relationship to that war was intimate and varied. In many senses he was as much a participant as those men he knew and loved who now are gone—Lucasz, Werner Heilbrunn, and the many anonymous dead of the glorious Twelfth International Brigade. The novelist gave freely of his substance and his spirit in the cause of Spain; he wrote and he spoke and he acted. And he commanded the admiration and respect of the men of many nationalities who fought there and who knew his name. It was during that war that he wrote a novel that represented what should have been—and what many thought was—a transition book: *To Have and Have Not.* It was both interesting and inevitable that that novel should have been the first work from his hand that was *not* greeted with unanimous enthusiasm by the critical fraternity of the bourgeois press. For in its pages a new note had been sounded. The old Hemingway of the postwar what-the-hell-boys and the old let's-have-another-drink was gone. A new Hemingway made his appearance, a new theme emerged. Whereas in his short stories and in two previous novels the author had exasperated his most perspicacious admirers by his inconclusive treatment of the necessity for manliness and the pervasive horror of death, a maturing artist found another subject— the problem of making a living, the necessity for human solidarity. "One man alone ain't got," whispered the dying Harry Morgan, an honest man who had found that he could not feed his wife and children by honest labor. "No man alone now." He stopped. "No matter how a man alone ain't got no bloody ——ing chance."

The critics deplored this new and serious note in their pet disillusioned author, an author they had praised for being above the political arena, who dealt with

* Alvah C. Bessie, Review of *For Whom the Bell Tolls, New Masses,* XXXVII (November 5, 1940), 25-29. Reprinted by permission of the author.

eternal realities in a "lean, athletic prose." It was whispered freely among these objective gentlemen that Hemingway was slipping; he was a member of the League of American Writers; he had discovered that non-existent figment of the Reds' imagination—the Class Struggle. But many who had thought Hemingway was dead (for more valid reasons) took new hope with the appearance in his work of this wider realization of man's humanity, this deeper understanding of his struggle. Sex and death were eternal verities, but it was not until 1937 that Hemingway discovered taxes. *To Have and Have Not* was a vastly imperfect work; the author's satirical treatment of the human parasites who lived on luxury yachts off the Florida keys was both brittle and jejune, and his old limitations were amply manifest: the interchangeability of his conversation; his feeble understanding of female character; his inability to fully explore and *plumb* character at all. For with the rarest of exceptions few characters that Hemingway has dealt with up to date have been more than pegs on which to hang those moods and intimations of mortality which have been the author's forte, and which reveal his greatest gifts.

That those gifts are considerable no sensitive person could doubt. He has an ear for the language (in dialogue) that is unique. No human being ever talked the way Hemingway's characters talk, but every word they speak makes the reader say, "How true to life." This is a real artistic triumph. This man can create moods and crystallize certain fundamental emotions in a way few writers have ever been privileged to achieve. And it is these moods and these emotions that the reader generally remembers, not the people who live through them—the futility of the life of the expatriate, his emptiness and his frantic search for a kick; the horror of the retreat from Caporetto; the loneliness that surrounds the death in childbed of the heroine of *A Farewell to Arms,* the brutality of *The Killers,* and the frustration of *Fifty Grand;* the loneliness and incon-

gruity of drunkenness, and the sense of decay that pervaded all his work up to *To Have and Have Not,* where the wider significance of living made a momentary appearance.

Many expected that Hemingway's experience in Spain would so inflame his heart and his talents, that his long-announced novel of that war would be both his finest achievement and "the" novel about Spain. It is not. It is his finest achievement only in the sense that he has now perfected his extraordinary technical facility and touched some moments of action with a fictional suspense that is literally unbearable. But depth of understanding there is none; breadth of conception is heartbreakingly lacking; there is no searching, no probing, no grappling with the truths of human life that is more than superficial. And an astounding thing has happened, that anyone who was even remotely concerned with what happened in Spain will find almost incredible: Hemingway has treated that war (in an essential way) exactly as he treated the first world war in *A Farewell to Arms.* Touched in his own flesh and spirit by the horror of that first great imperialist conflict, struck into a mood of impotent despair by its utter lack of meaning and its destruction of everything all decent human beings value, Hemingway proclaimed the futility of life and love and happiness. He killed his heroine and in a memorable evocation of utter human loneliness, his hero "walked home in the rain." The *Farewell* was so bitter a condemnation of imperialist war that it aroused the ire of Archibald MacLeish, who found that it had been largely responsible for destroying the new generation's faith in its misleaders.

Let us examine *For Whom the Bell Tolls,* and see what the author (who only recently aptly replied to MacLeish) has done with one of the greatest human facts of our century—the two and a half years during which [25/26] the Spanish people held in check, with their bare hands, the forces of international fascism. His hero this time is Robert Jordan, American volunteer in Spain who is a *partizan* fighter —one of that small band of extremely courageous men who worked behind the fascist lines. Jordan is sent behind the lines again to blow up a strategic bridge—his signal for the explosion is to be the beginning of a government attack upon Segovia.

The action takes place in three days' time. Jordan makes contact with a group of Spanish *guerilleros,* meets a Spanish girl who had been captured and raped by the fascists, falls in love with her, makes his plans to blow the bridge—a difficult enterprise in which he fully expects to lose his life. His guerrillas attack the fascist garrisons, and he blows the bridge as what is to be a futile attack gets under way—for the fascists have learned of the plans for the offensive and are prepared to meet it. In escaping, Jordan's horse is wounded, falls upon the man, and breaks his leg. He is too badly injured to be carried, and must be left behind to do what damage he can with a light machine-gun, and then to end his life.

This is a story of action, and the action is fast and furious, fused with a suspense that is magnificently handled in every incident. But this is also *A Farewell to Arms,* slightly in reverse. For the total implication of the novel is, again, the necessity for virility, the pervasive horror of death, the futility—nay, the impossibility of love. Given only seventy-two hours in which to live, Robert Jordan must live his life within that span. He accepts that fate, but the reader's disappointment in his fate is Hemingway's disappointment with life— for there is no tragedy here, merely pathos. Here, again, are long and fruitless and somewhat meaningless disquisitions upon the significance of death and killing (in war, in murder, in the bull-ring, by accident, by design). Here again is the small and personal (and the word *personal* is the key to the dilemma of Ernest Hemingway's persistent lack of growth) frustration of the individual, and here again is the author's almost pathological preoccupation with blood and mutilation and sex and death—they all go together and are part and parcel of his attitude toward life, and they are the *only* facts of life with which he has consistently dealt. I do not mean to imply that these subjects are unworthy or incapable of profound treatment, singly or together; I do mean to insist that in Hemingway's hands they have never achieved the stature of universality, perhaps because Hemingway cannot see them in perspective, cannot see them more than sentimentally.

It must be clearly stated that Hemingway's position in this novel is unequivocally on the side of the Spanish people; there can be no question of his defection from that cause. It is, however, a tragic fact that the cause of Spain does not, in any *essential* way, figure as a motivating power, a driving, emotional, passional force in this story. In the [26/27] widest sense, that cause is actually *irrelevant* to the narrative. For the author is less concerned with the fate of the Spanish people, whom I am certain that he loves, than he is with the fate of his hero and his heroine, who are *himself.* They are Hemingway and Hemingway alone, in their (say rather *his,* for Jordan is the mainspring of the narrative, and the girl Maria is only lightly sketched) morbid concentration upon the meaning of *individual* death, *personal* happiness, *personal* misery, *personal* significance in living and their personal equation is not so deeply felt or understood as to achieve wide significance. For all his groping, the author of the *Bell* has yet to integrate his individual sensitivity to life with the sensitivity of every living human being (read the Spanish people) ; he has yet to expand his personality as a novelist to embrace the truths of other people, everywhere; he has yet to dive deep into the lives of others, and there to find his own.

This personal constriction has long been evident and has made inevitable other aspects of Hemingway's personality that are, to say the least, reprehensible. I refer to his persistent chauvinism, as referred to the Italian people, and to women; to the irresponsibility he has shown in publishing in Hearst's *Cosmopolitan* such a story as *Below the Ridge,* a story whose implications gave deadly ammunition to the enemy—Hemingway's enemy, the fascist-minded of America; to the irresponsibility he demonstrated in permitting his play, *The Fifth Column,* to be mutilated and distorted out of all semblance of what he originally wanted to say, to the point where it was actually a slander of the Spanish people.

There are many references in the *Bell* to various political aspects of the struggle in Spain. And few of these references do more than *obscure* the nature of that struggle. Robert Jordan, his American anti-fascist fighter, wonders "what the Russian stand is on the whole business." If Jordan, who is pictured as an utterly inflexible anti-fascist, did not understand what the Soviet Union felt about Spain, surely his creator did and does. And just as in his story *Below the Ridge,* Hemingway's sins of omission in the *Bell* allow the untutored reader to believe that the role of the Soviet Union in Spain was sinister and reprehensible. For certainly he must himself know—and it is his obligation to clearly state—that that role was clear and well-defined, and so honest as to command the entire respect and adherence of the Spanish people, who hung banners in their towns which read: *Viva La U.R.S.S.; Mejor Amigo del Pueblo Espanol* (Long Live the Soviet Union, Best Friend of the People of Spain!).

Now this concentration, this constriction of Hemingway's indubitable genius, to the purely personal, has resulted in a book about Spain that is not about Spain at all! It has resulted in the intensification of his idiosyncratic tendencies to the point where he, an inflexible supporter of the loyalists and an avowed admirer of the International Brigades, can conceive and execute as vicious a per- [**27/28**] sonal attack upon Andre Marty, the *organizer* of the International Brigades, as could be and has been delivered upon him by French fascist deputies themselves! This attack upon Marty, who is portrayed in the novel under his own name, and upon whom Hemingway exercises the presumption (both personal and artistic) of *thinking for him,* is entirely irrelevant to the narrative. To understand it at all, one would have to know, at first hand, the nature of Hemingway's personal contact with this man—a revolutionary figure of the first magnitude, organizer of the Black Sea mutiny of the French navy (an achievement that could scarcely have been conceived and executed by the criminal imbecile Hemingway portrays), a monolithic representative of the French working class, and the man who was the organizational genius and spirit of the Brigades Hemingway makes such protestation of admiring. Both as novelist and reporter Hemingway had an obligation to understand this man, whatever his personal experience with Marty, whatever his personal opinion of Marty's personality might have been. He cannot plead that his intentions in attacking Marty were good; that it was his honest conviction that Marty was a part of the incompetence, the red tape, and the outright treachery that strangled Spain, for such "facts" simply will not hold water; they are lies. And I am afraid that Hemingway will live to see his book hailed by our universal enemy *precisely because of* his attack upon Marty; I am afraid he will live to see every living and dead representative of the Abraham Lincoln Battalion attacked and slandered because of the great authority that attaches to Hemingway's name and his known connection with Spain.

Yet this man Marty is the man the author portrays as a fool, a madman, and categorically indicts as a murderer! And I wonder, when he wrote these pages, whether he considered for a moment that he was attacking him with the very terms that have been leveled at him by the French fascists who sold France down the river to Hitler. I wonder if he considered he was accusing him in the very same way and with the very same words that were used by American deserters who appeared before the Dies committee and attempted to smear the Veterans of the Lincoln Brigade, with the very words of the Hearst press which, throughout the war in Spain, characterized the Internationals as the scum of the earth, international bums, gangsters, and murderers.

This is the trap into which the individualism Hemingway's bourgeois critics so admired, has led a man who is still one of our most greatly endowed creative artists. For he has written a novel of Spain without the Spanish people, a *Hamlet* without the Dane. And he has forgotten the words he wrote earlier this year: "There are events which are so great that if a writer has participated in them his obligation is to try to write them truly rather than assume the presumption of altering them with invention." For the author [28/29] of the *Bell* does not convince us, with this novel, that "any mans death diminishes me, because I am involved in Mankinde." He only convinces us—no matter how tenderly he may write of the love of Robert Jordan and Maria—that the imagination of his own death may yet destroy him as an artist.

It seems certain that Hemingway did not intend to write a *Cosmopolitan* love story against a background of the Spanish Civil War; yet this is what he has done. It is certain that he did not intend to slander the Spanish people or the Soviet Union; yet his method of telling the story has resulted in both. With minor exceptions, the Spanish people portrayed here are cruel, vindictive, brutalized, irresponsible. Throughout the long narrative there is evidence of much confusion: Hemingway praises the individual heroism of individual Communists, and impugns and slanders their leadership, their motives, and their attitudes. He admires the Brigades, and assails their leadership (and surely he knows enough about military affairs to realize that no soldier can fight well unless his officer commands his respect).

Already this greatly endowed writer, who on innumerable occasions has placed himself without equivocation on the side of the people against their enemies, has been readmitted by the most reactionary critics to the Valhalla of the Literary Giants. J. Donald Adams of the New York *Times* has forgiven him for writing *To Have and Have Not;* the defected liberal, John Chamberlain, absolves him for having (in the same novel) made "a common murderer of inferior sensibility and no moral sense whatever . . . do duty as a symbol of downtrodden humanity," cheers the fact that "If Archibald MacLeish still thinks of Hemingway as an underminer of the soldierly virtues he will have to change his mind," and becomes shrill with joy over the attack on Marty, Hemingway's "turn (ing) on the politicos of Moscow" and finally arriving at the point announced by John Dos Passos in *Adventures of a Young Man.* (This should be news to Hemingway, for Dos Passos ultimately became an avowed enemy of the republican government of Spain.) Edmund Wilson also points the Dos Passos parallel in the *New Republic,* lauds Hemingway for being more interested in "The *kind* of people . . . rather than their social-economic relations. . . ."

But this is strange company for a man like Hemingway, a man who transcended the futility created in him by the first world war, was vitalized, as a man and as an artist, by Spain; a man who won the respect and admiration of almost every International Brigade man who met him, and who gave liberally to these men of his own substance. For at the moment he is found in bad company; in the company of his enemies, and the people's enemies— clever enemies who will fawn upon him and use him, his great talents and his passion for the people's cause, to traduce and betray those talents and those people.

"Mechanized Doom": Ernest Hemingway and the American View of the Spanish Civil War*

ALLEN GUTTMANN, who has written extensively about the literary aspects of the Spanish Civil War, teaches at Amherst College.

I

The Spanish Earth, a documentary film written by Ernest Hemingway and directed by Joris Ivens, begins with the camera focused upon the soil itself. From the very beginning the film is an assertion of an intimate relationship between men and the land: "This Spanish earth is dry and hard and the faces of the men who work on [this] earth are hard and dry from the sun." The land must be defended against an enemy armed, in the film as in reality, with the most up-to-date weapons of mechanized war. The land *is* defended, and the film ends with the waters rushing through the newly constructed irrigation ditch, bringing life to the sun-baked soil. Floods of American aid never reached the Spanish Loyalists, but that is history's irony and not Hemingway's. In For Whom the Bell Tolls, there is a similar structure in that the novel begins and ends with the "pine-needled floor of the forest." In the novel as in the film, there is a struggle between men and machines.

Considering the historical facts, it is not surprising that there should be this common element in the novel and in the film. When the Spanish army revolted on the afternoon and evening of July 17, 1936, the Republic was saved from immediate destruction by the action of poorly armed and often unarmed civilians. As massive shipments of German and Italian equipment reached the Rebels, it became obvious to military observers that mechanized weapons were likely to be a decisive factor. Military historians studied the war as a testing ground for the newest theories of mechanized warfare: General Duval wrote Les Leçons de la Guerre d'Espagne; Hoffman Nickerson commented upon the obsolescence of the unmechanized "mass armies" in The Armed Horde; and Basil Henry Liddell Hart, in a series of books and articles, analyzed the new importance of Blitzkrieg and Panzerdivision. As documents captured after the fall of the Reich testify, Hermann Goering was particularly anxious to test his newly created Luftwaffe. Popular magazines such as Life, The Saturday Evening Post, and Time discussed Giulio Douhet's theory that methodical bombardment would demoralize civilian populations.

Since the London Non-Intervention Committee and the American embargo were effective in reducing the imports of the Republicans and quite ineffective in halting the flow of men and munitions to General Franco, the disparity in equipment grew increasingly greater. It was, therefore, perfectly natural that bombing planes and armored tanks should become, in the writings of Loyalist-sympathizers, symbols for the enemy; the symbols corresponded to the historical situation. At a time when much of the American public was stunned by the horror of aerial bombardment, it was natural that pro-Loyalist writings should emphasize the plight of the badly armed or unarmed Republicans, especially when these Republicans were

* Allen Guttmann, a revision of an article entitled, " 'Mechanized Doom': Ernest Hemingway and the Spanish Civil War," Massachusetts Review, I (May, 1960), 541-561. Printed by permission of the author and the Massachusetts Review. (No page numbers are supplied in the text because this revised version has not been published heretofore.)

the peasants whose primitive conditions of life left them almost completely helpless when attacked by the weapons of a technological civilization. It is, therefore, not unnatural that, in *The Spanish Earth* and in *For Whom the Bell Tolls,* a symbolic struggle between men and machines forms an important part of Hemingway's vision of reality, a vision which is, in the complex way that art is related to the rest of experience, based upon the historical facts. This essay is an attempt to treat two questions: (1) To what degree was Hemingway's interpretation of the fight against Fascism dramatized and particularized in the struggle of men against machines? (2) Can Hemingway's interpretations be helpful in exploring other interpretations and in suggesting one of the sources of the extraordinary concern which thousands of Americans felt for the fate of the Spanish Republic? The first step is to look at Hemingway's work.

From his earliest stories, from the Nick Adams episodes of *In Our Time* to the fable of *The Old Man and the Sea,* Ernest Hemingway has dealt with man in the natural landscape. Even within the general lostness of *The Sun Also Rises,* the characters find themselves briefly while fishing in Spain, near Pamplona. For Hemingway, Spain is an elemental symbiosis of man and nature. What are the rituals of Hemingway's paean to bullfighting, *Death in the Afternoon,* if not a stylized representation of man's organic relationship to nature? Remembering the proverb about Europe's being cut off at the Pyrenees, Hemingway looks upon Africa and Spain as a unit, and, in *The Green Hills of Africa,* shows the mechanized world entering insidiously to destroy the hitherto uncorrupted world of nature. The book opens with a hunt ruined by the passing of a truck. This is put into the simplest possible language: "The truck had spoiled it." Later, the theme is generalized:

A continent ages quickly once we come. The natives live in harmony with it. But the foreigner destroys. . . . A country wears out quickly unless man puts back into it all his residue and that of all his beasts. When he quits using beasts and uses machines, the earth defeats him quickly. The machine can't reproduce, nor does it fertilize the soil.

What Hemingway seemed to discover in the Spanish war was that the machine is not merely passively destructive in that it cannot perform biological functions; the machine can also become an agent of destruction:

There is nothing so terrible and sinister as the track of a tank in action. The track of a tropical hurricane leaves a capricious swath of complete destruction, but the two parallel grooves the tank leaves in the red mud lead to scenes of planned death worse than any the hurricane leaves.

Before dramatizing the conflict between the values associated with the natural landscape and the values associated with the tank and other machines, Hemingway wrote four short stories and also a play— all concerned with the Spanish Civil War. Three of the stories, set in Madrid, deal with the correspondents and the "Internationals" who made Chicote's bar their place of rendezvous. Hemingway himself feels that these stories are inferior in technique and has refused requests to print them anew. The fourth story, "The Old Man at the Bridge," dramatizes the flight of the peasant from the artillery and the planes of the Fascists. *This* story has become a part of the Hemingway canon. The play, *The Fifth Column,* was written at the urging of the foreign correspondents in Madrid. Set in Madrid's Hotel Florida, it is a wooden play about a Vassar girl (with long legs) and a counterspy for the International Brigades. If the play has any enduring meaning, it is to make clear that Hemingway could not dramatize the Spanish war with these stick figures; the play violates its author's own often-repeated rule—the writer must always tell the truth as he sees it, and the truth for Ernest Hemingway was not to be seen in Chicote's and not to be seen in the Hotel Florida. It was not even in Madrid; it was closer to the peasants and gypsies, closer to the earth, closer to the pine-needled floor of the forest.

The first thing one notices about *For Whom the Bell Tolls* is, usually, the epigraph taken from a meditation by John Donne. Ordinarily, we remember best the lines which give the book its title: "And therefore never send to know for whom the *bell* tolls; it tolls for *thee*." Hemingway uses the epigraph as a statement of the theme of brotherhood, of human solidarity, of the involvement of all men in a common humanity. The statement, however, is not separable from the imagery of the passage:

No man is an *Iland* intire of it selfe; every man is a peece of the *Continent*, a part of the *maine*; if a *Clod* bee washed away by the *Sea*, *Europe* is the lesse. . . .

The images of the earth, of island, continent, the main, a clod, are not accidental and not unimportant. Nathaniel Hawthorne, in his story "Ethan Brand," described all men as linked in a "magnetic chain of humanity" and Herman Melville, in Chapter LXXII of *Moby-Dick*, used a rope tied between Queequeg and Ishmael to symbolize "the precise situation of every mortal that breathes," the "Siamese connexion with a plurality of other mortals." Hemingway's use of Donne's metaphor of the earth, rather than the more obvious metaphors of chain or rope, would be scant grounds on which to base a thesis if it were not for the accumulation of such seemingly trivial bits of evidence. Consider, for instance, Hemingway's elegy for "The American Dead in Spain":

The dead sleep cold in Spain tonight and they will sleep cold all this winter as the earth sleeps with them. But in the spring the rain will come. . . . This spring the dead will feel the earth beginning to live again. For our dead are a part of the earth of Spain now and the earth of Spain can never die. Each winter it will seem to die and each spring it will come alive again. Our dead will live with it forever. . . . The dead do not need to rise. They are a part of the earth now and the earth can never be conquered. For the earth endureth forever.

One need only to finish the quotation from *Ecclesiastes*, "And the sun also riseth," to feel the unity of Hemingway's best writing.

Robert Jordan, a "peece of the *Continent*, a part of the *maine*," does *not* join the International Brigades. Two British soldiers described fighting in the wreckage of Madrid's University City, beneath busts of "Plato, Spinoza, Aristotle and Voltaire," behind the bullet-proof barricades of "Indian metaphysics and early nineteenth-century Germany philosophy," but Robert Jordan joins a guerrilla band in the mountains—a band which fights on horseback, a band whose previous accomplishments include chiefly the destruction of a troop-train. Robert Jordan fights side by side with Anselmo, a man of natural wisdom. The two trust each other by instinct, but Pablo, the leader of the band, is suspicious and grants the American a tentative approval only after witnessing his knowledge of horses, the same horses which subsequently bring out what little kindness is left in Pablo. (Hemingway's portrayal of Pablo indicates that the book is not a naive affirmation of the Noble Savage.) Later, the horses play a vital role in the climax of Chapter XXVI, in the terrifying conflict between El Sordo's band, sprawled behind the dead bodies of their mounts, and the Fascist patrol. El Sordo's men hold out until the dive bombers come. Then all is determined. On a hillside, where men are naturally accustomed to survey their dominions, the band is uncovered and helpless. They are all killed.

Those less grim sections of the novel, the episodes which concern the affair with Maria, have been condemned as extraneous, but, looking specifically at the theme of the earth and the machine, one notes that Maria, Roberto's beloved "rabbit," is somehow identified with the Spanish earth that was then violated figuratively as Maria was violated literally. Maria's shaved head is so realistic a detail that one is surprised to see an obvious symbolism as well. The *least* one can say is that the story of Maria, taken prisoner, raped, rescued from a troop-train, and, finally, saved by Roberto from the approaching tanks of the enemy, parallels certain aspects of Spanish history from 1936 to 1939. Paired with Maria is Pilar, a kind of Iberian Earth-Mother who is proud that the world itself moved during her love-making, who had lived nine years with three of the worst-paid matadors in the world, who reminds us again and again of the love-making and bull-fighting that represent Spain as it should have been.

In symbolic opposition to the cluster of values represented by the two bands, their mounts, and the earth itself, we have the steel bridge, the bombers, and the approaching tanks. In the documentary film, the flow of water onto the hard, dry Spanish earth parallels the movement of mechanized equipment on the successfully defended Madrid-Valencia road. The bridge, in the film, is held by the Loyalists and preserved from capture by a counterattack of Loyalist tanks and troops. In *For Whom the Bell Tolls,* Hemingway exercises the greater freedom of the novelist and changes the values of bridge and tank. The Fascists hold the bridge. It is their armor which must not cross.

Just as the lighthouse dominates the action of Virginia Woolf's novel, so the bridge controls and unifies the action of Hemingway's. In one sense, it is the center of a series of concentric circles; in another, it is the point toward which the elements of the plot converge. No matter what geometric metaphor is used to plot the book upon a plane surface, it is certain that the bridge is central. Robert Jordan thinks of it as "the point on which the future of the human race can turn." The character of each person is determined by his or her relation to the bridge. Pablo is, of course, against the demolition of the bridge. Pilar is for it because she understands its significance: "I am for the Republic . . . And the Republic is the bridge." Robert Jordan defines himself

by the bridge: "You're a bridge-blower now. Not a thinker." At the end, he once more identifies himself with the emblem of technological civilization: "As Jordan goes, so goes the bloody bridge." The bridge *is* destroyed, but Robert Jordan, escaping on horseback, is hit by a shell from an enemy tank. Mortally wounded, he waits to confront the enemy.

One need not, however, rely exclusively upon the action of the novel or upon the symbolic oppositions, for the characters speak out. Anselmo asserts bitterly, "We must take away their planes, their automatic weapons, their tanks, their artillery and teach them dignity." Pilar is completely explicit: "The sight of those machines does things to one. . . . We are nothing against such machines." Looking up at the Heinkels overhead, Robert Jordan thinks they are like "sharp-nosed sharks of the Gulf Stream," but only for a moment does he link the machine with the natural menace. As the tank was, in the *New Republic* dispatch, worse than the hurricane, so the bombers are worse than the worst of nature:

But these, wide-finned in silver, roaring, the light mist of their propellers in the sun, these do not move like sharks. They move like no thing there has ever been. They move like mechanized doom.

Clearly then, for Hemingway, the Spanish Civil War was, among other things, a struggle waged by men close to the earth and to the values of a primitive society against men who had turned away from the earth, men who had turned to the machine and to the antithetical values of an aggressive and destructive mechanical order. When Hemingway addressed the American Writers Congress in 1937, he spoke of Spain and of the writer's responsibility to "write truly and having found what is true, to project it in such a way that it becomes a part of the experience of the person who reads it." Considering the facts both of Spanish history and of Hemingway's own career prior to 1936,

For Whom the Bell Tolls seems the natural result of Hemingway's urge to write as truly as he could.

II

Ernest Hemingway was not the only writer to see the Spanish war as the opposition of man and machine. Waldo Frank praised "the profoundly *whole* culture of Spain" and glorified the land and the peasant who worked the land: "The peasant of Spain is real Spain. In no other country of Europe has culture and historic action sprung so directly from the humble human soil." At the same time, Frank shuddered to imagine "tens of thousands of bare breasts of simple men and women . . . there to confront the machine guns and bombing planes. . . ." Elliot Paul, John Dos Passos, and Josephine Herbst all emphasized the primitive village as the heart of Spain, the peasant or the fisherman as the truest Spaniard, as the victim of a mechanized enemy. In an early version, John Howard Lawson's film, *Blockade,* began with Marco, the peasant-hero, laboring in his vineyard. Norma, the soon-to-be-discovered Fascist, makes a destructive entry; she drives her motor-car through Marco's vines. But the car runs into a placid pair of oxen and expires with a smashed radiator. The scene was a preview of the triumph of the primitive over the mechanical order.

Still other men and women, who did not necessarily share Hemingway's affirmation of the Spanish earth, shared this vision of the tank and the bomber as images of doom. Edwin Rolfe, poet and historian of the Lincoln Battalion, wrote that "There is something about an enemy tank approaching, its machine guns spitting uninterrupted death, which throws fear into the heart. . . ." *The New Republic,* which had printed Hemingway's dispatches from the front, presented in an editorial the image of the machine as menace:

Women and children torn to pieces by aerial bombs as they go to market, crowded buildings and boulevards . . . shattered by artillery, suburbs and outlying parks made into playgrounds for grinding tanks, men and women . . . sprayed to death . . . by machine guns in power-diving pursuit planes—this is Madrid today.

There is no sense of human agency behind the weapons of the Fascists; there is only the sense of impotent humanity beneath omnipotent machines. This sense of impotence and this image of conflict between men and machines runs through a wide variety of writings and is found in the visual arts as well. For the sake of simplicity and clarity, I shall concentrate on the most nearly ubiquitous symbol of technological warfare—the bombing plane.

Herbert Matthews of *The New York Times* described his own feelings of powerlessness beneath the then-experimental *Luftwaffe:* "It is a terrible moment when one can hear a bomber directly overhead, knowing its power of destruction and feeling so helpless." Lester Ziffren, another correspondent, found air-raids the most frightful aspect of the Spanish war: "My dreams," he wrote, "were of horrors." Irving Pflaum, of United Press, admitted that his "one real fear" was that "methodical, systematic, terroristic bombing . . . may be one of the decisive factors in future wars. With me it was decisive. It licked me." Frank Pitcairn told the readers of *Travel* about the fantastic risks taken in the hopeless but still necessary effort to even out the difference between a German-manned Junker's plane with bombs and machine guns, and a peasant lad with eight days' training, a rifle and a few rounds of ammunition. Similar observations were made by Jay Allen and Katherine de Carreras in broadcasts over C.B.S., by Erskine Caldwell in his contribution to *Salud!,* by Alvah Bessie in his account of the last days of the Lincoln Battalion, and by Edwin Rolfe in his history of that battalion.

As names like Bessie, Caldwell, Dos Passos, and Herbst suggest, bombing planes were symbolically present in novels as well as in factual accounts of the war. The bomber quickly became a part of the sound effects, of the backdrop, for scenes of conflict. John Dos Passos uses this image of terror in *Adventures of a Young Man* and Michael Blankfort uses it in *The Brave and the Blind.* Upton Sinclair's *No Pasaran!* comes to a dime-novel close in which two Americans, cousins who have volunteered for opposing sides, fight it out. The quality of the novel is reflected faithfully in the triumph of the foot-soldier (Loyalist) who vanquishes his airborne relative (Fascist).

The importance of this image as a metaphor for our times becomes even more obvious when we see that the only American novelist of any merit whatsoever to take General Franco's side—the Baroness de Zglinitzki, *née* Helen Nicholson—also dramatized the opposition of man and machine. In her account of the war in Andalusia, she refers to "Franco's army in overalls, fighting in the snow of the Guadarramas," and comments that they have shown "how far an intrepid spirit can triumph, even over the might and the machine-guns of Russia." The coming of the bombers ends her one-act play, *Shelter for the Night.* Her novel of the Spanish War, *The Painted Bed,* comes to a climax when an air-raid brings death and a vision of Christ upon the cross.

Numerous one-act plays make symbolic use of the bombing plane. Barrie Stavis wrote *Refuge,* a play set in a bomb-shelter, and William Merrick's *Forgot in the Rains* (a Columbia Workshop play) concludes with the bombing of a village. Archibald MacLeish, who had joined Lillian Hellman in raising money for *The Spanish Earth,* wrote *Air Raid,* a verse-play broadcast by C.B.S., in which bombers are described by the narrator as a form of dehumanized menace:

> They swing like steel in a groove:
> They move like tools not men:
> You'd say there were no men:
> You'd say they had no will but the
> Will of motor on metal.

Implications of this vision become clearer as one recalls the visions of endangered primitivism that are found in MacLeish's earlier poem, *Conquistador.* Lacking this element of overt primitivism, but quite as bitterly written, Norman Corwin's play, *They Fly Through the Air With the Greatest of Ease,* was also broadcast by C.B.S. It was, like dozens of poems and hundreds of editorials, written as a response to the bombing of Guernica.

When history contained horrors such as Guernica, it is hardly odd that bombing planes appeared in the poetry of the Spanish war. Norman Rosten's "Fragments for America" is a disquieting poem. He wrote of a

> peasant who tried to stop an enemy plane
> rising; ran cursing into the swift propeller
> to stop it with his hands; the plane rising
> . . . the sun shining on the stained steel. . . .

Langston Hughes wrote that "A bombing plane's / The song of Spain," and added further poems to illustrate, poems in which he associates airplanes and death and undercuts the traditional connotations of moonlight: "Moonlight in Valencia: the moon meant planes. / The planes meant death." Edwin Rolfe, in "A City in Anguish," described Madrid under bombardment:

> All night, all night
> flared in my city the bright
> cruel explosions of bombs.
> All night, all night,
> there, where the soil and stone
> spilled like brains from the sandbag's head,
> the bodiless head lay staring;
> while the anti-aircraft barked,
> barked at the droning plane . . .

In "Casualty," Rolfe told how "one bomb, shrieking, / found the thin axis of his whirling fears, / the exact center." In an epitaph for an American volunteer, he used the imagery of the earth:

> This is the plot where the self-growing seed
> sends its fresh fingers to turn soil aside,
> over and under earth ceaselessly growing,
> over and under earth endlessly growing.

Another poet, Boris Todrin, wrote in a manner greatly reminiscent of Hemingway's elegy on the American dead and the Spanish earth:

> Worn out fields where bomb and shell
> Scattered iron seeds of hell
> Grow their scarecrow crops. The torn
> Bones will keep the roots of corn.

John Berryman's more complex poem, "1938," contains bitter comments on the Spanish war and on the war that was still in preparation:

> Across the frontiers of the helpless world
> The great planes swarm, the carriers of death,
> Germs in the healthy body of the air,
> And blast our cities where we stand in talk
>   By doomed and comfortable fires.

Randall Jarrell, who wrote several poems on the Spanish war, described in "The Winter's Tale" the collapsing world of the late thirties. His metaphor for fragmentation was the "disintegrating bomber" that had sown death "without hate or understanding."

In this helpless world beneath the iron bombers, poets found a metaphor grounded in reality. They found a still more specific metaphor when the "necessities" of modern warfare sanctioned the bombing of cities, for then it became "necessary" that children die with their elders. Harold Rosenberg's eight-line "Spanish Epitaph" is representative:

> O tall men of Hades
> Have pity on this little one!
> His speech was not formed yet
> All he knew of life was laughing and growing
> Till the iron dropped on him out of the sky.
> O gaunt horses of Hades
> He has not even one weapon
> With which to defend himself.

Muriel Rukeyser had been in Spain and had written several poems on the Spanish Civil War (which she characterized as one of "humans against guns") when she wrote "M-Day's Child." This short poem contains the particular theme of the men-aced child within a broader denunciation of military horror:

> M-Day's child is fair of face,
> Drill-day's child is full of grace,
> Gun-day's child is breastless and blind,
> Shell-day's child is out of its mind,
> Bomb-day's child will always be dumb,
> Cannon-day's child can never quite come,
> but the child that's born on the Battle-day
> is blithe and bonny and rotted away.

Poets like Charles Norman were infuriated by the defense of the raids on Spanish cities:

> ... empty now the schoolhouse stands,
> And empty since the planes went by;
> Children in school in other lands
> Will mark this victory.

Langston Hughes, Aaron Kramer, and Norman Rosten are three poets of the many more who wrote of the bombers and the children.

If bombing planes are almost ubiquitous in the written accounts, they are scarcely less so in the visual arts. Anton Refregier attempted a surrealist's vision of a bomber, a grotesque mixture of fiend and machine, but most American painters followed the lead of Luis Quintanilla, the Spanish artist whose drawings of the war expressed the simplicity of the slaughter. Quintanilla's drawings were exhibited and published in this country. In his preface to Quintanilla's book, Ernest Hemingway refers to the artist's combat experiences in places "where men with rifles, hand grenades, and bundled sticks of dynamite faced tanks, artillery, and planes. . . ." We find the same stark opposition graphically transformed, in the book, into images of peasants fleeing in ox-carts from planes that hover over ruined villages and slaughtered animals. Louis Ribak's *Refugees*, Zoltan Hecht's *Air Raid*, and Ione Robinson's sketches, *In a Refugio, Watching Enemy Planes*, and *After Bombardment*, represent scores of American paintings, drawings, cartoons. In an era when reading "morals" into paintings is sus pect, it is useful to have Ernest Brace's comment on William Gropper's *Air Raid:*

One senses . . . the terror of implacable, blind force, the senseless and indiscriminate destruction of human beings by other human beings too remote, too mechanically indifferent to wonder who or why.

Just as the contrast between men and bombers becomes in literature most striking when the child is opposed to the Heinkel or Caproni, so in the iconography of the Spanish war, the contrast is most awful when represented in these images. Photographs of the dead children of Madrid appeared as "photomontages," as covers of pamphlets denouncing the bombing of cities, as frontispieces for poems, and, paired with a picture of Cardinal Hayes flanking General Franco, as Ernest Hemingway's indictment of the Church.

Paintings and drawings embody the same theme of conflict. Aldous Huxley, editing Oxford University's edition of drawings *by* Spanish children, noted the following:

To the little boys and girls of Spain, the symbol of contemporary civilization, the one overwhelmingly significant fact in the world today is the military plane. . . . For hundreds of thousands of children . . . the . . . plane, with its bombs and its machine guns, is the thing that . . . is significant and important above all others. This is the dreadful fact to which the drawings in our collection bear unmistakable witness.

The briefest examination of the pictures convinces us that the children did indeed live in dread of the air raids. In drawing after drawing, we see ruined cities, the little figures of fleeing people, and the disproportionately enlarged bombers. The Spanish children did not, of course, trail clouds of Wordsworthian glory or understand international relations better than the diplomats, but children do often see certain things in a more immediate and less prejudiced way than adults do. It was the tough-minded Romans and not the Romantics who noted that *verba sapienta* came often *ex oribus infantum.*

Coming to America to speak for Spain, André Malraux told an anecdote about the distribution of toys to the children of Madrid.

When it was all over, there remained in the immense empty space one little heap, untouched. . . . It was a pile of toy airplanes. It lay there in the deserted bull ring, where any child could have helped himself. The little boys had preferred anything, even dolls, and had kept away from that little pile of toy airplanes . . . with a sort of mysterious horror.

Pablo Picasso's *Guernica* is no more pertinent to our theme, no more disturbing a revelation of *la condition humaine* in the twentieth century of the Christian era.

III

These quotations are only a few instances of the theme of conflict between men and machines, and of the image of the machine as the appropriate symbol for the terrible realities of the Spanish war. If we stop now to compare Hemingway's work with that of several European novelists, we can, perhaps, observe certain differences between the American and the European imaginations. It must be said, of course, that the American and the European imaginations are very similar. From the point of view of someone *outside* the western tradition, the similarities are undoubtedly more obvious and important than the dissimilarities, but we are *within* the western tradition and can profitably look for the subtler distinctions.

Gustav Regler's work is representative of the European radical tradition. His novel, *The Great Crusade,* is a novel of the International Brigades. Specifically, it is a novel of the XIIth International Brigade (made up of Germans, Frenchmen, and Italians of the Thaelmann, Marty, and Garibaldi Battalions). Paul, the commander of the brigade, is an authoritarian determined to make Madrid the "tomb of Fascism." Werner, the doctor in charge of the brigade's medical detachment, represents the more humane aspects of the radical tradition. Albert, modeled on Regler himself (as the other two are drawn from General Lucasz and from Werner Heilbrunn), is the brigade's commissar and the novel's central character. Albert observes and learns from Paul, Werner, and the other men and women of the brigade. The characters are international but quite unlike the allegorical polyglots of most novels of the International Brigades. These exiles from Germany are real exiles. Regler himself was one of them. Unlike American fiction, *The Great Crusade* is riveted with allusions to European radicalism, to Bukharin, Dimitroff, Kamenev, Radek, Trotsky, Zinoviev. And the book is shadowed by the noonday darkness of the Moscow Trials. The most sophisticated of the Internationals knew that Stalin had betrayed their cause. Nevertheless, they fought Fascism and accepted the discipline that made the fight possible. In C. Day Lewis's phrase, they "defended the bad against the worse."

The novel is episodic. It moves from the struggle in the lecture rooms of the University of Madrid, where the Fascist advance was finally halted, to the Jarama Front and thence to the Battle of Guadalajara. The conflict between men and machines is present here as in Hemingway's fiction, but the terms of the conflict are reversed. Now it is the Internationals who represent the future, the Fascists who represent the past. At the Jarama River, the French are attacked by General Franco's Moors. Werner watches the Moors advance and thinks of "the forest primeval." He thinks of "bestial Africans with the knife between their teeth. In reserve [for the French were] Italian proletarians. If the boys succeed in driving back that herd of beasts today, they must be sent home. To Lyons, to Ville-Juif, to Brussels, to Dunkirk. . . ." Not to Montana, not to the wilderness. But the Moors are not turned back. They swarm like animals over the overwhelmed French. They press forward then toward the positions held by the Dombrowski Battalion (Poles who had replaced the Germans of the Thaelmann Battalion). In a scene which seems to reverse the end of *For Whom the Bell Tolls*, the Loyalist armor arrives. The Moorish cavalry is stopped.

Now the tanks came wobbling in from both sides of the ravine in front of the line of Poles. Their guns felt out their targets for a moment, then as the machines rumbled slowly forward, the blue explosion burst.

Regler's novel, to which Hemingway wrote an introduction, is quite unlike *For Whom the Bell Tolls* or any other American novel of the Spanish Civil War. There was, however, one European of note who seemed to share something of Hemingway's vision. Ralph Bates, who lived in Spain as Hemingway had done, wrote —as Hemingway had—of Spanish life before the civil war. His novel, *The Olive Field*, describes the tumult of the years preceding the actual outbreak of the war. It is set, for the most part, in the agricultural south. The peasants are pitted against the effete landowners who collect ancient manuscripts; the peasants receive no help from the ascetic priests who do not understand that "the olive [trees are] the very spirit of the land." The action leads to the Left revolution of 1934, where the spontaneous action of the workers is overmatched by tanks and planes.

When, in 1936, the Right tried *its* hand at revolution, Bates joined the Republican side and fought through what he later called "the legendary time." The hastily organized militias stood up to the enemy's machines. In the preface to one book on Spain, Bates wrote of a "docker who had charged through rifle, machine-gun and *artillery* fire, with a broken plank through which he had hammered nails as his sole weapon." In *The New Republic* he wrote of "Unarmed men [who] leap on the gunners, wrestle with them, strangle them, drag them to the ground and stab them with knives. Men dive at the machine guns . . . and upset them with their hands." The article ends with the plea of a Spanish peasant: "Compañero Americano, will you *sell* us rifles? Italian aircraft . . . roar overhead." In "Spanish Improvisation," he wrote of a plowman who sang folksongs. Bates speculated, "I suppose he is dead now, because he would certainly have tried to defend the Republic, with a shotgun, against those Caproni and Junkers which nightly raid us."

Of all the writings on the Spanish war, Bates' short stories, collected in *Sirocco and Other Stories,* are closest to Hemingway's in tone and theme and diction. The protagonists are usually close to the land; their antagonists are associated with mechanized authoritarianism. In "The 43rd Division" (also published in two issues of *Harper's*), Pere, the undisciplined peasant-hero, insists on fighting the war on *his* very individualistic terms. He fights alone and is in constant trouble with his commanding officer. Moreover, he condemns the newer modes of war:

The mechanical aid to the rebels was violating the nature of the Spaniard, he felt. Man to man, valor against valor; that was the Spanish way of fighting. Not factory against factory, bald-head engineer against peasant.

The crucial episode of the story embodies this theme. An izard (a type of chamois) gives birth and a Fascist equipped with a panoply of technical implements—Luger, Mannlicher-Cacano, Zeis range-finder, Leitz binoculars—kills the animal. Pere realizes that Fascism means the destruction of the natural order, that undisciplined battalions cannot hope to withstand the enemy offensive. Returning to his unit, he is first reprimanded and then given command of a guerrilla force. Asked if he wants a political commissar, Pere replies, "Yes . . . it won't be necessary, but I'd like one." He chooses the commissar who had reprimanded him. Through indiscipline, Pere learns, paradoxically, to accept discipline. In "The 43rd Division," as in other stories by Ralph Bates, we catch a glimpse of the promised land, a socialist Spain in which the machine and the olive tree will be forever reconciled.

Excellent as many of these stories are,

André Malraux's *L'Espoir* is the only piece of writing which compares well with *For Whom the Bell Tolls* and with George Orwell's *Homage to Catalonia.* No other European novel contains so much of the complexity of the Spanish Civil War. No other novel so well suggests the differences between the European and the American views of the Spanish war.

In *L'Espoir,* Hemingway's theme of primitivism—the affirmation of the natural man in the natural landscape—is sounded with a marvelous sense of the ambiguous overtones, and then subordinated to another theme. The subtle distinction that is apparent in Bates' work and obvious in Regler's becomes, in Malraux, the theme. True to the European revolutionary tradition, Malraux debates and finally decides against the values of a primitive society. As Joseph Warren Beach noted, "The most inspiring moments in the book are those in which . . . individualists discover their community of feeling and prove themselves as efficient in action as the mechanized units of fascist violence. This theme is . . . underscored . . . in the critical struggle between men and property, men and machines." But, this affirmation of the primitive community does not persist throughout the novel. The conflict between man and machine becomes less important as Russian equipment arrives. Scenes of heroic struggle against a mechanical enemy give way to descriptions of victory won by those who turn from the land to fight steel with steel. The somehow humanized "crates" of the circus-like volunteer air-force are replaced by modern aircraft. The pilots learn the necessity of strict obedience. As Malraux's spokesman argues, "Our modest function . . . is to organize the Apocalypse." Realizing the hopeless situation of unarmed human beings, Malraux finds in this realization a call to action. The *milicianos* must be mechanized. Russian *chatos* climb the air over Malraux's Madrid as they did over the Madrid of historical fact. It is true that the theme of discipline and the dramatic victory of the International Brigades at Guadalajara are interwoven with another strand, with the theme of primitivism and the uncoerced action of the peasants who, late in the novel, carry down from the mountains, in ritual procession, the survivors of a wrecked airplane; nevertheless, despite this extraordinary episode, Malraux's explicit approval is with the organizers of the Apocalypse, with the Stalinists whose ultimate goal was the socialization and the industrialization of a "Progressive" Spain.

In taking this position, Malraux was anticipating historical developments. As the war continued, discipline *was* imposed upon militiamen and modern weapons *were* placed in the hands of the peasants. Ludwig Renn, German novelist and commander of the Thaelmann Battalion, told *Esquire* readers, "Today we have a modern army, well equipped, with planes, tanks and the latest anti-tank guns. Today, with the disappearance of the last of the party troops, we have a unified command, discipline, and up-to-date training." James Hawthorne of *New Masses* praised the "brand-new beauty" of the Loyalists' airplanes and Louis Fischer of *The Nation* began a statement by announcing that the war was one of "flesh against steel" only to continue by boasting that the "Loyalist army is better equipped than ever; airplanes have been imported." Poets wrote elegies for Ben Leider, an American killed while flying in Spanish combat: "O Icarus, / Welcome him, / wingless now and a wanderer," and

> No hawk, no eagle dies
> But broken lies—
> Ashes will stir,
> The phoenix shall arise.

And even Ralph Bates sounded the harsh call to discipline and insisted that the "legendary time" of undisciplined heroism was over. A realistic attitude was needed. Changes had been made and the army had become "a cleanly machine."

In taking this position, however grudgingly, men like Regler, Bates, and Malraux are representative of the mainstream of European radicalism, a tradition which has, for the most part, rejected the strong element of primitivistic anarchism found in American *and* in Spanish radicalism. The leading student of Spanish political history has this to say of Spanish anarchism:

> Spanish anarchism . . . is . . . dominated by that nostalgia for the past that is so characteristic of Spain. . . . It voices more clearly and intelligently than any other Iberian movement the resistance offered by the whole Spanish people to the tyranny and soullessness of the modern machine-serving age.

Voiced by the Spanish, this resistance to mechanized society was listened to by Europeans and by Americans. Europeans then shut their ears, but a few Americans—men like Hemingway—continued to listen, to remember the virgin land of the American past, and to hope. Although Karl Marx characterized modern man in industrial society as living in a state of alienation, Marxian socialism looks forward to a classless society in which technology is used for the benefit of mankind and not as the instrument of exploitation, and *not* backwards, to a vision of primitivistic anarchism. At the end of his chapter on "The Pond in Winter," Henry David Thoreau created a symbol which suggests the distinction between the two traditions. Thoreau described the voyage of the ice cut from Walden Pond.

> The pure Walden water is mingled with the sacred water of the Ganges. With favoring winds it is wafted past the site of the fabulous islands of Atlantis and the Hesperides, makes the periplus of Hanno, and, floating by Ternate and Tidore and the mouth of the Persian Gulf, melts in the tropic gales of the Indian seas, and is landed in ports of which Alexander only heard the names.

The movement of this passage is toward Asiatic shores, and the flow of metaphors carries us backwards in time. It is, perhaps, an oddity of the history of ideas that the influence of *Walden* was felt in Asia and in Eastern Europe, by anarchists distrustful of industrialism (such as Mahatma Gandhi and Leo Tolstoy), and far less strongly in industrialized Europe; Friedrich Engels and Karl Marx dreamed not of the past but of the future, and never saw the "pure Walden water" mingle with the waters of the Thames.

IV

Considering this theme of conflict between men and machines, it seems reasonable to suggest that at least *part* of the extraordinary fascination of the Spanish Civil War is related to a widespread if barely articulated (or even unarticulated) fear of the implications and the actualities of technological society. We can ask two questions: (1) Does this theme of opposition represent a fear of machines *as such* or only the fears of those for whom the machines were not yet available, or novel, or in the hands of an enemy? (2) Does this fear have a counterpart in the affirmation of man in a natural, organic relationship to the land, in a tendency toward that stream of primitivism that has run, underground for the most part, through western civilization since the time of Montaigne's essay on the cannibals?

Any answers to these questions are, of course, extremely inconclusive, but the evidence indicates that most men, for one reason or another and *despite* their fears of a mechanized enemy, were quite willing to equip themselves with modern weapons and to use them to the utmost. When the Spanish war ended and the Second World War began, most of those who condemned the *Luftwaffe* became enthusiastic over the R.A.F. and, eventually, the United States Air Force. Hiroshima caused less of a stir than Guernica.

Nevertheless, to say that most men were willing to mechanize or to condone mechanization (which is, of course, to say that most men were not primitivists) is *not* to say that they are untouched by the fear of mechanization or by the values of primitivism, by a desire for the spontaneity and

the freedom from repression which we associate with an organic relationship to the natural landscape.

What Ernest Hemingway has done in *For Whom the Bell Tolls* and in *The Spanish Earth* has been to orchestrate and make central a theme which runs through scores of other writers and artists. He has, to change the figure, turned the various images of value into the characters of a drama, his version of the Spanish tragedy. Although the greatest caution must be exercised, we can surely study Hemingway's ordering of the historical events and speculate whether or not there is, within a vast complex of other and often contradictory values, an association of freedom with the earth, of tyranny with machines; on the one hand, fertility and spontaneity, and on the other, sterility and repression.

The spectre of an urbanized, industrialized, mechanized and regimented world— a spectre which has haunted the Romantic imagination since Blake's dark Satanic mills and Melville's Tartarus of Maids— seemed, to Hemingway, Dos Passos, Frank, MacLeish, and a few men like them, to have materialized, to have become the bombing planes over Madrid and Barcelona. Perhaps this is but the symbolmaker's way of saying that capitalism was, in some countries, becoming Fascism. The problem is that the Marxists' vision of a Spain dotted with Magnitogorsks and Pittsburghs is not easily harmonized with the primitivists' vision of the Spain of Don Quixote, Sancho Panza, and Rosinante.

Looking back on the Spanish war, we can see now that Hemingway's primitivistic Spain was doomed the minute that the British Foreign Office warned Léon Blum that his siding with the Republic meant the end of the Franco-British alliance. Faced then by the mechanized armies of Germany and Italy, the Loyalists had either to secure modern weapons or go down to defeat. The failure of the Spanish Republic to arm itself and to achieve political unity meant the coming of a Spanish version of Fascism; *and,* had the Loyalists succeeded in their efforts, the

Spanish peasants would have been forced in the process to accept limitations on their famous individualism, to adopt the mechanized weapons of modern war, to surrender their archaic relationship with the hard, dry Spanish earth, to become members of a technologically-based mass-society that might or might not have evolved eventually into the Marxist utopia. In either case, the result would have been a curtailment of freedom and an increase in repression.

In other words, there was in Spain as in nineteenth-century America the dilemma and the paradox of primitivism and progress which Henry Nash Smith has assayed in *Virgin Land*. Just as the dream of America as an industrial Titan contradicted the dream of America as a new Garden of Eden, so the attempt to discipline and organize and mechanize "feudal" Spain contradicted the desire to preserve a spontaneous, organic, archaic relationship of man and nature. Joy Davidman wrote bravely about the unarmed men in the Republican armies:

We have only the bodies of men to put together,
the wincing flesh, the peeled white forking stick,
easily broken, easily made sick,
frightened of pain and spoiled by evil weather;
we have only the most brittle of all things the man
and the heart the most iron admirable thing of all,
and putting these together we make a wall.

But Hemingway's interpretation seems closer to the truth when Robert Jordan is left, crippled and alone, waiting for the onslaught of the newest *conquistadores*. Perhaps the novel is closer to historical fact *because The Spanish Earth* failed to move Americans, *because* there were too many time-serving diplomats and too few volunteers for liberty, *because* the western democracies abandoned Spain to a choice between two forms of totalitarianism. Confronted by the mechanized enemy, Hemingway's primitivism became an impossible vision, but that is not to say that the values associated with primitivism are not still valid ones; one need not be a primitivist today to feel that technological

mass-society is both repressive and frighteningly unstable. Perhaps we can thank the "practical" men of the 1930's that, in an era of abiding tension, in a time of ballistic missiles and atomic warheads, we are all as helpless as the children beneath the bombing planes.

At any rate, the extraordinary thing about the Spanish war is that the historical facts seemed almost of themselves to dramatize the conflicts of the age. The material facts did, as in nineteenth-century America, correspond to the spiritual facts, or, to continue in Emerson's language, the situation was such that the poet could attach the word to the thing. Within the labyrinth of events which historians have agreed to call the "Spanish Civil War," there was once again, on foreign soil, as so often before in our *literature,* that opposition of the "two kingdoms of force" which Leo Marx sees as central to our experience: "For the contrast between the two cardinal images of value, the machine and the native landscape, dramatizes the great issue of our culture. It is the germ, as Henry James put it, of the most final of all questions about America." In other words, Hemingway's vision of the Spanish war has its roots in a very *American* tradition of thought and feeling. The Spanish war was, among other things, a fight against the desecration of that relationship between man and nature which Natty Bumppo sought in forest and prairie, which Henry Thoreau found while floating quietly on Walden Pond, which Herman Melville pursued in his quest for an "authentic Eden in a pagan sea," which Walt Whitman contemplated in a blade of summer grass, which Huck and Jim discovered while drifting down the Mississippi on a raft, which William Faulkner finds in the mule-powered and horse-swapping South, which John Dos Passos envisioned when he wrote that the "villages are the heart of Spain," which Ernest Hemingway located in upper Michigan and in an African Spain. We found in the Spanish war a mirror which reflected the image of our own unquiet desperation.

The Spanish Tragedy*

CARLOS BAKER. For information about the author, see "Place, Fact, and Scene in *The Sun Also Rises*," by Carlos Baker, reprinted on page 11.

"Hemingway . . . is obviously the person who can write the great book about the Spanish War."
—*Cyril Connolly, 1937*[1]

I. A MATTER OF CHOICE

When Hemingway spoke to the Second American Writers' Congress in Carnegie Hall, New York City, the evening of June 4, 1937, he was newly back from two months' reporting on the Spanish Civil War. It was his first public speech. Since, in the course of it, he denounced the native and foreign fascists then operating in Spain, some of his large audience supposed that they were witnessing the wonderful transformation of a non-political writer to one who was socially conscious.[2]

Two days later, in one of the closing speeches of the Congress, Joseph Freeman thought he saw an important lesson in Hemingway's "conversion." He drew his text from an anecdote about Napoleon and Goethe. When Goethe said that he was writing a play about the destiny of man, Napoleon answered that politics is destiny. In an epoch like our own, said Freeman, politics, in its broadest sense, *is* destiny. "Even if you begin as Hemingway began, with a simple emotional desire to transmit experience, to find and convey the truth, if you follow the truth to its logical conclusion, you will end where Hemingway has ended now, in the People's Front."[3]

All this about "logical conclusions" (with the implication that the logic of history eventually forces a writer to support a political party-line) was Marxist language and typical Marxist thinking. The explosion of political circumstances in Spain had presumably blasted Hemingway out of his non-political lethargy and deposited [223/224] him safely in the camp of the Spanish Loyalists. Gone was his "simple emotional desire to transmit experience," and perhaps his wish "to find and convey the truth." At any rate, these desires were now channelized in a political direction. According to Freeman, Hemingway was espousing a Cause. The political left, though very supercilious about his former childishness, was ready to welcome this talented if prodigal son back into the state of political awareness.

The only trouble with Freeman's conclusion was that Hemingway was still of Goethe's persuasion. "A writer's problem does not change," he told his audience. "It is always how to write truly and having found out what is true to project it in such a way that it becomes a part of the experience of the person who reads it." As to forms of government, he frankly continued, really good writers seem to have been rewarded under almost any system of government which they could tolerate. "There is only one form of government," said he, "that cannot produce good writers, and that system is fascism. For fascism is a lie

[1] Cyril Connolly, *New Statesman and Nation* 14 (October 16, 1937), p. 606.
[2] *Writers' Congress proceedings:* published in book form with a selection of the speeches, *The Writer in a Changing World*, ed. Henry Hart, New York, Equinox Cooperative Press, 1937.
[3] *Goethe and Napoleon:* ibid., pp. 234-235.

*Carlos Baker, "The Spanish Tragedy," *Hemingway: The Writer as Artist* (Princeton, N. J.: Princeton University Press, 1956), pp. 223-263. Copyright 1956 by the Princeton University Press.

told by bullies. A writer who will not lie cannot live and work under fascism." [4] Although, as a friend of Spanish democracy, Hemingway believed in the Republican side, his statement did not mean that, *as an artist,* he was pro-Republican or pro-Communist. What it emphatically meant was that as artist and man, he was anti-fascist, and had been for years.

Hemingway had followed political developments in Spain from the beginning of his career. The almost medieval country he had known in the nineteen-twenties during Alfonso's eight-year dictatorship-by-royal-decree had begun to change rapidly in 1931 with the overthrow of the monarchy and the establishment of the Democratic Republic of Workers.[5] As a student of revolutions [224/225] who had watched, with an artist's eye, the development and decline of the troubles in Cuba during the early nineteen-thirties, he had regretted not being on hand for the events which took place in Spain during April and May of 1931, though he was in Spain that summer and learned from his friends what had happened. As an American and as a Catholic convert of some years' standing, he had in general approved the separation of the Church and the State achieved by the Democratic Republic, though he had naturally deplored the anti-clerical riotings which preceded it.[6] He had welcomed in principal, if not in all details, the extensive program of long-overdue reforms, covering nearly every aspect of Spanish civil life, which was instituted by the same government.

He was in Africa when the conservative reaction—largely the work of the landed aristocracy, the Army, and the Church—countermanded many of the reforms accomplished in the Cortes between the spring of 1931 and the spring of 1933.[7] In Spain before the African trip he had gone shooting in Estremadura with Luis Quintanilla, an ardent Republican who was later jailed by the conservatives for his political activities.[8] At the same time Hemingway had been embarrassed by a newspaper article which called him "the friend of Spain" in bold capitals. The country, he pointed out, was split wide open, and was "inhabited by too many politicians for any man to be a friend to all of it with impunity." Under the Republic, he saw, the country was more prosperous; more money was coming in from taxes. But the peasants, like some he had recently seen in Estremadura, were still the forgotten men. Despite the newfound evidences of prosperity it was clear to Hemingway that much of the money was going where it had always gone—into the pockets of those in power. The aims of the Republic were just and sound, but the "great new bureaucracy" [225/226] was not, strictly speaking, selflessly devoted to the welfare of Spain. "Politics," said Hemingway, "is still a lucrative profession." To the ironist, the rise of Spain's new bureaucracy made the spectacle of Spanish government "more comic than tragic." To the friend of Democratic Spain, however, the comedy did not seem like something that would last. "The tragedy," said Hemingway, "is very close." [9]

The first act of the Spanish tragedy was in fact only a month off when Hemingway made his prediction. The failure of Spain in 1933 to extend the revolution of 1931

[4] *Hemingway's speech:* ibid., pp. 69-73.
[5] The period covered was September 16, 1923, through the election of April 12, 1931. This was roughly the period of Hemingway's closest association with Spain and the Spanish, until the Civil War. The Democratic Republic was established April 14, 1931, with a new flag of red, yellow, and purple—irreverently described by Pilar and others as "blood, pus, and permanganate" (*FWBT*, p. 66). The old flag of yellow and gold had been referred to as "pus and blood." The flag under Franco is referred to in terms not generally printable.
[6] *Anticlerical riots:* In Madrid on May 12, 1931, mobs burned churches and convents. At this time also anticlerical activity was widespread in other Spanish cities. Martial law was proclaimed. This is the period referred to by the guerrillas in the novel as "the start of the movement."
[7] *Conservative reaction:* General election of November 19, 1933.
[8] Quintanilla, the Republican artist (born 1905) who painted Hemingway's portrait. Dos Passos and Hemingway jointly sponsored an exhibition of Quintanilla's excellent work in New York City, November 20 to December 4, 1934. See Hemingway's article, *Esquire* 3 (February 1935), pp. 26-27.
[9] "Friend of Spain": See Hemingway's letter of that title, *Esquire* 1 (January 1934), pp. 26, 136. Cf. Hemingway's remark that "Spain is an open wound in the right arm that cannot heal because the dust gets in it." *Gattorno*, foreword, Havana, 1935, p. 12.

came about, he afterwards observed, because "the mass of the people were not ready for it and they did not want it." As late as 1937, the leftist Joseph Freeman could corroborate Hemingway's earlier view. One must face the issue frankly, Freeman told the Writers' Congress: "The majority of the Spanish people" did not even then "want socialism." They were fighting for "a democratic republic." [10] What made the events of the autumn of 1933 tragic in their results was the degree to which socialism had infiltrated the republican bureaucracy, and fascist thinking the minds of the reactionary army officers. The tragedy was launched in Spain.

Between 1933 and 1936, while Hemingway watched with care, the second act of the tragedy built up. Conservative elements formed a strong anti-Marxist alliance. The restive reform groups, including both moderates and extremists, banded together in a Popular Front organization, precipitating the bloody and desperate general strike of October 1934, which further widened the gap between the workers and the conservative groups. But when the 1936 elections produced a decisive Republican majority, the long-frustrated reformers moved rapidly to enforce the terms of their program. Further civil disorders followed. In March, the Army threatened to seize the government if order were not restored. In April the government countered with a thorough shake-up of the Army command, including the exile of some of the more dangerous general officers who showed Hitlerite ambi- [226/227]tions. But the efforts of the Popular Front, which was torn by internal dissensions, were neither strong nor extensive enough. On July 17, 1936, insurrections of army garrisons began all over Spain. Despite reprisal action and the immediate mobilization of a Loyalist militia, Mola and Franco moved quickly and according to a carefully prepared plan. The third act of the Spanish tragedy burst out in civil war.

To Hemingway, who had watched and commented on Acts One and Two, Act Three was no surprise. He had heard talk of the next European war in the Montparnasse cafés in the fall of 1933, and had been distressed, as any old soldier must be, by the widespread assumption that it was inevitable. In the summer of 1935 he had stated forthrightly that a war was "being prepared and brought closer each day with all the premeditation of a long-planned murder." This veteran correspondent knew that Europe had always fought; the intervals of peace were only armistices. Hitler's desire for war in Europe was obvious. Although Mussolini, Hemingway's old enemy through the 1920's, was not especially anxious for a war in Europe, he was very busy making Ethiopia "fit for Fiats." The general war, said Hemingway, would not come in 1935 or 1936, but in 1937 or 1938, "they [would] fight." He did not foresee, publicly at least, that Spain would become a sort of international testing-ground for Germany, Italy, and Russia before the Spanish Civil War was a year old. Otherwise, in selecting 1937 as a possible date for the outbreak of a war involving several European nations (which of course happened in Spain) he had made a fairly sound prediction.[11]

He began the year 1936 with a condemnation of the Ethiopian campaign, calling Mussolini "the cleverest opportunist in modern history," and noting that while the sons of the dictator were aviators in action against a non-existent Ethiopian air-force, the poor men's sons of Italy were dying as foot-soldiers. When would the poor men's sons learn who their real enemy was, and why? Hemingway had always regarded Mussolini, says Dean Gauss, as "a fakir and a grandstand player." The march on Rome in 1922 had [227/228] been possible owing to the "wave of disgust," Hemingway said, which "followed

[10] Joseph Freeman in *The Writer in a Changing World*, p. 237.
[11] See Hemingway, "A Paris Letter," *Esquire* 1 (February 1934), pp. 72, 156; "Notes on the Next War," *Esquire* 4 (September 1935), pp. 19, 156; and "The Malady of Power," *Esquire* 4 (November 1935), pp. 31, 198.

the farcical failure of the Italian radicals to cooperate."[12] But for a good many years now the Italian situation had been anything but a farce, and the grandstand player, though still a fakir, was also a dangerous force. Hemingway could not foresee that within a year of his public condemnation of Mussolini's activities in Ethiopia, the opportunist Mussolini would be moving his legions into Spain. Still less could he foretell the feelings with which former Tenente Ernesto Hemingway of the Italian infantry would walk through the scrub oak woods of Brihuega in the spring of 1937, inspecting the bodies of the poor men's sons who had died in the name of their real enemy, Il Duce.[13]

Hemingway's temperamental and long-term distrust of all behind-the-scenes "deals" and "arrangements" in Europe found ample evidence to support it among the Italian dead at Brihuega. The world was not run as the statesmen said it was run; one had to be able to distinguish between the poor players and the true owners. The "starry-eyed" of all countries, not to mention the conscripted sons of the Italian poor who would never see any more stars or anything else, were more than likely to be "sucked in." Both these phrases came frequently to Hemingway's mind whenever he wrote about European politics.

Why, then, did he bother with a country which was torn with "deals" and "arrangements"? Hemingway's answer is forthright. "There were at least five parties in the Spanish Civil War on the Republic side. I tried to understand and evaluate all five (very difficult) and belonged to none. . . . I had no party but a deep interest in and love for the Republic. . . . In Spain I had, and have, many friends on the other side. I tried to write truly about them, too. Politically, I was always on the side of the Republic from the day it was declared and for a long time before."[14] When the Civil War broke out, it was necessary for him to make a choice of proper action. [**228/229**]

II. THE BIG STAGE

He soon made up his mind, though not without some of the qualms which usually attend the realist in reaching such decisions. By the end of 1936 he had raised $40,000 on personal notes to help equip the Loyalists with ambulances and medical supplies. In January 1937 he became chairman of the Ambulance Committee, Medical Bureau, American Friends of Spanish Democracy. The name of the organization fairly described Hemingway's position and the reasons behind it.

Once you are fighting a war, as he said in 1942, you have no choice but to try to win it.[15] On this principle, he worked hard for the Loyalists, among whom were many native Spaniards who shared his interest in and love for the Republic, whatever their buried feelings about the foreign communists who were moving into Madrid to join the war against the fascist aggressors, native and foreign. From the money-raising activities of 1936 through the end of the war in 1939, he was either in Spain, or working for the Republic outside Spain, or writing about the course of the conflict. His labors took him into the heart of the war on four separate occasions.[16]

His first trip began on February 27, 1937, when he sailed on the *Paris* to report the war for the North American Newspaper Alliance. From Toulouse in mid-March he flew south to Barcelona. From there a plane carried him down the east coast, over the yellow sprawl of Valencia far below, and into the airfield at Alicante, where he found the Loyalists in a holiday mood

[12] *Ethiopian Campaign:* See Hemingway, "Wings Always Over Africa," *Esquire* 5 (January 1936), pp. 31, 174-175. CG to CB, 12/26/50.

[13] See the reprinting of EH's NANA despatch in *New Republic* 90 (May 5, 1937), pp. 376-379. The crushing defeat of Mussolini's troops occurred in the period of March 11-23, 1937.

[14] EH to CB, 4/1/51.

[15] *Men At War,* introd., p. xi.

[16] *Four trips to Spain:* Besides the newspaper reports of Hemingway's arrivals and departures as listed in *New York Times Index* for these years, see the further reprintings of NANA despatches in the *New Republic:* Vols. 93 (January 12, 1938), pp. 273-276; 94 (April 27, 1938), pp. 350-351; and 95 (June 8, 1938), pp. 124-126.

over the recent defeat of the Italians at Brihuega.

When Hemingway reached the battle-field, getting up at dawn of a late March morning and driving up from Valencia, the Italian dead still lay where they had fallen. As an objective reporter, he was compelled to conclude that, whatever his own low opinion of Mussolini, and whatever Loyalist propaganda might say to the [**229/230**] contrary, the Italian poor men's sons had died bravely, the victims of superior fire-power, strong air attacks, and inadequate protection from the rocky terrain. These dead did not look to an objective observer like fascist devils cowering in death before the Marxist angels of destruction. They were men who had been killed. They were another example of *Los Desastres de la Guerra*. One more of Europe's intermittent periods of armistice had ended and these were among the victims.

As a friend to the Spanish Republic, Hemingway was ready to help with the development of a documentary film, *The Spanish Earth*.[17] During April and early May he joined the young Dutch director, Joris Ivens, and his cameraman, John Ferno, working in and near besieged Madrid. Wearing a Basque beret, wind-breaker, and heavy field boots, the American guide made a picturesque figure. The film-makers had set up an observation post only ten minutes' walk away, and they watched Miaja's Loyalist strikes in the depression below the city, or photographed the mangled bodies of the Madrileños in the streets and squares where Rebel artillery had permanently interrupted their civilian lives. Like every other Loyalist sympathizer who saw the results, Hemingway resented the totalitarian tactics of murdering non-participant citizenry with high explosives. The Rebels, as he told the Writers' Congress in [**230/231**] June, had been beaten in every major engagement up to that date; what they could not win in the military way, they sought to win by the mass-murder of civilian populations.

Often, at considerable personal risk, Ivens, Ferno, and Hemingway moved out into the hills of Morata de Tajuña to get pictures of tanks and infantry in action. Ivens and Ferno sometimes distressed their companion by unrealistically exposing themselves to enemy fire. Hemingway cabled MacLeish that there was some doubt about Ivens' survival because he was taking the daily risks of a regular infantry officer. In his turn, Hemingway distressed his companions by carrying strong Spanish onions in the pockets of his field-jacket as a means of assuaging hunger. For battle-thirst, the trio carried a large flat silver flask of whiskey. It was always empty by four in the afternoon until they discovered the wisdom of bringing along an auxiliary bottle.

In 1940, looking back on this spring of 1937, Hemingway said that "the period of fighting when we thought that the Republic could win was the happiest period of our lives." For the duration of that war, except for writing his play, he contented himself with NANA despatches, a few short stories, and the brief script of *The Spanish Earth*.[18] He might have agreed, if

[17] *The Spanish Earth:* 1000 copies of the sound-film text (it was exhibited in silent form, with spoken commentary by Ivens, at the Writers' Congress) were published in Cleveland, Ohio (J. B. Savage Company, June 1938), The 60-page book contains an emotional and somewhat inaccurate introduction by Jasper Wood and decorations by Frederick K. Russell. Besides the introduction, the text consists entirely of a transcript of Hemingway's sound-track commentary, and "The Heat and the Cold," a short reminiscence of experiences in Spain during the filming, written by Hemingway and reprinted from *Verve* (Spring 1938). The film was undertaken in aid of the people of Spain by an organization called *Contemporary Historians*, including John Dos Passos, Lillian Hellman, Archibald MacLeish, and Ernest Hemingway. All of these had early recognized the threat of fascism to the free world. The film itself was designed to show the efforts of the Spanish peasantry to reclaim for agricultural purposes land which had been misused and neglected for many generations. Because of the war, their efforts were defeated and they were betrayed. The film's six-reel message could be summed up in the directive: get rid of war. The film seeks dramatic focus by recounting in part the experiences of a young Spaniard named Julian who comes from the village of Fuenteduena.

[18] See "The Heat and the Cold" reference in note 17, and also the remarks by A. MacLeish, *The Writer in a Changing World*, p. 206. Ivens had left the U.S. December 26, 1936, and was in and near Madrid from January 1, 1937, until early May. See also Hemingway's preface to Gustav Regler, *The Great Crusade*, New York, 1940, p. viii.

A brief glimpse of Hemingway in Spain is pro-

confronted with it, to the sentiments of Philip Freneau's couplet:

> An age employed in edging steel
> Can no poetic raptures feel.[19]

Poetic raptures in Freneau's sense of the phrase had never much engaged Hemingway. But during the long armistice between his discharge from the Italian base-hospital and the outbreak of new hostilities in Europe, he had felt justified in learning to write and in continuing to mind it as his proper business. Having served [231/232] time "for society, democracy, and the other things quite young," he had felt no compulsion to enlist in the French Foreign Legion or to aid the Chinese in throwing back the Japanese invaders. His clear responsibility, as he saw it, was to the art of writing well, and he willingly exchanged the "pleasant, comforting stench of comrades" for the job of the individualist artist who must work alone if he is to get his work done.[20]

Now, however, he reversed the procedure, declining further writing until the war could be won and the fascist menace —with its enmity towards all honest writers—could be reduced in scale. It was a reasonably happy period for him because it was something like the old times in Italy along the lower Piave where he had served nearly twenty years earlier. The stench of brave comrades was as pleasant and comforting in the spring of 1937 as it had been in the spring of 1918. The cause was at least as good and possibly better. There was also the reasonable expectation that if one survived, with all that he had learned about the art of writing during the long armistice, he had a chance of writing a book about this war which would be better than any of the earlier books.

Though politics had brought the war on, it had little to do with the comradeship among the Loyalist soldiers in whose company Hemingway now moved. They were of all political persuasions from militant Comintern communism to the point

around the center where—as artist, American, semi-detached observer, student of war, and unpartied supporter of the Spanish Republic—Hemingway stood. The Eleventh and Twelfth Brigades (really the First and Second) were his chief centers of operation. The Eleventh was German. Though they were ardent anti-Nazis and had a remarkable commander named Hans, "most of them were communists" and "they were a little serious to spend much time with." Hemingway's Republican heart was with the Twelfth Brigade, a very mixed group politically, a memorably gay assemblage as comrades. One staunch friend was Werner Heilbrun, the medical officer of the outfit. He could always provide transport, good cheer, or a hot meal at night for the dusty and famished wayfarers. Heilbrun was killed in a strafing attack at Huesca soon after the Carnegie Hall speech, and Hemingway donated to his widow the [232/233] proceeds from the printed version of *The Spanish Earth*. Another friend was Gustav Regler, calm, cheerful, tough, and one of the ablest fighting officers in the brigade. His novel, *The Great Crusade,* was published in the United States in 1940, translated by Whittaker Chambers and Barrows Mussey, and with a preface by Hemingway. The commander of the Twelfth, General Lucasz, was one of Hemingway's good friends, and a good gay man at their party of May 1, playing a tune on a pencil held against his teeth. A month later, Lucasz, too, was dead.[21]

By May 19, Hemingway was back in the United States. Between this date and his departure again on August 14 he was extremely busy. He had accepted an invitation to speak before the general assembly of the forthcoming Writers' Congress. With this out of the way he pre-

vided by Constancia de la Mora, *In Place of Splendor*, New York, 1939, p. 290. See also the vignette in Stephen Spender, *World Within World*, New York, 1951, pp. 229-231.
[19] Philip Freneau, "To an Author" (1788), lines 35-36.
[20] *GHOA*, p. 148.
[21] Hemingway's preface to Regler, *Great Crusade*, pp. vii-x.

pared the sound-track for *The Spanish Earth,* working with Ivens throughout. By July 8, the film was ready and that evening, on invitation from the White House, Ivens and Hemingway showed the film to President and Mrs. Roosevelt. Later showings brought thousands of dollars in voluntary contributions to Loyalist Spain, and the public release came in New York in August. The brawl with Max Eastman on August 11 in the office of Maxwell Perkins was a comic interlude.[22] Three days later Hemingway sailed back to the tragedy.

On this second visit (August 14, 1937–January 28, 1938) he found that the third act of the tragedy had moved well along. "Où sont les amis d'antan?" he might now have asked himself, except that he already knew. Lucasz and Heilbrun were dead and buried; Regler, wounded by a pound and a half of steel which un- [233/234] covered his kidneys and exposed the spinal cord, lived to be put in a French concentration camp after the Spanish war was over. Madrid itself, "the capital of the world," was a tangle of bitter and cynical intrigue. If the winter and spring of 1937 had been the golden age of the International Brigades, now was the winter of their discontent.

This second trip produced *The Fifth Column.* Despite its historical interest, it is a bad play. Written in the Hotel Florida in a dollar-a-day room (low price: high danger) exposed to the German batteries on Garabitas Hill, the play was completed and sent out of the country late in December 1937, just before the taking of Teruel. It sought to present Hemingway's tough-minded apprehension of the state of things in Madrid that fall. Civilians were dying in the daily bombardments, food was becoming scarcer, hopes of lifting the siege were growing dim, and the malignant growth of treason operated deep in the city. By comparison and in retrospect, the spring of 1937 had been gay.

Whatever its dramatic shortcomings, *The Fifth Column* was an attempt to draw the actual Madrid of the fall of 1937 as

it might have appeared in the uncensored despatches of a very objective war correspondent. Like the film, the play showed that war is hell. Unlike the film, the play showed that at some level and out of necessity, war is waged by demons. Though still nominally sympathetic to the Republic, *The Fifth Column* could hardly be described as a vehicle for Loyalist propaganda. When he published it in 1938 (before the end of the war), Hemingway answered those "fanatical defenders of the Spanish Republic" who protested that his play did not sufficiently emphasize "the nobility and dignity of the Spanish people." This was a play about the regrettable necessity of fanaticism. It was not intended to show nobility and dignity. To present any adequate idea of the complex Spanish temperament or the even more complex Spanish predicament would require many plays and many novels. *The Fifth Column,* meanwhile, was in the nature of an on-the-spot report, and a prediction of things to come. Hemingway did not pretend that it was much more than that.[23] [234/235]

The background action of *The Fifth Column* is, in the play, what it was in the cellars of Madrid in 1937, a cloak-and-pistol, spy-and-counter-spy struggle of the

[22] For a dispassionate account of what happened in the office of Maxwell Perkins on the fifth floor at 597 Fifth Avenue on August 11, 1937, see the *New York Times* for August 14 (p. 15), August 15 (p. 31), and August 16 (p. 21). Of comic interest is an item in the catalogue of the House of Books, Ltd., *First Editions of Modern Authors with a Notable Hemingway Collection,* New York, n.d., p. 40. A copy of Max Eastman's *Art and the Life of Action,* New York, 1934, is there offered for $75. According to the note, this damaged copy (lacking pp. 7-84) shows on p. 95 a spot caused by contact "with Mr. Eastman's nose when Mr. Hemingway struck him with it in a gesture of disapproval of the critical essay 'Bull in the Afternoon.'" In the lower right hand corner is a presentation inscription in Hemingway's hand, "For Arnold [Gingrich] from Papa [Hemingway]," witnessed by the signature of Maxwell Perkins, August 12, 1937.

[23] See Hemingway's preface to *The First Forty-nine Stories,* New York, 1938, for a short account of the composition of the play and of the author's views on his material. "While I was writing the play," he says (p. v), "the Hotel Florida . . . was struck by more than thirty high explosive shells. So if it is not a good play perhaps that is what is the matter with it." His view of the play in November 1951 was that it is probably the most unsatisfactory thing he ever wrote. After much bad luck and several false starts, the play was adapted by Benjamin Glaser and produced by the Theatre Guild in New York in the winter of 1940.

most ruthless and melodramatic kind. In the foreground of the play, however, are two of Hemingway's familiar oppositions: home against war, and the lover against the lonely and essentially womanless worker. The hero is an Anglo-American soldier of fortune named Philip Rawlings. Ostensibly a blasé war-correspondent more given to playboying than to workhorsing, he is secretly a Republican agent in the fight against fascist infiltration. Though his job sometimes nauseates him, he believes that he understands its importance. He performs creditably and coldly. His human sensibilities are stirred, however, by an American named Dorothy Bridges. While she plays at being a war-correspondent, she too has secret plans: to marry Philip. One might construe her name as a pun. She bridges the gap back to the past, the years before fascism turned imperialistic, and when man's inhumanity to man was at least somewhat less spectacular than at present. "Her name," says Hemingway, "might also have been Nostalgia."

Philip's choice is between home and war—leaving Madrid with the girl or continuing to fight fascism. "If the play has a moral," writes Hemingway, "it is that people who work for certain organizations have very little time for home life." Without concurring in the politics or G.P.U. methods of the organization he serves (and he resembles Robert Jordan in that respect), Philip chooses to stay on in Madrid. In the closing scene he sums up the kind of life he might conceivably live with Dorothy Bridges:

"A thousand breakfasts . . . on trays in the thousand fine mornings of the next three years. . . . Auteuil steeplechasing . . . and nip back into the bar for a champagne cocktail and ride back in to dinner at La Rue's and weekends go to shoot pheasants in the Sologne. . . . And fly out to Nairobi and the old Ma- [**235/236**] thaiga Club . . . [or] . . . to Lamu where the long white beach is, with the dhows beached on their sides, and the wind in the palms at night. . . . Or . . . Malindi

where you can surfboard on the beach . . . [or] the Sans Souci in Havana . . . to dance in the Patio. . . ."

Sans-Souci is the word for it. Dorothy wants to know why they can't visit these places together. But they are all behind Philip like a distant past. "Where I go now I go alone, or with others who go there for the same reason I go." This is the region of man at work, man without woman. Rawlings, soldier of fortune, has given up the pursuit of happiness for the pursuit of enemies of liberty. "We're in for fifty years of undeclared wars," he tells Comrade Max, "and I've signed up for the duration."

Hemingway is not, of course, to be confused with Rawlings. As an artist whose books had been banned in Fascist Italy, and as the friend of many honest Spaniards who had suffered heavily in trying to inaugurate and consolidate the Republic, he had personal reasons for hating fascism. Russian-style communism was scarcely better, though friends of the Spanish Republic, once the war broke out, had no choice but to work with this wing of the popular front coalition. But the writer's problem was different from that of Philip Rawlings. Whatever happened to soldiers of fortune during a half-century of undeclared wars, Hemingway's obligation was still to tell the truth as he saw it.

To learn the truth he made two more extended visits to Spain. The third trip began on March 19, 1938. When he returned for the summer on May 31, he told American reporters that the Loyalists would win, though they were now clearly on the defensive. Privately, however, he must have known that they were doomed. Too much of Spain had fallen to Franco and company. Too many foreign powers were pouring in men and material on the wrong side. Fifth columns were at work in major cities. The Madrileños were starving. By far the gloomiest trip of all was the fourth, beginning September first. That winter saw the collapse. Barcelona fell late in January, and Madrid followed at the end of March.

One had no feeling of tragic catharsis when the curtain came down on Act III of Spain's tragedy. You could already hear them shifting the scenery in preparation for the gigantic epilogue. [236/237]

III. PARTISAN

The publication of *For Whom the Bell Tolls* on October 21, 1940, raised again (as Freeman had raised it in 1937) the question of Hemingway's political colors. Once more, as in the 1930's, certain critics failed to take his position as artist sufficiently into account. Mr. Edmund Wilson, for example, referred (quite erroneously) to Hemingway's "Stalinism." Hemingway flatly denies the allegation: "I had no Stalinist period." To Mr. Edwin Burgum, on the other hand, *For Whom the Bell Tolls* seemed to offer evidence that Hemingway was a fascist in spite of himself. Such claims stood at the extremes.[24]

One of the editors of *Time* magazine hailed the story of Robert Jordan as the work of a great and sensitive artist who had now safely recovered from the Red rash.[25] In spite of the compliment at the beginning of the sentence, it ended with a statement which still misrepresented Hemingway's position. He had never caught the Marxist measles. His devotion to truth in art was too effective a means of self-immunization. He knew that to propagandize is to lie, and that the complications which accompany lying may turn a simple rash to a fatal disease. He was immunized, so to speak, by esthetic principle, even if he had not been immunized by lengthy study of the European scene.

He had long since declared against the writer's making a career of politics. But to describe the effect of political forces on the individual life was quite another matter. Where the finger or the fist of power brings pressure on the human being, the artist may [237/238] legitimately move to his work. This was the situation with the old man at a bridge across the Ebro

on Easter Sunday 1938. In his lone retreat from San Carlos, this old Spaniard had been obliged to abandon a cat, two goats, and eight pigeons. He was concerned for their welfare.

"What politics have you?" asked Hemingway.

"I am without politics," said the Spaniard. "I am seventy-six years old. I have come twelve kilometers now and I think I can go no further."

Because of the weather, the fascist air force was neither bombing nor strafing that day. This fact, together with the probability that the abandoned cat, at least, could look out for itself, was the grand total of the old man's Easter luck.[26]

One displaced person in the spring of 1938 helped to dramatize for Hemingway the artist the predicament of the Spanish people. About the middle of March 1939 he began to write his great novel on the predicament of the Spanish people during their Civil War. He chose as his focal point a group of Republican partisans, drawn from many parts of Spain, and living under very primitive conditions in a cave on the high forested slopes of the Sierra de Guadarramas sixty miles northwest of besieged Madrid and behind the fascist lines. The time he chose was the sixty-eight-hour period between Saturday afternoon and Tuesday noon of the last week of May 1937. He worked on the book steadily for a period of eighteen months, rewriting it every day and doing the final revisions on galley proof. When his labors

[24] For Mr. Wilson's reference to Hemingway's "Stalinism" see McCaffery, *Ernest Hemingway: The Man and His Work*, p. 256. Hemingway has, it is alleged, "largely sloughed off his Stalinism" and reverted "to seeing events in terms of individuals pitted against dumb odds." Hemingway denied the implication, EH to CB, 4/1/51. Burgum's essay is in McCaffery, pp. 308-328, and is generally inaccurate. Among the pejorative judgments on *FWBT* is Alfred Kazin's. He calls this novel "among the least of Hemingway's works." McCaffery, p. 202. Maxwell Geismar said of *FWBT* that it "remains inchoate in its comprehension of the central social issues of our time." McCaffery, p. 186. Malcolm Cowley, on the other hand, agrees with the judgment of the present writer that *FWBT* is Hemingway's best novel.

[25] *Time* 36 (October 21, 1940), p. 95.

[26] *The First Forty-nine Stories*, p. 177. Mr. Kazin suggests, quite rightly, that "it was in something of this spirit" (*i.e.* of "Old Man at the Bridge") that Hemingway wrote *FWBT*.

were over he had written the great book about the Spanish Civil War. One could not call it a book "without politics." Yet it was important to point out that the politics had been dramatically embodied in a work of fiction whose moral values transcended political affiliations.[27] [238/239]

The driving emotion behind *For Whom the Bell Tolls* is Hemingway's sense of the betrayal of the Spanish people. Not only were they "killed in vast numbers, starved out, deprived of weapons" but they were also "betrayed."[28] Worst of all was the betrayal. In a decade of notable betrayals the events in Spain between 1936 and 1939 dwarfed the betrayals of the Abyssinians and the Czechs. The nature of the betrayal of the Spanish people was complex in the extreme. What had chiefly caused it—internal cancer or rape by international hoodlums? The intervention of foreign powers was clearly an important factor in the prolongation of the war and the ultimate fascist victory. The wanton destruction of Guernica—an excellent example of betrayal—was evidently undertaken as a test of German bombing equipment. Hemingway's *Spanish Earth* commentary was quite possibly correct in maintaining that the Army insurrection which opened the war could have been put down in six weeks if German and Italian aid had not been made available to Franco's professionals.

Hemingway's own perspective on the fascist-communist struggle, which had been going on sporadically throughout Europe since the close of World War I, might have indicated a kind of [239/240] tragic inevitability to foreign intervention in Spain's internal troubles. Yet these troubles had been serious before the foreign powers moved in, as Hemingway had duly noted in 1933. The outbreak of the war did not suddenly make an efficient machine from a somewhat inefficient and internally divided republican bureaucracy. Nor was it likely that the native Spanish conservatives would reject the advances of their foreign allies. Any genuinely true picture of the Spanish struggle would need

somehow to embody all of these considerations, and to bring them to dramatic focus in the lives of a group of people whose backgrounds and present mode of behavior would fairly represent the total betrayal of Spain.

As he worked through the complexities of his task, Hemingway was sustained by a belief he had long held to: the job of the artist is not to judge but to understand. No matter how hard it may be to believe it in our political age, there is such a thing as the artistic "neutrality" of one who puts humanity above politics and art above propaganda. What Melville said of Captain Vere, the hero of *Billy Budd,* is applicable to the artist Hemingway. "There had got to be established in him some positive convictions which . . . would abide in him essentially unmodified so long as his intelligent part remained unimpaired. . . . His settled convictions were as a dyke against those invading waters of

---

[27] Hemingway's progress with his novel may be summarized for the record. By March 25, 1939, he had done about 15,000 words. On May 10, he was still going well, averaging 700-1000 words daily. At this time he reiterated to Perkins that the thing to do with a novel was to finish it, as the thing to do with a war was to win it. By July 10, his MS stood at 56,000 words (14 chapters) ; and by July 26, 64,000. He spent the summer in the west, working steadily, and by October 27 had 90,000 words. He [238/239] now told Perkins that the book was designed to contain what people with party affiliations could never write, or even perhaps know, or (if they knew) allow themselves to think. He was then on the point of writing a "part about Madrid" (possibly the present Chapter 18, where Madrid material is inserted as a flashback).

Chapter 23 was finished on January 18, 1940, in Havana. About this time he told Perkins that while under arms he was faithful and loyal to his side, but that, once a war was over, he was a writer—not a Catholic writer or a Party writer or anything but a writer. February 18 found him in the midst of the El Sordo story (Chapter 27). By April 6 he was well into Chapter 33, and thought briefly of *The Undiscovered Country* as a title. By April 22, however, he had settled on *For Whom the Bell Tolls* (Donne's devotion, located in *The Oxford Book of English Prose,* p. 171).

Late in May the end was in sight. He finished Chapter 40 on May 21 and ten days later was in the midst of Chapter 42. Between early June and July 12 he finished Chapter 43 (the last) and worked through his manuscript. For the next two weeks, as copy began to go to the printer, he continued reworking, chapter by chapter. The book was in galley proof by August 13. On September 10, he air-mailed the final 18 galleys from Sun Valley, Idaho, to New York. The total time for writing and revision was thus almost exactly eighteen months.

[28] Hemingway's preface to Regler, *Great Crusade,* p. vii.

novel opinion, social, political, or otherwise, which carried away as in a torrent no few minds in those days."[29] Hemingway's "dyke" is a belief in the artist's obligation to truth and to art, and to humanity in its extra-political dimension.

For Whom the Bell Tolls offers many examples of the author's determination to maintain that balance without which art may degenerate into propaganda. One of the most conspicuous is Pilar's account of the massacre of the leading citizens of a town near Avila by Pablo and his mob. Pilar has the artist's observational and almost clinical interest in how each of the fascists will die. Deeper than this interest runs her sense of the humanity of the killed and the strange furious mixture of bestiality and humanity among the killers. She watches the spectacle with a cold fascination. But her humanity is revealed in the sick disgust which [240/241] assails her from time to time, as it troubles some of the individuals in the mob itself. One finds explicit recognition of how far out of the line of right human action this mob-murder is. But there is also a strong implicit suggestion of the criminal neglect, the inhuman apathy which has allowed the social situation in the villages of Spain to deteriorate so far that such mob action is now the sole recourse of the underdogs. After the massacre, says Pilar, "I went back inside the room and I sat there and I did not wish to think, for that was the worst day of my life until one other day." The "other day" was the day of reckoning. It came seventy-two hours later when the Fascists took the town.[30]

Pilar has led a hard life and is as tough as an old eagle. Yet the heart still beats for humankind even when the head coldly admits the need for violent activity against the enemy. Pilar's sentiments find many echoes among the more sympathetic characters of the novel. When they are put together, they show clearly that, unlike Picasso's "Guernica," *For Whom the Bell Tolls* is not a study in black and white. It is a study of the betrayal of the Spanish people—both by what lay within them and

what had been thrust upon them—and it is presented with that special combination of sympathetic involvement and hardheaded detachment which is the mark of the genuine artist. One could not rightly call the novel bipartisan. Yet it is partisan in a larger way than the modern use of the term ordinarily suggests. Its partisanship is in the cause of humanity.

The artist behind his dyke of conviction must likewise be able to understand the nature of these minds which the torrent of opinion carries along in its sweep. Hemingway's grasp of the motivations which strengthened and united, but also split, the extreme leftists is well illustrated in Jordan's contrast between the two communisms of Madrid.[31] One was symbolized in Velázquez 63, the palace which served as headquarters for the International Brigades. Here was the almost puritanical, religious-crusader's side of party feeling. It gave its adherents something like "the feeling you expected to have and did not have when you made your [241/242] first communion. . . . It gave you a part in something that you could believe in wholly and completely and in which you felt an absolute brotherhood with the others who were engaged in it." The religious reference emphasizes how far this secular substitute for religion—a substitute with its own propaganda-built hagiology and its own liturgy—had been able to go in capturing the devotions of foreign idealists.

Six months of the fighting effectively dissipated such devotions for any who kept their eyes and ears open. The idealist involved was shortly aware of the other symbol—the hotel called Gaylord's where the Russian directors of the Republican movement had congregated. Gaylord's symbolized the cold, practical, hardheaded, cynical ruthlessness of the Comintern mind, completely unsentimental and

---

[29] Melville, *Billy Budd, Foretopman*, Chapter 6.
[30] Pilar's account of the massacre occurs on pp. 99-129.
[31] *FWBT*, pp. 234-235. Cf. Jordan's view (p. 230): "He liked to know how it really was, not how it was supposed to be."

in no way deceived by the propaganda which it daily originated and disseminated. A part of the struggle in Spain lay in the attempt of the idealist to keep his devoutness whole in the face of the actualistic education he got at Gaylord's.

Another of the tensions at work under the surface of Spain's tragedy is dramatized through the boy Joaquín, one of the republican partisans on El Sordo's chancre-like hilltop. This is the conflict between the Catholic faith and the secular pseudo-religion of the communists. At eighteen, Joaquín is just old enough in 1937 to have been raised under the wing of the Church, and just young enough to have suffered irreparably when the fascists shot his parents in Valladolid. Joaquín is imbued now with party doctrine. He especially reverences La Pasionaria, the secularist Joan of Arc in Marxist Spain.

While El Sordo's men prepare their hilltop position, Joaquín admiringly quotes La Pasionaria's slogan: *Resistir y fortificar es vencer*—to hold out and to fortify is to win. The boy is obliged to endure some good-natured raillery from those of his companions to whom such propagandist watchwords are a dirty joke. Yet through the early stages of the fight on the hilltop La Pasionaria sustains him well. Then the planes come. Joaquín has not considered the vulnerability of even Pasionaria-built fortifications to attack from the air. While the drone of the fascist bombers grows in intensity, Joaquín, heavy with dread, begins to invoke [**242/243**] La Pasionaria once again. This time her words stick in his dry throat.

Then he shifted suddenly into "Hail Mary, full of grace, the Lord is with thee; Blessed art thou among women and Blessed is the fruit of thy womb, Jesus. Holy Mary, Mother of God, pray for us sinners now and at the hour of our death. Amen, Holy Mary, Mother of God," he started, then he remembered quick as the roar came now unbearably and started an act of contrition racing in it, "Oh my God, I am heartily sorry for having of-

fended thee who art worthy of all my love. . . ."

When the explosions of the fascist bombs roll under the boy at the very moment of his losing consciousness, he is still repeating the petitional phrase, "Now and at the hour of our death." La Pasionaria is for other times.[32]

La Pasionaria is for bringing passionately inspired news of Marxist victories. She is the occasion for a fine travesty on sentimental propagandists like the *Izvestia* correspondent at Gaylord's hotel.

"She was here with the news and was in such a state of radiant exultation as I have never seen. The truth of the news shone from her face. That great face . . ." says the correspondent happily. . . . "It was one of the greatest moments of the war to me when I heard the report in that great voice where pity, compassion and truth are blended. Goodness and truth shine from her as from a true saint of the people. Not for nothing is she called La Pasionaria."

"Not for nothing," says the other correspondent in a dull voice. "You better write it for *Izvestia* now, before you forget that last beautiful lead."[33]

In the welter of opposed hatreds and in the company of sentimental mystics, the artist must keep his human and moral values unimpaired. Of the native Spaniards in the book, none better exemplifies the right human norm than Anselmo, Jordan's sixty-eight-year-old guide and friend. Other members of Pablo's band show the range of political and moral attitudes across the popular [**243/244**] front. At one extreme is the blood-thirst of Pablo, not unlike that of the moonfaced Cuban revolutionist in *To Have and Have Not*. Near him, though at a higher level, stands the brave, relentless, fanatical hater, Agustín, who fiercely says that he would like to swim ten leagues in a broth made from the *cojones* of all the fascists.[34] At the opposite extreme stands, or rather lolls, the irresponsible paganism of the gypsy

[32] *FWBT*, p. 134.
[33] *FWBT*, pp. 357-358.
[34] *FWBT*, p. 286.

Rafael. But Anselmo willingly endures discomfort out of loyalty to Jordan's trust, as Rafael would obviously never do. And unlike Pablo or Agustín, Anselmo, with the wisdom of his years, still hates killing even while he admits that it is necessary.

Anselmo's important function is to serve as a yardstick of human values, as Kent does in *King Lear*. "That we should win the war and shoot nobody," he fiercely cries. "That we should govern justly and that all should participate in the benefits according as they have striven for them. And that those who have fought against us should be educated to see their error." The Republic must win and Anselmo will fight for the Republic. Yet much that he must do cuts cruelly across the absolute Christian grain of this admirable old man. With Anselmo as a norm, the tragedy of Spain shows all the darker.[35]

Like Anselmo, Robert Jordan is capable of working for a cause without allowing its heretical errors to eat their way like acid into his deeper convictions. Knowing the inside of both Velázquez 63 and the hotel called Gaylord's, Jordan can qualify as the educated man who is in no way "sucked in." Working efficiently as a dynamiter with the Republican guerrillas, loving Spain, hating fascism, sympathizing with the people who have been and are being betrayed, Jordan still manages to be temperate without being at all tepid. His brain is neither dominated nor deceived by the propagandistic. He remains the free man, the man not taken in, the man doing the necessary job but also making the necessary mental reservations.

Jordan's soliloquy—as he listens from below to the hilltop bat- [**244/245**] tle in which El Sordo's partisans die—is a key passage in this connection. He reflects that he is in love with Maria, even though "there isn't supposed to be any such thing as love in a purely materialistic conception of society." Then he catches himself. Since when did he really entertain any such conception?

"Never. And you never could have. You're not a real Marxist and you know it.

You believe in Liberty, Equality, and Fraternity. You believe in Life, Liberty, and the Pursuit of Happiness. Don't ever kid yourself with too much dialectics. They are for some but they are not for you. You have to know them in order not to be a sucker. You have put many things in abeyance to win a war. If this war is lost all of those things are lost. But afterwards you can discard what you do not believe in. There is plenty you do not believe in and plenty that you do believe in."[36]

Robert Jordan is with, but not of, the communists. For the duration of the war he is under communist discipline because they offer "the best discipline and the soundest and sanest for the prosecution of the [Spanish] war."[37] This is simple common sense, just as (though Robert Jordan did not live to see it) it was probably common sense for the Allies to fight side by side with the Russians in the second World War—in order to win it. But where the communist dialectic runs contrary to the older dialectics of the French and the American Revolutions, Jordan will remain as an essential nonconformist, a free man not taken in, though doing his part in the perennial attempts which free men must make if the concept of freedom is to last.

IV. THE EPIC GENRE

The structural form of *For Whom the Bell Tolls* has been conceived with care and executed with the utmost brilliance. The form is that of a series of concentric circles with the all-important bridge in the middle. The great concentration which Hemingway achieves is partly dependent on his skill in keeping attention [**245/**

[35] *FWBT*, p. 285. Cf. Jordan's comment (p. 287) that Anselmo is "a Christian. Something very rare in Catholic countries." And see the excellent Chapter 15 (pp. 191-201), containing Anselmo's soliloquy on the sin of killing.
[36] *FWBT*, p. 305. With this compare Willard Thorp's remark: "Where does the democratic faith live and speak if not in the pages of *For Whom the Bell Tolls?*" See Margaret Denny and William H. Gilman, eds., *The American Writer and the European Tradition*, Minneapolis, 1950, p. 100.
[37] *FWBT*, p. 163.

246] focussed on the bridge while projecting the reader imaginatively far beyond that center of operations. Chapter One immediately establishes the vital strategic importance of the bridge in the coming action. Frequent allusions to the bridge keep it in view through the second chapter, and in Chapter Three Jordan goes with Anselmo to make a preliminary inspection. From that time onwards until its climactic destruction, the bridge continues to stand unforgettably as the focal point in the middle of an ever widening series of circles.

The brilliance of execution becomes apparent when the reader stands in imagination on the flooring of the bridge and looks in any direction. He will see his horizons lifting by degrees towards a circumference far beyond the Guadarrama mountains. For the guerrillas' central task, the blowing of the bridge, is only one phase of a larger operation which Hemingway once called "the greatest holding action in history." Since the battle strategy which requires the bridge to be destroyed is early made available to the reader, he has no difficulty in seeing its relation to the next circle outside, where a republican division under General Golz prepares for an attack. The general's attack, in turn, is enough to suggest the outlines of the whole civil war, while the Heinkel bombers and Fiat pursuit planes which cut across the circle—foreign shadows over the Spanish earth—extend our grasp one more circle outwards to the trans-European aspect of the struggle. The outermost ring of the circle is nothing less than the great globe itself. Once the Spanish holding operation is over, the wheel of fire will encompass the earth. The bridge, therefore—such is the structural achievement of this novel—becomes the hub on which the "future of the human race can turn."[38] Wherever the reader moves along the circumferences of the various circles, all radial roads lead to and from this bridge.

If the reader of *For Whom the Bell Tolls* is hardly cramped for space, he is also free to range in time. Jordan's action,

particularized though it is, has also a significance *sub specie aeterni-* [246/247] *tatis.* The timelessness of the central event invites the reader to compare it with all those other small and local holding actions which are stuck like gems in the web of history and tend to assume an importance out of all proportion to their size. One civil war easily suggests another, as in Jordan's memories of his grandfather who bore arms in America's war of the rebellion. Behind that, in the long perspective, is the bridge where the republican (and anti-monarchist) "peasants" of Concord fired the shot heard round the world. On a bridge across the Tiber young Horatius delayed briefly the advance of a superior force. Still farther back is the action of Leonidas against the Persian host at the hot gates of Thermopylae. The terrain and the odds were not, after all, far different from those of Robert Jordan. There is even the prediction, comparable to Pilar's, that Leonidas will die, and there is a lone Persian cavalryman who comes, like the fascist horseman in Hemingway, to reconnoitre the mountain pass. Jordan could never complain with Eliot's Gerontion that he had not fought at "the hot gates." His bridge is at the center of the history of holding actions; and although his problem is small in scale, it is so conceived and projected as to suggest a struggle of epical dimensions.

In making such a claim for Hemingway's novel, one must reckon with his own assertion that "all bad writers are in love with the epic." Even a few gifted writers have fallen into the error of attempting too much or going about it in the wrong way. The conscious striving for an epic magnitude, as in some of Whitman's poetry and much of Wolfe's prose, may reduce the writing to rhetoric and enlarge the people to set-piece characters whose resemblance to human beings is merely co-

[38] *FWBT*, p. 43. Cf. Sinclair Lewis's view that *FWBT* crystallizes "the world revolution that began long ago . . . and that will not cease till the human world has either been civilized or destroyed." Lewis, introd., Limited Editions Club reprint of *FWBT*, Princeton University Press, 1942, p. ix.

incidental. There is also the danger that the struggle for the cosmic may backslide into the comic. The grand manner too easily inflates to the grandiose; good sense may be sacrificed to size; quantity may be mistaken for quality; and what was meant to be great will become simply gross.

As a prose epic of the Spanish people, *For Whom the Bell Tolls* commits none of these errors. Indeed the novel is a living example of how, in modern times, the epic quality must probably be projected. The failure of certain modern practitioners of the [247/248] epic manner rests perhaps primarily upon ignorance of the uses of synecdoche, the device by which a part can be made to function for the whole, and the fact to gain an emblematic power without the loss of its native particularity. Hemingway's war novel, rich as it is in symbolic extensions, is somewhere near a synecdochist's triumph.

What elements of the epic manner may be successfully adapted to modern needs? Despite the obvious gap between Spain and Ilium, the student of the epic may find part of his answer in considering the Homeric parallel. A primitive setting, simple food and wine, the care and use of weapons, the sense of imminent danger, the emphasis on masculine prowess, the presence of varying degrees of courage and cowardice, the rude barbarisms on both sides, the operation of certain religious and magical superstitions, the warrior codes—these, surely, are common ties between the two sets of protagonists. Jordan is not to be scorned as the type of Achilles, and one can recognize in Pablo the rude outlines of a debased and sulking Ajax. Pilar the gypsy, though she reads the life-line in Jordan's palm instead of consulting the shape and color of animal entrails, makes the consciousness of the supernatural an operative factor.

Nor should the technical comparisons be overlooked. One of the most interesting of these is the intentionally heightened language. Mr. Edward Fenimore has published a valuable essay on the subject. He remarks, for instance, on "the Elizabethan

tone" of a number of phrases and sentences.

"That such a tone should haunt Hemingway's pages is [he goes on] inevitable. His tale has much of the epic in its breadth, in the plain fact that his characters mean more than themselves alone, the action they are engaged upon [being] unmistakably a culminating point pushed up by profound national or . . . universal forces. In the Elizabethan, the English possesses an epic language, and it is into the forms of this language that Hemingway, through the very nature of the world he is creating . . . constantly passes."[39] [248/249]

Yet, as Fenimore observes, this language is carefully tempered. A purely colloquial modern English and an English which belongs in its essence to the King James version of the Bible are brought together to mutual advantage. One example is a brief interchange between the rough-spoken Agustín and the supremely dignified Fernando—who is, incidentally, one of Hemingway's best-drawn minor characters.

"Where the hell are you going?" Agustín asked the grave little man as he came up.

"To my duty," Fernando said with dignity.

"Thy duty," said Agustín mockingly. "I besmirch the milk of thy duty. . . ."[40]

Several of Hemingway's short stories had made a similar collocation of the old and dignified with the new and crass. In "The Gambler, The Nun, and The

[39] "English and Spanish in *For Whom the Bell Tolls*," McCaffery, pp. 205-220. See especially pp. 212 and 217. In spite of his criticism of Melville (*GHOA*, p. 20) for the over-use of rhetoric as a substitute for ob-[248/249]servation, Hemingway had now reached the point where an admixture of Marlovian and Shakespearean language served him in the elevation of language tone towards the epic level. Yet *FWBT* never falls into rhetoric in the expository passages, as happens frequently in *Moby-Dick*. The Elizabethan-Jacobean tone in *FWBT* is communicated exclusively through dialogue, and even there is carefully "corrected" towards modernity by the intermixture of the contemporary *lingua communis* with the slang removed. Hemingway had been speaking Spanish for 15 years, and his ear was awake to its tempos and its delicate or indelicate formalities.
[40] *FWBT*, p. 92.

Radio," for example, the contrast is used to underscore the humor of character. Now, however, with his temperamental sensitivity to the tone of language, and an intuitive feel for what would constitute the proper blend of ancient and modern idiom in the conduct of key scenes, whether they were comic or not, Hemingway developed a language suitable to his epic purposes. The masculine vigor in the march of the narrative comes about, not alone from the author's skill in the unfolding of events but also through his responsiveness to language values.

Outside the technical aspects of language one finds an over-all seriousness of conception which, though high enough to meet even Arnold's stringent requirements, does not preclude rough humor and soldierly badinage. As a means of giving depth to his characterizations, Homer knew and used (if indeed he did not invent) the device of the flashback. As for synecdoche, Homer [**249/250**] was very far from limiting his range of significance by carefully centering his attention on the action before Troy. All bad writers may love the epic. A few good ones, working somewhat after the fashion of Hemingway, can succeed in keeping the epic genre in a state of good health by adapting transferable elements to the needs and expectations of the modern reader.

The principle of characterization-in-depth is strong in *For Whom the Bell Tolls*—more so than in any of Hemingway's previous work. If touch-and-go is the mark of the apprentice and the journeyman, stay-and-see may well be one of the attributes of the master. Even though the qualities which distinguished the younger writer still serve Hemingway at forty, he is now ready to move beyond them. Without, for example, sacrificing the value of *suggestion* (where the reader is required to supply his own imaginative clothing for an idea nakedly projected), Hemingway has come round to an appreciation of the value of *ingestion*. This signifies a bearing within, a willingness to put in, and to allow to operate within the substance of a piece of writing, much that formerly would have been excluded in favor of suggestion.

The result of this willingness is a notable gain in richness and depth without sacrifice of the values inherent in the principle of suggestiveness. What Hemingway allows us to know of Pilar's past, for example, enriches, activates, and deepens our sense of her vital performance in the present. The willingness, even the eagerness, to invent that past, to stay and see how it informs the present, is a mark of the transition achieved by the fully mature artist in Hemingway. The will to report has given place to the willingness to invent, though the values of the will to report have not been sacrificed in the process. There were formerly only limited vistas back through time. Now the full panoply of time past is at work in time present. This mode of operation is likewise habitual to the epic genre.

V. THE PATTERN OF TRAGEDY

If *For Whom the Bell Tolls* is a kind of epic, it is above all a tragic epic. Like the *Iliad*, it may be seen as a study in doom. Madrid, like Troy, was fated to fall. Seventeen months of hind- [**250/251**] sight on the Spanish war helped to mature in Hemingway a feeling that the republican defeat had been virtually inevitable. "The Spanish civil war was really lost, of course, [he wrote in 1940] when the Fascists took Irun in the late summer of 1936. But in a war you can never admit, even to yourself, that it is lost. Because when you admit it is lost you are beaten."[41]

Hemingway's choice of the early summer of 1937 as the time of Jordan's action thus takes on special importance. He wanted a period deep enough into the war so that the possibility of republican defeat could be a meaningful psychological force. But the time must also be far enough removed from the end of the war

[41] Hemingway's preface to Regler, *Great Crusade*, p. vii.

so that some of his people could still believe in a republican victory. The struggle could not seem to be hopeless. Yet, as a study in doom, the novel must early isolate and dramatize those adverse powers and power-failures which would ultimately combine to defeat the Spanish republic.

Robert Jordan's first sight of Pablo gives him an insight into the nature of one power-failure. No republican, at the beginning of the movement, was more in command of himself or the situation than Pablo. Now the guerrilla leader is so far gone in defeatist "sadness" and moral cowardice as almost to doom in advance any undertaking in which he is to play a part.

"I don't like that sadness [Robert Jordan thought]. That sadness is bad. That's the sadness they get before they quit or before they betray. That is the sadness that comes before the sellout."[42]

Pablo is a specific Judas, as his stealing of the detonator will later show. But he is also a recognizable symbol for the general canker of defeatism, gnawing the tissues of republican morale from within, and leading to the larger betrayal.

A second internal danger is the inefficiency of the Republican bureaucracy. A third is an aspect of the Spanish temperament. One gets the impression that a radical inefficiency stretches all the way from the higher echelons in Madrid down to the gypsy Rafael, who is so irresponsible that he runs off to shoot rabbits when he should be standing guard near Pablo's cave. The Rus- [251/252] sian General Golz, only half-believing that his attack will not be doomed to failure before it even starts, points up the larger difficulties.

"They are never my attacks [says Golz]. I make them. But they are not mine. The artillery is not mine. I must put in for it. I have never been given what I ask for even when they have it to give. That is the least of it. There are other things. You know how those people are. It is not necessary to go into all of it. Always there is something. Always some one will interfere."[43]

Tangled in red tape like Laocoon in serpents, Golz is not free enough to prosecute a war successfully. The Rafaels of the republican side are too free, and too irresponsible. Bureaucracy and temperament, two more internal foes of the republic, help to fix the doom.

But the most awesome symbol of doom is the air-power of the foreign enemy. All the Spaniards hate it, as they hate the foreigners for interfering in their civil war. When the fascist planes roar over the mountain hide-out, it is always in threes, like the weird sisters, or in those multiples of three with which practitioners of black magic used to conjure.

"The three passed and then came nine more, flying much higher in the minute, pointed formations of threes and threes and threes . . . He could still hear the receding drone. . . . By now they're well beyond the pass with Castile all yellow and tawny beneath them now in the morning . . . and the shadows of the Heinkels moving over the land as the shadows of sharks pass over a sandy floor of the ocean."[44]

When the planes return, Jordan revises his simile into something even more sinister. They have the shape but not the motion of sharks. "They move like no thing that has ever been. They move like mechanized doom."[45] It is by three such planes that [252/253] El Sordo's band will be wiped out at three o'clock of the following Monday afternoon.

Hemingway's linking of the modern bombers with the ancient magic-symbol of number three greatly enhances the emotional effectiveness of the plane-passage. The old epics and the great dramatic tragedies could employ supernatural agents in the full expectation that they would intensify the emotions of pity and terror in the spectator. The rise of naturalism, and the

---

[42] *FWBT*, p. 12.
[43] *FWBT*, p. 5. Compare Golz's almost elegiac acceptance of reality, as he speaks over the telephone to Duval at the other end of the novel, when it is known that the plan of the bridge will not work: "*Nous sommes foutus. Oui. Comme toujours. Oui. C'est dommage. Oui. . . . No. Rien à faire. Rien. Faut pas penser. Faut accepter. . . . Bon. Nous ferons notre petit possible.*" *FWBT*, pp. 428-430.
[44] *FWBT*, pp. 74-76.
[45] *FWBT*, p. 87.

partial decay of superstition, denied the tragic artist direct access to one of his most evocative instruments. Yet within the shadowy subconscious, the perennial human capacity for fear and awe remained to be touched by any artist who could empower new symbols with old terrors.

The book touches the edge of the supernatural also by a considered use of premonition. The primary human agent is the gypsy Pilar, who is both a woman and a kind of witch, though a witch very naturalistically portrayed and very womanly in her witchhood. Her function in part is to sharpen the reader's foreboding and thus to deepen his sense of impending tragedy. Having watched Pablo's degeneration through fear, she is both too wise and too fond of Jordan to reveal that she has seen his coming death in the lines of his hand. (Like the Circean "witch" of *The Sun Also Rises,* she is a good judge of quality.) But the reader's knowledge of Jordan's coming death gives special point to the passage in which Pilar describes, with naturalistic precision, the three blended odors of the smell of death to come.

The woman-witch dialectic is marked often in the book. In this instance, the woman withholds what the witch has gloomily discovered. Her certainty that Jordan will die has motivated her in bringing the lovers together. This is done both for the therapeutic effect of a healthy love affair on Maria, and in order to give Jordan, through Maria, as much of life as three days will hold. This, one might guess, is the tender side of Pilar. But in the passage on the smell of death to come, she adopts the very tone which will arouse Jordan's doubts as to the truth of what she is saying. He doubts and he argues, and the doubting arguments divert his thoughts at least from the probability, if not from the possibility, of death. The rough railing humor of her presentation [253/254] is meant to save him from a fear which might undo his resolution, or, at any rate, spoil the closing hours of his short, happy life.[46]

This entire aspect of the novel may well remind some readers of the problem which Henry James set himself in *The Wings of the Dove*—though, as always, there is little or no overt resemblance between the two books. "The idea, reduced to its essence," said James of his own major effort, "is that of a young person conscious of a great capacity for life, but early stricken and doomed, condemned to die under short respite, while also enamoured of the world."[47] A marked "capacity for life," a full acceptance and love of the world, is always a driving motive with the Hemingway hero. It grows even stronger as one moves with Hemingway's work through the nineteen-thirties. Yet Nick Adams has it, Jake Barnes has it, Frederick Henry has it. It is strong in Harry Morgan, though he is not very articulate in expressing what he feels. The love of life—the good life—gives special point to the dying reminiscences of that other Harry, the writer on safari in Africa. Yet the two men called Harry are stricken and doomed, condemned to die under short respite, as is Colonel Richard Cantwell, a lover of life, in *Across the River and Into the Trees.*

There are other premonitions in *For Whom the Bell Tolls* than those we owe to Pilar's supersensory gifts. Jordan, as a partisan soldier, must often consider that he may die at the affair of the bridge. He is compelled to recognize the possibility of death. His life among the Guadarramas may well total three-score hours and ten—seventy hours as a substitute for seventy years.[48] In the meteorological bad luck which brings an unseasonal snowfall, in Pablo's defection, and in the bombing of El Sordo, there is a discernible "pattern of tragedy" which he is too sensible to ignore. But he has also a special soldier's talent "not to ignore but to despise whatever bad endings there could be."[49] From the point of view of the reader, therefore, Jordan's predicament is some- [254/255] thing like that of the torero who knows that he may

---

[46] *FWBT*, pp. 250-257.
[47] *Works*, New York edition, vol. 19, preface, p. v.
[48] See Jordan's soliloquy, *FWBT*, p. 166.
[49] *FWBT*, p. 393.

be killed but despises death and enters the ring in spite of the possibility. The knowledge, derived through Pilar, that Jordan not only *may* but *will* die gives every incident in Jordan's seventy-hour span of life the special poignancy that would be felt by a spectator who knew in advance that he was watching the last fight of a torero. Through this double perspective, Hemingway gets into his novel the very "feeling of life and death" which he was seeking when he first went to watch the Spanish bullfights.

But the idea that a sane consciousness of death will give added depth and meaning to the events of life is only one of the familiar Hemingway themes in *For Whom the Bell Tolls*. Sparing but effective use is also made of the men-without-women, the father-and-son, and the home-versus-war themes. Jordan, for example, shows a kind of spiritual relationship to Pilar in that he can be, by turns, both tender and tough-minded. In one of his aspects, he can love human beings and allow himself to become involved with them, as in his good companionship with Anselmo or his love for Maria. At the other extreme, he must be the cold-minded and detached commander, reserving part of himself in all human relationships so that the necessary job can be done. It is in this detachment that he coldly judges his companions, estimating their relative dependability and expendability, and perfecting his battle-plan in accordance with these estimates. He cannot often expand warmly; as soldier he must contract coldly within himself. "I cannot have a woman, doing what I do," he tells Maria. "But thou art my woman now." After one of their encounters, Maria observes that he is now thinking of something else than love. "Yes," Jordan says, shortly. "My work." On another occasion, talking with Pilar, the men-without-women idea emerges very clearly. "You are a very cold boy," says Pilar. Jordan disagrees. "No," says Pilar. "In the head you are very cold." Jordan replies that he is preoccupied with his work. "But you do not like the things of life?" asks Pilar. "Yes. Very

much. But not to interfere with my work." It is not now a liking for hardy masculine comradeship in hunting or fishing or skiing which motivates the Hemingway hero, but a preoccupation with the work a man must do, where women have no place and may even be in the way. The morning [255/256] Jordan kills the fascist cavalryman, Maria is still beside him in the sleeping-bag. As he quickly and coldly issues orders to Anselmo and Primitivo, he is aware of Maria behind him, dressing herself under the robe. "She had no place in his life now." At the end of the book, both elements are still visible. He is the republican soldier coolly drawing a bead on the fascist Lieutenant Berrendo, and the husband covering his wife's escape.[50]

The closing scene also rounds off the father-and-son theme which has been introduced in Jordan's soliloquies at various earlier times. Jordan's grandfather fought bravely and successfully in the American Civil War. His father, like the father of Nick Adams, died by his own hand. Jordan has long since forgiven his father for the act, but he is still as ashamed of it as he is proud of his grandfather's soldierly bravery. Now, at the end of the line, as Jordan lies nearly fainting under the ballooning pain from his fractured leg, the father-grandfather opposition once more commands his mind. Suicide would be permissible under the circumstances. But the memory of his grandfather, his true spiritual ancestor, helps him to hold onto his courage and to die in combat.[51]

The significance of Maria, when she is seen in the light of such other heroines as Catherine Barkley, Marie Morgan, and even Dorothy Bridges, is finally symbolic. In the lonely alien region of the Guadarramas, she comes to stand as the image of "home." Most of Hemingway's women tend to take on this special symbolic meaning. Dorothy Bridges (a fairly unsympathetic portrait) is explicitly equated with nostalgia, a somewhat untrustworthy reminder of the comforts and the joys which

[50] *FWBT*, pp. 73, 161, 91, 267.
[51] *FWBT*, especially Chapter 30, pp. 334-340.

are so rarely possible in a world besieged by the ideology of terror. Catherine Barkley and Marie Morgan, though in different ways, represent normal domesticity vanquished by war and by the economic struggle for survival. Similarly, Maria stands for the normal in the midst of a terrible abnormality. She has been subjected to all sorts of outrages by her fascist captors. The rape is an act of supreme brutality; only the true tenderness of Jordan, as Pilar well knows, can erase the psychological scars the fascists have left. The cut- [256/257] ting of Maria's hair is a symbol of her loss of normal womanhood or girlhood, just as its growing-out indicates her gradual return to balance and health.

One might argue, of course, that the normal male-female situation in Hemingway is something like what took place in the Garden of Eden just after the eating of the fruit of the tree, but before the malediction. All these Eves are as pleasurably ductile as the Adams are hirsute and sexually vigorous. Like all travesties, such a characterization would have its element of truth. But it would tend to ignore the real tenderness with which the "good women" in Hemingway are treated. The fate of the heroines is that they are almost never at home; their virtue is that the best of them carry the home-image with them wherever they go.

A fourth well-tried theme handsomely adapted to the uses of the Spanish tragedy is that of *nada,* or nothingness militant. By placing his action among the high slopes of the Sierra de Guadarramas, a clean, well-lighted place where the weather is cold and the air clear, Hemingway has achieved a kind of idyll in the midst of war, an island (like that of Nick Adams in his afternoon grove on the way to the Big Two-Hearted River) surrounded by the sinister. It is there that Maria, raped and venereally infected by fascist soldiery, is restored to health and sanity. This is a mountain fastness like Burguete in *The Sun Also Rises,* or like the priest's homeland of Abruzzi in *A Farewell to Arms,* or like the Alpine sanctuary to which Fred-

erick and Catherine retire for their short happy life together. One sees again the lowland-versus-highland image; on the plain before Madrid the fascists are deployed, but here are high slopes, concealment, and something like the good life, a veritable island in the midst of *nada*. Still, in the words of Donne's devotion, "no man is an island." In this savage war, no mountain can serve as a permanent sanctuary. El Sordo, on his high hilltop position, finds no good life. Fascist cavalry surround it, and three fascist planes destroy it from above. Similarly, when the bridge is blown, Pablo's mountain cave becomes untenable as a refuge. The partisans plan to retreat across the war-swept lowlands to another mountain fastness in the Sierra de Gredos. But the planes of the enemy, in sinister "threes and threes and threes," can presumably come there, too. "I am tired of the [257/258] mountains," says Pilar in a moment of despondency. "In mountains there are only two directions. Down and up, and down leads only to the road and the towns of the Fascists." And up, one might add, leads to the foreign bombers, assaulting even the highest and loneliest peaks.[52]

Hemingway's sense of fascism's betrayal of the Spanish people has in fact much of the nightmare quality of Picasso's allegorical painting. The mountain-sanctuary, an essentially private symbol in Hemingway's earlier books, is now shown to be open to invasion and destruction by fascist bombers, which the artist carefully establishes as symbols of the power of evil. If one follows Picasso's pictorial allegories through the order of composition from the "Minotauromachy" through the "Sueño y Mentira de Franco" up to the "Guernica," he will see how an essentially private set of symbols is made to take on political significance. In the "Minotauromachy" of 1935, Picasso employs motifs from the bullfight to express symbolically a struggle no doubt personal to himself as artist and Spaniard. The "Guernica" of 1937, occasioned by the bombing of an open

[52] *FWBT*, p. 97.

Spanish city by foreign planes, regrouped the symbols of the bull and the horse and broke the calm human figures of the *Minotauromachy* into fragments of anguish and fear. In one postwar interview, Picasso refused to identify the bull-figure of the "Guernica" with fascism, though he did give it the generic meaning of "brutality and darkness"—something like Goya's "Nada." The horse, transfixed by a spear which has fallen from above, is however for Picasso a specific symbol for the Spanish people. In somewhat the same way, the destruction of El Sordo's band on the hilltop, like the roar of Heinkel bombers above Jordan's high sanctuary, suggests the horror of brutality and darkness unleashed against a betrayed people.[53]

Among those whom fascism will betray are the artists. Robert Jordan is not only a teacher of Spanish and a lover of Spain; he is also a writer. As an artist he is fully aware of the threat of fascist domination. If fascism were the kind of force which fed upon itself, remaining relatively limited in its dimensions, Jor- [258/259] dan's manifest duty would belong to the development of his art—a task so huge that it takes a lifetime to accomplish. During the years of peace, Jordan wrote one book on Spain and the Spanish people.[54] Presumably he would not be averse to doing another. But this is not the time.

In the deeper meaning of *For Whom the Bell Tolls,* the invasion of the high sanctuary *from above* marks a transition in the affairs of the artist. Unless the force is stopped, it can mean the death of art as it can mean the death of everything else the artist values and needs. Fascism has become militant, imperialistic, and international. The artist, devoted though he must be to the development of his art, can no more ignore it than he could ignore a storm blowing in at his study window and scattering the pages of his work in progress. His move must be to shut the window against the storm. Still it will not leave him alone. The lightning strikes his house, and it is his obvious duty to save his manuscript and put out the fire.

The *blitz* is not what he asked for or what he wanted. Since it has come, he must take arms against it, and end it as soon as possible by opposing it. Then he can go back to his work, if he survives.

VI. THE GREAT WHEEL

In his account of how he went about writing *The Awkward Age,* James says that he "drew on a sheet of paper . . . the neat figure of a circle consisting of a number of small rounds disposed at equal distances about a central object."[55] This central object was his "situation." The small rounds disposed about it were like a series of small searchlights centering on the situation, and seeking to illuminate it from all sides. As often in James, the problem of the artist was to draw, by a geometry of his own, the limited circle in which his demonstration would transpire. If he drew his circle well and directed his searchlights with a sufficient intensity, the human relations on which he concentrated would "stop nowhere."[56] [259/260]

The central organizing image of *For Whom the Bell Tolls* is also geometrical. We have, of course, in the chief characters, a series of smaller rounds disposed at equal distances about the central object or situation. But beyond these, and spreading out to the edge of the world, we have a whole series of concentric circles. The human relations of the war in Spain "stop nowhere,"—any more than the tragic implications of the art of the bullfight stay confined within the two hours' traffic of a particular afternoon. In fact Hemingway's novel follows an architectural plan comparable to that of a Spanish bullring, which is constructed in a series of concentric circles, so arranged that from any point one can watch the action taking place at the center.

Remembering that Picasso and Hem-

[53] See Alfred H. Barr, Jr., *Picasso: Fifty Years of His Art,* New York, 1946, p. 202.
[54] *FWBT*, p. 248.
[55] Henry James, *Works,* New York edition, vol. 9, preface, p. xvi.
[56] *ibid.,* vol. 1, p. vii.

ingway have as artists a common interest in the bullfight, and noting that their separate reactions to the Spanish Civil War produced so remarkable a set of symbolic parallels, one might expect to find Hemingway making use of symbolism derived from the bullfight. That is, one might find both the geometrical *and* the pictorial use of images. To a limited extent this happens, and as usual the pictorial images are fully justified by the psychological situation. All the native Spaniards in the book are of course well acquainted with the terminology of their national sport, as a similar group of Americans might be with that of baseball or football. A few even know the sport from the inside. Before the war began, Pablo worked around bullrings. The boy Joaquín planned a career as torero. And by her own boast, Pilar lived for "nine years with three of the worst-paid matadors" in the business.

One of the most striking and memorable parts of the novel is organized in terms of a pictorial metaphor of the bullfight.[57] This is Pilar's account of the murder of the fascists in the village square at the hands of Pablo's lynch-mob. The natural resemblance between the square and an arena has been furthered by piling carts before the several street-entrances to the square. This is the usual custom in preparation for a *capea,* or amateur bull-baiting show, at the time of a fiesta. The resemblance to a feast-day celebration is emphasized by the fact that some of the peasants, just in from the country, are dressed in their Sunday clothes. The [**260/261**] caretaker of the plaza hoses down the dust as would be done for a *capea,* and when the dust has settled a peasant shouts, "When do we get the first fascist? When does the first one come out of the box?"

The eyes of the whole company are fixed on the doorway of the *Ayuntiamento,* where the fascists have been herded, as if by sweating workers at a bullring. The concentration is comparable to that with which a *capea* crowd would watch the cage-door through which a bull was to be released. Once the crowd has tasted blood through the murder of the first fascist, Mayor Don Benito Garcia, it is as though they waited tensely and impatiently for the second bull. Howling in a great voice, a drunkard summarizes the sentiments of a considerable part of the crowd. *"Qué salga el toro!* Let the bull out!"

But this is one of those almost unendurable "bullfights." It will produce no sense of tragic catharsis, no genuine purgation of the emotions. Pilar says that after it was over she felt sick, hollow, ashamed, and oppressed. There was no experience, as happens in a good bullfight, of anything "profound as any religious ecstasy." The total effect was as nasty as that of a jungle grove through which a tribe of baboons have just passed.

Even though, as such affairs often will, this *capea* produced some isolated instances of courage, *pundonor,* and the allied virtues—instances which Pilar describes along with the rest—these are not enough to redeem the total performance. Pilar's feeling is itself a fitting symbol for the reaction of many a reluctant observer to the tragedy of the Spanish war, the international bullfight with a poorly armed matador arrayed against the "brutality and darkness" of Pan-European fascism. If one at this instant remembers "Guernica," he sees that the artists Picasso and Hemingway, drawn as by a magnetic attraction to the pictorial imagery of the bullfight, move along lines precisely parallel. The major difference is that Hemingway, working with a different and more extendable medium, can take care to paint both sides of the picture. He has, to return to the Jamesian metaphor, an opportunity to draw more circles, more wheels of fire.

Within the scope of man's world, turning like a great wheel through empty space, there are in fact many small and large [**261/262**] wheels turning for ever. In the quiet of his last Sunday evening inside the cave of Pablo, while Jordan draws his circles and makes his mathe-

[57] *FWBT*, pp. 109-129. See also p. 55.

matical computations for the dynamiting of the bridge, the simile of a wheel comes into his mind.

"It is like a merry-go-round, Robert Jordan thought. Not a merry-go-round that travels fast, and with a calliope for music, and the children ride on cows with gilded horns, and there are rings to catch with sticks, and there is the blue gas-flare-lit early dark of the Avenue du Maine, with fried fish sold from the next stall, and a wheel of fortune turning with the leather flaps slapping against the posts of the numbered compartments, and the packages of lump sugar piled in pyramids for prizes. No, it is not that kind of a merry-go-round; although the people are waiting, like the men in caps and the women in knitted sweaters, their heads bare in the gaslight and their hair shining, who stand in front of the wheel of fortune as it spins. Yes, those are the people."

Those are the people, French or Spanish or any other, watching the two revolving circles—the temporal merry-go-round and the wheel of fortune. But Jordan has in his mind yet another wheel.

"This [he reflects] is like a wheel that goes up and around. It has been around twice now. It is a vast wheel, set at an angle, and each time it goes around and then is back to where it starts.

"One side is higher than the other and the sweep it makes lifts you back and down to where you started. There are no prizes either, he thought, and no one would choose to ride this wheel. You ride it each time and make the turn with no intention ever to have mounted.

"There is only one turn; one large, elliptical rising and falling turn and you are back where you have started. We are back again now, he thought, and nothing is settled." [58]

Call it the wheel of human conflict. For Jordan, as for all men, the turn of the wheel shows tragic implications. When it has completed its revolution, the rider is back where he started, as on the little wheel of Jordan's relations with Pablo. He has been twice now on *that* wheel, "and twice it has gone around and come back to where it started." Jordan wants no more rides with Pablo, though he will have them before his day is done. In the giant [262/263] clockwork of human relations, the turning wheels may be as small as the arguments with Pablo, or as vast as the elliptical rise and fall in the action of a year of war.

In either of these instances, in three days or three years, you come back to where you began—"and nothing is settled." This is the wheel-like turn of Spain's tragedy, indeed, that after all the agony and all the blood, nothing should be settled, and that Spain should be back where it began, in a medieval situation.

[58] *FWBT*, pp. 225-226.

PART FOUR

THE OLD MAN AND THE SEA

With Grace Under Pressure*

MARK SCHORER. For information about the author, see "The Background of a Style," by Mark Schorer, reprinted on page 87.

The only guts that are mentioned in this story are the veritable entrails of fish, but we are nevertheless reminded on every page that Hemingway once defined this favorite word, in its metaphorical use, as "grace under pressure." Grace, in the fullest sense, is the possession of this old man, just as grace was precisely what Colonel Cantwell, in *Across the River and Into the Trees,* was totally without. But here it is, complete and absolute, the very breath of this old man, so thoroughly his in his essence as in his *ambiente,* that it can only be there under pressure as at all other times, and indeed, even under the greatest pressure, he hardly alters. Grace, by which one means now not the old stuff [*sic*] upper lip (this old man's upper lip is not so very stiff) which came to some of the older heroes a little easily sometimes, a quality more nearly a manner of speaking than of being; not that now, but benignity, nothing less, and beautifully, masterfully presented, so that the satisfaction one has in this creation is plain happiness, and then, I suppose, gratitude.

The old man has a Franciscan quality that so prevades [*sic*] his habit of thought as to support and give the body of dramatic plausibility, even inevitability to the suggestion of Christian martyrdom which comes at the end. Early in the story, when the old man is being helped by the boy, he thanks him for the food he gives him. "He was too simple to wonder when he had attained humility. But he knew he had attained it and he knew it was not disgraceful and it carried no loss of true pride." Humility—the assumption, without self-consciousness and therefore without sentimentality—is the old man's strength.

He was very fond of flying fish as they were his principal friends on the ocean. He was sorry for the birds, especially the small delicate dark terns that were always flying and looking and almost never finding, and he thought, "The birds have a harder life than we do except for the robber birds and the heavy strong ones. Why did they make birds so delicate and fine as those sea swallows when the ocean can be so cruel? She is kind and very beautiful. But she can be so cruel and it comes so suddenly and such birds that fly, dipping and hunting, with their small sad voices are made too delicately for the sea."

And again, now of porpoises, and then of the marlin itself:

"They are good," he said. "They play and make jokes and love one another. They are our brothers like the flying fish."
Then he began to pity the great fish that he had hooked. He is wonderful and strange and who knows how old he is, he thought. Never have I had such a strong fish nor one who acted so strangely. Perhaps he is too wise to jump. He could ruin me by jumping or by a wild rush. But perhaps he has been hooked many times before and he knows that this is how he

*Mark Schorer, "With Grace Under Pressure," New Republic, CXXVII (October 6, 1952), 19-20. Reprinted by permission of the author.

should make his fight. He cannot know that it is only one man against him, nor that it is an old man. But what a great fish he is. . . . I wonder if he has any plans or if he is just as desperate as I am?

And thus, with a kind of Biblical abstraction that always assumes the independence of all things in their own character from his character, which is likewise independent and separate (in this recognition lie the true sources of brotherhood as of pity) , he speaks to a bird, to his fish, and to the parts of his own body, his hands and his head. With a few wavering exceptions, Hemingway sustains the perilous poise of all this with great beauty over pits of possible bathos.

Everywhere the book is being called a classic. In at least one sense, the word cannot be applied, for here and there, where the writing wavers, its pure lucidity is muddied by all that hulking personality which, at his worst, Hemingway has made all too familiar. I do not have in mind the talk about baseball, which has bothered at least one reviewer. "The baseball" is a near obsession with most Caribbean natives, but we do not have to know this to accept the old man's interest as his own rather than as Hemingway's. (After all, DiMaggio's father *was* a fisherman, as the old man tells us, and the sword of the marlin is "as long as a baseball bat.") But a murky paragraph that has to do with "mysticism about turtles" is a case in point. Or a sentence such as this: "He did not truly feel good because the pain from the cord across his back had almost passed pain and gone into a dullness that he mistrusted"—is it a quibble to suggest that the word "truly" and its location spoil this sentence, jar us out of the mind of the old man whom we are coming to know into the reflection that we've read Hemingway before? Or a brief passage such as this:

After he judged that his right hand had been in the water long enough he took it out and looked at it.

"It is not bad," he said. "And pain does not matter to a man. . . .

"You did not do so badly for something worthless," he said to his left hand. "But there was a moment when I could not find you."

Why was I not born with two good hands? he thought. Perhaps it was my fault in not training that one properly. But God knows he has had enough chances to learn. He did not do so badly in the night, though, and he has only cramped once. If he cramps again let the line cut him off.

The last sentence tells us with dramatic concreteness what the generalization, "pain does not matter to a man," which is really Hemingway's, does not tell us at all. It should not have been written, precisely because what *is* written must make *us* speak that conclusion, it should be our generalization from his evidence.

But the old man seldom lapses into dramatic falseness. In his age, alone at sea, he has taken to speaking aloud, and instead of dialogue between characters by which most fictions [sic] moves, this story moves by little dialogues in the old man himself, the exchange of what is spoken and what is not spoken. This is almost a running drama between that which is only possible and that which is real:

"Fish," he said, "I love you and respect [19/20] you very much. But I will kill you dead before this day ends."

Let us hope so, he thought.

The threat of over-generalization is almost always in the spoken words, which, then, are immediately rooted in actuality by the reservations of the unspoken. And of course, Hemingway's incredible gift for writing of the natural life serves the same function. Whether he is describing plankton, jelly fish, the sucking fish that swim in the shadow of the marlin, the gutting of a dolphin that contains two flying fish, or turtles, they are all always there before us, actualities, and the old man is an actuality among them.

The novel is nearly a fable. The best

fiction, at its heart, always is, of course, but with his particular diction and syntax, Hemingway's stories approach fable more directly than most, and never so directly as here. It is the quality of his fiction at its very best, the marvelous simplicity of line. (" 'Be calm and strong, old man', he said.") There has been another strain in his fiction, to be sure—his personal ambition to become a character in a tall tale, folklore as opposed to fable. That is the weaker man pushing aside the great novelist. The strain glimmers once in this story, when we are told of the old man's feat of strength in his youth: "They had gone one day and one night with their elbows on a chalk line on the table and their forearms straight up and their hands gripped tight." Take it away.

The true quality of fable is first of all in the style, in the degree of abstraction, which is not only in some ways Biblical but is always tending toward the proverbial rhythm. ("The setting of the sun is a difficult time for fish.") Next, it is in the simplicity of the narrative, and in the beautiful proportion (about three-fourths to one-fourth) of its rise and fall. Finally, of course, it is in the moral significance of the narrative, this fine story of an ancient who goes too far out, "beyond the boundaries of permitted aspiration," as Conrad put it ("You violated your luck when you went too far outside," the old man thinks), and encounters his destiny:

His choice had been to stay in the deep dark water far out beyond all snares and traps and treacheries. My choice was to go there to find him beyond all people. Beyond all people in the world. Now we are joined together and have been since noon. And no one to help either one of us.

In this isolation, he wins a Conradian victory, which means destruction and triumph. We permit his martyrdom because he has earned it. His sigh is "just a noise such as a man might make, involuntarily, feeling the nail go through his hands and into the wood." He stumbles under the weight of his mast when he carries it across his shoulder, up a hill. He sleeps, finally "with his arms out straight and the palms of his hands up." There is more than this and for those who, like this reviewer, believe that Hemingway's art, when it is art, is absolutely incomparable, and that he is unquestionably the greatest craftsman in the American novel in this century, something that is perhaps even more interesting. For this appears to be not only a moral fable, but a parable, and all the controlled passion in the story, all the taut excitement in the prose come, I believe, from the parable. It is an old man catching a fish, yes; but it is also a great artist in the act of mastering his subject, and, more than that, of actually writing about that struggle. Nothing is more important than his craft, and it is beloved; but because it must be struggled with and mastered, it is also a foe, enemy to all self-indulgence, to all looseness of feeling, all laxness of style, all soft pomposities.

"I am a strange old man."
"But are you strong enough now for a truly big fish?"
"I think so. And there are many tricks."

Hemingway, who has always known the tricks, is strong enough now to have mastered his greatest subject. "I could not fail myself and die on a fish like this," the old man reflects. They win together, the great character, the big writer.

Hemingway: The Matador and the Crucified*

MELVIN BACKMAN, who teaches Liberal Studies at Clarkson College of Technology, has written extensively about both Hemingway and Faulkner.

Running through Ernest Hemingway's work, from *In Our Time* to *The Old Man and the Sea,* are two dominant motifs—the matador and the crucified. The matador represents a great force held in check, releasing itself proudly in a controlled yet violent administering of death. The crucified stands for the taking of pain, even unto death, with all of one's courage and endurance so that it becomes a thing of poignancy and nobility. Although it was not until *The Old Man and the Sea* that Hemingway achieved a perfect blending of his two themes, the continual tension and interplay between those forces represented by the matador and the crucified create a pattern in the Hemingway canon against which the individual works of fiction may be profitably studied.

In Our Time sets forth the pain and brutality of our world, recorded apparently without comment in a terse, telegraphic style. Yet underneath the tight-lipped writing a current of protest and repressed brooding threads its secretive way. This is violence caught in the stifled shock of its initial impact. The stories and inter-chapters have the effect of painful memories of which one must rid himself to exorcise their evil spell, to drive them from the night into the day.

Recoiling from these memories of a sick world, the discharged soldier Nick Adams sought retreat in the Big Two-Hearted River. In this story, Hemingway omits rather ominously all mention of the war and of the people and places of Nick's past, so that a strange aloneness and suspension of time are created. Nick's only function was to fish, to immerse himself so completely in the physical sensations and details of his fishing that there was no need to think. This became, therefore, a strange idyl. Nick called it "the good place," but it was the good place because of its associations with a certain part of his past—fishing and hunting, the river and the woods—which had not been excised from his life as he was trying to do with all the rest. It was as though he wanted to rub out his immediate past and begin clean again here in the woods. But even [2/3] the woods had been burned over—now there were just charred stumps and black grasshoppers. Yet here amid the shelter and quiet of the trees and the river, with the sun warm on his back and his line trailing in the water, was a moment of separation, of forgetfulness, of peace.

If Nick Adams was trying to withdraw from his world in "Big Two-Hearted River," it was in "Soldier's Home" that the Hemingway protagonist was officially separated. The soldier Krebs found himself hopelessly alienated from the conventional, middle-class American town to which he returned. Living with a kind of flat despair from day to day, holding in abeyance the inevitable decision, he dwelt

* Melvin Backman, "Hemingway: The Matador and the Crucified," in *Hemingway and His Critics; An International Anthology,* ed. Carlos Baker (New York: Hill and Wang, 1961), pp. 245-258 (a corrected version of Melvin Backman, "Hemingway: The Matador and the Crucified," *Modern Fiction Studies,* I [August, 1955], 2-11). Reprinted by permission of the author and the Purdue Research Foundation.

in uneasy isolation in the midst of his family. Pushed to action finally by family pressure, he decided to sever the last clinging thread of his filial bond. It was a curiously cold, passionless rebellion, as though he had long since worn out his emotions and given up his hope.

In cutting the human bonds that tie one to his world there is the danger of cutting into the very will to live. The threat of this infection hovers over the three stories "Mr. and Mrs. Elliott," "Cat in the Rain," and "Out of Season," each concerned with an American couple characterized by sexual sterility and impotence. Marked by a strangely bloodless discord, without intensity or love, their lives follow a drifting purposeless course. But like green wooded mountains rising abruptly out of barren plains, the descriptions of matadors (interspersed between the stories) emerge in sharp relief:

When he started to kill it was all in the same rush. The bull looking at him straight in front, hating. He drew out the sword from the folds of the muleta and sighted with the same movement and called to the bull, Toro! Toro! and the bull charged and Villalta charged and just for the moment they became one. Villalta became one with the bull and then it was over. Villalta standing straight and the red hilt of the sword sticking out dully between the bull's shoulders. Villalta, his hand up at the crowd and the bull roaring blood, looking straight at Villalta and his legs caving.

From the unvoiced fears of disintegration of Nick Adams, from the weary despair and apathy of Krebs, and from the scorn, which may mask a secret dread, of the passionless and sterile union of impotent lovers, Hemingway has turned to the violence of the matador.

The theme is developed more fully in *The Sun Also Rises*. If *In Our Time* recorded, for Hemingway, the waves of man's violence effacing the recognizable outline of the shore of one's home, *The Sun Also Rises* depicts the human wreckage that had been left behind. The time was one of irresponsibility, drunkenness, and promiscuity. As Mike pursued his drunken way, trailing his mounting debts like a banner, Brett preceded her escort, trailing her mounting amours, like a Don Juan turned weary bitch. Jake and Bill Gorton joined in the drunken camaraderie. Yet the endless rounds of drinks seemed to be accompanied by endless rounds of useless quarrels, and the camaraderie was broken by animosities and malice. There was, nevertheless, a certain measure of fellowship, loyalty, and even gaiety. Cohn was outside of it, not merely because he did not belong but because he seemed too self-centered to participate in friendship. Friendship or not, there is no denying the essential futility of their lives. It was a life without purpose or direction, without intensity or passion, without faith in themselves or their world. Nor did they seem truly to believe in the hedonism by which they [3/4] lived. It seemed that at the bottom of their hearts there lay such a cold dead despair that they drank in order not to think of it; they drank to wind themselves up, like a clock that must be wound every twenty-four hours. So they got through their days.

Whatever fault may be found, however, with the character of these people, it is Cohn for whom Hemingway reserved his most damning portrait. Cohn lacked true identity. His personality was without a core; in place of its center there was only a sickly ego expressing itself in the spurious martyrdom of the weak and self-pitying. Woman-dominated, he was without the vital maleness which Hemingway, like Lawrence, deems absolutely essential to the true man. There was no true pride, no resistance to Cohn. In his love of Brett he was childish in his possessiveness and unmanly in his abject pursuit. What a sharply contrasting picture Hemingway has painted of Pedro Romero as he paid suit to Brett by fighting his bull in front of her. "Never once did he look up. He made it stronger that way, and did it for himself, too, as well as for her. Because he did not look up to ask if it pleased he did it all for himself inside, and it strengthened him, and yet he did it for her too.

But he did not do it for her at any loss to himself." A polarity has been established between Cohn, unmanly representative of the lost generation, and the primitive, Pedro Romero. When these two fought, the hard male core of the young bullfighter could not be touched by Cohn's punches, and he reduced Cohn to a whimpering child.

Pedro was exempt from the *mal de siecle* that beset the others, for his fighting with the bulls brought him into a fundamental relationship with life, which involved the pitting of his maleness against that of the bull. It is a life and death struggle that reveals not only the steel of his young manhood but a certain passion with which he met life—an intensity, a seriousness, a dedicated quality. Pedro had a place in the scheme of existence—and a role to fulfill. With the instinctive sureness of a primitive who need never question his reason for living, he pursued his natural course. And it was this which even Brett came to recognize. There was an absolute center to him. He did not have to drink, he did not have to keep running away. His inner core was brought into a vital active relationship with life. As Jake commented, it is only a bullfighter who lives life to the hilt, bringing to his work all his courage, intelligence, discipline, and art.

The crisis for Pedro came not in the fight with Cohn but in the invasion of his world by Brett. Jake, the only one of the blighted moderns who was truly aware of this other world, served to bridge them. When he agreed to act as go-between in the proposed seduction of the primitive by this woman of the lost generation, he was knowingly betraying all that the matador represented. No wonder that Montoya, the *aficinado* [sic], no longer acknowledged Jake as one of them, for he knew that the two worlds had to stand forever apart if the bullfight was to retain its truth. Oddly enough, it was Brett's remnant of a conscience that, touched by shamed awareness of the desecration she threatened, brought to an end this unnatural conjunction of two separate worlds.

A purer, more natural kind of love is celebrated in *A Farewell to Arms*. Less sustained in movement and less orchestrated than *The Sun Also Rises*, *A Farewell to Arms* is a more emotional and subjective novel. It seems to be based upon the memory of a lost love and a lost youth; one's first love, dramatized like that of Romeo and Juliet, destroyed by the "they" that Hemingway in Byronic [4/5] fashion has cast as the enemy that ever seeks to crush the individual. Although there is no primitive, like Pedro Romero, in this novel, there is, in contrast, to the comparatively disillusioned picture of the war, the love itself—tender and idyllic. Glowing with the first flush of the lovers' physical discovery of each other, their love overarches the lovers themselves, who remain essentially passive. Lyrically conceived by the author, it is a small fire of life dampened by a sense of doom and threatened by the cold rain of death.

In *The Sun Also Rises* and *In Our Time*, Pedro Romero and Villalta—as their swords go all the way in, the men leaning after—become one with the bull, united for a single instant by death. This is the "moment of truth." It is an intense, almost an ecstatic moment of communion, involving an abnegation of self before the final merging. The only other experience analogous to this in Hemingway's work is sexual union. Both are experiences of controlled violence that demand a tight holding on of self until the last moment, then the yielding, merging, and flooding ecstasy. Sexual implications may be seen in the matador's domination of the bull that leads to the climax, the final thrusting of the sword; after the sword's entry the caving in of the bull suggests, by a curious transfer of roles, the collapsed tension, the death-like state of the spent male after ejaculation. Hemingway usually describes love as the act of becoming one: both Maria and Catherine try to become one with their lovers, Robert Jordan and Frederic Henry. While the killing of the bull ends in union, the making of love, as Hemingway has often remarked, becomes a kind of killing, the good killing. The famous love passage in *For Whom the Bell Tolls,* when the earth seems to move, is so filled with death imagery that it might be taken for a description of dying:

For him it was a dark passage which led to nowhere, then to nowhere, then again to nowhere, once again to nowhere, always and forever to nowhere, heavy on the elbows in the earth to nowhere, dark, never any end to nowhere, hung on all time always to unknowing nowhere, this time and again for always to nowhere, now beyond all bearing up, up, up and into nowhere, suddenly, scaldingly, holdingly all nowhere gone and time absolutely still and they were both there, time having stopped and he felt the earth move out and away from under them.

The feeling of soaring suggests a mystic ascension and recalls the soaring of the airplane in "The Snows of Kilimanjaro" that symbolized death.

It is this twining of sex and death, both fundamental crises of life, that is central to Hemingway's work. Both killings and sexual union are basic primitive experiences in which the male asserts his will and proves his manhood. In the primitive mind, both love and death are surrounded by religious and fearful influences. Because of a sense of danger and evil attending both marriage and death, ceremonies are instituted and taboos and restrictions imposed as safeguards. And Hemingway—defying Christianity's condemnation of killing and its concept of sex as a sort of necessary sin—has presented love as a mystic ceremonial experience and killing (killing cleanly with honor, pride, and humility) as a spiritual experience.

Killing cleanly and in a way which gives the aesthetic pleasure and pride has always been one of the greatest enjoyments of the human race . . . when a man is still in rebellion against death he has pleasure in taking to himself one of the God-like attributes; that of giving it. This is one of the most profound feelings in those men who enjoy killing. [5/6] These things are done in pride and pride, of course, is a Christian sin, and a pagan virtue.

In a world from which Hemingway has sought to dissociate himself, the only sacred subjects left for him have proved to be love and death—experiences which he has sought to invest with the quality of ancient mysteries.

One remembers the cold rain of *In Our Time* associated with an evil violence, the rain of the fiesta in *The Sun Also Rises* that became part of a Walpurgis-like nightmare, the black rain of the Caporetto retreat and of the death of Catherine Barkley in *A Farewell to Arms*. But in *For Whom the Bell Tolls* there is no rain. The sun dominates the novel—the sun shining through the trees and warming the pine needled earth. The setting—except for the occasional huddling within the cave, where the atmosphere was close, sullen, as Pablo brooded drunkenly on his lost manhood, as tempers flared darkly, and death stalked ominously—the setting is of the out-of-doors. There love was made and the soldier's death received. And there was the sun, the warm life-giving sun, the sun that heralded the coming of spring after the snow, the sun that was Maria illuminating the life of Robert Jordan. Maria is a child of the sun, with her hair "the color of ripe wheat," her face the "color of burnt gold," and her eyes "gold with the dark flecks in them." And the sun is identified with their love. On the day that Jordan and Maria made love, the hot gold of the sun commingled with the heather smell of the earth and the cropped golden hair of Maria—blending into a Van Gogh-like celebration of the sun so that the pulsing energy of the sun beat through the lovers into the earth and the earth moved. For Robert Jordan, Maria was the sun driving away the night and abolishing loneliness; she was the life that held off death. Finally love itself became a soaring union in which for a moment *la gloria* was realized, a glory like that "in Greco and in San Juan de la Cruz."

That their love should achieve some measure of mystical glory is not completely unprepared for. Maria—her very name suggests the Virgin—was the violated virgin who by the force of her love and will obliterated the violence that had been done her and recaptured her virginity. Borne by the men of Pablo's or rather Pilar's band from the scene of the train disaster, she had been restored to life by Pilar. Although Pilar was her support and protector, all had had a hand in her restoration, and all approached her with tenderness and love. And despite the Loyalists' official disproval of the Church, it is to the Virgin that many turned in the presence of death.

When El Sordo's band, surrounded and isolated on a hill, were facing annihilation, El Sordo in his last moment thought: 'Dying was nothing and he had no picture of it nor fear of it in his mind. But living was a field of grain blowing in the wind." This image of life may suggest association with the recurring description of Jordan's running his hand through Maria's close-cropped hair like the wind blowing through the tawny wheat. But Sordo did not pray; it was Joaquín—the boy who just the day before had been teasing Maria like a brother—who, as the planes swooped down, uttered a "Hail Mary" at the hour of his death. The bombs dropped, splitting the air apart, hitting the earth with a red black roar; "and the earth rolled under him with the roar. Then it came again and the earth lurched under his belly and one side of the hilltop rose into the air and then fell slowly over them where they lay." For him too the earth had moved. [6/7]

After the action only the enemy was left. Lieutenant Berrendo, riding at the head of the column, thought of his friend Julian, dead on the hill, and prayed to the Virgin for the soul of his friend. At almost the same moment Anselmo caught sight of the enemy column, and frozen by fear he prayed to the "most kind, most sweet, most clement Virgin." Unknowingly these two men, pledged enemies and destined to die the next day, were united in their prayer.

It would seem, then, that while Maria is associated with the sun, and the sun generally with life, she is also associated with the Virgin,[1] and the Virgin with death. Yet in the last chapter—when all that has gone before has led us painstakingly and inevitably to the destruction of the bridge —the sun is curiously twisted together with death. The scene is the opening of the chapter, just prior to the commencement of the Loyalist attack at dawn, the bombing to serve as signal for the blowing of the bridge. Jordan, who had always loved the coming of the sun, lay on the pine-needled earth and watched the first light of the sun dispelling the light mist that obscured the outline of the bridge. As the bridge shone clear in the morning light he heard the bombs drop, and he drew a long breath, as if to expel the lonely feeling that came with the dealing of death, and he prepared to shoot the sentry. The sentry stood in the road with the sun shining on him. "There was no mist on the road now and Robert Jordan saw the man, clearly and sharply, standing there on the road looking up at the sky. The sun shone bright on the trees." And gently Robert Jordan squeezed the trigger. After the death of the sentry came the wiring of the bridge. With the sound of shots in his ear, suspended under the trestle of the bridge, Jordan worked with a tense quick deliberateness against time, lashing the grenades to the girders. But for a moment the noise of the white bubbling stream below him drowned out the war, and looking down he saw a trout nibbling on the chip he had dropped, and through the metal of the bridge he saw

[1] Other evidence that might be offered is the reference to the "Blessed Virgin of Pilar" in the letter of the cavalryman shot by Robert Jordan. There is also the ambiguous evidence of the Fascists' conferring of the title of "Red Bride of Christ" upon Maria, and the scene in which Maria, in the Mary Magdalen tradition, serves Jordan, "The Lord and Master."

the sunlight on the green slope that had been brown but three days ago. It was a green moment of peace that could not be, and it had to yield to the twisting of sun and bridge into destruction.

And the sunlight played over Fernando, the good cigar-store Indian Fernando with all his fine wooden dignity, as he lay wounded against the bank. "In front of him was one of the whitewashed stones that marked the edge of the road. His head was in the shadow but the sun shone on his plugged and bandaged wound and on his hands that were cupped over it. His legs and his feet also were in the sun. The rifle lay beside him and there were three clips of cartridges shining in the sun beside the rifle." Then there was Anselmo —loyal Anselmo, the good old man who did not want to kill, believing that killing men was sin—with the wire pulled tight around his fist, waiting for the signal from the *Inglés*. The sun weighed heavy on his back. Then came the blowing of the bridge —and Anselmo lay face down behind the white marking stone, that shone in the sunlight like a common gravestone for the good and the brave.

If the sun represents the exposure that spelled death for some, for Robert Jordan it meant still more. The novel opens with Jordan lying on the pine-needled floor of the forest, planning the destruction of the bridge that arched peacefully [7/8] over the stream, white in the summer sunlight. And the novel ends:

> Lieutenant Berrendo, watching the trail, came riding up, his thin face serious and grave. His submachine gun lay across the saddle in the crook of his left arm. Robert Jordan lay behind the tree, holding onto himself very carefully and delicately to keep his hands steady. He was waiting until the officer reached the sunlit place where the first trees of the pine forest joined the green slope of the meadow. He could feel his heart beating against the pine-needle floor of the forest.

We have come full circle. The pine trees and the sun and Robert Jordan have become inextricably mingled with the giv-ing and receiving of death. Yet there the moving memory of the love in the h« sunlight and the love on the pine bough in the cool nights in the sleeping bag. is as though death in some subtle fashio has not only twisted itself about love bi has become a secret forbidden attractio that the Hemingway hero finds hard t resist. But resist it he must, even if resis ance requires the inflicting of violenc upon others. Or it may be that by h administering of death he takes uncor scious revenge for the violence inflicte upon the young manhood of Nick Adan and Jake Barnes and Frederic Henry.

Yet death in this novel is different from death in *The Sun Also Rises* or *Death i the Afternoon*. In those earlier works th dominating point of view was that of th matador, because killing was the means c proving one's manhood. The identificatio was chiefly with the killer; there was deep fundamental enjoyment, Hemingwa said, to be had from killing. In *For Whon the Bell Tolls*, however, there is an an biguity of attitude. In only one instanc did Robert Jordan identify himself, pa tially at least, with the desire to kill. Th took place at the scene when Robert Jo dan and Augustín, tense and still behin their guns, were watching the enemy ca alry depart. Augustín, speaking of th necessity to kill that was on him like "o a mare in heat," said that there was n stronger thing in life. Jordan, in siler thought, called it the Spanish "extra sac rament" that, repressed by Christianit. had welled forth in wars and inquisition: and Jordan admitted that he too and "a who are soldiers by choice have enjoye it at some time whether they lie about i or not." Yet throughout the story Jorda never killed with pleasure but always wit reluctance. He could not bring himself t "assassinate" Pablo, he shot the sentr with sadness, and his defensive killing c the cavalryman initiated a long searchin of his conscience in which he questione his right to kill. (Even the old man in *Th Old Man and the Sea* continues this ques tioning of one's right to kill.) Jordan

position seems to lie between that of Anselmo and Pablo. Although Augustín had
spoken of killing as an instinct, only with
Pablo had this "instinct" become an inordinate lust, revealed in the brutally
sadistic executions and the blood-drunken
slaughter initiated by Pablo during the
taking of his town. Part of Robert Jordan
—the greater part, it would seem—was in
accord with Anselmo, who felt that "in
those who like it [killing] there is always
a rottenness." Hating to kill, Anselmo is
a foil to Pablo in other respects, manifest-
ing loyalty as against treachery, courage
as against fear, gentleness as against
cruelty. Something of the quality of the
old man in "Old Man at the Bridge" invests Anselmo. Idealized, of course, he
represents a position toward which part of
Hemingway was drawn, just as the priest in
A Farewell to Arms had served as a similar attraction for Frederic Henry. [8/9]

But the most crucial experience for Robert Jordan lay not in the killing but in the
preparing to be killed. Although he had
to face up to his ordeal with courage and
dignity, like all the Hemingway heroes
who live by the "code," the reason for this
code is now made clear. Submerged in the
back of Jordan's mind was the guilt of
his father's suicide, which compelled Jordan to live in such a manner as to annul
his father's cowardice. Just as he had to
rid himself of the pistol by which his
father had shot himself, so had he to rid
himself of his father—that is, to obliterate
his father from his consciousness, as if he
had never been, and to replace him with
his grandfather, the soldier in the family.

Although Jordan must die to make the
"code" live, to wipe out the stain of his
father's cowardice, may there not be an-
ther explanation for his pain and death?
Jordan, after all, is but part of a pattern
into which all the Hemingway protagonists fall. At the end of *In Our Time* Nick
Adams, having been initiated into a painful world, was left in a curious state of
suspension; Jake Barnes resigned himself
hopelessly to a miserable lot in a futile

world; Frederic Henry, stripped by death
of his love, was left alone with his despair
and misery in a war-torn world. Always
the Hemingway protagonist was left alone
and always a victim, his world a torturing
wheel upon which he was stretched. *Death
in the Afternoon, Green Hills of Africa,*
and *To Have and Have Not* recorded the
seeking of violence as a means of asserting
oneself in despite of the world. But Harry
Morgan received only pain and death.
And death came to Robert Jordan and
Richard Cantwell. This pattern of agony
and death, with the protagonist as a sort
of crucified victim[2]—is it not a curious
complement to the matador going in for
the kill? Or are these two faces to a single
coin? On one side there is the matador
who in his administering of death, Hemingway has said, takes on the attributes
of a god. Is there an old primitive truth
here: the welding of the act to the unviti-
ated passion, like an Oedipus rising in pure
wrath to strike down his father; the god-
like taking to oneself one of the power [*sic*]
to judge and punish, like a Zeus dealing
out divine punishment to a transgressing
Prometheus; the mingling of sadism with
power, like a Moloch demanding sacrifice? On the other side there is the glorifying of the victim, the seeking of brotherhood out of weakness and life out of
death, like a Prometheus transformed
into helper of mankind, like a Yahweh
become Christ. But Hemingway's works
do not reflect any true belief in the glory
of martyrdom; they reflect only the tendency to see oneself as victim and life as
pain. Nor do they manifest any true desire for brotherhood, for the Hemingway
protagonist is always an island, separated
by his pain and despair and, in the last
resort, by death. In a life that is pain,
death may come to represent release—the
final sleep that knits up souls, the sleep
that cannot be had by a Nick Adams
haunted by the nightmare of his wound-

[2] Both Robert Jordan and Colonel Cantwell are
invested occasionally with a vague Christ symbolism. And in a short early play of Hemingway's,
"Today Is Friday," the Roman soldier's comment
on the crucified Christ—"He was pretty good in
there today"—echoes and re-echoes throughout the
works.

ing, by an old man living with a nameless dread ("A Clean Well-Lighted Place"), or by a Frazer ridden with physical pain. The despair that lies at the bottom of so many of the Hemingway protagonists leads either to passive suffering or to a defiant seeking of violence.

When we reach *The Old Man and the Sea*, we seem to have come a long way from the early works, but there is a pattern into which all of them fall. It is true that [9/10] the old man is the only hero who is not left alone, at the end of the story, with death or despair. He is old and womanless and humble. Yet in him we have a blending of the two dominant motifs—the matador and the crucified.

At first glance it may not seem that what the matador represents is in the old man too. Yet just as the matador pits himself against the bull, so does Santiago pit himself against the great fish; in their killing they achieve a rebellion against death. In this combat both men must call upon their pride and courage, their skill and knowledge of their craft. Whereas the bullfight terminates with the final sword thrust between the shoulders of the bull, the fight with the fish terminates with the thrusting of the harpoon into his heart. And the old man, his hands lacerated and mushy, raises himself out of his pain to bring down the harpoon, in the same way as the matador Maera in *Death in the Afternoon*, disregarding his broken wrist, goes in for the sixth time over the horns of the bull. Nevertheless, there are differences. The artificial setting of the bullfight, its spectators, and its ceremony leave one with the sense that this is but violence on exhibit, that it is not a natural struggle between man and animal, and that the emotions produced seem strained and self-induced. But Santiago's struggle with the fish is natural. As he says, he was born to be a fisherman and the fish was born to be a fish. The killing of fish is an old accepted livelihood. And the setting for Santiago's struggle is the most natural in

the world: overhead move the sun and the stars and the moon; beneath sways the sea, *la mar,* and about the boat move the birds and fish. The sea is the old man's home and the others are his friends and brothers. The old fisherman himself—his skin blotched brown by the friendly sun, his eyes "the color of the sea," the scars on his hands "old as erosions in a fishless desert"—is part of this natural universe. It is a complete and closed universe, a friendly one—its Creator neither hostile nor beneficent but mysteriously just. And the old man talks to the fish and the birds and the stars just as primitive man might have done long ago.

Yet more remarkable than Santiago's killing of the fish is his suffering. (Santiago is Spanish for Saint James—the fisherman, apostle, and martyr from the Sea of Galilee.) Etched on the reader's mind is the image of the old man as he settled against the wood of the bow—the big fish towing the cord tight across the old man's back—and took his suffering as it came, telling himself, " 'Rest gently now against the wood and think of nothing.' " "The old man rode gently with the small sea and the hurt of the cord across his back came to him easily and smoothly." Suffering and gentle and wood blend magically into an image of Christ on the cross. Then as he was pinned to the bow, dreaming for a few minutes of the lions on the long yellow beach, he woke suddenly with a jerk, the line burning his right hand, his left without feeling. He leaned against the line and tried to brake it, while it burned his back and cut deeply into his left hand. "Just then the fish jumped making a great bursting of the ocean . . . jumped again and again." The straining line pulled the old man face down into the slice of dolphin at the bow. He got his head out of the fish, which was nauseating him, and rose slowly to his knees. Taking the strain with his left hand, he washed the dolphin off his face and let his bleeding right hand trail clean in the salt water, reassuring himself the while, " 'Pain does not matter to a man.' " The fish circled slowly, while "the old man was wet with sweat and tired deep into his bones" and his hands were mushy and he was seeing only in flashes and he [10/11] was feeling himself go. [*sic*] It was then that he prepared for the kill, pitting "all his pain and what was left of his strength and his long gone pride" against the agony of the fish. When he thrust and pushed his harpoon into the fish's heart, "Then the fish came alive, with his death in him, and rose high out of the water showing all his great length and width and all his power and beauty. Then he fell into the water with a crash that sent spray over the old man and all of the skiff." For a moment after the death of the fish, the tension relaxed, but the pain continued and then the sharks came. " 'Ay,' he said aloud. There is no translation for this word and perhaps it is just a noise such as a man might make, involuntarily, feeling the nail go through his hands and into the wood." He fought the sharks through the afternoon, into the evening and the night, until he was almost dead; but the "pain of life" in his hands and shoulders told him otherwise. He fought until he was weaponless. Then he knew he was beatened [*sic*] and turned the skiff home. The sharks bit into what was left of the great fish, but the old man did not heed them. He was past everything now. Finally sailing into the little harbor, making the boat fast, and stepping ashore, he shouldered the mast and started to climb. "It was then that he knew the depth of his tiredness," as he looked back at the head and the white skeleton of the great fish. He climbed again, bearing his mast like a heavy cross, "and at the top he fell and lay for some time with the mast across his shoulder." He got up again. Then reaching his shack, he put the mast against the wall and lay down on his bed. The next morning the boy found him—"his face down on the newspapers with his arms out straight and the palms of his hands out."

Yet that afternoon the old man was dreaming of the lions on the white beaches of Africa. The dream may represent, as Philip Young had suggested, not only a nostalgic return to the strength of one's youth but also a desire for immortality— like the meaning of the frozen leopard on the summit of Kilimanjaro. Despite the suffering and seeming defeat of the old man, the final effect is that of a triumph which is invested not with the violent ritualized quality of the bullfights of *Death in the Afternoon* or the uneasily insistent and belligerent note of *Green Hills of Africa,* but with a warm autumnal glow. The old man beating off the sharks is like life rebelling against death—as though the old man and the great fish who are lashed together and steering as one toward home, just as earlier they had been bound by the "pain of life," have become the symbol of life; while the sharks (scavengers like the vultures and hyena who are symbols of death in "The Snows of Kilimanjaro") have become the death which must be resisted even though it will win.

Combined with this triumph is a tenderness not usually found in Hemingway's work. For all of Hemingway's glorifying of love between man and woman, too much of the author seemed involved, as Edmund Wilson and Philip Young have noted, with a repudiation of woman. But now in the relation between man and boy, Hemingway achieves a new gentleness. This turning to male companionships seems characteristically American, recalling the paired Huck Finn and Jim, Natty Bumppo and Chingachgook, Ishmael and Queequeg. Curiously, with the exception of Ishmael, they are all variations of primitives. And in Santiago Hemingway has created as fine a primitive as the twentieth century has revealed, one who seems worthy of comparison with Mark Twain's Huck Finn or Jim. But the old man is more richly endowed than most primitives: bearing the name of Saint James, who was fisherman and martyr, he strangely unites the matador and the crucified.

Confiteor Hominem: Ernest Hemingway's Religion of Man*

JOSEPH WALDMEIR is a member of the Department of American Thought and Language at Michigan State University.

In recent years, critics have become increasingly suspicious that it is necessary to read Ernest Hemingway's work on the symbolic as well as on the story level in order to gain a full appreciation of its art.[1] Since the publication of *The Old Man and the Sea,* the suspicion has become first an awareness, then a certainty. Of all Hemingway's work, this one demands most to be read on both levels; and the story, its details, its method of presentation, are sufficiently similar to the balance of his work as to suggest strongly the possibility of a similar reading and perhaps a similar interpretation.

The Old Man and the Sea is, as story, very good Hemingway. It is swiftly and smoothly told; the conflict is resolved into a struggle between a man and a force which he scarcely comprehends, but which he knows that he must continue to strive against, though knowing too that the struggle must end in defeat. The defeat is only apparent, however, for, as in "The Undefeated," it becomes increasingly clear throughout the story that it is not victory or defeat that matters but the struggle itself. Furthermore, *The Old Man and the Sea,* while reasserting the set of values, the philosophy which permeates all of Hemingway, is built upon the great abstractions—love and truth and honor and loyalty and pride and humility—and again speaks of the proper method of attaining and retaining these virtues, and of the spiritual satisfaction inevitably bestowed upon their holder.

The Christian religious symbols running through the story, which are so closely interwoven with the story in fact as to suggest an allegorical intention on Hemingway's part, are so obvious as to require little more than a listing of them here. The Old Man is a [**349/350**] fisherman, and he is also a teacher, one who has taught the boy not only how to fish—that is, how to make a living—but how to be have as well, giving him the pride and humility necessary to a good life. During the trials with the great fish and with the sharks his hands pain him terribly, his back is lashed by the line, he gets an eye-piercing headache, and his chest constricts and he spits blood. He hooks the fish at noon, and at noon of the third day he kills it by driving his harpoon into its heart. As he sees the second and third sharks attacking, the Old Man calls aloud " 'Ay,' " and Hemingway comments: "There is no translation for this word and perhaps it is just such a noise as a man might make, involuntarily, feeling the nail go through his hand and into the wood."[2] On landing, the Old Man shoulders his mast and goes upward from the sea toward his hut, he is forced to rest several times on his journey up the hill, and when he reaches the hut he lies on the bed "with his arms

[1] The two most recent comprehensive examinations of Hemingway symbolism are: Carlos Baker, *Hemingway: The Writer as Artist* (Princeton: Princeton University Press, 1952), and Philip Young, *Ernest Hemingway* (New York: Rinehart, 1952).

[2] Ernest Hemingway, *The Old Man and the Sea* (New York: Scribners, 1952), p. 118.

*Joseph Waldmeir, "Confiteor Hominem: Ernest Hemingway's Religion of Man," *Papers of the Michigan Academy of Science, Arts, and Letters,* XLII (Ann Arbor, Mich.: The University of Michigan Press, 1957), 349-356. Reprinted by permission of The University of Michigan Press.

out straight and the palms of his hands up."[3]

The Christian symbolism so evident here shifts from man to fish—a legitimate symbol for Christ since the beginning of Christianity, as it was a legitimate religious symbol before Christianity—and back to man throughout the story. This apparent confusion is consistent not only within the Hemingway philosophy as an example of the sacrificer-sacrificed phenomenon (a point which I will discuss later in this paper) but within formal Christianity as well, if the doctrine of the Trinity be accepted. Furthermore, the phenomenon itself closely parallels the Roman Catholic sacrifice of the Mass, wherein a fusion of the priest-man with Christ takes place at the moment of Transubstantiation.

Along with the Christ symbols, reinforcing them, but depending on them for its importance, is a rather intricate numerology. It is not formalized—neither is the numerology of Christianity—but it is carefully set forth.

Three, seven, and forty are key numbers in the Old and New Testaments, and in the religion, and Hemingway makes a judicious use of them. The Old Man, as the story opens, has fished alone for forty-four famine days and with the boy for forty more. The Old Man's trial with the great fish lasts exactly three days; the fish is **[350/351]** landed on the seventh attempt; seven sharks are killed; and, although Christ fell only three times under the Cross, whereas the Old Man has to rest from the weight of the mast seven times, there is a consistency in the equal importance of the numbers themselves.

But, once it has been established that *The Old Man and the Sea* may be read on the symbolic as well as on the story level, a new problem presents itself, a problem which grows out of the nature of the symbolic level and out of the disturbing realization that the two levels exist harmoniously in the work. I think that the problem may best be expressed by two questions which the discerning reader

must have asked himself as he put *The Old Man and the Sea* down: Is the story, as it appears at first glance to be, a Christian allegory? Has the old master tough guy decided, in the words of Colonel Cantwell, "to run as a Christian"? If neither of these questions can be answered with an unqualified affirmative—and I submit that they cannot—then a further question must be asked: Just what is the book's message?

The answer assumes a third level on which *The Old Man and the Sea* must be read —as a sort of allegorical commentary by the author on all his previous work, by means of which it may be established that the religious overtones of *The Old Man and the Sea* are not peculiar to that book among Hemingway's works, and that Hemingway has finally taken the decisive step in elevating what might be called his philosophy of Manhood to the level of a religion.

Two aspects of the total work, including *The Old Man and the Sea,* must be considered at this point in order to clarify the above conclusion on the one hand, and to answer the questions concerning Hemingway's Christianity on the other.

The first of these aspects is Hemingway's concern with man as man, with man in his relation to things of this world almost exclusively. The other world, God, does not often enter into the thoughts, plans, or emotions of a Hemingway character. God exists—most of the characters are willing to admit His existence, or at least, unwilling to deny it—but not as an immanent Being, not ever benevolent or malevolent.

God is sometimes prayed to by the Hemingway hero at moments of crisis, but His aid or succor are never depended upon, never really expected. Thus we have Jake Barnes in the Cathedral at Pamplona, on the eve of his great trial, praying for everybody he can think of, **[351/352]** for good bullfights and good fishing; and as he becomes aware of himself kneeling, head bent, he

[3] *Ibid.*, p. 134.

was a little ashamed, and regretted that I was such a rotten Catholic, but realized that there was nothing I could do about it, at least for awhile, and maybe never, but that anyway it was a grand religion, and I only wished I felt religious and maybe I would the next time. . . .[4]

And thus, too, we have the Old Man, who, after twenty-four hours of his monumental struggle have passed, prays for heavenly assistance mechanically, automatically, thinking, "I am not religious," and "Hail Marys are easier to say than Our Fathers." And after forty-five hours, he says:

"Now that I have him coming so beautifully, God help me to endure. I'll say a hundred Our Fathers and a hundred Hail Marys. But I cannot say them now."
Consider them said, he thought, I'll say them later.[5]

But when the struggle is ended and the full ironic impact of his "victory" is clear, he asks himself what it was that beat him, and answers, "Nothing . . . I went out too far."[6]

He who depends too heavily on prayer, or for that matter on any external aids when faced with a crisis, is not very admirable to Hemingway. In *Death in the Afternoon,* when he wants to describe the unmanliness of a "cowardly bullfighter" girding himself for action, Hemingway places him in church

in his bullfighting clothes to pray before the fight, sweating under the armpits, praying that the bull will embiste, that is charge frankly and follow the cloth well; oh blessed Virgin that thou wilt give me a bull that will embiste well, blessed Virgin, give me this bull, blessed Virgin, that I should touch this bull in Madrid to-day on a day without wind; promising something of value or a pilgrimage, praying for luck, frightened sick. . . .[7]

A man must depend upon himself alone in order to assert his manhood, and the assertion of his manhood, in the face of insuperable obstacles, is the complete end and justification of his existence for a Hemingway hero. The Old Man *must* endure his useless struggle with the sharks;

Manuel, in "The Undefeated," *must,* in spite of his broken wrist and a terrible goring, go in on the bull six times and [352/353] accept the horn at last; Jake *must* continue to live as "well" and "truly" and "honestly" as he is able in spite of his overwhelming frustration. And each must face his struggle alone, with no recourse to otherworldly help, for only as solitary individuals can they assert their manhood.

And significantly they must go it alone without regard to otherworldly blame. As far as sin is concerned, Jake would probably say along with the Old Man, "Do not think about sin. It is much too late for that and there are people who are paid to do it. Let them think about it."[8] And Manuel would probably nod agreement.

However, in spite of such obvious rejections of otherworldly Christianity in his affirmation of Manhood, Hemingway has formulated as rigid a set of rules for living and for the attainment of Manhood as can be found in any religion. These rules, along with the detailed procedure for their application, constitute the second aspect of Hemingway's total work to be considered in this paper.

The rules are built upon the great abstractions mentioned above. They are so

[4] Hemingway, *The Sun Also Rises* (New York: Scribners, 1926), pp. 99-100.
[5] *The Old Man and the Sea,* p. 96.
[6] *Ibid.,* p. 133.
[7] Hemingway, *Death in the Afternoon* (New York: Scribner, 1932), p. 90.
[8] *The Old Man and the Sea,* p. 116. Hemingway has always had a deep respect for Christians—provided they *live* like Christians. His great abstractions are also great Christian virtues; and when he finds a believer, such as the priest in *A Farewell to Arms* or Anselmo in *For Whom the Bell Tolls,* who lives in accord with the abstractions, he praises him as "a Christian," and adds, for the benefit of the hypocritical, "something very rare in Catholic countries."
There is no evidence of intentional blasphemy in any of his work; the deeply religious are frequently exalted, not in the terms of Christianity, but in Hemingway's own terms. In the one-act play, "Today is Friday," Christ's Manhood is given far greater importance than His Godhead with no blasphemous overtones. The First Soldier, speaking for Hemingway and offering the highest praise he is capable of, answers, "He was pretty good in there today," each time the cynical Second Soldier minimizes Christ's manliness. The words are not only directly addressed to the cynic, but indirectly to the emotionally disturbed Third Soldier as well, who has had a religious experience which the First cannot share, but which he comprehends and sympathizes with.

bound up with the procedure for their application that the procedure itself might be considered to be a rule—or better, that neither rules nor procedure exist without one another. Hemingway's philosophy of Manhood is a philosophy of action; a man is honest when he acts honestly, he is humble when he acts humbly, he loves when he is loving or being loved. Thus, taking an awareness of the rules as he has taken an awareness of the abstractions for granted, Hemingway concerns himself primarily with the presentation of procedure. [353/354] The procedure is carefully outlined; it is meticulously detailed. If no part of it is overlooked or sloughed off, it must result in a satisfying experience almost in and of itself.

This procedure, this ritual—for such is what the procedure actually amounts to—is most clearly evident in Hemingway's treatment of the bullfight. *Death in the Afternoon* is devoted to an evaluation of the manhood of various bullfighters on the basis of their ability to abide by the rules, and to a description of the ritual by means of which they prove possession and communicate the satisfaction to be gained from a proper performance of function to the spectator. War, the prize ring, fishing, hunting, and making love are some of the other celebrations by means of which Hemingway's religio-philosophy of Man is conveyed. But the bullfight is the greatest because, besides possessing, as the others do also, a procedure inviolate, intimately related to the great abstractions, it always ends in death. It assumes the stature of a religious sacrifice by means of which a man can place himself in harmony with the universe, can satisfy the spiritual as well as the physical side of his nature, can atone for the grievous omissions and commissions of his past, can purify and elevate himself in much the same way that he can in any sacrificial religion. The difference between Hemingway's religion of man and formal religion is simply—yet profoundly—that in the former the elevation does not extend beyond the limits of this world, and in the latter, Christianity for example, the ultimate elevation is totally otherworldly.

The bullfighter is in a sense a priest, performing the sacrifice for the sake of the spectator as well as for his own sake, giving each that "feeling of life and death and mortality and immortality" which Hemingway described in *Death in the Afternoon,* and, as does the Roman Catholic priest on the ideal level, the bullfighter actually places his own life in jeopardy. This curious phenomenon of the sacrificer gambling on becoming the sacrificed serves to clarify the terms of Hemingway's system, rather than, as at first glance it might seem, to confuse them. The bullfighter recognizes the possibility and immanence of death when he steps into the ring, and he must face it bravely. He must perform the sacrifice cleanly, with one true stroke, preserving both his honor and the bull's dignity. If he kills out of malice or out of fear his actions will show it, and the spectator will be distracted from concentration upon the sacrifice to awareness of the man, and no satisfaction will result. [354/355]

There must be a cognizance of death both from the standpoint of killing and from that of being killed; there must be more than a cognizance actually; there must be an acceptance. Knowledge of death's inevitability so that he does not react to its immediacy, coupled with unconcern for the possibilities of life after death, are necessary attributes of the ideal bullfighter. His aim can extend no further than the great abstractions themselves, how he earns them and how he communicates them. He must realize that it is not *that* one dies but *how* one dies that is important. And equally important, that it is not *that* one kills but *how* one kills.

It is not only in his treatment of the bullfight that this second aspect of Hemingway's total work is evident, though there it may be most immediately apparent. The abstractions, the rules, the ritual, the sacrifice dominate the details of *The Old Man and the Sea* as they dominate those of "The Undefeated" and *The Sun*

Also Rises.[9] We are told carefully, painstakingly, how the Old Man performs his function as fisherman; how he prepares for the hoped-for struggle:

Before it was really light he had his baits out and was drifting with the current. One bait was down forty fathoms. The second was at seventy-five and the third and fourth were down in the blue water at one hundred and one hundred and twenty-five fathoms. Each bait hung head down with the shank of the hook inside the bait fish, tied and sewed solid and all the projecting part of the hook, the curve and the point, was covered with fresh sardines. Each sardine was hooked through both eyes so that they made a half-garland on the projecting steel.

. . . Each line, as thick around as a big pencil, was looped onto a green-sapped stick so that any pull or touch on the bait would make the stick dip and each line had two forty-fathom coils which could be made fast to the other spare coils so that, if it were necessary, a fish could take out over three hundred fathoms of line.[10]

We are told how he hooks the fish and secures the line, waiting suspensefully for the fish to turn and swallow the bait, then waiting again until it has eaten it well, then striking, "with all the strength of his arms and the pivoted weight of his body," three times, setting the hook; then placing the line across his back and shoulders so that there will be something to give when the fish lunges, and the line will not break. We are told specifically, in terms reminiscent of such descriptions of the bullfight, how the kill is made:

The old man dropped the line and put his foot on it and lifted the harpoon as high as he could and drove it down with all his strength, and more strength he had just **[355/356]** summoned, into the fish's side just behind the great chest fin that rose high in the air to the altitude of a man's chest. He felt the iron go in and he leaned on it and drove it further and then pushed all his weight after it.[11]

The immanence of death for the sacrificer as well as for the sacrificed, and his total disregard of its possibility, are made clear at the climax of the struggle when the Old Man thinks: "You are killing me, fish . . . Come on and kill me. I do not care who kills who." [12]

It is at this point I think that the questions asked earlier in this paper can be answered. Has Hemingway decided to "run as a Christian"? I think not; the evidence in *The Old Man and the Sea*, with the exception of the Christian symbolism indicates that he is no more Christian now than he was when he wrote *The Sun Also Rises.* But the Christian symbolism in the book, and it *does* appear to constitute a Christian religious allegory. Yes, but on a superficial level. The religious allegory, attached to the two aspects of the total body of Hemingway's work as they appear in *The Old Man and the Sea* which have been the subject of most of my discussion thus far, actually constitute a third level on which *The Old Man and the Sea* must be read—as the allegorical interpretation of the total body of the work.

I said above that Hemingway is no more Christian now than he was thirty years ago; it has been my intention in this paper to show that he was *no less religious* thirty years ago than he is now. The evidence which I have presented adds up to something more than a philosophy or an ethic, the two terms which have most often been used to describe Hemingway's world view.

[9] With the possible exception of sacrifice, the dominate the details of *Across the River and Into the Trees* as well. If examined from the point of view of the religion of Manhood, this is not really as poor a book as most critics have insisted. It is a gentle story, intended to give a procedure for dying to fellow members of the Order who realize that they are going to die in bed. Colonel Cantwell experiences in fact many of those things which have contributed to the happiness of his life—the beauties of nature and of art, the taste of properly prepared food and drink, the pleasures of the hunt, the give and take of sexual love—and in memory, he re-lives the pleasure he had gained from a proper performance of his function as a soldier.

The reviewers chose to look upon this procedure for dying as little more than nostalgic sentimentalism; but even granting the tendency of the story this direction, it still fits neatly into the Hemingway religio-philosophical mold. And at its climax there is the usual refusal to turn to the supernatural, a more pointed refusal than ever: "You going to run as a Christian?" the Colonel asks himself and answers, "Maybe I will get Christian toward the end. Yes, he said, maybe you will, Who wants to make a bet on that?" (p. 291). [This footnote has been added at the author's request and did not appear in the original publication. Footnotes through 12 have been renumbered.]

[10] *The Old Man and the Sea*, pp. 33-34.
[11] *Ibid.*, pp. 103-104.
[12] *Ibid.*, p. 102.

it adds up to what I would call a Religion of Man. Hemingway did not turn religious to write *The Old Man and the Sea.* He has always been religious, though his religion is not of the orthodox, organized variety. He celebrates, he has always celebrated, the Religion of Man; *The Old Man and the Sea* merely celebrates it more forcefully and convincingly than any previous Hemingway work. It is the final step in the celebration. It is the book which, on the one hand, elevates the philosophy to a religion by the use of allegory, and on the other, by being an allegory of the total body of his work, enables us to see that work finally from the point of view of religion.

The Old Man and the Sea: Hemingway's Tragic Vision of Man*

CLINTON S. BURHANS, JR., author of a number of essays in American literature, teaches at Michigan State University.

I

In *Death in the Afternoon,* Hemingway uses an effective metaphor to describe the kind of prose he is trying to write: he explains that

If a writer of prose knows enough about what he is writing about he may omit things that he knows and the reader, if the writer is writing truly enough, will have a feeling of those things as strongly as though the writer had stated them. The dignity of movement of an iceberg is due to only one-eighth of it being above water.[1]

Among all the works of Hemingway which illustrate this metaphor, none, I think, does so more consistently or more thoroughly than the saga of Santiago. Indeed, the critical reception of the novel has emphasized this aspect of it: in particular, Philip Young, Leo Gurko, and Carlos Baker have stressed the qualities of *The Old Man and the Sea* as allegory and parable. Each of these critics is especially concerned with two qualities in Santiago—his epic individualism and the love he feels for the creatures who share with him a world of inescapable violence —though in the main each views these qualities from a different point of the literary compass. Young regards the novel as essentially classical in nature; Gurko sees it as reflecting Hemingway's romanticism; and to Baker, the novel is Christian in context, and the old fisherman is suggestive of Christ.[2]

Such interpretations of *The Old Man*

and the Sea are not, of course, contradictory; in fact, they are parallel at many points. All are true, and together they point to both the breadth and depth of the novel's enduring significance and also to its central greatness: [446/447] like all great works of art it is a mirror wherein every man perceives a personal likeness. Such viewpoints, then, differ only in emphasis and reflect generally similar conclusions—that Santiago represents a noble and tragic individualism revealing what man can do in an indifferent universe which defeats him, and the love he can feel for such a universe and his humility before it.

True as this is, there yet remains, I think, a deeper level of significance, a deeper level upon which the ultimate beauty and the dignity of movement of this brilliant structure fundamentally rest. On this level of significance, Santiago is Harry Morgan alive again and grown old; for what comes to Morgan in a sudden and unexpected revelation as he lies dying is the matrix of the old fisherman's climactic experience. Since 1937, Hemingway has been increasingly concerned with the relationship between individualism

[1] Ernest Hemingway, *Death in the Afternoon* (New York, 1932), p. 183.
[2] On the other hand—though not, to me, convincingly—Otto Friedrich, "Ernest Hemingway: Joy Through Strength," *The American Scholar,* XXV (Autumn, 1957), pp. 470, 513-30, sees Santiago's experience as little more than the result of the necessities of his profession; Philip Young, *Hemingway* (New York, 1952), p. 100; Leo Gurko, "The Old Man and the Sea," *College English,* XVII, 1 14 (Oct., 1955); Carlos Baker, *Hemingway* (Princeton, 1956), p. 299.

*Clinton S. Burhans, Jr., "The Old Man and the Sea: Hemingway's Tragic Vision of Man," American Literature XXXI (January, 1960), 446-455. Reprinted by permission of the author and Duke University Press.

and interdependence;[3] and *The Old Man and the Sea* is the culminating expression of this concern in its reflection of Hemingway's mature view of the tragic irony of man's fate: that no abstraction can bring man an awareness and understanding of the solidarity and interdependence without which life is impossible; he must learn it, as it has always been truly learned, through the agony of active and isolated individualism in a universe which dooms such individualism.

II

Throughout *The Old Man and the Sea*, Santiago is given heroic proportions. He is "a strange old man,"[4] still powerful and still wise in all the ways of his trade. After he hooks the great marlin, he fights him with epic skill and endurance, showing "what a man can do and what a man endures" (p. 64). And when the sharks come, he is determined " 'to fight them until I die' " (p. 116), because he knows that " 'a man is not made for defeat. . . . A man can be destroyed but not defeated' " (p. 103). **[447/448]**

In searching for and in catching his big fish, Santiago gains a deepened insight into himself and into his relationship to the rest of created life—an insight as pervasive and implicit in the old fisherman's experience as it is sudden and explicit in Harry Morgan's. As he sails far out on the sea, Santiago thinks of it "as feminine and as something that gave or withheld great favors, and if she did wild or wicked things it was because she could not help them" (p. 27). For the bird who rests on his line and for other creatures who share with him such a capricious and violent life, the old man feels friendship and love (pp. 26, 46). And when he sees a flight of wild ducks go over, the old man knows "no man was ever alone on the sea" (p. 59).

Santiago comes to feel his deepest love for the creature that he himself hunts and kills, the great fish which he must catch not alone for physical need but even more for his pride and his profession. The great marlin is unlike the other fish which the old man catches; he is a spiritual more than a physical necessity. He is unlike the other fish, too, in that he is a worthy antagonist for the old man, and during his long ordeal, Santiago comes to pity the marlin and then to respect and to love him. In the end he senses that there can be no victory for either in the equal struggle between them, that the conditions which have brought them together have made them one (p. 92). And so, though he kills the great fish, the old man has come to love him as his equal and his brother; sharing a life which is a capricious mixture of incredible beauty and deadly violence and in which all creatures are both hunter and hunted, they are bound together in its most primal relationship.

Beyond the heroic individualism of Santiago's struggle with the great fish and his fight against the sharks, however, and beyond the love and the brotherhood which he comes to feel for the noble creature he must kill, there is a further dimension in the old man's experience which gives to these their ultimate significance. For in killing the great marlin and in losing him to the sharks, the old man learns the sin into which men inevitably fall by going far out beyond their depth, beyond their true place in life. In the first night of his struggle with the great fish, the old man

[3] This direction in Hemingway's thought and art has, of course, been pointed out by several critics, particularly by Edgar Johnson in the *Sewanee Review*, XLVIII, 3 (July–Sept., 1940) and by Maxwell Geismar in *Writers in Crisis* (Cambridge, Mass., 1942). With prophetic insight, Johnson says that "the important thing about Hemingway is that he has earned his philosophy, that he has struggled to reach it, overcome the obstacles to attaining it. . . . He has earned the right to reject rejection. For the good, the gentle, and the brave, he now tells us, if they do not try to stand alone and make a separate peace, defeat is not inevitable. His life-blood dripping into the bottom of the boat, Harry Morgan realized it at the end of his career. Philip Rawlings realized it in the blood and terror and tragedy and splendor even of a dying Madrid. Hemingway has realized it there too, and the realization may well be for him the very beginning of a new and more vital career."

[4] Ernest Hemingway, *The Old Man and the Sea* (London, 1952), p. 10.

begins to feel a loneliness and a sense almost of guilt for the way in which he has caught him (p. 48) ; and after he has killed the marlin, he feels no pride of accomplishment, no sense of victory. Rather, he seems to feel al- [448/449] most as though he has betrayed the great fish; "I am only better than him through trickery," he thinks, "and he meant me no harm" (p. 99).

Thus, when the sharks came, it is almost as a thing expected, almost as a punishment which the old man brings upon himself in going far out "beyond all people. Beyond all people in the world" (p. 48) and there hooking and killing the great fish. For the coming of the sharks is not a matter of chance nor a stroke of bad luck; "the shark was not an accident" (p. 99). They are the direct result of the old man's action in killing the fish. He has driven his harpoon deep into the marlin's heart, and the blood of the great fish, welling from his heart, leaves a trail of scent which the first shark follows. He tears huge pieces from the marlin's body, causing more blood to seep into the sea and thus attract other sharks; and in killing the first shark, the old man loses his principal weapon, his harpoon. Thus, in winning his struggle with the marlin and in killing him, the old man sets in motion the sequence of events which take from him the great fish whom he has come to love and with whom he identifies himself completely. And the old man senses an inevitability in the coming of the sharks (p. 101), a feeling of guilt which deepens into remorse and regret. "I am sorry that I killed the fish . . ." (p. 103), he thinks, and he tells himself that "You did not kill the fish only to keep alive and to sell for food. . . . You killed him for pride and because you are a fisherman" (p. 105).

Earlier, before he had killed the marlin, Santiago had been " 'glad we do not have to try to kill the stars' " (p. 74). It is enough, he had felt, to have to kill our fellow creatures. Now, with the inevitable sharks attacking, the old man senses that in going far out he has in effect tried "to kill the sun or the moon or the stars." For him it has not been "enough to live on the sea and kill our true brothers"; in his individualism and his need and his pride, he has gone far out "beyond all people," beyond his true place in a capricious and indifferent world, and has thereby brought not only on himself but also on the great fish the forces of violence and destruction. " 'I shouldn't have gone out so far, fish . . . ,' " he declares. " 'Neither for you nor for me. I'm sorry, fish' " (p. 110). And when the sharks have torn away half of the great marlin, Santiago speaks again to his brother in the sea: " 'Half-fish,' he said. 'Fish that you [449/450] were. I am sorry that I went too far out. I ruined us both' " (p. 116).

The old man's realization of what he has done is reflected in his apologies to the fish, and this realization and its implications are emphasized symbolically throughout the novel. From beginning to end, the theme of solidarity and interdependence pervades the action and provides the structural framework within which the old man's heroic individualism and his love for his fellow creatures appear and function and which gives them their ultimate significance. Having gone eighty-four days without a catch, Santiago has become dependent upon the young boy, Manolin, and upon his other friends in his village. The boy keeps up his confidence and hope, brings him clothes and such necessities as water and soap, and sees that he has fresh bait for his fishing. Martin, the restaurant owner, sends the old man food, and Perico, the wineshop owner, gives him newspapers so that he can read about baseball. All of this the old man accepts gratefully and without shame, knowing that such help is not demeaning. "He was too simple to wonder when he had attained humility. But he knew he had attained it and he knew it was not disgraceful and it carried no loss of true pride" (pp. 9-10).

Santiago refuses the young boy's offer to leave the boat his parents have made him go in and return to his, but soon after he hooks the great marlin he wishes increasingly and often that the boy were with him. And after the sharks come and he wonders if it had been a sin to kill the great fish, the old man thinks that, after all, "everything kills everything else in some way. Fishing kills me exactly as it keeps me alive." But then he remembers that it is not fishing but the love and care of another human being that keeps him alive now; "the boy keeps me alive, he thought. I must not deceive myself too much" (p. 106).

As the sharks tear from him more and more of the great fish and as the boat gets closer to his home, the old man's sense of his relationship to his friends and to the boy deepens: "I cannot be too far out now, he thought. I hope no one has been too worried. There is only the boy to worry, of course. But I am sure he would have confidence. Many of the older fishermen will worry. Many others too, he thought. I live in a good town" (p. 115). In the end, when he awakens in his shack and talks with the boy, he notices "how pleasant it was to have someone to talk to instead of speaking only [450/451] to himself and to the sea" (p. 125). This time he accepts without any real opposition the boy's insistence on returning to his boat, and he says no more about going far out alone.

This theme of human solidarity and interdependence is reinforced by several symbols. Baseball, which the old man knows well and loves and which he thinks and talks about constantly, is, of course, a highly developed team sport and one that contrasts importantly in this respect with the relatively far more individualistic bullfighting, hunting, and fishing usually found in Hemingway's stories. Although he tells himself that "now is no time to think of baseball" (p. 37), the game is in Santiago's thoughts throughout his ordeal, and he wonders about each day's results in the *Gran Ligas*.

Even more significant is the old man's hero-worship of Joe DiMaggio, the great Yankee outfielder. DiMaggio, like Santiago, was a champion, a master of his craft,

and in baseball terms an old one, playing out the last years of his glorious career severely handicapped by the pain of a bone spur in his heel. The image of DiMaggio is a constant source of inspiration to Santiago; in his strained back and his cut and cramped left hand he, too, is an old champion who must endure the handicap of pain; and he tells himself that he "must have confidence and . . . be worthy of the great DiMaggio who does all things perfectly even with the pain of the bone spur in his heel" (p. 66).

But DiMaggio had qualities at least as vital to the Yankees as his courage and individual brilliance. Even during his own time and since then, many men with expert knowledge of baseball have considered other contemporary outfielders—especially Ted Williams of the Boston Red Sox—to be DiMaggio's equal or superior in terms of individual ability and achievement. But few men have ever earned the affection and the renown which DiMaggio received as a "team player"—one who always displayed his individual greatness as part of his team, one to whom the team was always more important than himself. It used to be said of DiMaggio's value as a "team player" that with him in the line-up, even when he was handicapped by the pain in his heel, the Yankees were two runs ahead when they came out on the field. From Santiago's love of baseball and his evident knowledge of it, it is clear that he would be aware of these qualities in DiMaggio. And when Manolin re- [451/452] marks that there are other men on the New York team, the old man replies: " 'Naturally. But he makes the difference' " (p. 17).

The lions which Santiago dreams about and his description in terms of Christ symbols further suggest solidarity and love and humility as opposed to isolated individualism and pride. So evocative and lovely a symbol is the dream of the lions that it would be foolish if not impossible to attempt its literal definition. Yet it seems significant that the old man dreams not of a single lion, a "king of the beasts," a lion proud and powerful and alone, like the one from which Francis Macomber runs in terror, but of several young lions who come down to a beach in the evening to play together. "He only dreamed of places now and of the lions on the beach. They played like young cats in the dusk and he loved them as he loved the boy" (p. 22). It seems also significant that the old man "no longer dreamed of storms, nor of women, nor of great occurrences, nor of great fish, nor fights, nor contests of strength, nor of his wife" (pp. 21-22) — that is that he no longer dreams of great individualistic deeds like the one which brings violence and destruction on him and on the marlin. Instead, the lions are "the main thing that is left" (p. 65), and they evoke the solidarity and love and peace to which the old man returns after hunting and killing and losing his great fish.

These qualities are further emphasized by the symbolic value of the old fisherman as he carries the mast crosslike up the hill to his shack and as he lies exhausted on his bed. His hands have been terribly wounded in catching the great marlin and in fighting the sharks, and as he lies sleeping "face down on the newspapers with his arms out straight and the palms up" (p. 122), his figure is Christ-like and suggests that if the old man has been crucified by the forces of a capricious and violent universe, the meaning of his experience is the humility and love of Christ and the interdependence which they imply.

Such, then, are the qualities which define man's true place in a world of violence and death indifferent to him, and they are the context which gives the experience of the old fisherman its ultimate significance as the reflection of Hemingway's culminating concept of the human condition—his tragic vision of man. For in his understanding that "it is enough to live on the sea and kill our true brothers," the fellow creatures who share life with us and whom he loves, the old man is expressing Hemingway's conviction that de- [452/453] spite the tragic necessity of such a condi-

tion, man has a place in the world. And in his realization that in going alone and too far out, "beyond all people in the world," he has ruined both himself and also the great fish, the old man reflects Hemingway's feeling that in his individualism and his pride and his need, man inevitably goes beyond his true place in the world and thereby brings violence and destruction on himself and on others. Yet in going out too far and alone, Santiago has found his greatest strength and courage and dignity and nobility and love, and in this he expresses Hemingway's view of the ultimate tragic irony of man's fate: that only through the isolated individualism and the pride which drive him beyond his true place in life does man develop the qualities and the wisdom which teach him the sin of such individualism and pride and which bring him the deepest understanding of himself and of his place in the world. Thus, in accepting his world for what it is and in learning to live in it, Hemingway has achieved a tragic but ennobling vision of man which is in the tradition of Sophocles, Christ, Melville, and Conrad.

III

It is not enough, then, to point out, as Robert P. Weeks does, that "from the first eight words of *The Old Man and the Sea* . . . we are squarely confronted with a world in which man's isolation is the most insistent truth."[5] True as this is, it is truth which is at the same time paradox, for Santiago is profoundly aware that "no man was ever alone on the sea." Nor is the novel solely what Leo Gurko feels it is—"the culmination of Hemingway's long search for disengagement from the social world and total entry into the natural" (p. 15). If the old man leaves society to go "far out" and "beyond all people in the world," the consciousness of society and of

[5] Robert P. Weeks, "Hemingway and the Uses of Isolation," *University of Kansas City Review,* XXIV, 125 (Winter, 1957).

his relationship to it are never for long out of his thoughts; and in the end, of course, he returns to his "good town," where he finds it pleasant "to have someone to talk to instead of speaking only to himself and to the sea." To go no further than Santiago's isolation, therefore, or to treat it, as Weeks does, as a theme in opposition to Hemingway's concern with society, is to miss the deepest level of significance both in his novel and in Hemingway's writing generally. [453/454]

For, surely, as Edgar Johnson has shown, the true direction of Hemingway's thought and art from the beginning and especially since 1937 has been a return to society—not in terms of any particular social or political doctrine, but in the broad sense of human solidarity and interdependence. If he began by making "a separate peace" and by going, like Santiago, "far out" beyond society, like the old man, too, he has come back, through Harry Morgan's " 'no man alone,' " Philip Rawlings's and Robert Jordan's "no man is an island," and Santiago's "no man is ever alone on the sea," with a deepened insight into its nature and values and a profound awareness of his relationship to it as an individual.[6]

In the process, strangely enough—or perhaps it is not strange at all—he has come back from Frederic Henry's rejection of all abstract values to a reiteration for our time of mankind's oldest and noblest moral principles. As James B. Colvert points out, Hemingway is a moralist: heir, like his world, to the destruction by science and empiricism of nineteenth-century value assumptions, he rejects equally these assumptions and the principle underlying them—that intellectual moral abstractions possess independent supersensual existence. Turning from the resulting nihilism, he goes to experience in the actual world of hostility, violence, and destruction to find in the world which destroyed the old values a basis for new ones—and it is precisely here, Colvert suggests, in reflecting the central moral problem of his world,

that Hemingway is a significant moralist.[7]

But out of this concern with action and conduct in a naturalistic universe, Hemingway has not evolved new moral values; rather, he has reaffirmed man's oldest ones —courage, love, humility, solidarity, and interdependence. It is their basis which is new—a basis not in supernaturalism or abstraction but hard-won through actual experience in a naturalistic universe which is at best indifferent to man and his values. Hemingway tells us, as E. M. Halliday observes, that "we are part of a universe offering no assurance beyond the grave, [454/455] and we are to make what we can of life by a pragmatic ethic spun bravely out of man himself in full and steady cognizance that the end is darkness."[8]

Through perfectly realized symbolism and irony,[9] then, Hemingway has beautifully and movingly spun out of an old fisherman's great trial just such a pragmatic ethic and its basis in an essentially tragic vision of man; and in this reaffirmation of man's most cherished values and their reaffirmation in the terms of our time rests the deepest and the enduring significance of *The Old Man and the Sea.*

---

[6] This development in Hemingway's thought and art is further illustrated in a story which he wrote in 1939 and which, prompted by the recent Cuban revolution, *Cosmopolitan*, CXLVI, 4 (April, 1959), pp. 78-83, has reprinted. "Nobody Ever Dies!" is the story of a Spanish-speaking young man and a girl who have given themselves with selfless devotion to the cause of social liberty in a revolt in Cuba. The young man is trapped and killed by governmental forces, and the girl faces the torture of questioning with "a strange confidence. It was the same confidence another girl her age had felt a little more than five hundred years before in the market place of a town called Rouen."

[7] James B. Colvert, "Ernest Hemingway's Morality in Action," *American Literature*, XXVII (Nov., 1955), pp. 372-85.

[8] E. M. Halliday, "Hemingway's Ambiguity : Symbolism and Irony," *American Literature*, XXVIII (March, 1956), p. 3.

[9] Halliday's comment on Hemingway's ironic method is particularly applicable to *The Old Man and the Sea:* "the ironic gap between expectation and fulfillment, pretense and fact, intention and action, the message sent and the message received, the way things are thought or ought to be and the way things are—this has been Hemingway's great theme from the beginning ; and it has called for an ironic method to do it artistic justice" (*ibid.*, p. 15).

Hemingway's Ancient Mariner*

CARLOS BAKER. For information about the author, see "Place, Fact, and Scene in *The Sun Also Rises*," by Carlos Baker, reprinted on page 11.

I. TRUTH AND POETRY

Goethe called his autobiography *Dichtung und Wahrheit,* Poetry and Truth. The reverse of Goethe's title, as a strategy of emphasis, admirably fits the collected works of Hemingway. From the first he has been dedicated as a writer to the rendering of *Wahrheit,* the precise and at least partly naturalistic presentation of things as they are and were. Yet under all his brilliant surfaces lies the controlling *Dichtung,* the symbolic underpainting which gives so remarkable a sense of depth and vitality to what otherwise might seem flat and two-dimensional.

The literary histories commonly credit Hemingway with being the "archpriest of naturalists." This is something less than a half-truth because it tends, as a designation, to ignore what is always taking place down under. That Hemingway the technician achieves effects simply impossible to his naturalistic forebears or current imitators has sometimes been noticed. The cause behind the majority of these effects, the deep inner *Dichtung* which runs through all of his work from *The Sun Also Rises* to *The Old Man and The Sea,* has not until very recently been fully recognized or systematically explored.

Hemingway's conception of the meaning of *Wahrheit* has steadily increased in breadth and depth over the past thirty years, attaining a kind of apogee in *The Old Man and The Sea.* His earliest conviction, to which he still adheres with one facet of his artistic consciousness, is well summed up in a remark of Albert Schweitzer's on the *Naturphilosophie* of Goethe: "Only that knowledge is true which adds nothing to nature, either by thought or imagination; and which recognizes as valid only what comes from a research that is free from prejudices and preconceptions, from a firm and pure determination to find the truth, from a meditation which goes deeply into the heart of nature."

As a partial summary of Hemingway's esthetic and moral position, Schweitzer's statement would have to be qualified only by adding human nature to the rest of nature. Hemingway has rarely been interested in the passing show of the non-human universe unless it could serve him in some way to gain further understanding of one of nature's more complex phenomena, the human mind. A meditation which goes deeply enough into the heart of nature, whether along the banks of the Big Two-Hearted River, on the high slopes of the Guadarramas, or among the vast waters of the Gulf Stream, will often end, as it does in Hemingway, with a meditation which goes deeply into the heart of man.

Its grasp of reality, its content of *Wahrheit,* is one guaranty of the survival power of Hemingway's art. A second guaranty, not less important, is the use and control of *Dichtung.* The *Dichtung* in Hemingway might be provisionally defined as the artist's grasp of the relation-

---

* Carlos Baker, revision of "The Ancient Mariner" from *Hemingway: The Writer as Artist* (Princeton, N. J.: Princeton University Press, 1956), pp. 289-320. Copyright by the Princeton University Press. (No page numbers are supplied in the text since this revised version has not been published heretofore.)

ship between the temporal and the eternal. That grasp is expressed, in his fiction, through the considered use of imaginative symbols. Most of these come, by way of the artist's imagination, from the visible material universe—the mountains and the plains, the rivers and the trees, the weather and the seasons, the land and the sea. To such natural images Hemingway has attached the strong emotional power of his artistic apprehension of them. With Wordsworth, he knows that natural "objects derive their influence, not from properties inherent in them, not from what they are actually in themselves, but from such as are bestowed upon them by the minds of those who are conversant with or affected by those objects. Thus the poetry ... proceeds, whence it ought to do, from the soul of man, communicating its creative energies to the images of the external world." At the same time, Hemingway has generally managed to render with fidelity each of the natural objects or scenes precisely for what, in itself, it really is. As a result of their union with imagination and emotion, the various phenomena rise up as operative symbols in all his art. They become thereby not less real but more real than they are in themselves because of the double or triple significations with which they have been imbued.

Hemingway hinted strongly at this point when he said in 1942 that the writer's "standard of fidelity to the truth should be so high that his invention, out of his experience, should produce a truer account than anything factual can be." The *invention* here could be defined as that form of symbolic logic which is the artist's rough equivalent to the rational logic of the philosophers. Hemingway well knows, with Niebuhr, that "the relation of time and eternity" cannot be expressed in simple rational terms, but "only in symbolic terms." In some writers, the symbols are made over from antecedent literatures. In Hemingway they are usually, though not invariably, derived from the nexus of nature by means of the imag-inative apprehension of human experience in natural environs. ...

II. ANCIENT MARINER

The Old Man and The Sea earned its author the Pulitzer Prize in Fiction for 1952, and was instrumental in winning him the Nobel Prize two years later. This short novel, in the words of Eliot, explores yet "another intensity" beyond those which can be located in Hemingway's previous fictions. Among the vast waters of the petrel and the porpoise, he seemed to many of his readers to have found the means of establishing "a further union" and "a deeper communion" between *Wahrheit* and *Dichtung* than he had achieved before.

The old man of the title is a fisherman by trade. He bears the fitting name of Santiago. Early one morning after months of bad fishing luck, he rows out alone into the mile-deep Gulf Stream where it swings in above the long island of Cuba. Towards noon of the first day out, he hooks a gigantic marlin. For two days and two nights, it pulls him in his boat far to the northward and the eastward, while he hangs for dear life onto the heavy line, a human towing bitt, fighting a battle of endurance against the power of the fish. On the third day out, again nearly at noon, he succeeds in bringing the marlin to the surface and killing it with his harpoon. Since it is too large to put aboard, he lashes it alongside his skiff and sets his small, patched sail for the long voyage home. Then, one by one, two by two, and later in rapacious ripping packs, the sharks move in on his trophy. By the time he has reached his native harbor, there is nothing left of it except the skeleton, the bony head, and the proud, sail-like tail.

Heads or tails, the old man loses the battle he has won. The winner takes nothing but the sense of having fought the fight to the limits of his strength, of having shown what a man can do when it is necessary. Like many of the rest of us, he is undefeated only because he has gone on trying. There is no need for the corrupting forces of moth and rust: thieves have broken through Santiago's lines of defence and made off with all there is. As for the mariner himself, he has reached a condition of absolute physical exhaustion as well as, on the moral plane, an absolute but not an abject humility. Both have cost him very little less than everything, which is of course the price one must always finally pay. Santiago's victory is the moral victory of having lasted without permanent impairment of his belief in the worth of what he has been doing.

In its main outlines, the story is simple in the extreme. Stripped, like the marlin, down to its bare bones, it looks not unlike the 200-word version which Hemingway first recorded in an article on the Gulf Stream during the spring of 1936.

An old man fishing alone in a skiff out of Cabanas hooked a great marlin that, on the heavy sash-cord handline, pulled the skiff far out to sea. Two days later the old man was picked up by fishermen 60 miles to the eastward, the head and forward part of the marlin lashed alongside. What was left of the fish, less than half, weighed 800 pounds. The old man had stayed with him a day, a night, a day and another night while the fish swam deep and pulled the boat. When he had come up the old man had pulled the boat up on him and harpooned him. Lashed alongside the sharks had hit him and the old man had fought them out alone in the Gulf Stream in a skiff, clubbing them, stabbing at them, lunging at them with an oar until he was exhausted and the sharks had eaten all they could hold. He was crying in the boat when the fishermen picked him up, half crazy from his loss, and the sharks were still circling the boat.

The difference between this anecdote and the finished work of art is of course immense. What makes the difference is the manner of the narration. Concentrating on the shape of the anecdote alone, the unsympathetic reader might argue that, except for its presumptive basis in historical fact, the story is nearly incredible. Or he might find too neat a balance in the narrative of a determined old man doing battle, first against an almost equally de-

termined marlin, and then against a band of predators determined to make off with the catch. Such a reader might ask what the whole matter comes to. After the sharks' assault, the tangible loss precisely cancels out the tangible profit, leaving the reader neither in the red nor in the black, neither plus nor minus, but exactly at zero.

Yet the novel does not leave us that cold. The manner of its telling controls, one might say, the thermogenetic factor. The warmth of our sympathy can be traced in part to the way in which the portrait of Santiago himself has been drawn.

He was an old man, [the story begins,] who fished alone in a skiff in the Gulf Stream and he had gone eighty-four days now without taking a fish. In the first forty days a boy had been with him. But after forty days without a fish the boy's parents had told him that the old man was now definitely and finally *salao,* which is the worst form of unlucky, and the boy had gone at their orders in another boat which caught three good fish the first week. It made the boy sad to see the old man come in each day with his skiff empty and he always went down to help him carry either the coiled lines or the gaff and harpoon and the sail that was furled around the mast. The sail was patched with flour sacks and, furled, it looked like the flag of permanent defeat. The old man was thin and gaunt with deep wrinkles in the back of his neck. The brown splotches of the benevolent skin cancer the sun brings from its reflection on the tropic sea were on his cheeks. The blotches ran well down the sides of his face and his hands had the deep-creased scars from handling heavy fish on the cords. But none of these scars were fresh. They were as old as erosions in a fishless desert. Everything about him was old except his eyes and they were the same color as the sea and were cheerful and undefeated.

In a strictly objective view, the man Santiago is only a simple fisherman, like his namesake the son of Zebedee, mending his nets by the shore of Galilee. As Laurence Housman remarked of Wordsworth's leech-gatherer, another old man going about his lonely professional work on the undulating stretches of a British moorland, he is probably not in himself an exceptionally noble character. What has happened is that in both instances an individual has been singled out against such ancient backdrops of sea or moorland, and then staged so memorably, and in terms of a contest of endurance that seems itself a paradigm of human life, that he enters immediately, and perhaps not even tentatively, into the gallery of literary immortals.

Sean O'Faolain once commented on Hemingway's love for the spirit of gallantry, which has made him rove the world "in search of the flame of the spirit in men and beasts." Within the structure of the story, it may be said at once, the gallantry of Santiago is defined in part by the gallantry of his adversary. Aside from the essential valiance of the marlin's towing operation, which Santiago knows all too well because he is on one end of it, the adversary's courage and power are underscored in three stages. When he first sees one of his bobbing green sticks dip sharply, and feels the slight, nibbling, tentative yank on his line, Santiago knows that an event of some importance is in the offing. For this is the line set for a hundred fathoms, and six hundred feet down in the darkness a marlin is eating the sardines impaled on the point and shank of the hook.

After the gentle tugging comes the hard pull and heavy weight when the huge fish swims off with the bait in its mouth. As Santiago braces himself against the thwart and leans against the pull, weight against weight, the skiff moves slowly off towards the northwest. Four hours later the fish is still swimming steadily and the old man is still solidly braced with the line across his back. Like other Hemingway characters in not dissimilar positions, he is by now trying "not to think but only to endure." By sunset it is still the same. "I wish I could see him only once," thinks Santiago, "to know what I have against me." And again, near midnight: "We are joined together and have been since noon. And no one to help either of us." Gallantry against gallantry: but neither of them has seen his adversary.

The second stage comes with Santiago's first sight of the fish, in royal purple as befits a king, near noon of the second day. "The line rose slowly and steadily and then the surface of the ocean bulged ahead of the boat and the fish came out. He came out unendingly and water poured from his sides. He was bright in the sun and his head and back were dark purple and in the sun the stripes on his sides showed wide and a light lavender. His sword was as long as a baseball bat and tapered like a rapier and he rose his full length from the water and then re-entered it, smoothly, like a diver and the old man saw the great scythe-blade of his tail go under and the line commenced to race out." With awe, Santiago observes that the marlin is two feet longer than the skiff.

But Santiago knows, has known all along, that there are other standards of measurement than feet or inches on steel tape. That morning, at first light, while the boat still moved steadily, inexorable as the tick of time, he had spoken to the fish of his love and respect: "But I will kill you dead before this day ends." It is the huntsman's code—as in the pursuit of the kudu among the green hills of Africa—to admire the courage and the strength of that which one is out to kill. Breakfasting on raw bonito, the old man had reflected that he would like to pass some down to the fish his brother. Yet he knew he must kill the fish and keep strong to do it, and that by the same token the fish's strength must be worn down.

From his new knowledge of "what I have against me" Santiago becomes newly aware of what he has inside him that will enable him to win. It is this sense of proving worth against a worthy adversary which, as much as any other means at his disposal, sustains the old man in his time of stress. The first breaching, like the various slight changes in the slant of the line, suggest that by almost imperceptible degrees Santiago is gaining the advantage. The sight of the fish itself is a further spur, for here at last, expansed before his eyes, is the enormous quarry, the goal towards which he moves. But the chief way in which the power outside enlarges the power inside is through Santiago's resolute comparisons. "Let him think I am more man than I am, and I will be so." Or again: "I will show him what a man can do and what a man endures." If the old man wins, he has proved his own worth to himself once more, which is the proof men need in order to continue with the other and perpetual endurance contest into which birth precipitates them all.

Stage the third, the zenith of Santiago's struggle, which is also close to the nadir of his strength, comes on the morning of the third day. Now the marlin rises and slowly circles the boat while the old man sweats and strains to get him close enough for harpooning. "You are killing me, fish, the old man thought. But you have a right to. Never have I seen a greater, or more beautiful, or a calmer or more noble thing than you, brother. Come on and kill me. I do not care who kills who." But he does care. Though his hands are pulped and he is nearly blind with fatigue, he tries one final time on the ninth circle. "He took all his pain and what was left of his strength and his long gone pride and he put it against the fish's agony and the fish came over onto his side and swam gently on his side, his bill almost touching the planking of the skiff." Now Santiago drives home the harpoon, the fish leaps and falls in death, and the first forty-eight hours are over.

In this movement of the story, as in the phase of the sharks that is yet to come, Santiago bears a significant relationship to other characters in the Hemingway canon. For many years prior to the composition of *The Old Man and The Sea,* Hemingway had interested himself in the proposition that there must be a resemblance, in the nature of things, between Jesus Christ in his human aspect as the Son of Man and those countless and often nameless thousands in the history of Christendom who belong to the category of "good men,"

and may therefore be seen as disciples of Our Lord, whatever the professed degree of their Christian commitment. The young priest, friend to Lieutenant Henry in *A Farewell to Arms,* is an early example; the old Spaniard Anselmo, friend to Robert Jordan in *For Whom the Bell Tolls,* is a more recent instance.

Santiago shows, in his own right, certain qualities of mind and heart which are clearly associated with the character and personality of Jesus Christ in the Gospel stories. There is the essential gallantry, a kind of militance. There is the staying-power which helps him in his determination to last to the end of whatever is to come. There is the ability to ignore physical pain while concentrating on the larger object which is to be achieved. "Etched on the reader's mind," writes a recent commentator, "is the image of the old man as he settled against the wood of the bow . . . and took his suffering as it came, telling himself, 'Rest gently now against the wood and think of nothing.' " The suffering, the gentleness, and the wood, it is noted, "blend magically into an image of Christ on the cross." So it may be. As the old man moves into and through the next phase of his operation, the force of the crucifixion idea is gradually intensified.

Besides the qualities already enumerated, three others deserve particular notice in this connection: Santiago's humility, his natural piety, and his compassion. His humility is of that well-tested kind which can co-exist with pride. "He was too simple to wonder when he had attained humility. But he knew he had attained it and he knew it was not disgraceful and it carried no loss of true pride." When his own disciple, the boy Manolo, calls him, as Jesus has many times been called, "the best fisherman," Santiago answers in character:

"No. I know others better."
"Qué va," the boy said. "There are many good fishermen and some great ones. But there is only you."
"Thank you. You make me happy. I hope no fish will come along so great that he will prove us wrong."

The great fish that Santiago is soon to be engaged with will not, of course, prove Manolo to be in error. Quite the contrary. But when the old man finally outfights his marlin, we are told that his pride has been gone for a long time—forced out through the openings in the sieve of his suffering. The humility remains as the natural companion of his immense fatigue.

However jocular he may be about his religion, however much, in his humility, he may deny himself the guerdon, Santiago is evidently a pious old man. The piety appears unobtrusively in his constant, accepted, and unquestioning awareness of supernal power, at once outside and potentially inside his personal struggle. His allusions to Christ, to God, and to the Virgin are never oaths, as one might expect to find them in the mouth of a professional fisherman out of Havana. They are rather simple petitions to a presumably available source of strength of which he feels the need. "Christ knows he can't have gone," he exclaims in the parlous interval before the fish is actually hooked. "God let him jump," he prays, soon after dawn on the second day, for if God will permit or urge the great fish to leap high and twist, "he'll fill the sacs along his backbone with air and then he cannot go deep to die." "God help me to have the cramp go," says Santiago once again, when his left hand has become temporarily useless. But he does not depend solely on God's intercession: he massages the hand, he exposes it to the sun, he eats raw tuna in the expectation of benefit. If he has to compel the hand to open, he will. He prefers to "let it open by itself and come back of its own accord." But like sun, diet, and massage, prayer may help.

One finds also the more formal prayers. "I am not religious," says the old man untruly. "But I will say ten Our Fathers and ten Hail Marys that I should catch this fish, and I promise to make a pilgrimage to the Virgen de Cobre if I catch him. That is a promise." As he begins to say his prayers, he discovers that he is so fatigued that he cannot always remember the word-

sequences. Concluding that "Hail Marys are easier to say than Our Fathers," he tries one of the former and completes it, appending a further petition to the Blessed Virgin: "Pray for the death of this fish. Wonderful though he is." Then, "with his prayers said, and feeling much better, but suffering exactly as much and perhaps a little more," he leans once more against the wood of the bow of his boat, mechanically working the fingers of his recently uncramped left hand. Much later, at the battle's climax, prayer enters his mind again. This time he raises the ante of promised prayers tenfold. "Now that I have him coming so beautifully, God help me to endure. I'll say a hundred Our Fathers and a hundred Hail Marys. But I cannot say them now."

According to the ancient mariner of Coleridge, "he prayeth best who loveth best all things both great and small." Along with humility, pride, and piety, Hemingway's ancient mariner is richly endowed with the quality of compassion. Of course he is not so foolish as to love all creatures equally. He dislikes, for example, the Portuguese men-of-war, whose beautiful "purple, formalized, iridescent, gelatinous" bubbles serve to buoy up the "long deadly purple filaments" which trail a yard behind them in the water and contain a poison which will paralyze unwary passersby. *"Agua mala,"* says the old man to one of them. "You whore." Outwardly handsome, inwardly lethal, these beings strike him as the falsest things in the sea. It is his landside sport to "walk on them on the beach after a storm and hear them pop when he stepped on them with the horny soles of his feet." He has another set of enemies in the waters of the tropic sea. For he genuinely hates, and gladly destroys, the voracious sharks which attack and disfigure the marlin he has fought so long to win.

But his hatred is more than overbalanced by his simple love and compassion for all those creatures which swim or blindly soar. His principal friends on the ocean are the flying fish. He loves the green turtles and the hawksbills "with their elegance and speed," and though the loggerheads are huge and stupid, happily gobbling the Portuguese men-of-war with shut eyes and an air of heavy contentment, the contempt he feels for them is friendly. Porpoises delight him. "They are good," he says. "They play and make jokes and love one another. They are our brothers like the flying fish." Several times in the course of his struggle he feels pity for the great marlin he has hooked—so "wonderful and strange" in his power to pull the skiff for so many hours, without sustenance, without respite, and with the pain of the hook in his flesh.

For the lesser birds his compassion is greatest, "especially the small delicate dark terns that were always flying and looking and almost never finding." The birds, he reflects, "have a harder life than we do except for the robber birds and the heavy strong ones. Why did they make birds so delicate and fine as those sea swallows when the ocean can be so cruel? She is kind and very beautiful. But she can be so cruel and it comes so suddenly and such birds that fly, dipping and hunting, with their small sad voices are made too delicately for the sea."

His grateful sense of brotherhood with the creatures of the water and the air is, though full of love, essentially realistic and unsentimental. His implied or overt comparisons between subhuman and human brothers often open out, therefore, in as many directions as our imaginations wish to follow. A memorable example of this tendency appears in the incident of the land-bird, a warbler, which comes to rest on Santiago's skiff far out at sea.

A small bird came toward the skiff from the north. He was a warbler and flying very low over the water. The old man could see that he was very tired. The bird made the stern of the boat and rested there. Then he flew around the old man's head and rested on the line where he was more comfortable.
"How old are you?" the old man asked the bird. "Is this your first trip?"

The bird looked at him when he spoke. He was too tired even to examine the line and he teetered on it as his delicate feet gripped it fast.
"It's steady," the old man told him. "It's too steady. You shouldn't be that tired after a windless night. What are birds coming to?"
The hawks, he thought, that come out to sea to meet them. But he said nothing of this to the bird who could not understand him anyway and who would learn about the hawks soon enough.
"Take a good rest, small bird," he said. "Then go in and take your chance like any man or bird or fish."

This gently humorous monologue with its serious undertone of implied commentary on the human condition encourages the old man at this stage of his struggle. "Stay at my house if you like, bird," he said. "I am sorry I cannot hoist the sail and take you in with the small breeze that is rising. But I am with a friend." It is just at this point that the marlin gives a sudden lurch, the tautened line jerks, and the warbler flies away—towards whatever it is that awaits him on the long voyage home. Hawks or sharks, the predators wait, whether for tired young birds or tired old men.

Coleridge's ancient mariner comes, one might say, to share with Hemingway's this quality of compassion. A major difference between the novel and the poem is that Santiago already owns compassion as by a natural gift; Coleridge's wanderer must achieve it through an ordeal. The act of shooting the albatross is in no way comparable to Santiago's killing of the marlin. One is meaningless and wanton; the other is professional and necessary. In Coleridge's poem, the broken circuit, the failure of spiritual electricity, leads immediately and sequentially to the ordeal, which is by hunger and thirst, cold and heat (like Santiago's), but is chiefly an ordeal by loneliness. Precisely balancing the horror of aloneness is the sense of brotherhood and at-one-ment which floods in upon the mariner when by a simple act of contrition he subconsciously blesses the watersnakes as they coil and swim in the phosphorescent ocean of Coleridge's imagination. The central theme of the poem resides exactly here: in that projected sense of a breakable but reparable solidarity between us and the other life that is around us on the earth, or in the waters beneath the earth.

To their hazard or their sorrow, Hemingway's heroes sometimes lose touch with nature. Jake Barnes in the Parisian café-circle and Fred Henry in the toils of war on the plains of Italy are two memorable examples. Their health ordinarily returns when they re-ally themselves with the natural laws and forces which wait unchanged for the errants' return. But Santiago is never out of touch. The line which ties him to the fish is like a charged wire which guarantees that the circuit will remain unbroken. Saint Francis with his animals and birds is not more closely allied to God's creation than this Santiago with his birds and his fish. These are his brothers, in all the sizes. "I am with a friend," he cheerfully tells the warbler. When the bird has departed, he is momentarily smitten by a sense of his aloneness on the vast waters. Then he looks ahead of his skiff to see "a flight of wild ducks etching themselves against the sky over the water, then blurring, then etching again." Once more he is convinced of what he has only momentarily forgotten: no man is ever alone on the sea. This sense of solidarity with the visible universe and the natural creation is another of the factors which help to sustain him through his own long ordeal.

III. THE BOY AND THE LIONS

In the light of the experiment in symbolic representation which Hemingway tried in *Across the River and Into The Trees,* the meaning of the Santiago-Manolo relationship becomes clear. Renata stands, in one of her aspects, for Colonel Cantwell's lost youth. Manolo fulfills a similar purpose, and with greater success in that we do not have to overcome the doubt raised by the difference of sexes. To say this is not, of course, to discount Manolo's dramatic function, which is to heighten our sympathy for the old fisherman. At the beginning and end of the story, we see Santiago through the boy's sympathetic eyes. From the charitable and again fittingly named Martin, owner of the Terrace, Manolo brings Santiago a last supper of black beans, rice, fried bananas, stew, and two bottles of beer. On the morning of the expedition, Manolo arranges for the simple breakfast of coffee in condensed milk cans, and procures the fish and sardines which Santiago will use for baits. He helps launch the skiff, and sees Santiago off in the dark with a wish for luck on this eighty-fifth day. At the end of the story, after the ordeal, Manolo brings coffee and food for the old man's waking, and ointment for his injured hands, commiserating on the loss, planning for a future when they will work side by side again. The love of Manolo for Santiago is that of a disciple for a master in the arts of fishing; it is also the love of a son for an adopted father.

But from Santiago's point of view, the relationship runs deeper. He has known the boy for years, from the period of childhood up to this later time when Manolo, strong and lucky, stands confidently on the edge of young manhood. Like many other aging men, Santiago finds something reassuring about the overlay of the past upon the present. Through the agency of Manolo he is able to recapture in his imagination, and therefore to a certain degree in fact, the same strength and confidence which distinguished his own young manhood as a fisherman and earned him the title of *El Campeón.*

During his ordeal, the two phrases, "I wish the boy was here," and "I wish I had the boy," play across Santiago's mind nine separate times. In each instance, he means exactly what he says: the presence of the boy would be a help in a time of crisis. But he is also invoking by means of these phrases the strength and courage of his youth. Soon after he has hooked his marlin and knows that he must hang onto the line for some time, Santiago says, "I wish I had the boy." Immediately his resolution tightens. During the first night he says it again, reflecting that "no one should be alone in their old age," although in this case it is unavoidable. As if the mere mention of the boy were a kind of talisman, he then resolves to eat the tuna he has caught "in order to keep strong." Later the same night, he says aloud, "I wish the boy was here," and promptly settles himself against the planks of the bow for another period of endurance. Near dawn he says again, "I wish I had the boy." Then he upbraids himself for wishful thinking. "But you haven't got the boy, he thought. You have only yourself and you had better work back to the last line now . . . and cut it away and hook up the two reserve coils." So he does exactly that.

As he summons courage to eat the raw tuna for his breakfast on the second day, he links the boy and salt in what amounts to an image with double meanings: "I wish the boy were here and that I had some salt." Then he proves to himself that he has enough of both in their metaphorical meaning to eat the tuna and renew his waning strength. While he wills to unknot the cramp, he thinks that "if the boy was here" a little massaging would loosen the forearm and maybe help the still useless gnarled claw of the hand. Yet when, soon afterwards, his great marlin breaches, Santiago summons the strength he needs to play his fish.

On the next breaching it is the same. While the marlin leaps again and again in an attempt to throw the hook, and while the old man and his line are both strained and stretched to the breaking-point, he triples the refrain: "If the boy was here he would wet the coils of line . . . Yes. If the boy were here. If the boy were here." Once more the effect of the invocation is nearly magical as if, by means of it, some of the strength of youth flowed in to sustain the limited powers of age. Always, we notice, just after he has said the words, Santiago manages to reach down into the well of his courage for one more dipperful. Then he goes on.

From this point onwards, having served its purpose, the refrain vanishes. It is not until the return voyage, while the old man reflects Job-like upon the problem of the connection between sin and suffering and while the sharks collect their squadrons in the dark waters, that the boy's image returns again. "Everything kills everything else in some way," he tells himself. "Fishing kills me exactly as it keeps me alive." Then he corrects the misapprehensions that can come from false philosophizing. "The boy keeps me alive . . . I must not deceive myself too much." It is good, at this point, that the old man has the thought of the boy to keep him alive. The sharks wait, and a very bad time is just ahead.

In the night in which he is preparing for betrayal by the avaricious sharks, Santiago has recourse to another sustaining image—a pride of lions he has seen at play on the beaches of Africa when he was a young man like Manolo. Hemingway early establishes a clear symbolic connection between the boy and the lions. "When I was your age," Santiago says, "I was before the mast on a square rigged ship that ran to Africa and I have seen lions on the beaches in the evening." Manolo's answer —"I know. You told me."—indicates not only that the reminiscence has arisen before in their conversations, but also that the incident of the lions is a pleasant obsession in Santiago's mind. "There is for every man," writes the poet Yeats, "some one scene, some one adventure, some one picture that is the image of his secret life, and this one image, if he would but brood over it his life long, would lead his soul." Santiago finds such an image in the lions of his youthful experience.

The night before his ordeal, after the boy has left him to sleep, the old man dreams of the lions.

He was asleep in a short time and he dreamed of Africa when he was a boy and the long golden beaches and the white beaches, so white they hurt your eyes, and the high capes and the great brown mountains. He lived along that coast now every night and in his dreams he heard the surf roar and saw the native boats come riding through it. He smelled the tar and oakum of the deck as he slept and he smelled the smell of Africa that the land breeze brought at morning. Usually when he smelled the land breeze he woke up and dressed to go to wake the boy. But tonight the smell of the land breeze came very early and he knew it was too early in his dream and went on dreaming to see the white peaks of the Islands rising from the sea and then he dreamed of the different harbours and roadsteads of the Canary Islands.

Santiago "no longer dreamed of storms, nor of women, nor of great occurrences, nor of great fish, nor fights, nor contests of strength, nor of his wife. He only dreamed of places now and of the lions on the beach. They played like young cats in the dusk and he loved them as he loved the boy."

Early in the afternoon of his second day out, having said his prayers and strengthened his resolution by this means, Santiago thinks again about his lions. The marlin is pulling steadily. "I wish he'd sleep and I could sleep and dream about the lions," thinks Santiago. "Why are the lions the main thing that is left? Don't think, old man . . . Rest gently now against the wood and think of nothing. He is working. Work as little as you can." Much later that day, "cramping himself against the line with all his body," and "putting all his weight onto his right hand," the old man manages to sleep. Presently then, he begins to dream "of the long yellow beach." In the dream, we are told, "he saw the first of the lions come down onto it in the early dark and then the other lions came and he rested his chin on the wood of the bows where the ship lay anchored with the evening off-shore breeze and he waited to see if there would be more lions and he was happy." In his old age and the time of his suffering, Santiago is sustained by the memory of his youth and the strength of his youth. Living so, in the past, he is happy. Luckily for him, he has also the thought of the strength of the boy Manolo, a young lion of just the age Santiago was when he first sailed to Africa. These together enable

him to go on.

They help in a very notable way. For the boy and the lions are related to one of the fundamental psychological laws of Santiago's—and indeed of human—nature: the constant wavelike operation of bracing and relaxation. The boy braces, the lions relax, as in the systolic-diastolic movement of the human heart. It is related, as a phenomenon, to the alternation of sleep and waking through the whole range of physical nature. But it is also a law which operates on the level of mentality, and its effects can be seen in our reactions to works of literature like this story of the acquisition and the loss of the great marlin. In its maritime sections, at any rate, the basic rhythms of the novel resemble those of the groundswell of the sea. Again and again as the action unfolds, the reader may find that he is gradually brought up to a degree of quiet tension just barely endurable, as in the ascent by a small craft of a slow enormous wave. When he has reached the presumptive peak of his resistance, the crest passes and he suddenly relaxes towards a trough of rest. The rhythm of the story appears to be built on such a stress-yield, brace-relax alternation. The impression is furthered by the constant tension which Santiago and his fish maintain on the line which joins them. Again and again one finds the old man telling himself that he has stretched the cord to a tension just short of the breaking-point. Then and only then, the stress relaxes, and the involved reader relaxes with it. This prolonged tug-of-war involves not only the fisherman and his fish but also the reader and his own emotions.

The planned contiguity of the old man with the boy and the lions pulls the story of Santiago, in one of its meanings, in the direction of a parable of youth and age. There is a distinct possibility that Hemingway, who read the whole of Conrad during the days of his writing apprenticeship in Paris and Toronto, has recollected if not the details at least the central strategy of Conrad's long short story, "Youth." For that story is brilliantly organized in terms of the contrast of age and youth. The ill-fated voyage of the barque *Judea,* out of London, bound for Bangkok, shows young Marlow, with all the illusions and prowess of his youth, side by side with old Captain Beard, the ship's master and a brave man. "He was sixty, if a day," says Marlow of the captain. "And he had blue eyes in that old face of his, which were amazingly like a boy's, with that candid expression some quite common men preserve to the end of their days by a rare internal gift of simplicity of heart and rectitude of soul." Again Marlow says, as the fated ship beats her way through a sea of trouble, that Beard was "immense in the singleness of his idea." It may of course be a coincidence that these are qualities which Santiago shares. Two "quite common men" rise to the level of the heroic through simplicity of heart, rectitude of soul, and that immensity in the singleness of their respective ideas which enables each to stick out the voyage to the end. "Do or die," the motto which adorns in flaking gilt the stern-timbers of the old *Judea,* might with equal justice be carved into the weather-beaten wood of Santiago's skiff.

Conrad's story depends for its effects not only upon the contrast of young Marlow and old Beard but also, since the story is told some twenty years after the event, upon the contrast of the aging Marlow and his own remembrance of his youthful self. The aging Santiago happily recalls the lions on the shore of Africa. The aging Marlow recollects, with mingled happiness and sorrow, that time, far back now, when the small boats from the wrecked *Judea* at last pulled into a port on the Javanese coast. "I remember my youth," says Marlow, "and the feeling that will never come back any more—the feeling that I could last for ever, outlast the sea, the earth, and all men; the deceitful feeling that lures us on to joys, to perils, to love, to vain effort—to death; the triumphant conviction of strength, the heat of life in the handful of dust, the glow in the heart that with every year grows dim, grows cold, grows small, and expires." This feeling, which Hazlitt has well described as "the feeling of immortality in youth," is closely associated in Marlow's mind with the East—"the mysterious shores, the still water, the lands of the brown nations." For me, he tells his auditors, "all the East is contained in that vision of my youth. It is all in that moment when I opened my young eyes on it. I came upon it from a tussle with the sea—and I was young—and I saw it looking at me. And this is all that is left of it! Only a moment; a moment of strength, of romance, of glamour—of youth!"

For Santiago it is not the coast of Java but that of Africa, not the faces of the brown men crowding the jetty but the playing lions, which carry the associations of youth, strength, and even immortality. "This is all that is left of it," cries Marlow of his youthful vision. "Why are the lions the main thing that is left?" says Hemingway's old man in the midst of his ordeal. For both of them, in Marlow's words, it is "the time to remember." But Santiago, luckily, is able to do more with his vision than remember it. He puts it to work once more in the great trial of his old age. "I told the boy I was a strange old man," he says. "Now is when I must prove it." And the author adds: "The thousand times that he had proved it meant nothing. Now he was proving it again. Each time was a new time and he never thought about the past when he was doing it." But if he does not, at these times, think about the past to brood upon it, he periodically calls back what it means to him through the double vision of the boy and the lions. If he can prove his mettle for the thousand-and-first time, there is no reason why he cannot prove it again and again, as long as his vision lasts.

Of how many events in the course of human life may this not be said? It is Marlow once more who reminds us of the way in which one account of one man on one journey can extend outwards in our imaginations until it easily becomes a paradigm of the course of men's lives. "You fellows know," says Marlow, beginning his account of the *Judea*, "there are those voyages that seem ordered for the illustration of life, that might stand for a symbol of existence. You fight, work, sweat, nearly kill yourself, sometimes do kill yourself, trying to accomplish something—and you can't. Not from any fault of yours." If it is so with the *Judea*, out of London bound for Bangkok, do or die, it is so likewise with Santiago of Havana, bound for home, with the sharks just beginning to nose the blood of his great fish. Do or die. In such works as this we all put to sea, and sitting well in order smite the sounding furrows. Santiago makes his voyage on what used to be known as the Spanish Main. But it is also, we are persuaded, that more extensive main or mainstream where we all drift or sail, with or against the wind, in fair weather or foul, with our prize catches and our predatory sharks, and each of us, perhaps, like the ancient mariner of Coleridge, with some kind of albatross hanging around his neck.

IV. THE CAUTERY OF CIRCUMSTANCE

It is provided in the essence of things, writes the stoical philosopher, that from any fruition of success, no matter what, shall come forth something to make a greater struggle necessary. With such a sentiment Santiago would no doubt agree. For the second major movement of the novel confronts him with a struggle which, though shorter in duration, is at least as intense as the fight with the marlin just brought to a successful conclusion. This comes, too, at a time when he has used all his strength, and as much more as he could summon, to attain his object; when his hands are stiffening round the edges of his wounds, when the muscles of his back and shoulders are knotted with pain, and when his fatigue runs bone-deep.

Having secured his catch alongside, stepped his mast, rigged his boom, and moved off with the beneficent tradewind towards the southwest and home, Santiago enjoys (though not to the full because of his tiredness) that brief respite which follows work well done. Side by side like brothers the old man and the marlin move through the sea. Up to now, they have been, as Santiago believes, friendly and mutually respectful adversaries. Now they join together in league against the common enemy. "If sharks come," the old man has long ago reflected, "God pity him and me." It is a full hour before the first shark arrives.

With its arrival begins a tragedy of deprivation as piteous as that which King Lear undergoes at the hands of his shark-hearted daughters. Lear's hundred knights, the only remaining sign of his power and the badge of his kingly dignity, are taken from him in batches of twenty-five. A series of forty-pound rippings and tearings are now gradually to reduce Santiago's eighteen-foot, fifteen-hundred-pound marlin to the skeleton he brings finally to shore.

The first of the sharks is a Mako. "Everything about him was beautiful except his jaws . . . Inside the closed double lip . . . all of his eight rows of teeth were slanted inwards. They were not the ordinary pyramid-shaped teeth of most sharks. They were shaped like a man's fingers when they are crisped like claws. They were nearly as long as the fingers of the old man and they had razor sharp cutting edges on both sides." Santiago, standing poised with his harpoon, hears the clicking chop of these great jaws and the rending and tearing of the marlin's flesh just before he drives the point of his weapon "with resolution and complete malignancy" into the Mako's brain. Death is immediate but the loss is heavy. When the shark sinks, he takes with him forty pounds of the marlin, the harpoon, and all the rope. The marlin's blood will attract other sharks. But worse than this is the mutilation of the long-fought-for prize. Santiago "did not like to look at the fish anymore since he had been mutilated. When the fish had been hit it was as though he himself were hit." The process of crucifixion is now intensified.

At first sight of the second shark, Santiago utters the single word *Ay*. "There is no translation for this word," writes Hemingway, "and perhaps it is just a noise such as a man might make, involuntarily, feeling the nail go through his hands and into the wood." For some hours now, of course, Santiago's hands have shown the fisherman's equivalent of the stigmata of a saint. Both have been cut in the "working part," which is the palm, by the unpredictable lurchings of his quarry. The right hand is cut first, at a time when the old man's attention is momentarily diverted by the warbler's visit. Another of the marlin's sudden accelerations awakens him from the only sleep he permits himself. The line is burning out through his already wounded right hand. When he brings up his left for use as a brake, it takes all the strain and cuts deep.

The old man's involuntary epithet, and Hemingway's explanation of it, is fully in line with what has gone before. Throughout the ordeal, Santiago has been as conscious of his hands as any crucified man might be. He speaks to them as to fellow-sufferers, wills them to do the work they must do, and makes due allowances for them as if they were, what he once calls them, "my brothers." He also carefully distinguishes between them in a manner which should not be lost on any student of paintings of the Crucifixion. The right hand is, the good one, dextrous and trustworthy. The left hand, the hand sinister, has "always been a traitor."

Our Lord might well have entertained a similar reflection about the man who was crucified on his own left. The allusions to Santiago's hands are so carefully stylized that such a statement becomes possible. On the naturalistic plane, of course, the meaning of the distinction between the two hands is apparent to all normally right-handed persons; the left is never as good as the right. But on the plane of what we have called *Dichtung,* and in the light of the tradition of Christian art as it pertains to the Crucifixion, it is clear that a moral judgment is to be inferred. Of the two who were crucified with Jesus Christ, the one on the left failed Him, insulting and upbraiding him. But the man crucified on Jesus' right hand rebuked his companion, and put his fortunes into the hands of the Savior. In paintings of the Crucifixion, as Hemingway is well aware, the distinction between the two malefactors is always carefully maintained. It even carries over into pictures of the Last Judgment, where those who are to be saved are ranged on the right hand of the Savior, while the damned stand dejectedly on the left.

Santiago vanquishes the second and third sharks, hateful, bad smelling, "scavengers as well as killers" with his knife lashed to an oar. But when the *galanos* sink into the sea, they take with them fully a quarter of the marlin's best meat. "I wish it were a dream and that I had never hooked him," says the old man. "I'm sorry about it, fish. It makes everything wrong." The fourth shark, a single shovel-nose, adds yet another degree to our sense of wronged rightness. "He came like a pig to the trough if a pig had a mouth so wide that you could put your head in it." This one breaks Santiago's knife, bearing the blade in its brain-pan as it follows the *galanos* to death.

By the time the old man has clubbed the fifth and sixth sharks into submission just at sunset, a full half of the marlin has been gouged away. "What will you do now if they come in the night?" asks the voice inside Santiago. "Fight them," says the old man aloud. "I'll fight them until I die." But when he tries to stand off a whole ravaging pack at midnight, striking at whatever heads he can see, he knows the fight is almost useless. Something seizes his club and it disappears; he hits out with the unshipped tiller until it breaks, and then lunges at another of the sharks with the splintered butt. When this one lets go of the marlin and rolls away, the massacre is ended. A few more come to hit the carcass in the night, "as someone might pick up crumbs from the table." But the old man ignores them and sails on. There is nothing left of the great fish except the skeleton, the bony head, and the vertical tail.

This story of great gain and great loss is esthetically satisfying partly because of its symmetry. Hemingway has little trouble, either, in persuading his readers of the inevitability of the process. For with so fine a prize in a tropical sea where hungry sharks constantly swim, Santiago's return with a whole fish would be nothing short of miraculous. In assessing the old man's total experience, one is reminded of the experiences of younger men in some of Hemingway's earlier novels: Lieutenant Henry's gain and loss of a new wife, for example, in *A Farewell to Arms,* or Robert Jordan's gain and loss of a new life in *For Whom the Bell Tolls.* Yet in this latter-day return to the theme of winner-take-nothing, on which Hemingway has so often and so successfully played his variations, he seems to have added a new dimension. This is the dimension of transfiguration, anticipated (it is true) in the story of Robert Jordan, but never made quite so nearly explicit as in the instance of Santiago.

Santiago's experience is a form of martyrdom. We do not object: it is his by right of eminent domain. The old man's only fault, if it is a fault, consists in doing to the best of his ability what he was born to do. When the man on the right rebuked his companion for crass raillery at the expense of Jesus Christ, he raised the essential moral problem. "We receive," said he, "the due reward of our deeds: but this man [Jesus Christ] hath done nothing amiss." Neither has Santiago, but this does not prevent his martyrdom. Tried out through an ordeal by endurance comparable to a crucifixion, he

earns, by virtue of his valiance, a form of apotheosis.

His humility and simplicity will not allow entry to any taint of conscious martyrdom. "Man is not made for defeat," he says at one point. "A man can be destroyed but not defeated." His resolution is always stiffened by some such thought as this, and he acts in accordance with it. Being native to his character, these qualities of resolution and action sustain him up to that point when he knows that his only remaining recourse is to take what comes when it comes. Arrival at this point does not unbalance him. He is not a rebel, like the mariner Ahab, against the ruling powers of the universe. Nor does he imagine, as he drives his harpoon into the marlin's heart, that he is destroying anything except a prize fish with whom he has fought long and fairly. The arrival of the sharks on the scene does not surprise him. He does not expect for a moment that they will let him run their saber-toothed gauntlet unscathed. Santiago is a moral realist.

Yet he is too human not to be troubled, like Job before him, by certain moral and metaphysical questions. One is the problem of whether any connection exists between sin and suffering. "It is silly not to hope," he thinks to himself after the killing of the Mako shark. "Besides I believe it is a sin." In this way he launches himself into a consideration of the problem. At first his realistic capacity for self-criticism cautions him that this is dangerous ground. "There are enough problems without sin. Also I have no understanding of it and I am not sure that I believe in it . . . Do not think about sin. It is much too late for that and there are people who are paid to do it. Let them think about it."

The problem will not be put down so easily. "Perhaps," he speculates, "it was a sin to kill the fish. I suppose it was even though I did it to keep me alive and feed many people." After all, "San Pedro was a fisherman," and who would accuse him of sin? But once more the cautionary voice chimes in. "You did not kill the fish only to keep alive and to sell for food, he thought. You killed him for pride and because you are a fisherman. You loved him when he was alive and you loved him after. If you love him, it is not a sin to kill him. Or is it more?"

On this double allusion to pride and to love, greatest of sins and greatest of virtues, hangs the philosophic crux of the problem. Was his real motivation the blameless one of doing his professional duty and feeding people? Probably not basically. He did it for pride: to show that he was still El Campéon. "I'll kill him," he boasted during the battle. "In all his greatness and his glory . . . I will show him what a man can do and what a man endures." Yet all through the struggle he was never without love and compassion for his marlin, or for most of the lesser creatures in God's marine creation.

As in other tragic literatures, the whole process consists ultimately in the readjustment of moral proportions. What begins as a balanced mixture of pride and love slowly alters through the catalysis of circumstance. When Santiago brings his marlin to the gaff, his pride has been gone for a long time. Statements like "I'll fight them until I die," made during the encounter with the sharks, are not so much the evidence of pride as of the resolute determination to preserve something loved and earned from the distortion that comes with mutilation. The direction of the process then comes clear. Where pride and love exist together, the pride must be burned out, as by the cautery of fire. Love will remain as the natural concomitant of true humility.

Though Santiago admits to pride and lays claim to love, his moral sense is not fully satisfied by this way of resolving the problem. He looks for some other explanation of the profit-and-loss pattern. What he seems finally to settle on is the notion that he has gone, as he often puts it, "too far out." This concept of "too-far-outness" is not simply what Colonel Cantwell might describe as over-extension: lines of communication stretched past the breaking-point, possible support abandoned, danger courted for its own sake, excess of bravery spilling over into foolhardiness. It is rather what Melville described as "the intrepid effort of the soul to keep the open independence of her sea"—a willingness to take the greater risk where the greater prize is involved.

Very early in the book the contrast is established between the lee shore and the Gulf Stream. There are the inshore men, those who work within sight of land because it is easier, safer, and less frightening, and those like Santiago who have the intrepidity to reach beyond the known towards the possible. "Where are you going?" Manolo asks him, on the eve of the eighty-fifth day. "Far out," replies Santiago, "to come in when the wind shifts." The boy hopes to persuade his father to work far out that day in order to provide help for Santiago if it should be necessary. But this will not happen. Manolo's father is plainly an inshore man, one who does not like to work far out, one who prefers not to take chances, no matter how great the potential gain might be.

Santiago does not hesitate. On the morning of the eighty-fifth day, we are told that he "knew he was going far out." This is why he passes over, even before dawn, the inshore fishing-ground which fishermen call "the great well"—an easy place teeming with provender, where thousands of fish congregate to feed and to be caught. By seven he is already so far out that only three fishing boats are remotely visible inshore; by noon only the tops of the blue Cuban hills show on the horizon. No other boats are now in sight. Here, somewhere, lurk the great fish of this September season. When Santiago is passed by a school of dolphin, he guesses that marlin may be nearby. "My big fish," he tells himself, "must be somewhere."

Even as he speaks the marlin is approaching, the lordly denizen of this far-out domain. In coming there, in the process of invasion, the old man has made his choice—not to stay inshore where the going might be easier but to throw out a challenge to what might be waiting, far out and down deep at the hundred-fathom level. As for the marlin, "his choice had been to stay in the deep dark water far out beyond all snares and traps and treacheries." Yet he accepts, in effect rises to, the old man's challenge. From then on Santiago is tied by a strong line to his doom. "My choice," he reflects, "was to go there to find him beyond all people. Beyond all people in the world. Now we are joined together." The long battle is also joined. Since it came about through Santiago's free choice, he has no alternative but to accept the consequences.

These follow inevitably. For to have gone far out is to have invited the depredations of the sharks on the equally long homeward voyage. When the first three have done their work, Santiago apologizes. "I shouldn't have gone so far out, fish. Neither for you nor for me. I'm sorry, fish." When the mutilation has developed to the point where he cannot bear to look at it, he apologizes again. "You violated your luck," says his speaking self, "when you went too far outside." Inshore again, with the marlin destroyed and the old man's weapons gone, there is another dialogue of the soul with itself. "And what beat you?" "Nothing," answers the second voice. "I went out too far." Urged on by pride, by the love of his trade, by his refusal to take continuing bad luck as his portion, and by a resurgent belief that he might win, Santiago made trial of the impossible. In the tragic process he achieved the moral triumph.

It is not necessarily a Christian victory. Yet it is clear that Hemingway has artfully enhanced the native power of his tragic parable by enlisting the further power of Christian symbolism. Standing solus on the rocky shore in the darkness before the dawn of the fourth day, Santiago shows the wounded hands. Dried blood is on his face as from a crown of thorns. He has known the ugly coppery taste in his mouth as from a sponge filled with vinegar. And in the agony of his fatigue he is very much alone. "There was no one to help him so he pulled the boat up as far as he could. Then he stepped out and made her fast to a rock. He unstepped the mast and furled the sail and tied it. Then he shouldered the mast and started to climb."

Once he paused to look back at the remains of his fish. At the top of the hill "he fell and lay for some time with the mast across his shoulder. He tried to get up. But it was too difficult and he sat there with the mast on his shoulder and looked at the road. A cat passed on the far side going about its business and the old man watched it. Then he just watched the road." The loneliness of the ascent of any Calvary is brilliantly emphasized by the presence of the cat. The Old Masters, as Auden wrote long ago, were never wrong about suffering. "How well they understood its human position; how it takes place while someone else is eating or opening a window or just walking dully along . . . They never forgot that even the dreadful martyrdom must run its course anyhow in some corner, some untidy spot where the dogs go on with their doggy life"—and where the innocence of ignorance never so much as bats an eye. The cat on the far side of the road from Santiago is also proceeding about its private business. It could not help the old man even if it would. Santiago knows and accepts this as he has accepted the rest. There is nothing else to be done—except to reach home, which he manages at last to do, though he has to sit down five times to rest between the hilltop and the door of his shack.

On the newspapers that cover the springs of the bed, and below the colored chromos of the Sacred Heart of Jesus and the Virgin of Cobre, the old man now falls heavily asleep. He sleeps face down with his arms out straight and his body straight up and down: cruciform, as if to sum up by that symbolic position, naturally assumed, all the suffering through which he has passed. *In hoc signo vinces.* Santiago has made it to his house. When Manolo looks in next morning, he is still asleep. There is a short conversation as he drinks the coffee the boy brings, and they lay plans for the future even as they allude laconically to the immediate past. "How much did you suffer?" Manolo asks. "Plenty," the old man answers. Outside, a three-day blow has begun. Inside the shack, the book concludes, the old man falls again into the deep sleep of renewal, of diurnal resurrection. "He was still sleeping on his face and the boy was sitting by him watching him. The old man was dreaming about the lions." In my end is my beginning.

PART FIVE

SYNOPTIC ESSAYS

Hemingway's Narrative Perspective*

E. M. HALLIDAY. For information about the author, see "Hemingway's Ambiguity: Symbolism and Irony," by E. M. Halliday, reprinted on page 61.

The limitations and privileges which go with telling a story in the first or in the third person are patent, to an extent, and are to be found listed in nearly anybody's manual on The Technique of the Novel. What is often missed is the effect of these limitations and privileges in relation to the intent of a particular work of fiction; that is, just how they may support or weaken the kind of artistic illusion the author seems to have been aiming at, and how they may implement or impede his theme. The technical problem is one not simply of choice, but of management.

Hemingway's novels—leaving out of account *The Torrents of Spring,* which is a special case—offer some interesting sights when examined in this light. *The Sun Also Rises* (1926) and *A Farewell to Arms* (1929) are both told in the first person; *To Have and Have Not* (1937) is decidedly mixed in its narrative perspective; *For Whom the Bell Tolls* (1940) and *Across the River and Into the Trees* (1950) are third-person. It is well known that the autobiographical element in the first two is large, and it might be supposed that this sufficiently explains, for them, the choice of method. Yet only two of the fifteen stories of *In Our Time* (1925), most of which are as certainly private in origin, are told in the first person. There were better rea[s]ons for the choice.

"Sometimes the novelist feels himself like God," Somerset Maugham observes in *Cakes and Ale,* "and is prepared to tell you everything about his characters; sometimes, however, he does not . . . and since as we grow older we feel ourselves less and less like God I should not be surprised to learn that with [**202/203**] advancing years the novelist grows less and less inclined to describe more than his own experience has given him. The first person singular is a very useful device for this limited purpose." It may be doubtful whether Hemingway has felt less and less like God as he has grown older; but it is certain that Jake Barnes, the hero and narrator, feels as little as possible like God in *The Sun Also Rises.* Impotent from a battle wound, hopeless, therefore, in his love for the predatory Brett Ashley, and mixed up with a group of expatriates whose spiritual anthem is the cynical refrain of *Ecclesiastes,* Jake moves through life with a kind of desperate caution. "Perhaps as you went along you did learn something," he tells himself. "I did not care what it was all about. All I wanted to know was how to live in it. Maybe if you found out how to live in it you learned from that what it was all about." What Jake seems to learn in the course of the novel propels him steadily in the direction of emotional insularity. Brett exploits him cruelly in the interest of a series of egotrophic affairs involving several of his friends and acquaintances, and at the end he stands quite alone, thrown into himself for whatever consolation he can find. This withdrawal, as a matter of fact, is the ironic source of the only sense of catharsis we may feel: possibly he is through, we think—despite his trip to Madrid to help her out of her latest fiasco—

*E. M. Halliday, "Hemingway's Narrative Perspective," *Sewanee Review,* LX (Spring, 1952), 202-218. Copyright © 1952 by The University of the South and reprinted with the permission of the author.

with the particular cycle of vanity personified by Brett. "Oh Jake, we could have had such a damned good time together." "Yes," Jake answers, pronouncing the famous last line in the book, "isn't it pretty to think so?"

What is pertinent here about the first-person method of narration is the remarkably effective way in which it implements and reinforces the theme of *The Sun Also Rises*. The very limitations of the technique, and its concomitant virtues, combine to produce an effect of *singularity;* and singularity, in the sense of emotional isolation, is inseparable from the novel's theme of moral atrophy. Not only do we find it easy to identify our- [203/204] selves with Jake Barnes, because all the action is seen through his eyes, and all the reaction through his mind—he being perforce our only medium of contact with the other characters. This would be true to some degree of any competent first-person narrative; but because Jake, as protagonist, is a man drawing himself inward and apart from others, becoming, as the story unfolds, constantly more self-sufficient and alone, this effect of singularity is made extremely telling and powerful. All of Jake's protective reserve, his individualism, and his bitter honesty, are explored and reinforced by a technical perspective which in effect is itself necessarily exclusive, individual, limited (confined to Jake's point of view), and authentic (having the tone of an eye-witness report). Thus theme, characterization of the hero, and technique are mutually supporting.

But this bounty did not fall at once to Hemingway merely by reason of his having chosen the first-person method. For in addition to its inherent limitations, which he turns so well to his advantage, there are certain features of that method which conceal dangers, particularly to a writer who aims at realism.

It is necessary to digress briefly here, because "realism" is one of those floating terms in our critical vocabulary which remain to be usefully anchored, and because currently it is fashionable to regard Hemingway as not basically a realist. I do not mean to argue the point in this essay beyond a partial definition of realism which includes two limitations. One of these is familiar and, I should think, easily acceptable: that realism in fiction attempts to re-present life, through an artistic illusion, as it is "normally" experienced—that is, with as much probability and immediacy as possible. The other, which I advance more tentatively, is that literary realism, like epistemological realism in the vocabulary of philosophy, should make a distinction between the objective and subjective worlds, presupposing and emphasizing the existence of things independent of our experience of them.

The first-person narrative technique, however, for the very [204/205] reasons that made it valuable to Hemingway in the support of his theme of emotional insularity, tends toward a phenomenalistic or impressionistic view of the universe. It may create the illusion of a world existing only by reflection in the consciousness of one man—its use in *Robinson Crusoe,* for instance, is interesting: it may be that it contributes a good deal to the almost hypnotic and dream-like quality (despite the abundance of concrete detail) of the early part of that epic of solitude. Unless precautions are taken to emphasize the objective as distinct from the subjective, the first-person method may lead to a solipsistic confusion of inner and outer worlds; and this is, in fact, what we get (and quite in accordance with the author's intentions) in such a writer as Proust, where the convolutions of the narrator's introspection frequently fuse the world of reality and the world of dreams.

In *The Sun Also Rises* there is no such fusion. Its objectivity, indeed, is one of its most celebrated features, though the exact functioning of this feature in restricting the point of view within realistic limits is not usually noticed. Ordinary opportunities for explicit subjective insights, such as are relished by the average novelist, are forgone by Hemingway; yet his method is equally removed from that of the writer who attempts to materialize experience by means of a naturalistic catalogue of objective detail. Selecting his objective facts carefully, Hemingway manages to convey accurately his hero's subjective states by implication: not only through what Jake does under given circumstances, but also through what, as narrator, Jake chooses to report from his perception of outward reality. Early in the story, for example, the hero has arranged a rendezvous with Brett at the Crillon, in Paris. The reader knows that for him the keeping of the appointment has a decided emotional weight: "Try and be there," he says to her the night before. "Don't worry," Brett says, "I've never let you down, have I?" The next chapter opens: [205/206]

At five o'clock I was in the Hotel Crillon waiting for Brett. She was not there, so I sat down and wrote some letters. They were not very good letters but I hoped their being on Crillon stationery would help them. Brett did not turn up so about quarter to six I went down to the bar and had a Jack Rose with George the barman. Brett had not been in the bar either, and so I looked for her upstairs on my way out, and took a taxi to the Café Select. Crossing the Seine I saw a string of barges being towed empty down the current, riding high, the bargemen at the sweeps as they came toward the bridge. The river looked nice. It was always pleasant crossing bridges in Paris.

There are subjective touches in this passage: "They were not very good letters. . . . It was always pleasant crossing bridges in Paris." But these touches consistently turn away from the central subjective fact which must be supposed to exist, and from any introspective examination of it: Jake's feelings at having Brett fail to keep the date. It is, nevertheless, piercingly suggested; and not alone by the sparse description of the kind of outward action most of us would perform in a similar situation. Hemingway has made use of the curious psychological truth that in such circumstances, when the emotions are abrasively disturbed, the panorama of objective reality often has a kind of insistent clarity and sharpness, apparently peripheral as it may be to what concerns us most at the

moment. The secret of this insistence is partly that our minds tend to establish a metaphorical correlation between certain details of that panorama and our emotional state at the moment; and this too Hemingway has exploited. In this case, Jake's perception and reporting of the empty barges being towed down the current suggests his feelings with a strange poignancy; and thus, without blurring the realistic distinction between objective and subjective worlds, Hemingway arranges to convey, obliquely, an accurate indication of his hero's state of mind.

This method, which might be called objective epitome, is held [206/207] to even for the emotionally climactic scenes of the novel: for instance that in which, near the end of the Pamplona fiesta, Jake presents Brett to Pedro Romero. Everything about the situation, we must infer, makes it acutely painful for the hero-narrator; but he describes it with scarcely a word about his feelings. These do not escape us, however; a few scrupulously chosen objective details take care of that:

When I came back and looked in the cafe, twenty minutes later, Brett and Pedro Romero were gone. The coffee-glasses and our three empty cognac-glasses were on the table. A waiter came with a cloth and picked up the glasses and mopped off the table.

The special felicity for Hemingway was that this additional limiting of the first-person technique not only fulfilled its function of avoiding the non-realistic tendency to confuse objective and subjective; it also lent further reinforcement to the Spartan tone of the novel. Jake's refusal, as narrator, to discuss his emotions, is perfectly in keeping with his characterization as a strong but physically and morally injured man, drawing farther and farther into a shell of disillusionment, yet stubbornly retaining his hold on outward reality.

Still, *The Sun Also Rises* is not a novel without subjective passages. Though few, there are some important ones; and they show another significant aspect of Hemingway's handling of narrative perspective. For they are almost without exception dealt with by means of a device which protects the realistic illusion against a fault peculiar to the first-person method. The difficulty has to do with the license we conventionally grant the first-person narrator. We are willing that he shall have a most extraordinary memory, reporting in detail actions long since past, and delivering verbatim accounts of involved conversations. But when it comes to prolonged introspection, cogitation, or analysis of emotion, we are less generous; at least if we are prejudiced [**207/208**] in favor of realism. Probability and immediacy are both threatened when a first-person storyteller presents such subjective action by ordinary narrative statement: the artistic illusion is in danger of collapse. The workings of the human mind are too intricate, kaleidoscopic, and elusive to permit an accurate retrospective report at any considerable distance in time; and an attempt to give one, though it may be ever so probable in content, is extremely likely to smack of ex post facto reconstruction—that is, to be lacking in probability with respect to technique, and therefore in immediacy. The third-person narrator, conventionally granted an Olympian knowledge of both future and past, is not bothered with this: his omniscience vouches for the thoughts and feelings of his characters however complex and finely distinguished they may be. The first-person narrator, on the other hand, is inescapably fixed in his dual role of storyteller and human character; and though we are generous to him when it comes to his recollection of objective phenomena, we carry our skepticism of *subjective* reminiscence to the realm of fiction, and modify his privileges with penalties. The penalties are of course acceptable to many authors: they simply involve a shift away from realism in the direction of romance.

The device used by Hemingway to give his hero's subjective interludes a palpable immediacy, protecting them from the stigma of retrospective reconstruction, was one borrowed from impressionism (very likely through Joyce) : the now common device of interior monologue. But in *The Sun Also Rises* he uses this machine with interesting reservations. He does not, like Joyce and his forerunner Dujardin, attempt to imply objective action by representing corresponding subjective action— the reversal, that is, of his technique of objective epitome. No: whenever an objective action occurs which is itself significant for the narrative, he describes it by means of an interpolated return to objective narrative. When, however, a subjective action is not accompanied by any significant outward action or perception, [**208/209**] Hemingway turns to the interior monologue, avoiding a retrospective account. A fair example is the long passage in Chapter IV, where Jake goes to bed pondering his unfortunate wound and his relationship with Brett. Immediacy is here preserved, yet there is no confusion between the subjective and objective as there is in Joyce, whose efforts to suggest objective behavior without deserting the labyrinth of his hero's mind sometimes submerge the reader in uneasy doubt as to where one leaves off and the other begins, to say nothing of any clear idea as to what is going on in either sphere. Dujardin, incidentally, despite his claim (in *Le Monologue Intérieur,* 1931) to be the progenitor of the stream-of-consciousness technique, took pains to escape such confusion by introducing remarks, ostensibly made by the hero of *Les lauriers sont coupés* to himself in the natural course of performing certain actions, which in fact nobody would conceivably make, but which do indicate clearly what is going on. Joyce hewed closer to experience by foregoing unlikely explanatory remarks to an impressive extent in his interior monologues: he thereby saved both probability and immediacy, but sometimes at the expense of being understood. Hemingway, choosing occasions where objective action and perception have come virtually to a standstill, uses the interior monologue in a manner which maintains all three real·

istic features of epistemological polarity, naturalistic probability, and immediacy. He was thus able to exploit fully the advantages offered by the first-person method in developing the theme of his novel, while at the same time avoiding the dangers to realism peculiar to that method when it undertakes the exposition of subjective states.

Most of the statements I have made about the technique of narrative perspective in *The Sun Also Rises* could be transferred, with some modification and extension, to *A Farewell to Arms*. As in the earlier novel, a motif of spiritual and emotional alienation is strongly buttressed and expressed by the choice of the first-person method of narration with its inherent [209/210] singularity and confinement. And again, to a marked extent, this harmony of theme and technique is made particularly effective by a careful use of certain precautions which insure the resilience of the realistic illusion. For brevity's sake I will only suggest certain differences which finally result, I believe, in a total effect rather less starkly realistic than that of *The Sun Also Rises*. There is, for one thing, a higher proportion of subjective passages where one might have looked for objective epitome; and although many of these are controlled by the same careful use of interior monologue which I have just described, some are not; and their occurrence slackens somewhat the objective tautness, the firm gaze upon outward reality, which is so characteristic of the earlier book. Moreover, some of these passages are particularly interesting, for they seem to be most obtrusive—most suggestive of retrospective reconstruction, and therefore most jarring to the sense of a continuous present—when they approach closest to specific thematic statement.

A prominent instance is the much-quoted paragraph beginning: "I did not say anything. I was always embarrassed by the words sacred, glorious, and sacrifice, and the expression in vain. . . ." Another occurs later in the book during Frederic

Henry's reunion with Catherine in an Italian hotel, after his desertion:

> I know that the night is not the same as the day: that all things are different, that the things of the night cannot be explained in the day, because they do not then exist, and the night can be a dreadful time for lonely people once their loneliness has started. But with Catherine there was almost no difference in the night except that it was an even better time. If people bring so much courage to this world the world has to kill them to break them, so of course it kills them. The world breaks every one and afterward many are strong at the broken places. But those that will not break it kills. It kills the very good and the very gentle and the very brave impartially. If you are [210/211] none of these you can be sure it will kill you too but there will be no special hurry.

There is a good deal of difficulty for the reader, it seems to me, about incorporating these interludes into the illusion of continuous action which, on the whole, is typical of *A Farewell to Arms*. One is likely to feel not so much that Frederic Henry thought these thoughts at the time, as that Frederic Henry—or Ernest Hemingway—thought them retrospectively, and is delivering short lectures with his eyes on the audience rather than on the story itself. Perhaps they were intended as interior monologues; but if so the intention has been defeated by the lack of proper transitions to indicate that these thoughts went through the hero's mind during the action of the story. Compare another well-known thematic passage, the description of the ants on the burning camp-fire log, and note how it emerges naturally from an interior monologue, thus successfully preserving the artistic illusion.

The thematic intrusions of *A Farewell to Arms* may be regarded as technical faults in the handling of narrative perspective, but they are hardly big enough to spoil the excellent over-all adjustment of perspective to theme, and its subordination to the demands of realism. At any rate one is hardly prepared for the exhibition of technical irresponsibility which is to be found in *To Have and Have Not*. Partly, of course, as Hemingway himself has said, the trouble was in the way half of the book was composed: pieced together out of two or three short stories. (The first five chapters were actually published in Cosmopolitan as "a complete short novel" called "One Trip Across.") In addition to producing obvious structural difficulties, this encouraged a wild eclecticism in narrative perspective throughout the entire novel. Those first five chapters are told in the first person by the hero, Harry Morgan; the next three are third-person; the ninth is related by Albert Tracy—who, by the way, [211/212] is dead before the end of the book, along with the hero—; the tenth is Harry's, and is entirely interior monologue; the rest is third-person. This diversity is not necessarily bad in itself, although it immediately cancels narrative perspective as a possible unifying force for the book. The trouble is that no positive justification can be found for the display of variety. An advantage often gained by the use of the third-person form is that it permits the reader to view the action from enough angles so that he sees it whole even if not steadily. In *To Have and Have Not,* however, the point of view flips back and forth so capriciously that the reader suffers from a kind of vertigo of the imagination which blurs the illusion. And there is something disconcerting about meeting the hero first as the story teller, and then having to readjust our conception of him in the light of his impression on an unknown "omniscient" narrator. No doubt the alteration can be managed, and for valid ends (one thinks of Faulkner's *The Sound and the Fury*); but it calls for more care than Hemingway has exercised.

Other unpleasant surprises await the reader. Some episodes which begin as objective narration, from the point of view of a disinterested observer quite outside the story, slip oddly, from time to time, into the manner of first-person narration:

"Take it easy," Harry said. Just then this goofy Cuban that drives a taxi came in with a fellow from the plane.... That Hayzooz is a character all right. Him and that other Cuban, Sweetwater.

Here the story-teller seems to have become some local hanger-on, but if so he is not only anonymous but has the useful faculty of invisibility:

The two of them stood there at the bar and neither one sad* anything until Big Rodger and the two or three others had drifted out. Then they went in the back. [212/213]
"You're poison," Harry said. "Everything you touch is poison."

It is hard to avoid a strain on the mind's eye in trying to keep the illusion in sharp focus under such circumstances as these; nor are we helped by the swarm of new characters who begin to appear midway in the book, and whose activities often take place when none of the already familiar characters is available as a center of vision. The affairs of the Gordons, Professor Mac-Walsey, Helene Bradley, *et al,* are related from as many points of view, with frequent shifts; and occasionally the narrator feels obliged to step in with his vastly superior knowledge, and explain things directly to the reader from *his* point of view:

Down the street Richard Gordon was on his way to the Bradleys' big winter home. He was hoping Mrs. Bradley would be alone. She would be. Mrs. Bradley collected writers as well as their books but Richard Gordon did not know this yet. His own wife was on her way home walking along the beach. She had not run into John MacWalsey. Perhaps he would come by the house.

This sort of intrusion from the narrator (or author), so jolting to realistic immediacy, reaches its height in chapter twenty-four, where we are introduced to several disagreeable members of the cosmopolitan yachting world. Here the narrator is not content to exercise as much omniscience in his expositions as Hawthorne, leaving the immediate scene for summaries of past events, thumbnail biographies, and a few ominous prophecies. Stretching the third-person narrator's privilege to the limit, he takes pains that the reader shall not miss the moral of all this in relation to the theme of the book:

* "said" in Hemingway.

The money on which it was not worth while for him [Henry Carpenter] to live was one hundred and seventy dollars more a month than the fisherman Albert Tracy [**213/214**] had been supporting his family on at the time of his death three days before.

The chapter ends, as if in compensation, with a kind of paroxysm of immediacy: the four-page interior monologue purporting to be the inward remarks of the beautiful Dorothy Hollis as she endeavors to put herself to sleep. While this is interesting for having more Joycean features than any seen before in Hemingway—fragmentary and incoherent, and allowing the picture of outward reality to blur into a series of hazy suggestions in the realm of mind—its novelty redeems neither the confusion of perspective of the remainder of the chapter, nor the seriously frayed illusion which is the result.

In reviewing the almost chaotic technique of *To Have and Have Not*, one is struck by the fact that the technical confusion is matched by a confusion of theme. Harry Morgan, despite his valor, his solid grip on the fundamentals of life, and his splendid domestic virtues, is established in the first section of the book as a thief and murderer, and he remains a curiously unadmirable hero throughout the rest of the story. Moreover, there seems to be some uncertainty about the consistency of Hemingway's intent in attacking such varied representatives of the leisure class as Richard Gordon and Dorothy Hollis, to name only two. The total impression is that of an author groping for his theme in a not-very-well-lighted place, and betrayed into unhappy technical tricks in spasmodic efforts to seize it firmly.

The relief offered by *For Whom the Bell Tolls*, in which Hemingway is again thoroughly in control of his narrative perspective, is correspondingly great. Here he is also much surer of his theme: the stumbling last words of Harry Morgan ("One man alone ain't got . . . no bloody f——ing chance") have been transmuted into the sonorous eloquence of the epigraph, from Donne, which furnishes the title. Now it would be too [**214/215**] pat to say that the theme of "No man is an island" could not have been adequately presented by means of first-person narrative. Nevertheless, if what has been said about the propriety of that method for the themes of *The Sun Also Rises* and *A Farewell to Arms* is true, it seems clear that the first-person would have imposed a considerable handicap on *For Whom the Bell Tolls*. The effect of singularity and isolation which it is possible to convey so admirably with that technique is not what is wanted to express the essential brotherhood of man. On the other hand, the third-person method, which Hemingway did choose, is very well suited to the investigation of human interdependence. Here the narrator is free to move from one character to another, showing the common elements in the respective views which each of them has of the action. In being thus equally at the disposition of the superhuman narrator, moreover, all existing objectivity on one plane and apart from him, they may be regarded technically as well as thematically as each "a peece of the continent, a part of the maine." And for the writer interested in maintaining sharply the realistic distinction between objective and subjective there is the added advantage that he need not treat subjective passages so cautiously either. For the narrator is not in this case another human being, with a humanly imperfect perception of just where the two realms divide: he can state positively, merely on the authority we conventionally grant him, what is subjective and what is objective in the view of each of the characters.

Hemingway takes judicious advantage of all this. While we see a good deal of the action from the points of view of Pilar, Anselmo, Maria, and several lesser characters, including a few Fascists, far and away the greater part of the whole is told as experienced by Robert Jordan, the hero. And for the most part Hemingway has resisted the temptation to reduce the integrity of effect thus gained by resorting to private knowledge of the [**215/216**] omniscient narrator—a technical triumph, after the obnoxious intrusions of *To Have and Have Not.*

The handling of subjective passages also shows close attention to technique. There is no danger here that exposure of a character's mental or emotional activity will violate the narrator's conventional license, to the detriment of illusion; but there is still a positive gain to immediacy if such passages are rendered by means of the interior monologue. And it can fairly be said that when he wishes to show Robert Jordan's mental reactions (Jordan is a surprisingly speculative fellow, even for a Spanish instructor from the University of Montana) Hemingway turns to this device as a matter of routine. In fact, the very frequency of its use raises a question with respect to realism: does not the preponderance of subjective passages in *For Whom the Bell Tolls,* by the shift in emphasis away from the solid specifications of the outward world, make that novel less eminently realistic than Hemingway's first two books?

In any case, it can be said that in its use of narrative perspective, *For Whom the Bell Tolls* is a competent novel, enjoying the advantage of a technique well chosen in the light of its theme, and applied with sufficient attention to the demands of realism to create, on the whole, a steady and powerful artistic illusion. I feel that for all its variety and excitement it does not give the reader the realistic sense of having "been there" as solidly as *The Sun Also Rises* and *A Farewell to Arms.* And I think the explanation is partly that in regard to narrative perspective there have seldom been, in the history of fiction, two books so fortunate as those in the thorough assimilation of technique to theme.

The faults of *Across the River and Into the Trees,* for which it has been duly belabored by the reviewers, are not principally matters of narrative perspective. The last days of Colonel Cantwell, an old soldier who refuses to fade away, somehow fail to realize a theme essentially valid and poignant: action is inade- [**216/217**] quate

to theme. Between a solid beginning and a solid end we meander through a spongy middle of prolonged conversation wherein the hero expresses to his dream-girl *contessa* numerous prejudices, often malicious and often irrelevant to what meaning the book could have.

Still, when one thinks about how it might, perhaps, have been saved, the problem of narrative perspective draws some attention. Particular passages which seem to distill the objectionable, or more accurately, the embarrassing qualities of the narrative, stand out. Colonel Cantwell, "forced to look in the mirror to check any traces of lipstick," studies his facial scars:

> He did not notice the old used steel of his eyes nor the small, long extending laugh wrinkles at the corners of his eyes, nor that his broken nose was like a gladiator's in the oldest statutes.* Nor did he notice his basically kind mouth which could be truly ruthless.

Since the Colonel does not notice these things, the responsibility for the observations is entirely the narrator's; and he is, unfortunately, the same intrusive commentator, gone sentimental, who plagued the reader of *To Have and Have Not.* "The hell with you," says the Colonel to the mirror, in the next line; and the reader may feel the same way toward the narrator.

> "*Have to?*" the Colonel said and the cruelty and resolution showed in his strange eyes as clearly as when the hooded muzzle of the gun of a tank swings toward you.

This communication, the style of which suggests *Western Romances,* is direct from narrator to reader—both, presumably, old combat men; for the Colonel is breakfasting with and looking at the *Contessa.* The point of view is outside the narrative, and whether you like or dislike the simile its effect is one of distraction. [**217/218**] Finally, this, with its curious non-narrative comment:

* "statues" in Hemingway

"I understand," the *Gran Maestro* said and he looked at Renata and his heart rolled over as a porpoise does in the sea. It is a beautiful movement and only a few people in this world can feel it and accomplish it.

All of these, in thought and style, fairly represent the unsatisfactory middle of *Across the River and Into the Trees,* and it is significant that all are likewise exploitations of special privilege by the omniscient narrator such as we have learned, from better novels by Hemingway and others, to regard suspiciously. *Où sont les neiges d'antan? Où sont les neiges d'autrefois? Dans le pissoir toute la chose comme ça,* quotes Colonel Cantwell to himself at one point, approvingly. But the value of Hemingway's narrative technique at its best is precisely its ability to save for us *les neiges d'antan.* For if they are anywhere, they are in art.

Ernest Hemingway: The Meaning of Style*

JOHN GRAHAM teaches English and American literature at the University of Virginia.

In memory of Leo Spitzer, 1887-1960

Hemingway, in the opening pages of *Death in the Afternoon,* insists that he, his characters, and, ultimately, his readers be aware of the active existence of persons, things, and actions. Too often, however, critics seem to accept this as meaning simply the accumulation of concrete details by a sensitive observer. Furthermore, the vitality of Hemingway's novels has been attributed to a number of factors ranging from his plots and characters to his simplicity of theme and control of language. These elements in their many aspects are, of course, contributory but are subordinate to a more constant cause: the active presentation of subject and object (observer and thing observed) and the continuous, intimate, and conscious relationship between subject and object. The characters' conscious reception of present fact (not judgment of or even response to fact) is so pervasive in Hemingway's novels that it appears to be a mode of thought for Hemingway, rather than a conscious artistic device. It is in this constant activity of sensory perception of active objects, and, still more important, in the subjects' awareness of relationship to these objects that the vitality of the writing is found.

The total effect of activity in the novels is gained by a simplicity of plot, a directness of human relations, and a basic impermanence of situation. The major circumstances are keynoted by impermanency: the hero is in a foreign land or, in the case of Santiago of *The Old Man and the Sea,* a foreign element. No matter how familiar the protagonist may be with the place, he is not expected to settle there. The characters "use" countries, hotels, cafes, and houses, but there is never a real act of possession. The reader waits for the next move. The main plot is dominated by violence of war, combat and/or erratic movement from place to place; the characters reflect these highly unstable conditions by their attention on the [298/299] immediate present and by their lack of demand on the future. They are active, direct and, one might argue, uncomplicated people with an almost fatalistic acceptance of life. Since they are so uncomplicated in their relations and attitudes, more of a burden falls on the "working out" of the action if the novel is not to die for lack of physical, emotional, or intellectual life.

These elements of circumstance, plot, and character achieve their effects of total vitality cumulatively rather than constantly. On the other hand, it is the continuous and aware relation of active subjects and objects that vivifies the novel at all times. By the nature of Hemingway's plot and characters, and his idea of conflict, the "movement" of this relation takes on added importance since, because of its pervasiveness, it sustains the vitality, giving more flexibility in the presentation of the other elements. Without going into extended detail, the plots of the novels are certainly no more vivid, often less so, than thousands of others. While the subject is often war or physical combat, which by their very nature are intensively active, such subjects, even when coupled with

*John Graham, "Ernest Hemingway: The Meaning of Style," *Modern Fiction Studies,* VI (Winter, 1960), 298-313. Reprinted by permission of the author and the Purdue Research Foundation.

credible participants, do not guarantee life but simply physical exercise. The characters may fade in and out of the action, emotionally alert but divorced from the source of the emotion. Hemingway, with the possible exception of some ruminations of Robert Jordan in *For Whom the Bell Tolls,* does not permit his characters to retreat so far from the facts of their existence that the reader concentrates on the emotion rather than on the motivating force.

A second negative point concerning the importance of this sustaining element of relation with the active concrete is the lack of development of Hemingway's characters. In a surprisingly brief time, Hemingway establishes character; in the first few chapters the reader learns all he is to know about the central actors, and these actors are as knowing about each other as they are ever to be. The action and relations which follow serve only as illustrative incidents which fix more firmly what was openly presented and readily grasped many pages before. There is nothing new to learn; even with the various crises, the characters observe simply. While they seem to understand what they do and what goes on about them, they never seem to assimilate this knowledge and, if they react, they do not change as a result.[1] There would be a real danger of stagnation in the characters if they were not intimately aware of and actively [299/300] connected with the active material world as well as the incidents in which they take part.

The final negative element that heightens the importance of movement is the lack of complexity in the conflicts presented in the novels. The simplicity, directness, and obviousness of the conflicts give the characters knowledge of the facts of their various situations. There is no challenge to the characters or the reader demanding extended mental activity, subtle or otherwise. The testimony of the participant's senses can be accepted as objective, if limited, fact. While such a simplicity is of value to a forward moving and well controlled narrative, it lessens the

possibility of establishing tensions which will keep the novel alive and meaningful as it moves through its rises and falls. Vitality is preserved by the constant and conscious reception of more, though basically unvaried, information concerning the living world in which the characters operate.

The *constant* effect of vitality is gained by the rather obvious quick shifts (particularly within the unit of the paragraph) from one type of expression to another. The writing ranges freely and briefly through narration, description and exposition, monolog and dialog, and first, second and third persons.[2] Shifting points of view add a more organic variation to these essentially artificial devices. But the real force of life is conveyed by the *consciousness* of the *relation* between characters and an *active* material world. These relations may be physical, emotional or mental, active or static, and actual, potential, hypothetical or desired.[3] They may be

[1] There is a prevailing doggedness, a form of passivity mixed with the major characters' acceptance of fact. They do not control their worlds but rather observe and react, accept and endure: Robert Jordan tenaciously follows orders (though admirably making the best of several bad bargains, i.e. the stolen exploder and his broken leg); Santiago does the usual and inevitable by trying to catch a fish and staying with one when it is hooked; Frederic Henry has only a negative solution by continuing "the retreat" from the war [299/300] after which he and Catherine reject the world which has only interfered; Jake and Brett continue an impossible, aimless existence in spite of the knowledge of experience. (Brett is so unstable in her relations that her "action" of sending Pedro Romero away is as much a different way of expressing her inability for real intimacy as a revelation of any basic goodness.)
There is, however, a deepening of the relations of the hero as the novels progress: Frederic and Catherine, Robert and Maria, and Santiago and the fish. But these relations have only an immediate and temporary unity, one which has no existence outside the present situation. It is difficult to take the love affairs seriously for there is never a sense of permanency, future, which, I venture, is a necessary note of love. There is a romantic conjuring up of the flames of love for a physical and an emotional security in the extremely unstable conditions in which the characters find themselves; there is an active attempt at getting what life may offer before life goes. It may be very gratifying and exciting, but it does not seem to be love.
[2] This type of activity is in a sense outside the world of the novel because it relies on the activity of the reader who is making subtle adjustments to the different types of presentation. It is not an activity within the world of the novel but rather a part of the direct process of artistic communication.
[3] In connection with the preceding note, no relation is "static" as long as there is an observer to

simple, one-directional relations, or become involved exchanges, expanding in both time and place. [**300/301**]

A consideration of this element of "movement" in the novels of Hemingway might well commence with one of the more simple and direct examples. In the description of the Russian, Karkov, there is a limited range of sensory perception, no present physical action on the part of the object, and a rather simple physical, emotional, and mental relation of subject to object:

He had liked Karkov but not the place. Karkov was the most intelligent man he had ever met. Wearing black riding boots, gray breeches, and a gray tunic, with tiny hands and feet, puffily fragile of face and body, with a spitting way of talking through his bad teeth, he looked comic when Robert Jordan first saw him. But he had more brains and more inner dignity and outer insolence and humor than any man that he had ever known.
For Whom the Bell Tolls, p. 231.[4]

Even in such a seemingly ordinary paragraph there is much conscious relation and active detail. The opening statement of Robert Jordan's reminiscence first connects him with Karkov and indicates generally the atmosphere of the relations; this is emphasized by the concluding phrase *but not the place,* which also forces the question "why?", then "why not?" to become prominent. This question leads to the second which explains the first and implies, by *most intelligent* and *ever,* an act of evaluation and the passage of time. *Had . . . met* is the direct physical and social act which leads to the description of Karkov. The description is brief, rather disorderly, but ranging progressively in detail from clothing to physique to typical action. The inanimate articles are given a type of life by their relation to Karkov, by the participles *wearing* and *riding* and by the reader's action of forming a uniform from the separate pieces of clothing. The mannerism, *a spitting way of talking through his bad teeth,* presents two actions with a relation between each other and a further relation to an audi-

ence, specific and general. The concluding detail, *his bad teeth,* is connected intimately with the verb *talking* by the preposition *through* which in itself is an "active" preposition denoting passage from one place to another. The independent clause presents an active judgment, *looked comic;* the temporal clause reveals an implied continuation of physical relation by the adverb *first. First* also anticipates the later change of Jordan's conclusion which is revealed in the next sentence, a concluding statement of Robert Jordan's opinion of Karkov. This statement has the implied comparison with other men, then a connection between Jordan and Karkov in *had ever known,* and a shift from *inner* to *outer* man. [**301/302**]

Robert Jordan, the subject, has a definite activity here of both the senses and the judgment; his relation to the object, Karkov, is not only logically set forth but is explicitly reiterated. Action for Karkov is restricted and potential, but he is the cause of the activities of Jordan. The interplay of the content and the implications of the perception present the basis for the mental activity of the reader.

Other descriptions are more complex, expanding in time and in place and presenting reciprocal relationships. While Karkov may be considered "potential activity," Santiago is the result of the passage of time and action:

The old man was thin and gaunt with deep wrinkles in the back of his neck. The brown blotches of the benevolent skin cancer the sun brings from its reflection on the tropic sea were on his cheeks. The blotches ran well down the sides of his face and his hands had the deep-creased scars from handling heavy fish on the cords. But none of

consider the relation, and Hemingway always has a direct observer. Even the "static physical," i.e. "the tree next to the house," demands an adjustment on the part of the observer. I do not wish to make too much of this point since it is not of immediate importance for the particular thesis at hand; it does, however, add one more constant to the present discussion.
[4] The editions cited in this study are *The Sun Also Rises* (New York, [1957]), *A Farewell to Arms* (New York, 1929), *For Whom the Bell Tolls* (New York, 1940), and *The Old Man and the Sea* (New York, 1955), all issued by Scribner.

these scars were fresh. They were as old as erosions in a fishless desert.
                    The Old Man and the Sea, pp. 9-10.

The activity and unity here is one of cause
and effect; the continuous action of nature
and of past experience on the old man has
produced the present figure. Although the
old man is "doing" nothing, the involvement of the relationships (indicated by
the blotches and scars, the results, which
exist in the present) gives a history of past
action and forces the reader to shift from
one point to another for his perspective
and evaluation of the scene and condition.

Both Karkov and Santiago are presented
with a sufficient amount of concrete detail
for the reader to gain a direct and concrete
picture of the characters. The approach to
Brett Ashley is, however, quite different.
In the entire novel, the only static details
we are given about Brett are that her hair
is short and her figure slender. She is attractive. Hemingway gives Brett "body"
by suggesting to the reader a type: he reveals her in settings, attitudes, and actions
that bring out a compulsive, jaded, uncon-
ventional animalism, and the reader may
choose, from imagination or experience,
the physical embodiment for these qualities. A pertinent quotation may be drawn
from Jake's observation in a Paris scene:
Jake and Bill have come up to a bar; Mike
strides forward and greets Jake cheerily;
the two talk socially:

Bill had gone into the bar. He was standing talking with Brett, who was sitting on a high stool, her
legs crossed. She had no stockings on.
                    The Sun Also Rises, p. 78.

The point of concentration which has existed for the long evening has been
broken; the reader no longer sees the relaxed Bill-Jake [**302/303**] combination
but an unsettled one of Mike-Jake. The
reader's line of observation moves from
Jake, one half of the original point of concentration, to Bill, the other half, who is
the immediate object of Jake's vision. Bill
Gorton has not waited for an introduction
to Mike (who certainly makes himself conspicuous) but goes straightway to Brett,

Brett who sits reigning insolently on a
high bar stool. This shift uses the person
we are with, Bill, to draw us closer to
Brett, who has just come into range.

The shift demanded is not only a physical one but an emotional one involving
change of tone. Jake, surrounded by the
alcoholic garrulity of Mike, is in sharp
contrast with the intimacy of the conversation at the bar. The present activity
of Brett and Bill *talking*, the past activity of shifting up onto the *high* stool and
of crossing her legs and the partially in-
completed past action of dressing *(no
stockings)*, fills the paragraph with an un-
dercurrent of physical activity contributing to the scene's vitality. A still further
note of vitality lies in Jake's either intellectual or emotional disapproval of this
scene, a scene which expands, reaching
through the novel and presenting Brett
for what she is: attractive, alcoholic, un-
conventional, loose and inclined to justify
her activities. The reader is given the
woman in her particular active relation to
particular friends, places, and actions; the
character and life are there, although
Brett herself is not defined overtly or given
a set, static description.

Within the limits of the paragraph, the
unit under discussion, vitality might be
achieved most easily and effectively in a
scene emphasizing the relationships of human beings who were reacting to each
other on a number of levels and with varying intensity. While this is true and important for complexity, Hemingway often
gains surprisingly active effects with the
simple relations of a human subject and
an inanimate object to preserve a sense of
continuous vitality and to instill an awareness of an immediate and direct contact
with the physical world. In an act of seemingly casual observation, Robert Jordan's
eyes shift from one point to another as he
looks at the snow stretched out before the
machine gun:

The sun was bright on the snow and it was melting fast. He could see it hollowing away from the
tree trunks and just ahead of the gun, before his
eyes, the snow surface was damp and lacily frag-

ile as the heat of the sun melted the top and the warmth of the earth breathed warmly up at the snow that lay upon it.

For Whom the Bell Tolls, p. 282.

Not only is Robert Jordan aware of the existence of the snow, but the snow is in active relation to the sun, the trees, and the earth, changing before the man's gaze. The sun and the earth act on the [**303/304**] snow, transforming it; the snow acts in relation to the trees, withdrawing from them; and the snow surface has a static relation (its position) *ahead of the gun, before his eyes*. The interconnected activity of the inanimate has its own life, independent of the observer yet in relation to him.

While Robert Jordan is rather passively conscious of the active snow object above, he is physically and emotionally very actively conscious of the view of his relation to it as he lies above the bridge waiting for dawn and the attack.

Robert Jordan lay behind the trunk of a pine tree on the slope of the hill above the road and the bridge and watched it become daylight. He loved this hour of the day always and now he watched it; feeling it gray within him, as though he were a part of the slow lightening that comes before the rising of the sun; when solid things darken and space lightens and the lights that have shown in the night go yellow and fade as the day comes. The pine trunks below him were hard and clear now, their trunks solid and brown and the road was shiny with a wisp of mist over it. The dew had wet him and the forest floor was soft and he felt the give of the brown, dropped pine needles under his elbows. Below he saw, through the light mist that rose from the stream bed, the steel of the bridge, straight and rigid across the gap, with the wooden sentry boxes at each end. But as he looked the structure of the bridge was still spidery and fine in the mist that hung over the stream.

For Whom the Bell Tolls, p. 431.[5]

The activity and relations here are many and varied, but the scene is dominated by Jordan's observation of and identification with the coming light and the hanging mist. In this fluid context, he shifts his gaze from detail to detail and watches as the objects grow clearer. He is acted upon (wet by the dew), reacts (feels) to an act

(the give of the forest floor). The vividness of the activity of light and of the connection of detail with detail in a static physical relation is ultimately dependent on the unity and vitality of Jordan's awareness of his sense perceptions.

To emphasize this intimate connection between subject and object, and their mutual relation to activity, Hemingway is fond of presenting a picture of the countryside as seen by a moving observer. Perhaps "picture" is inexact for it is rather an impression which reveals the movements of the observer on an equal scale with the general nature of the landscapes. The activity of the single observer's continually changing perspectives and objects is transferred to the rather disconnected details and unifies and vivifies them. A simple example of this [**304/305**] approach may be drawn from the trip that Jake and Bill take from Paris to Bayonne:

We ate the sandwiches and drank the Chablis and watched the country out of the window. The grain was just beginning to ripen and the fields were full of poppies. The pastureland was green, and there were fine trees, and sometimes big rivers and chateaux off in the trees.

The Sun Also Rises, p. 87.[6]

Here the vitality of the rich growth of the expanding vista is closely connected to the vitality of the aware and pleased observer, and the gain is mutually reinforcing.

An additional virtue of these travel episodes is that the action has a consciously sought goal of a destination which aids in the movement; "the bridge" in *For Whom the Bell Tolls* serves in a similar capacity, generating an almost compulsive drive toward a conclusion. The sense of conscious purpose in the activity of a character can increase the intensity of a scene, putting a particular demand on the person as, for example, during the retreat from Caporetto.

[5] The tactile element in this paragraph is balanced by the visual. For paragraphs of exclusively tactile awareness, see those presenting Jordan checking his packs (p. 48) and readying his submachine gun (p. 431).

[6] Compare Jake and Bill on the bus ride to Burguette (p. 108) and during their walk through the beech wood (p. 120) in *The Sun Also Rises*.

Crossing the field, I did not know but that someone would fire on us from the trees near the farmhouse or from the farmhouse itself. I walked
toward it, seeing it very clearly. The balcony of
the second floor merged into the barn and there
was hay coming out between the columns. The
courtyard was of stone blocks and all the trees
were dripping with the rain. There was a big
empty two-wheeled cart, the shafts tipped high up
in the rain. I came to the courtyard, crossed it,
and stood under the shelter of the balcony. The
door of the house was open and I went in. Bonello
and Piani came in after me. It was dark inside.
I went back to the kitchen. There were ashes of a
fire on the big open hearth. The pots hung over
the ashes, but they were empty.

A Farewell to Arms, pp. 229-230.

Here the goal of the subject is not simply
one of perception or destination but of
specific and necessary information. As he
crosses the field to reach the farmhouse,
Frederic describes the place in active terms
but the description is, in a sense, accidental to his act of peering for an enemy.
This farmhouse has a vital and direct significance to Frederic; it is not presented
simply as a concrete detail in a landscape.
The "purposeful observation" is the usual
method employed for the apparently "incidental" presentation of concrete surroundings. Sometimes the description will
have an immediate and specific significance; at others a very general one. This
utilitarian aspect of observation is one of
the strongest links between the characters
and their world. [305/306]

An interesting aspect of this purposeful
relation between the observer and the
world is the semi-professional view that the
characters often take of their world as if
they were evaluating it (and often are)
for an immediate or future specific use.
The major characters often reveal a handbook view of an object, a view conditioned
by their function as professional observers.
Santiago looks at sky, water, and light for
indications of future weather and fishing
conditions. Frederic and Robert, as soldiers, consider roads, bridges, and terrain
in terms of men, movement, and equipment, though Frederic Henry does so with
a dull and jaded eye while Robert Jordan
is always interested and often pleased;

finally, Jake, the newspaper man, views
spectacles in the colorful manner that
might be expected of a journalist and experienced traveler. These special variations of purposeful observation are the
results of two basic conditions of the
Hemingway protagonists that elicit the
consciousness of particular or professional
knowledge. The hero is often a foreigner;
even though he may know the language
fluently, he is in some way an outsider, not
really in the stream of tradition or daily
life. As a result he must learn rather consciously as much as possible about the
alien world if he is to deal with it; terrain
and customs must be assimilated. Furthermore, while the hero's senses are alerted in
his learning process, he, as a "professional," has something to teach the other
characters, whether it be bull fighting,
warfare, fishing, or eating and drinking.
The hero as either student or teacher
needs to be aware of the world around
him—persons as well as places and things
—if he is to survive as a personality and,
often, as a physical entity.[7]

[7] These teacher-learner relations function not
only within the world of the novel but extend to
the reader. The two premises—hero as foreigner
and hero as professional—encourage the reader's
identification with the protagonist as learner as
well as submission to his (teacher's) knowledge
and experience. The reader is inclined to identify
himself with the hero-foreigner since the reader himself is a stranger who accepts and welcomes information given by the author (either directly or
indirectly), the presentation of which he would
find obtrusive under other circumstances. This attitude is not limited to acceptance of fact, but after
conditioning the reader to accept him as guide to
the facts of the situation, the author is in a more
authoritative position in any statement he makes
or impression he conveys. In some particular
sphere, however, the author is often knowledge-
able. The "teaching" aspect in Hemingway's novels
may be divided into three basic facets: 1. Characters teach characters: Jake teaches Brett about
bullfighting (Ch. XIII), peasants teach Bill how to
drink wine from a skin (Ch. XI), Karkov teaches
Robert Jordan his politics (Ch. XVIII), Robert
Jordan teaches gun placement and observation (Ch.
XXII & XLIII); 2. Hemingway teaches reader indirectly: Afición, *The Sun Also Rises* (Ch. XIII),
France and tipping, *The Sun Also Rises* (Ch. XIX),
and fishing methods, *The Old Man and the Sea*;
3. Hemingway teaches reader indirectly: Jake prepares trout (Ch. XII), Santiago prepares fish
(p. 47), and Jordan makes a bough bed (Ch. XX)
and loads a gun (Ch. XLI). James B. Colvert, in
"Hemingway's Morality in Action," *AL*, XXVII
(1955), 384, quite rightly argues that Hemingway's
women are all "students" of the heroes, and references to Hemingway's concern for professional
knowledge and attitude may be found in Joseph
Beaver, "Technique in Hemingway," *College Eng-*

The final example of a presentation of the inanimate is an extremely carefully worked out picture of the bull corral in *The* [**306/307**] *Sun Also Rises*. An orderly interweaving of concrete detail and of the crowd's restrained activity carries the observing party from the ticket gate to the top of the wall; the simple, direct narration of activity and the orderly expanding description are such that neither could have existence (to say nothing of meaning and vitality) without the order. The eye does not stop at the top of the wall; the area is opened and expands up and out to the horizon, gathering more details and more aspects of life, in particular, people who are in turn focusing their gaze toward the center of the scene.

> "Look up there," I said.
> Beyond the river rose the plateau of the town. All along the old walls and ramparts people were standing. The three lines of fortifications made three black lines of people. Above the walls there were heads in the windows of the houses. At the far end of the plateau boys had climbed into the trees.
> *The Sun Also Rises*, p. 138.[8]

Just as the composition of a painting directs the viewer's eye to rest or to follow a certain direction, so this place, the first-person narrator, and Hemingway's description urge the reader to move from one concentric ring to another. It is as if the viewer were a sentient stone sending out ripples in a pool, aware of the expanding circles and the movement of points (i.e., people) on them.

Until this point the examples considered have been of relationships of persons, places, and things. These relationships have been active, significant, and recognized by the observer. The emphasis has been on the concrete fact and the observer's simple awareness of the existence of concrete fact rather than on incident. The following examples have been chosen as examples of action but they are more than that alone; the combination of narration and description does not make the distinction of "descriptive unit" or "narrative unit" simple and clearcut. But then this is just one more of the devices for integrating all aspects of the life presented in the novels.

Within the context of the regular plot of the novel, there will be many incidents of subordinate actions contributing toward the whole. To drive the point further, parts of incidents are again subordinate actions contributing to their particular whole. Obviously this can be pushed back to the sentence or phrase or even word, each element being filled with actual or potential movement. The extent to which the writer "packs" his action scenes is, of course, dependent on the precise effect he wishes to achieve, but Hemingway's tendency is [**307/308**] toward gaining as much internal action as possible and relating it closely to the characters.

The simplest form of action is the rather automatic performance of commonplace deeds. The flat economy of this narrative or type can achieve a variety of effects, especially when used for contrast, but more significantly the act described is the narrator's attempt to get out of his unrecognizable emotions, to establish contact with the non-self. (Unfortunately, this single facet of expression is taken by many of the hard-boiled, half-hour-radio-program school to be the genius of Hemingway.) The drained Jake retreats to San Sebastian after the fiesta:

> I unpacked my bags and stacked my books on the table beside the head of my bed, put out my shaving things, hung up some clothes in the big armoire, and made up a bundle for the laundry. Then I took a shower in the bathroom and went down to lunch. Spain had not changed to summertime, so I was early. I set my watch again. I had recovered an hour by coming to San Sebastian.
> *The Sun Also Rises*, p. 234.

Jake must "establish" himself in San Sebastian, must be consciously aware of his relation to a world just as he was aware

lish, XIV (1952-53), 325-328 and Charles A. Fenton, "No Money for the Kingbird: Hemingway's Prizefight Stories," *American Quarterly*, IV (1952), 339-350.
[8] Compare the view from the bus in *The Sun Also Rises* (p. 108).

when he and Bill walked through Paris or fished in a stream. It is a part of the self-centeredness of the Hemingway protagonist who must relate all things to himself if either self or thing is to have meaning. He must make a world of conscious relation. Slowly the detachment is overcome, slowly a richness of consciousness emerges, and Jake can again enjoy as well as perceive.

I walked around the harbor under the trees to the casino, and then up one of the cool streets to the Café Marinas. There was an orchestra playing inside the cafe and I sat out on the terrace and enjoyed the fresh coolness in the hot day, and had a glass of lemon-juice and shaved ice and then a long whiskey and soda. I sat in front of the Marinas for a long time and read, and watched the people, and listened to the music.
The Sun Also Rises, p. 235.

The world and Jake's orderly relation to it have been reasserted. The impersonality is gone, and Jake can contact only the life he wishes and come alive. The actions of the subject, the passage of time, the sights, sounds, tastes, and the transition from the heat of the day to the cool of the evening all fill this paragraph with a leisurely movement of quiet consciousness.

To the relaxed action of this scene an interesting contrast is the animal vigor and pleasure of Rafael, the gypsy, as he walks toward [308/309] Robert Jordan, who has just killed a cavalry man and is setting up a machine gun in anticipation of discovery and attack:

Just then, while he was watching all of the country that was visible, he saw the gypsy coming through the rocks to the left. He was walking with a loose, high-hipped, sloppy swing, his carbine was slung on his back, his brown face was grinning and he carried two big hares, one in each hand. He carried them by the legs, heads swinging.
For Whom the Bell Tolls, p. 474.

Not only is his walk animated but his whole body is working: arms, hands, face. Even the dead rabbits are a part of the action as they swing in the gypsy's grasp.

As satisfying as these presentations may be in their movement, restraint, and solidity, one turns with interest to the pres-

entation of violent action such as that of the bull's entrance in *The Sun Also Rises:*

I leaned way over the wall and tried to see into the cage. It was dark. Some one rapped on the cage with an iron bar. Inside something seemed to explode. The bull, striking into the wood from side to side with his horns, made a great noise. Then I saw a dark muzzle and the shadow of horns, and then, with a clattering on the wood in the hollow box, the bull charged and came out into the corral, skidding with his forefeet in the straw as he stopped, his head up, the great hump of muscle on his neck swollen tight, his body muscles quivering as he looked up at the crowd on the stone walls. The two steers backed away against the wall, their heads sunken, their eyes watching the bull.
The Sun Also Rises, pp. 138-139.[9]

The activity here is literally explosive as the bull bursts from the dark of the cage into the sunlight of the corral. Jake's anticipatory action establishes him as a concerned part of the scene; the heralding noises prepare for the entrance; then the charging, quivering bull dominates the picture. The bull defies the crowd; the steers wait with frightened resignation. Except for the crowd itself, all relationships here are active and intense, and anticipate future action.

The simplicity and directness of the lines of actions in the examples already cited give an immediacy of impact and a quick-paced reception of active fact. More complex devices of presentation vary and control this communication. One technique employed is the revelation by grammatical structure of separate but concurrent actions that become mutually involved. United by no logical relation or by cause and effect, the actions draw into closer relation characters [309/310] or things which reveal or clarify each other. One obvious use of this device may be observed in *For Whom the Bell Tolls:*

Robert Jordan unrolled the bundle of clothing that made his pillow and pulled on his shirt. It was over his head and he was pulling it down when he heard the next planes coming and he pulled his trousers on over the robe and lay still as three more of the Heinkel bimotor bombers

[9] Compare the description of the fish breaking water in *The Old Man and the Sea* (p. 69).

came over. Before they were gone over the shoulder of the mountain, he had buckled on his pistol, rolled the robe and placed it against the rocks, and sat now, close against the rocks, tying his rope-soled shoes, when the approaching droning turned to a greater clattering roar than ever before and nine more Heinkel light bombers came in echelons; hammering the sky apart as they went over.

For Whom the Bell Tolls, p. 75.[10]

The two actions are channeled grammatically—Robert Jordan's dressing in the independent clauses, the planes' flight in the temporal ones. The independent clauses present a base of commonplace activity and flat rhythm from which operates the harshly poetic flight and the climactic rhythm of the dependent clauses. It is through the earthborn, the personal, the individual of the guerrilla that we approach the diabolic symbol of distant, impersonal mechanization.

Another method of involving forward pace while keeping the action immediately alive is to shift from one object to another with a real or implied shift of subject.

The count was looking at Brett across the table under the gaslight. She was smoking a cigarette and flicking the ashes on the rug. She saw me notice it. "I say, Jake, I don't want to ruin your rugs. Can't you give a chap an ashtray?"

The Sun Also Rises, p. 57.

Jake, the subject, looked at the count who was watching Brett; the subject momentarily and implicitly shifts from Jake to the count, the object from the count to Brett. Then Brett's action of flicking the ashes occurred; "when she saw me notice it," the subject becomes Brett, the object Jake, and then is immediately reversed. Brett requested an ashtray in a vaguely guilty manner. The shifting of subject and object, and the limited action of the scene have combined to form a vital whole. The intimate relation of Jake and Brett, her attractiveness to other men and her awareness of that attraction, her carelessness and Jake's control over that carelessness, are all revealed in the conscious observations in these few lines. The significant interplay is alive and active within itself without having any direct role in a specific

incident in the usual meaning of the term. [310/311]

In the preceding scene, the people are conscious of themselves and of each other. A different type of consciousness, more introspective and articulated, is presented by Frederic Henry as he floats down the icy river, clinging to a heavy timber. Not only is he uncomfortably aware of the present and very much involved in it, but his thoughts range back and forth in time and place.

You do not know how long you are in a river when the current moves swiftly. It seems a long time and it may be very short. The water was cold and in flood and many things passed that had been floated off the banks when the river rose. I was lucky to have a heavy timber to hold on to, and I lay in the icy water with my chin on the wood, holding as easily as I could with both hands. I was afraid of cramps and I hoped we would move toward the shore. We went down the river in a long curve. It was beginning to be light enough so I could see the bushes along the shore-line. There was a brush island ahead and the current moved toward the shore. I wondered if I should take off my boots and clothes and try to swim ashore, but I decided not to. I had never thought of anything but that I would reach the shore some way, and I would be in a bad position if I landed barefoot. I had to get to Mestre some way.

A Farewell to Arms, p. 242.

The activity of the subject, both mental and physical, is continuous as is the contact with the reader. The lieutenant explains to the reader the sensation in the river and the problem of judgment, considers cause and effect, admits good fortune, fears, accounts, speculates, judges, anticipates, and then doggedly fixes his mind on getting "to Mestre some way." His is an observation and consideration of both the facts and the possibilities of the situation in which he finds himself.

This sense of involvement with the present action, as is leisurely revealed in the foregoing quotation, is nowhere more brilliantly dramatized than in the opening scene of Chapter XXI, pp. 265 ff. from *For Whom the Bell Tolls*, a section too long for inclusion here. In this incident, the

[10] Compare Jordan's concurrent awareness of his watch (time) and Maria in *For Whom the Bell Tolls* (p. 378).

vivid description and fast-moving action fuse into a whole in which the characters act, react, and are acted upon. After opening rather "idyllically" in the quiet peace of the morning, the sound of hoofbeats comes to Robert Jordan, anticipating the entrance of the young cavalryman. The dynamiter is caught up immediately in a three-way relation: he warns Maria, readies himself, and watches for a horseman. The rider appears and the pistol roars; the man is killed and the camp aroused to frantic activity.

The section is vivid, economical, and controlled. To consider just a part of it:

He reached his hand down toward the scabbard and as he swung low, turning and jerking at the scabbard, Robert Jordan saw the scarlet of the formalized [311/312] device he wore on the left breast of his khaki blanket cape.
Aiming at the center of his chest, a little lower than the device, Robert Jordan fired.
The pistol roared in the snowy woods.

For Whom the Bell Tolls, p. 265.

The brilliance of the movement, detail, and sound merge to give a piercing sensory impression. The simplicity of *the pistol roared in the snowy woods* has been prepared for in every respect: the quiet country setting with the snow melting and falling is shattered by the harsh shot ringing from the heavy automatic pistol held in both hands. The idyllic is broken by the ugly; we knew both existed but their juxtaposition gives us the drama. Both of these elements are picked up again as the scene is worked out: the cavalryman is dragged through the snow, the horse tracks are a matter of concern, and Robert Jordan nervously comments on the pistol and lanyard, as he replaces the expended round. The entire section is the perfect example of the union of vital parts in a living frame to produce a dramatic and significant reality. All facets previously discussed have been integrated in this passage.

There are three factors which have been examined in this study: one, the object which is under observation; two, the sub-ject, who, in one way or another, does the observing; and three, the nature of the relation between subject and object. Because of the usual integration of these three aspects, it has been unnecessary and impossible to prescind too sharply from any two. The conclusions reached from these discussions are briefly: the activity of the object and subject may be either physical, emotional, or mental. These activities may be presented as actual, potential, hypothetical, desired, past, or implied. The relation of the subject and object is most often one of conscious or effective recognition by one or more of the senses; the subject often seeks to observe the object for a specific, sometimes necessary, purpose. (The reader, acting as external subject, must make subtle adjustments to varying types of expression.) The sense of immediacy in Hemingway's novels is gained not by the reproduction of the object for itself or even in the perception of the object by the subject so much as by the subject's awareness of his act of perception and the activity of the object perceived.

These are the pedestrian facts by way of conclusion. The actual use of this view gives a concretely interrelated world to which the characters continually testify as present *now* and accounts for Hemingway's particular achievement in such vivid scenes as the fishing trip in *The Sun Also Rises*. Depending little on the cataloging of [312/313] static details in the manner of Zola and Norris, Hemingway constructs the connection of character and action which always enlivens and solidifies the characters and humanizes scenes and actions. Before, and below the level of, the formation of the Hemingway "code"—his ideal of action, courage, endurance, and technical competency—lies the involvement with and awareness of the material and interrelated world of character, action, and things. In the presentation of a moving, changing world and of the characters' recognition of that active world exists the constant movement which gives the novels their vitality.

PART SIX

TOPICS FOR STUDY AND RESEARCH

Suggested Topics for Controlled Research

An unopened book is like an unknown country. Its hills, valleys, cities, farms, lakes, and rivers lie there waiting, ready and open to any intrepid explorer who chooses to make the trip. If the book is well known, there is a strong likelihood that other explorers have paid previous visits. Many have gone to the trouble to set down how they felt at what they saw, how the land lay, what the citizens were like. They have drawn maps, let us say, of some parts of the terrain. These diarists and cartographers are the people we call critics. Their accounts are of use to us who follow them. Yet we cannot be certain that they have correctly reported the heights of the mountains, the depths of the rivers, the nature of the citizenry, until we too have made the journey, seen the land for ourselves, come back—so to speak—with our own measurements, our own reactions. To make that journey, supplementing and complementing our own observations with those of other people who have been there before us, is a necessary prerequisite in the preparation of any sound research paper.

No research paper, obviously, can tell the whole truth about a piece of fiction. This is why the topical approach is desirable. Yet the apprentice explorer is often baffled by the task of finding a suitable topic. How is he to discover one that will repay exploration? One way to do it is to read a novel with his eyes open and his senses alert.

Let us say that he selects *A Farewell to Arms.* In the final chapter he is much taken with Frederick Henry's gloomy analogy between the human situation and that of a colony of ants on a burning campfire log. Here is an excellent topic: "Fatalism in *A Farewell to Arms.*" He gathers all the passages from the novel which seem to bear upon this topic. He examines the critical essays in this anthology in order to find further evidence and other arguments to complement and supplement his own views on the idea of fatalism in Hemingway's work. Even though all of the critiques are not directly about *A Farewell to Arms,* they may offer clues and affirmations which will suit the researcher's purpose. As soon as this double task is behind him, as soon as he has achieved a satisfactory union between his own observations and those of others, he is ready to organize and write his research paper, following with care the procedures outlined by the general editor of this anthology.

Suppose, to take a second example, that he has read *The Old Man and the Sea.* He becomes curious about the function of the boy Manolo in the conduct and development of the story. Why is Manolo there? What was the author's purpose in placing the youth side by side with the old man? Manolo is present in person at the beginning and end of the tale. He is likewise present, though only in Santiago's memory, on several occasions in the middle. The student gathers his notes on all the passages in which Manolo appears, whether in flesh or spirit; checks his ideas against those of the critical essayists in this volume; organizes his materials; reaches his conclusions; and is prepared to write.

The examples cited above are only two among scores and even hundreds of available possibilities. But let us suppose, what is unlikely enough, that the student has read all the way through *The Sun Also Rises* or *For Whom the Bell Tolls* without having found a single research topic which strikes him as feasible. In that predicament, if he turns to the critical essays on those two novels which are reprinted here, he will find that the essayists have raised a number of important points, any one of which would serve the student very well as a topic for a research paper. Returning thus freshly armed from his foray into secondary sources, the student can re-examine the novels in the light of ideas derived from his reading of the essays.

Once more, now, he gathers his materials, organizes them according to the method outlined at the beginning of this volume, and begins to build his paper.

The essays here reprinted have been chosen in such a way as to illustrate and typify a considerable variety of approaches to the four major novels of Hemingway. A student who has chosen a topic like "Fatalism in *A Farewell to Arms*" will doubtless be most interested in topics which emphasize Hemingway's characteristic ideas and attitudes. On the other hand, the student who has chosen to write about Manolo will find useful hints and suggestions in what the various critics have had to say about minor or "contributory" characters elsewhere in Hemingway's work.

Yet another large family of available topics may be found under the general heading of "Recurrent Themes in Hemingway." Halliday calls attention to the "theme of moral atrophy" in *The Sun Also Rises*. The student should be alert for the possibility that the same theme may reappear in other forms and contexts in *A Farewell to Arms* or *For Whom the Bell Tolls*. The title of Hemingway's third collection of short stories is *Winner Take Nothing*. These three words imply much more than they say. One might ask whether and how this theme is exemplified in *The Sun Also Rises* or *The Old Man and the Sea*. Backman's essay distinguishes between the recurrent type of the matador, who gives death, and that of the crucified, who receives injury. This distinction operates thematically not only in *The Old Man and the Sea* but also at many other points in Hemingway. Guttmann discusses "the theme of conflict between men and machines" in *For Whom the Bell Tolls*. The student may wish to explore the same theme in Hemingway's earlier war-book, *A Farewell to Arms*. The invasion of the idyllic by the ugly is noted by Graham as a recurrent theme throughout Hemingway's fiction. In short, one of the uses of the essays in this volume is to identify themes in one novel which may be expected to re-

appear in other novels or short stories by the same author.

Many potentially fruitful research topics can be found in Hemingway's characteristic use of symbols and images. West, for example, quotes Malcolm Cowley's opinion that Frederic Henry's plunge into the icy Tagliamento River is a symbolic baptism, pointing the way to a new mode of life. Other essayists discuss the symbolic use of weather, seasons, landscapes, animals, hands, numbers, and various artifacts and art objects. Many of the characters seem to have been intentionally infused with symbolic significance. With this idea in mind, one is all the more interested in people like Pilar, Pablo, Anselmo, and Maria as they move through the crowded pages of *For Whom the Bell Tolls*. *The Old Man and the Sea* is often interpreted as a parable of human life, though critics disagree on its meaning as well as on the extent to which Hemingway may be justly described as a parabolical— or even a symbolic—writer.

Hemingway's Nobel Prize citation stressed his achievements as a prose stylist. Here is another large area for possible investigation. Readers of the essays in this volume will discover Anderson's fresh examination of stylistic counterpoint in *A Farewell to Arms*. Schorer speaks of the syntactic loosening of style in *For Whom the Bell Tolls* as over against the tighter and more laconic style of earlier novels. Beach discourses interestingly on the use of language in dialogue for the differentiation of characters. Graham devotes an entire essay to the problem of style in Hemingway. Despite the manifest difficulties of writing research papers on stylistic problems, the rewards in such investigations may be great, since the student compels himself (under critical guidance) to look very closely at those linguistic elements which, in unique combinations, distinguish Hemingway's prose and stamp it with the impress of his personality.

Considerations of form and structure are as important in fiction as they are in architecture. Schorer speaks admiringly of the structural proportions of *The Old Man and the Sea.* Young's analysis of *The Sun Also Rises* mentions the novel's rising and falling action. West argues that the physical form of *A Farewell to Arms* resembles that of a drama. Speaking of *For Whom the Bell Tolls,* Trilling remarks that it is Jordan's fate which provides the "intellectual architectonic" for the novel. The way a writer of fiction begins and ends his stories is frequently significant in a formal sense. The present volume prints for the first time Hemingway's original conclusion to *A Farewell to Arms,* inviting comparisons between this and the more familiar final paragraph in which the bereaved Frederick Henry leaves the hospital and walks back to his hotel in the rain. The exploration of formal patterns in Hemingway's fiction is always rewarding because the form is always there, though its full significance seldom comes clear except to one, like the archaeologist, who is willing to dig for it.

Finally, there is the important topic of character and motivation. In his essay on *The Sun Also Rises,* Spilka contrasts the "honest cripples" and "the pretenders." It is likely that similar contrasts may be found in other Hemingway novels. Light locates four "ideals of service" in *A Farewell to Arms.* Can one discern the opera-tion of other ideals or standards of behavior in, for example, the conduct of Santiago or that of Anselmo or that of Romero or that of Maria? Schorer asserts that *For Whom the Bell Tolls* is moti-vated throughout by Hemingway's "tre-mendous sense of man's dignity and worth." It would be worth while to look into the question of how this sense of hu-man dignity is manifested through the agency of such characters as Robert Jordan or El Sordo. One of Hemingway's rejected titles for *The Old Man and the Sea* was *The Dignity of Man.* What qualities vis-ible in Santiago demonstrate this dignity? What are the elements of the so-called "hero's code" in Hemingway's fiction and how are they embodied and dramatized?

To return to the point with which we began, topics for controlled research may be found everywhere in Hemingway's four major novels. If the student will work sys-tematically on the problem of finding those which best suit his tastes and current interests, keeping in mind the broad divi-sions outlined above, what could be a chore will emerge as a challenge. Ideas and attitudes, form and structure, language and style, recurrent themes and motifs, symbols and images, character and motiva-tion—under these rubrics a world of liter-ary values awaits discovery.

Suggested Topics for Library Research

Students who have access to extensive library resources should find many opportunities for useful research into the backgrounds of Hemingway's four major novels. To follow the geographical analogy of the preceding section, the researcher with a library at his disposal is like an explorer with unlimited funds. He has more of everything: more maps, more eyewitness reports, more sociological and anthropological data, and a far greater number of well-constructed roadways into the territories he wishes to investigate.

Since most of Hemingway's fiction is closely tied to his own experience, one suitable area for library research is that of the autobiographical element in his work. The adventures of Frederic Henry in *A Farewell to Arms* are based in part upon the author's youthful visit to Italy as an ambulance driver ten years earlier. Charles A. Fenton's *The Apprenticeship of Ernest Hemingway* (New York, 1954) is very helpful on this period in Hemingway's life. The same book describes his expatriate years in Paris after the first world war, years which culminated in the publication of *The Sun Also Rises*. Harold Loeb's *The Way It Was* (New York, 1959) provides an even more particularized background for the story of the fiesta in *The Sun*. Other books which offer biographical facts and opinions essential to the fuller understanding of the early work include Philip Young, *Ernest Hemingway* (New York, 1952); Carlos Baker, *Hemingway: The Writer as Artist* (Princeton, 1952, second edition, 1956); Leicester Hemingway, *My Brother, Ernest Hemingway* (Cleveland, 1962); and Marcelline Sanford, *At the Hemingways'* (Boston, 1962). A good study of Hemingway's experiences in the Spanish Civil War, and their bearing on *For Whom the Bell Tolls,* is that of David Sanders in the *American Quarterly,* XII (Summer, 1960), 133-143.

Library resources also make it far easier than it would otherwise be to investigate problems in literary parallels and influences. The critiques in this anthology suggest various literary ancestors for Hemingway, ranging all the way from Homer and Shakespeare down to James Fenimore Cooper, Herman Melville, Mark Twain, W. H. Hudson, Joseph Conrad, Stephen Crane, Henry James, and T. S. Eliot. Such allegations deserve careful checking. Nor is it wise to ignore the matter of parallels between Hemingway's work and that of some of the painters he most admired—in particular Goya, Cézanne, and Picasso. A good art library should enable the research student to look further into this subject.

Another useful approach is through the study of stylistic parallels. It is often argued that Hemingway's early style owes much to the examples of Gertrude Stein, Sherwood Anderson, and Ring Lardner. Miss Stein's *Three Lives,* Anderson's *Winesburg, Ohio,* and Lardner's *Gullible's Travels* are worth examining for the light they throw on Hemingway's narrative manner, vocabulary, and vernacular usage during the first ten years of his career. The author's own views on the subject of stylistic influence are set forth in George Plimpton's interview, printed in the *Paris Review,* XVIII (Spring, 1958), 61-82. Researchers will find other pertinent data in *The Torrents of Spring,* Hemingway's cruel parody of Anderson published in 1926, in Anderson's *A Story-Teller's Story* (1924), and in Gertrude Stein's *The Autobiography of Alice B. Toklas* (1933). The part played by newspaper work in the development of Hemingway's style is discussed in Fenton's book on the apprenticeship, mentioned above. For previous research on these and other topics, the student may consult the check list of Hemingway criticism (1925-1960) printed in Carlos Baker, ed., *Hemingway and His Critics* (New York, 1961), pages 279-298. The author's own pithy literary judgments appear in *Death in the After-*

noon and *The Green Hills of Africa,* as well as in the Plimpton interview already referred to. The best outline of his esthetic position, from which he did not afterwards significantly deviate, is to be found also in *Death in the Afternoon.*

Much has been made of Hemingway's evident liking for violence and his admiration for various forms of primitivism. A good introduction to the subject, both in Hemingway's fiction and elsewhere in American literature, may be found in W. M. Frohock, *The Novel of Violence in America* (Dallas, 1950, second edition, 1957). In this connection, it will be apparent from materials relating to the bullfight in both *The Sun Also Rises* and *For Whom the Bell Tolls* that this was almost a lifelong preoccupation of Hemingway. Valuable background commentary on the leading matadors, the animals, the ritualistic performances, and the tragic implications of the sport appears everywhere in *Death in the Afternoon.* The student may also consult Hemingway's bullfight article in *Fortune* magazine, I (March, 1930), 83-88, 139-150. The various violences involved in big-game hunting provide the substance of *The Green Hills of Africa,* which grew out of the author's safari in Kenya and Tanganyika in 1933-1934. Anyone interested in Hemingway's primitivistic outlook should read this book as well as a series of articles on the same subject which he contributed to *Esquire* magazine during the 1930's. A list of these is conveniently available in *Hemingway: The Writer as Artist,* second edition, 1956, pages 336-337. As background for *The Old Man and the Sea,* the *Esquire* articles on big-game fishing in the Caribbean are also worth attention. So is S. K. Farrington's *Atlantic Game Fishing* (New York, 1939), for which Hemingway wrote the introduction.

The fact that two of Hemingway's major novels focus on war, the most deadly and violent of sports yet devised by man, makes pertinent a study of his anthology, *Men at War* (1942), for which he organized the selections and provided a cogent introductory essay. Another topic of real potential interest would be the historical actualities which underlie *A Farewell to Arms* and *For Whom the Bell Tolls.* Such books as Herbert Vivian's *Italy at War* (New York, 1917) or Thomas Nelson Page's *Italy and the World War* (New York, 1920) provide useful material on the larger aspects of the conflict. Charles M. Bakewell, *The Story of the American Red Cross in Italy* (New York, 1920) is directly concerned with ambulances, hospitals, and wounded soldiers at a time when Hemingway, as a wounded and hospitalized ambulance driver, was absorbing the materials which would later appear in his first war-novel. Charles A. Fenton's article on ambulance drivers in France and Italy during the first world war may be found in the *American Quarterly,* III (Winter, 1951), 326-343. The literature relating to the Spanish tragedy of 1936-1939 is of course immense. *The Spanish Civil War,* by Hugh Thomas (New York, 1961), is the best over-all history to date. Other useful books include Herbert L. Matthews, *Two Wars and More to Come* (New York, 1938); Anna Louise Strong, *Spain in Arms* (New York, 1937); Alvah Bessie, *Men in Battle* (New York, 1939); and Gustav Regler's war-novel, *The Great Crusade* (New York, 1940), for which Hemingway wrote the introduction.

A fruitful field for exploration is the part played by the so-called "little magazines" in the development of Hemingway's reputation. The best book on the whole subject is *The Little Magazines,* edited by Frederick J. Hoffman, Charles Allen, and Carolyn F. Ulrich (Princeton, 1946, second edition, 1947). Hemingway's own contributions to these magazines are listed in Baker, *Hemingway: The Writer as Artist* (second edition, 1956, pages 335-340). Students interested in the critical reception of any of Hemingway's novels will find reviews listed and excerpted in the *Book Review Digest,* a series of annual volumes available in reference rooms of most college and university libraries.

Whatever phase of Hemingway's work he student chooses to explore, whether it s autobiographical and historical backgrounds, literary parallels and influences, he interest in violence, primitivism, hunting and fishing, war and death, critical reception or reputation, the imaginative use of a good library will open out into many possibilities for further investigation. "Controlled research," in which he uses only Hemingway's own writings and the materials of this anthology, is a logical first step. Beyond that stretches the immense and inviting domain of card catalogues, bibliographies, and books of our own and former times.

Bibliography

For library research, students may wish to consult the following:

Baker, Carlos. *Hemingway: the Writer as Artist.* Princeton, New Jersey: Princeton University Press, 1952. Second edition enlarged, 1956. Contains a checklist of Hemingway's writings.

—————, ed. *Hemingway and His Critics: An International Anthology.* New York: Hill and Wang, 1961. Contains a checklist of criticism on Hemingway's work.

Beach, Joseph Warren. *American Fiction, 1920-1940.* New York: The Macmillan Co., 1941.

Fenton, Charles A. *The Apprenticeship of Ernest Hemingway: The Early Years.* New York: Farrar, Straus, and Cudahy, Inc., 1954.

Hoffman, Frederick J. *The Modern Novel in America, 1900-1950.* Chicago: Regnery, 1951.

Kazin, Alfred. *On Native Grounds.* New York: Reynal and Hitchcock, 1942.

Loeb, Harold. *The Way It Was.* New York: Criterion Books, 1959. Mr. Loeb's autobiography.

McCaffery, John K. M., ed. *Ernest Hemingway: The Man and His Work.* Cleveland: World Publishing Company, 1950.

Samuels, Lee, comp. *A Hemingway Checklist.* New York: Charles Scribner's Sons, 1951.

Young, Philip. *Ernest Hemingway.* New York: Rinehart and Co., 1952. A critical study.

—————. *Ernest Hemingway.* University of Minnesota Pamphlets on American Writers, Number 1. Minneapolis: University of Minnesota Press, 1959. A short introduction to Hemingway's work.

Scribner Library Editions
(Paperbound)

THE SUN ALSO RISES

A FAREWELL TO ARMS

IN OUR TIME

A collection of Hemingway's earliest stories including "On the Quai at Smyrna," "Indian Camp," "The Doctor and the Doctor's Wife," "The End of Something," "The Three Day Blow," "The Battler," "A Very Short Story," "Soldier's Home," "The Revolutionist," "Mr. and Mrs. Elliot," "Cat in the Rain," "Out of Season," "Cross Country Snow," "My Old Man," "Big Two-Hearted River" (Parts I and II), "L'Envoi."

GREEN HILLS OF AFRICA

FOR WHOM THE BELL TOLLS

THE SNOWS OF KILIMANJARO AND OTHER STORIES

Including "A Clean, Well-Lighted Place," "A Day's Wait," "The Gambler, the Nun, and the Radio," "Fathers and Sons," "In Another Country," "The Killers," "A Way You'll Never Be," "Fifty Grand," and "The Short Happy Life of Francis Macomber."

College Editions
(Clothbound)

THE HEMINGWAY READER

An omnibus volume containing two complete novels: *The Torrents of Spring* and *The Sun Also Rises* and selections from Hemingway's five other novels and from *Death in the Afternoon* and *Green Hills of Africa*. Also includes the following short stories: "Big Two-Hearted River" (Parts I and II), "A Way You'll Never Be," "Fifty Grand," "A Clean, Well-Lighted Place," "The Light of the World," "After the Storm," "The Short Happy Life of Francis Macomber," "The Capital of the World," "The Snows of Kilimanjaro," "Old Man at the Bridge," "The Fable of the Good Lion." Selected, with a Foreword and twelve Brief Prefaces, by Charles Poore.

THREE NOVELS

The Sun Also Rises, intro. by Malcolm Cowley; *A Farewell to Arms,* intro. by Robert Penn Warren; *The Old Man and the Sea,* intro. by Carlos Baker.

THE SHORT STORIES OF ERNEST HEMINGWAY

This collection of the "First Forty-Nine" stories includes all those contained in *In Our Time, Men Without Women,* and *Winner Take Nothing* and additionally "The Short Happy Life of Francis Macomber," "The Capital of the World," "The Snows of Kilimanjaro," "Old Man at the Bridge," and "Up in Michigan."

THE OLD MAN AND THE SEA

*Trade Editions**
(Clothbound)

MEN WITHOUT WOMEN

A collection of short stories including "The Undefeated," "In Another Country," "Hills Like White Elephants," "The Killers," "Che Ti Dice La Patria?" "Fifty Grand," "A Simple Enquiry," "Ten Indians," "A Canary for One," "An Alpine Idyll," "A Pursuit Race," "To-day Is Friday," "Banal Story," "Now I Lay Me."

DEATH IN THE AFTERNOON

WINNER TAKE NOTHING

A collection of short stories containing "After the Storm," "A Clean, Well-Lighted Place," "The Light of the World," "God Rest You Merry, Gentlemen," "The Sea Change," "A Way You'll Never Be," "The Mother of a Queen," "One Reader Writes," "Homage to Switzerland," "A Day's Wait," "A Natural History of the Dead," "Wine of Wyoming," "The Gambler, the Nun, and the Radio," "Fathers and Sons."

TO HAVE AND HAVE NOT

ACROSS THE RIVER AND INTO THE TREES

*N.B. All titles listed under Scribner Library and College Editions are also available in clothbound trade editions.